ELIAS HICKS: *Quaker Liberal*

ELIAS HICKS, BY WILLIAM ORDWAY PARTRIDGE

BLISS FORBUSH

ELIAS HICKS
Quaker Liberal

with a Foreword by FREDERICK B. TOLLES

HATRED OF CANT AND DOUBT OF HUMAN CREEDS

MAY WELL BE FELT: THE UNPARDONABLE SIN

IS TO DENY THE WORD OF GOD WITHIN!—*Whittier*

NEW YORK COLUMBIA UNIVERSITY PRESS

To: *LaVerne Hill Forbush*

Foreword

". . . AND IF by reason of strength they be fourscore years, yet is their strength labor and sorrow." Elias Hicks, by reason of great strength, lived full fourscore years. If they were years of labor and sorrow—of tireless "gospel labor" in the Quaker ministry and bitter sorrow over the tragedy of a dividing Society of Friends, yet they were years of great joy too—joy in the serene conviction that "light has broken," the Divine Light, shed abroad, as Friends believed and still believe, in every human heart.

It was an eventful eighty years that Elias Hicks lived through —eventful for his country, eventful for his beloved Society of Friends. Consider for a moment the outward changes he saw: When he was born in 1748, the youngest of the thirteen colonies was barely sixteen years old, George II was still on the throne of Great Britain, and the final struggle with France for control of North America had not yet begun. When he died in 1830, the thirteen colonies had become twenty-four states in a proud, independent nation, Andrew Jackson was in the White House, and premonitory rumblings of the Civil

War could already be heard in the land. Or consider the changes in
the spiritual life of America: When Elias Hicks was a boy, the voices
of Jonathan Edwards and George Whitefield were strong in the
pulpit and the Great Awakening was at its height. When he was
old, William Ellery Channing was a powerful influence on men's
thinking and a young man named Emerson was about to abandon
the ministry for a new vocation as high priest among the Transcen-
dentalists. Or again, reflect on the changed climate in the little world
of the Society of Friends: In Elias's youth John Woolman of Mount
Holly was a familiar figure among the Quaker Meetings on Long
Island. In his old age John Greenleaf Whittier, the Quaker poet, was
already publishing his verses and maturing his antislavery convictions.

Mere longevity is no guarantee of historical importance. But Elias
Hicks in his own right was one of the most striking figures in the
history of American Quakerism, indeed in the history of religion
in America. As a preacher he demands comparison with Edwards
and Whitefield. As a liberal he deserves to stand in the same company
as Channing and Emerson. As a Friend, he is the spiritual brother
of both Woolman and Whittier, for his Quaker faith was as deep-
rooted and pervasive as theirs, his social conscience as tender, and if
his writings lack the literary qualities of Woolman's *Journal* and
Whittier's poems, his *Observations on the Slavery of the Africans
and Their Descendants* (1811) was unquestionably a major document in the development of the antislavery conscience in America.

Most Quakers, most students of American religious history know
—vaguely and inaccurately—only one thing about Elias Hicks: that
he somehow precipitated, even "caused" a disastrous schism in the
Society of Friends and became the founder of the Hicksite "branch"
of the Society. Hicks' relationship to that tragic chapter in Quaker
history—now hopefully drawing to a close—was indeed crucial, but
it was not simple. Never before has it been explained in such fullness, with such richness of documentation, as Bliss Forbush has now
explained it. If this book were notable for no other reason, it would

command attention for its careful examination into the cause and course of the "Separation" of 1827–28.

But Bliss Forbush has put us in an even greater debt: by tapping a rich vein of hitherto untouched source material, he has recovered for us a great human being, a refreshing personality, whose tonic, bracing effect Walt Whitman could compare only to that of a clear, cold mountain stream—"as if, indeed, under the smoke of battles, the blare of trumpets, and the madness of contending hosts . . . should come melting down from the mountains from sources of unpolluted snows, far up there in God's hidden, untrodden recesses, and so rippling along among us low in the ground, at men's very feet, a curious little brook of clear and cool, and ever-healthy, ever-living water."

FREDERICK B. TOLLES

*Howard M. Jenkins Research Professor of History
and Librarian at the Friends Historical Library,
Swarthmore College*

Swarthmore, Pennsylvania
December, 1955

Preface

IT IS FORTY-FOUR YEARS since Henry W. Wilbur wrote *The Life and Labors of Elias Hicks,* one hundred and twenty-two since the *Journal of the Life and Religious Labours* appeared in the first of five editions, and ninety-three years since a portion of the letters of the Jericho minister were printed. According to the author, Wilbur's book was based primarily on printed sources. Several hundred letters written by Elias Hicks are now available in the Friends Historical Library at Swarthmore College; several score are in the hands of individuals; nearly two hundred and fifty letters written to Elias Hicks, now in the Newell Collection, give the other side of his correspondence. The original manuscript of Hicks' *Journal,* containing approximately one hundred pages not found in the printed edition, is in Friends Historical Library. The passing of nearly half a century since Wilbur's book was published adds a new perspective to the Separation within the Society of Friends. Most of the bitterness caused by that tempestuous event has died away, but it remains the skeleton in the Quaker ecclesiastical closet. New issues confront

Quakerism in America. Today the most divisive issue involves the very purpose for which the Society of Friends came into being— the free and open group worship without clerical leadership, as opposed to the pastoral and churchly system practiced by a majority of Friends in America. In the wider relationship of American churches with the present resurgence of theological orthodoxy, the liberalism of Elias Hicks is still a healthy antidote.

Elias Hicks, 1748–1830, saw a tremendous sweep of American history. Growing up in the colonial province of New York he observed the rising temper which brought on the American Revolution; six times he passed through the lines of the contending armies. He experienced the failures of the Confederation and heard the proclamation of the new Federal Union. He protested the second war with Great Britain and died while the sonorous sentences of Daniel Webster filled the halls of Congress. He traveled over forty thousand miles in the ministry, following Indian trails on horseback and by carriage over the uncertain roads of early America; he journeyed from his home on Long Island as far west as Richmond, Indiana, and from northern Virginia into southern Canada. He knew the settled life of Eastern farmers, followed the advancing frontier westward, and watched the increasing shipping of New York, Boston, Philadelphia, and Baltimore turn those towns into substantial cities.

When Elias Hicks was born the first period of Quakerism was past, that glorious time of Enthusiasm when Friends went east and west presenting their message that God speaks directly to each human soul through a present, living experience of Christ, the Inner Light. Hicks was brought up and lived nearly to the end of the Quietistic period. The Quietist tenet that man must empty himself of all earthly thoughts before God can speak to him has its strength and weakness. It caused the believer to "center down" during individual as well as corporate worship, and frequently resulted in moments of spiritual exaltation. But some men and women, weary and harassed by worldly affairs, rarely succeeded

in breaking through the wrappings of everyday events to let the
Light shine in. Quietism, with its need for retreat from society, was
responsible for the isolation with which Friends surrounded themselves, prohibiting their members to marry those of other religious
bodies, their entrance into politics, or their holding of public office. It
was responsible, however, for a renewed interest in education,
though this was of a "select" or exclusive nature, both as to personnel
and curriculum.

Coming in the wake of political and social revolution, the religious
ferment of the first quarter of the nineteenth century profoundly affected the Society of Friends. A new liberal approach to the Bible
was in the air, which in the hands of Elias Hicks was used against
scepticism and Deism. A reaction also was evident in the form of
evangelicalism, spreading from John Wesley in England into the
Society of Friends; in America coming through the visiting English
Evangelical ministers and the entrance into Quaker circles of men,
like Stephen Grellet, who had previous Orthodox training. To combat what seemed to them to be both a social and religious revolution,
the elders in Philadelphia tried to nullify the essential democratic
conduct of Friends' affairs. Because he opposed this tendency, Elias
Hicks was regarded by rural Quakers, and by the majority of
Friends in New York City and Baltimore, as the champion of
religious freedom.

No Quaker can write impartially of the Separation in the Society
during 1827 to 1829. A historian should be as objective as is humanly
possible, which is here attempted, but the story of Elias Hicks obviously means a full presentation of the Liberal point of view. This
has not been amply presented by any modern Quaker historian.
The causes of the division among Friends have been pointed out;
they were the new currents of thought seeping into the Society, the
struggle to resist the encroaching power of the Quaker hierarchy,
and the widening differences between urban and rural Friends.
Rufus M. Jones adds, "It has been seriously questioned whether
there would have been a separation in 1827-28 if it had not been for

the aggressive influence of [Evangelical] visitors from England." [1]
It is maintained in this book that no division among American
Quakers would have occurred, certainly not outside of Philadelphia,
without the direct interference of English Evangelical ministers
traveling with the weight and authority of London Yearly Meeting.

It is difficult in any age to recapture the message of an earlier in-
terpreter of Christianity, and to understand its impact upon men
and women in a period long past. Emphases change, hot words grow
cold, moving phrases lose their power to reach men, and new ideas
thrust former battle cries into the background. In a day when
Quakers prefer ten-minute talks, and the typical Protestant minister
turns to ritual to fill half the time occupied by sermons in his grandfather's day, it is hard to appreciate how breathless congregations
numbering several thousand listened to Elias Hicks speak from
forty minutes to two hours or more. To those who heard him in a
frontier cabin, in a Maryland tobacco barn, a Pennsylvania stone
Meeting House, a district school, in an orchard, or beneath the
silver-grey shingles of a Long Island Quaker building, his words
came with soul-stirring power. As an orator he has been classed with
Webster, Clay, and Everett; but it was his message that drew people
to him—the message of the Light of God within man, the certainty
that there were hidden depths of personality which connect, through
channels beyond our tracing, with the Ultimate Reality. The perfectionism held by Hicks led him to reject the Calvinistic teaching
of Evangelicals concerning the depravity of man, and spurred his
effective work against slavery. He firmly maintained the Quaker
testimonies for simplicity, temperance, and peace. His message,
which combined the ancient mystical doctrine of the nearness and
willingness of God to guide the individual, with his fresh emphasis
on the full use of human reason, came to thousands with the power
of the first Publishers of Truth.

Elias Hicks' home life was tender; he was a good neighbor and a
welcomed visitor. Rufus Jones writes that he "was far and away the
most striking personality of the historical drama" of the Separation; [2]

and D. Elton Trueblood says, "In many ways, Elias Hicks is the most picturesque and dramatic figure that American Quakerism has produced." [3] Yet he was a man of his times, looking backward as well as forward. He opposed the building of canals and railroads, as well as the absorption of Quaker merchants in shipping and extensive trade, certain that these pursuits would cause the spiritual life to be neglected. He helped to build the "hedge" which for decades cut Friends off from the rest of the world. He was not a trained theologian, and some of his religious ideas are dated. His use of the Bible anticipates modern Biblical criticism, permitting the retention of eternal religious and ethical truths, freed from earlier and less worthy antecedents. Timeless is his insistence that revelation is progressive and continuous. On the whole, no Quaker Liberal, or twentieth-century mystic, need be ashamed of the logical thinking of Elias Hicks. As with all important forward-looking religious teachers, the implications of his words are carried to fuller conclusions by modern Liberals.

Some readers may feel the author has overindulged in quotations; the answer rests in the certainty that the personality of Elias Hicks, the setting of his life among a distinct and "separate" people, can be most effectively portrayed by the quaintness and beauty of words of an earlier day. It is hoped that in these pages the great Liberal of Jericho will return out of the mists of time, and that the reader may catch something of his strong character and dynamic message.

BLISS FORBUSH
Friends School

Baltimore, Maryland
December, 1955

Acknowledgments

ROBERT LIVEZEY, a Baltimore Friend, made a thorough collection of Quaker books, magazines, and pamphlets published between 1820 and 1845. Through the kindness of his relatives the library came to me. It has saved hours of work in distant places. Friends in Baltimore Yearly Meeting have added original or copied Hicks material. The Record Room at Stony Run Meeting was always available.

On Long Island, Friends were most helpful. The late Daniel Underhill, then Clerk of Jericho Monthly Meeting, and Bertha Underhill on a number of occasions opened their home that I might spend hours with the Jericho Records. Descendants of Elias and Isaac Hicks have supplied papers or answered questions concerning local traditions. These include Robert Seaman, Phebe U. Seaman, Marietta Hicks, Samuel J. Seaman, William Seaman, and Henry Hicks. Dr. Franklin Hicks of Halifax, Nova Scotia, added information on the Long Island Loyalists. At Westbury, Leon Rushmore, Recorder of the Meeting, made possible a study of those records, and here was found the original *Journal* of Elias Hicks. Mrs. Le Roy Newell of Glen Head permitted the reading of two hundred and fifty letters in her possession which were written to Elias Hicks.

Jesse Merritt, Nassau County Historian, supplied many photostats and gave sound advice.

In New York City, Gladys S. Seaman and Percy Clapp made available records in the Joint New York Yearly Meeting Records Room. Dr. Charles F. Gosnell, State Librarian at Albany, supplied a necessary list of books on early Long Island, arranging for the use of those not available in Baltimore. Anna B. Hewitt at Haverford College Library was helpful. William Bacon Evans sent advice, books, and leaflets bearing on the Separation. At Friends House, London, Muriel Hicks kindly opened the records of that Yearly Meeting and supplied diaries of Evangelical Friends who visited America before and during the Separation. At Friends Historical Library of Swarthmore College, Dorothy G. Harris, Assistant Librarian, was of invaluable assistance.

To the Friends General Conference I am beholden for assistance in making the publication of the manuscript possible; to John W. Seybold for photographs of the Partridge bust and the Inman portrait at Swarthmore College; to Elise Voysey for photographs taken on Long Island; and to Joan McQuary for assistance in seeing the book through the press.

To all the above I am deeply grateful, to four individuals I owe a special debt of gratitude: to my friend Dr. A. S. Chalfant for his constant encouragement and inspiration; to Dr. Sidney E. Mead of the Divinity School of the University of Chicago, who has read the manuscript and made many wise proposals; to Dr. Frederick B. Tolles, Librarian, Friends Historical Library of Swarthmore College, who is the godfather of this book and who has spent hours in reading various versions of the manuscript and who has made vital suggestions; and most of all to LaVerne H. Forbush, who has spent days transcribing material, hunting records, checking facts, and, above all, has had the not-too-easy task of living with Elias Hicks as a "house guest"—by constant reminder if not in person— these past nine years.

B. F.

Contents

Illustrations

MAPS

ELIAS HICKS: *Quaker Liberal*

1

A

Quaker Boyhood

ELIAS HICKS, turbulent prophet of Liberal Quakerism, was born, "the nineteenth day of the Third month, 1748," [1] on the Hempstead Plain of Long Island. Within a fifteen-mile circle he spent much of his rich life, although it seemed to his friends that for months and years the Island served only as a base of operations from which the great preacher traveled as far north as Canada, through the ever westward-moving frontier into Indiana, and south among the slave-tilled farms of Maryland and Virginia. Always Elias Hicks found it necessary to return to the Island and draw strength from contact with the land, affectionate encouragement from his family, and new insights received as he sat with his fellow worshipers in the Quaker Meeting House. Elias' parents, John and Martha, had established a home on land given to John in his twenty-fourth year by his father Jacob Hicks "for and in consideration of the Love Good Will and Affection," he held, "towards [his] Well Beloved Son." Here on "ye third part of [the] patent Right in ye sd town of Hempstead," [2] Samuel, John, Jacob, Elias, Stephen, and a younger brother spent their youth in the exciting days of the mid-century.

In later years, Elias Hicks referred to his forebears as of "reputable families"; [3] his heritage recorded in the early annals of Massachusetts and Long Island is a goodly one. Robert Hicks, who sailed for Plymouth in the *Fortune* in 1621, was the founder of the Hicks family in the new country. Robert was a friend of the first authorities in the Plymouth Colony—Miles Standish, Elder Brewster, and Governor Bradford—and died in 1647 on land formerly owned by John Alden of romantic fame. Robert's son John of Hempstead, Long Island, was the first of many Hickses who became magistrates, judges, captains of militia, treaty-makers with the Indians, and delegates to colonial assemblies. After John came Thomas, a Justice of the Common Pleas Court. Thomas defended Samuel Bownas, a Quaker in difficulty with the Hempstead churchmen, for attacking their doctrines and ceremonies. This defense, mentioned by Elias with satisfaction in his Journal, introduced the Hicks family to the enthusiastic Quakers then invading Long Island.

Jacob Hicks, son of Thomas the Justice, was impressed by the earnestness of the Friends although he, like his father, was a staunch Anglican, serving as a church warden and vestryman of St. George's Church at Hempstead. His wife, Hannah Carpenter, daughter of a founder of the Baptist Church in America, held Nonconformist views. Thomas Chalkley, an itinerant Quaker minister of power, made two visits in the neighborhood, lodging with Jacob and Hannah. After these visits Jacob ceased to be a vestryman, although he did not become a Quaker. It was not easy for a churchman to join a sect whose prophets in the previous generation created tumult and incited ridicule when preaching in the open fields. On occasions Friends were still moved by visions and revelations. This lingering emotionalism disturbed Jacob Hicks, yet he was willing to open his home for a monthly gathering of Friends for worship.

Jacob's son John, who was Elias' father, influenced by the gatherings held in Jacob's house, longed to possess the great joy which came to Friends through their certainty of the forgiveness and love of God. He felt that the Quakers were actually reviving Apostolic

Christianity by removing the layers of theological dust accumulated over the centuries, by cutting through the tradition and custom which had blanketed the primitive faith. He finally joined the Society by convincement a few years before the birth of Elias, and became a faithful member of Westbury Monthly Meeting.

Little is known of Martha Smith Hicks, Elias' mother. Elias wrote that she "was never in strict fellowship with any religious society, but was a Woman of Strict Morality and generally beloved and respected by her Neighbors, and acquaintance, of every profession." [4] As the Hickses had been repulsed in earlier days by the Enthusiasm of the Quaker exhorters walking the streets of Newtown and Hempstead, so Martha Smith was repulsed by the Quietism now dominant in the Society. The atmosphere of silent waiting upon God in Meetings for Worship, with all human impulses stifled, all "creaturely activities" set aside, did not appeal to her. She found it hard on First day mornings to achieve a spiritual vacuum within her soul that the Divine word might come to her. She was never sure whether the voice of God or her own instincts commanded her attention. Martha Smith was an individualist who could not bring herself to yield her own opinion to the judgment of the group as required by the Quaker Meeting for Business. Social mysticism did not "speak to her condition." [5]

On First and Fourth day mornings the Hicks family drove the three miles to the Westbury Meeting House for worship. Elias' sensitive nature was open to spiritual impressions and he "early felt the operation of divine grace." [6] At the age of seven he experienced a "night vision." He dreamed that on the way home from school he came to a certain hollow tree where a wren had her nest. As he reached in to draw out the eggs, a stream of flame issued from the hollow tree enclosing him in a blaze of pure fire about eight feet in diameter. In this flame he saw the face of an angel as he had seen one in pictures. Struck with amazement and horror he looked wildly about him for relief, then noted his father standing outside the flame. In a calm and assured manner Elias' father requested him to be still and the boy awoke to find himself safe in bed. The remembrance of this vision exerted a strong influence on Elias for many years, strengthening him "to resist evil for fear of the fatal consequences." [7] He thought of the experience as a revelation of the goodness of God sent to him as a special mark of Divine care.

When Elias was eight years old, John Hicks moved from the farm near Westbury to East Rockaway. This portion of his inheritance lay five miles southwest of Hempstead village, and was adjacent to acres belonging to the boy's uncles, Jacob and Thomas. John Hicks' farm included a creek, woods, orchard, marsh land, pasture land, a house, barn, smokehouse, and a third part of Long Beach. At one corner was the Hicks cemetery in which Elias' grandfather was buried, as well as a relative whose name the boy bore. With the move to Rockaway, Elias left behind the undulating fields and wooded dells of the north shore of the Island for the plains extending south to the salt marshes, bays, and narrow sand bars. These plains were treeless in colonial times, and in Elias' youth ten thousand acres were still kept as common pasture. Walt Whitman delighted in these "prairie-like vistas." [8] They stretched smooth and unbroken as the surface of a sea in calm, without tree or shrub, covered with a coarse high grass. As a boy, Elias took much delight in hunting and fishing in the great copper-colored marshes and in the bays full of fish and aquatic fowl. On the weird white-grey sand bars he, with his brothers, found many wrecked ships, gaunt witnesses to the power of the winter storms. They talked with descendants of the Indian tribes who once had their chief camping ground at Rockaway. The Indians, and the south Long Island whalers, were vanishing brotherhoods with tales fascinating to growing boys.

The education of boys in pre-Revolutionary days was informal. The struggle involved in subduing a new country; securing a livelihood from the land, forest, and sea was an education in itself. Formal schooling in Hempstead Town between 1748 and 1765, when Elias was growing up, was highly irregular. The intellectual interests of the Hempstead people were limited, as most had little book learning and only slight skill in reading, writing, and counting. At an early period, land was set aside for a school and for the house and garden of the schoolmaster, but the Annals of the town indicate that the schoolmaster's house was seldom occupied. The town minister frequently acted as teacher, and during the boyhood of Elias Hicks, the Reverend Samuel Seabury, whose wife was a distant relative, taught the school at Hempstead.[9] A catechist, sent by the Society for the Propagation of the Gospel in Foreign Parts, wrote of the children in Hempstead that they were, "for want of letters and education, as wild, uncultivated, and unimproved, as the soil when their forefathers first had it." [10] In such a school Elias learned his letters. He was advanced for his years and at an early age took pleasure in reading the Scriptures. When he was twelve, the Epistle from London, read in every Quaker Meeting in the colonies, urged parents to procure such useful learning for their children as their ability admitted. John Hicks gave his children all the useful learning that the environment provided, although such learning to him meant the knowledge necessary to gain a livelihood by craft, trade, or agriculture.

A Long Island farm provided most of the physical needs of those who cultivated the land. Elias learned to prepare the ground for wheat, to harvest and to grind it into flour. He helped to make butter and cheese, to preserve meat by smoking and pickling. Now and then he went on excursions to the beaches for lobsters and clams, or helped to salt and dry fish caught off the inlets. Flax was raised on the Hempstead farm and turned into linen cloth, wool became blankets and clothing. In the fall apple butter was made and barrels of cider were stored in the cellars for winter use, as the Quakers objected to the use of rum and fruit brandies. Except for tea and coffee, the rare white sugar, and spices, the needs of a Long Island family were supplied by land and water.

Political life at Hempstead, especially the town meeting, provided some unusual elements in the education of the Quaker boy. These gatherings exemplified democracy in action. The population assem-

bled at the beat of a drum, with every boy in the community on hand.
The boys put the town house in place, a movable booth which
rested beside the road during the year. Elias watched the election
of moderator, supervisor, and magistrates. He noted that decisions
were made by the lifting of hands, so unlike the method of reaching decisions in the Quaker Meeting where no vote was ever taken.
He listened to native orators, heard motions to set the dates for cutting the hay on the salt marshes, turning the cattle out to common
pasture, and parting of the sheep. He knew that his father's sheep
mark was "a latch ye fore side ye oaf Ear and two hapneys under
ye near Ear." [11] He heard decisions rendered involving the time when
fishermen might seine their catch, and watched as licenses were
granted for grist mills and taverns. In the stormy days preceding the
Revolution, the town meetings became the scene of heated debate
and created much excitement, especially as Queens County population was divided between Tories, Whigs, and pacifist Quakers.

The happiest days at Rockaway ended when Elias was eleven
with the death of Martha Hicks. His father, now with six growing
boys, depended during the next five years on a young niece with a
lively disposition who was ready when John Hicks was away to
join the boys in their merriment. Yet Elias was sensitive at this early
age to spiritual impressions. He wrote, "I can look back to my childhood, and see [God's] mercy and kindness toward me. How it often
softened my heart and clothed me with feelings of love. I knew not
from whence it came, but it caused me to look up and love him.
When I transgressed, I was ready to reprove and impeach myself for
my folly. My pillow was often wet with my tears, when I was very
young." [12]

In 1761, fearing that thirteen-year-old Elias would fall into bad
company, John Hicks sent him to live with the oldest married
brother who had settled at a distance from Rockaway. This was not
a happy experience for Elias. Long afterwards he expressed the
opinion that children should not be removed from under the watch-

ful notice of their parents, and that parents ought to consider "the right education and preservation of their tender offspring as the most important matter next to the care of their own souls." [13] While in the home of his brother Samuel, Elias joined with the young people in the neighborhood in all their pleasures. Walt Whitman's grandfather spent much of his time with Elias; together they went to the country balls, sang vain songs, joined in merrymakings and sleigh-rides in the winter over the plains. Whitman said that Elias was a thorough gunner and fisherman, a fine horseman, and a lad who knew horses and rode them successfully at races.

Annual races had been established by the English governor many years before, in 1665. The excitement of racing horses was in the blood of Hempstead boys. Many highly bred stallions and mares were introduced into Long Island from England, and across the Sound the most distinctive colonial breed of horses, the Narragansett pacer, was developed. Crowds came to the contests, and the New York *Gazette* frequently carried accounts of the events, the wagers, and the gentry in attendance at the race track at the Little Plains. The *Gazette* spoke of as many as "seventy chairs and chaises and many more horsemen" [14] passing over the ferry for a single sporting event. Elias enjoyed managing swift horses. On one occasion, when setting off at a fast clip, he was thrown over sixteen feet from his horse but, though stunned and very much shaken up, he was not badly hurt. This incident he was later to consider a most merciful and unmerited preservation.

In time, Elias' conscience was disturbed by the enjoyment which he took in racing horses, playing cards, and attending dances—all quite contrary to the Quaker discipline. He barely escaped becoming one of the "world's people," and in the time spent under his brother's roof "lost much of [his] youthful innocence," and "was led wide from the salutary path of true religion." [15]

When Elias was seventeen, his father married Phebe Powell. John Hicks arranged for Elias to be apprenticed to a carpenter who traveled in the Hempstead area. Elias' master was an orderly man who care-

fully taught the trade of carpenter and joiner to his assistants, but
he was a man in an "eager pursuit after temporal riches," and so
of little use, Elias thought, in his "religious improvement." Moving
from place to place with his master, Elias was "introduced into hurtful company . . . passed through many trials and much exposure";
he believed it was only "the interposition of divine mercy and goodness" [16] which kept him from falling prey to the various temptations
which surrounded him.

Elias Hicks was not as religiously precocious as his contemporaries,
John Woolman, the tailor of Mount Holly, or Job Scott of Rhode
Island; and yet about this time Elias began to read his Bible many
hours at a time, to give himself to solid meditations, to devote himself to religious improvement. Gradually becoming conscious of the
nearness of God, Elias had to make a decision whether the good or
evil seed, which the Friends taught was in every soul, should gain
ascendancy in his life. A long battle followed, with many retreats,
spiritual rallies, and a dearly won victory in the end. Eventually, Elias
turned his back on his beloved sports, fishing and hunting, deciding
that he would never "take the life of any creature, except it was
really useful and necessary when dead, or very noxious and hurtful
when living." [17] Dancing, which he greatly enjoyed, suddenly became odious to him, and with a heavy heart he decided to refrain
from it. He vacillated for a time, but finally decided that he must
cease from the amusement forever or go to his eternal ruin. He was
convinced on the dance floor that if he continued this gaiety he never
again would be forgiven. Struck by the thought, Elias stood still, his
limbs fettered to the wood, then walked to the side of the room and
told his companions he would never dance again as long as he lived.
He gave up playing cards, frolicking and gaming into the small
hours of the morning, and horse racing. He no longer consorted
with his old companions, but began to cultivate the acquaintance
and guidance of more Friends. He sought to attend Meetings for
Worship with greater frequency, and in the association of like-

minded people, he found the necessary strength to carry out his
newly formed resolutions.

In arriving at a state of manhood, Elias found a very pernicious
and hurtful custom prevailing, through the unwarranted indulgence of parents in his own and other parts of the country. The custom
of bundling grew out of the desire of young people to secure privacy
during the long winter evenings when the entire family assembled
in the main kitchen before the open fire. Elias described the custom
in censorious words:

Young people, more especially on the evenings of the first days of the
week, and after passing the evening until late in foolish and vain conversation would couple out as the young men and women could agree,
and retire in secret, where they spent the rest of the night frequently on
beds together.

Elias added that this custom was "sinful, indecent, and immodest,"
and was astonished that "Friends' children, likewise indulged in this
practice." [18]

Hints as to the wrestling in the soul of the Hempstead boy are
found in later reminiscences. It was "the fear of God that dwelt in
[his] soul" that kept him from falling into evil ways when in his
teens, and the growing assurance that God had called him to a
special task to be undertaken at some future day. During his apprenticeship, Elias sat in the home of his master and meditated upon
the law of God and waited in quiet until God showed him the direction in which to proceed. "All this he does for youth," Elias wrote.
"He makes them feel his goodness and love." [19] This he could testify
out of his own experience.

Elias did not show signs of religious leadership until after his
marriage. Meanwhile he gave more time to reading the Scriptures
and other religious books. The Bible became for him a source of
ancient history, a manual of style, and a book of spiritual revelation.
In a measure it took the place in his life, as a means of culture, of
higher education. Elias borrowed his father's books dealing with

the Quakers, the Journals of George Fox and Thomas Ellwood, William Sewel's *History of the Rise, Increase, and Progress of the Christian People called Quakers.* He secured the loan of books from his neighbors, and it was said that "a new book possessed for him such charm . . . that his friends who invited him for a social visit, knowing this, were careful to put the new books out of sight, lest he should become absorbed in them, and they lose his ever-welcome and very entertaining conversation." [20]

About this time Elias learned the science of surveying and began to practice it in the neighborhood. He also taught for a time in the village school. One of his pupils said of his proficiency in this field: "The manners of Elias Hicks were so mild, his deportment so dignified, and his conversation so instructive, that it left an impression for good on many of his pupils' minds that time never effaced." [21] Elias' religious thinking, like John Woolman's, developed from his study of the Bible, his knowledge of the ideas of Friends, and his own experimental faith. He probably did not realize as he sat in quiet Meetings for Worship and Business that he was gaining a rich spiritual heritage. He knew that he loved the Quaker ways and thrilled within when he heard ministers speak of the Indwelling Christ, the Inner Light which guided a man into all truth and gave him power to follow the truth. He felt a new dignity within himself and in his relation to others as he meditated upon the oft-repeated message of "that of God in every man." [22] Elias accepted the Quaker ideal of perfectionism. Reverence, chastity, honesty, temperance, integrity, and vocation were to young Hicks proper expressions of the Quaker way of life. He saw nothing odd in giving women an equality with men in matters religious. He heartily approved of the Quaker testimony against the taking of oaths and engaging in warlike activities. He felt that the use of titles was a mark of vanity, as was the adoption of the changing styles in dress. Elias Hicks found himself a convinced Friend.[23]

The home, the school, the political life of the Long Island community, the varied tasks that came to his hand on the farm and as an apprentice, all exerted a powerful influence upon Elias Hicks. It was the Society of Friends that provided the dominant force which determined his mental and emotional development.

II

Hand

in Hand

IN A CONVENIENT OPPORTUNITY I opened my mind to her, and receiving from her a mutual return of affection and good will therein . . . and after divers opportunities together, and duly weighing the subject as a matter of great importance, and feeling a continual increase of mutual love, we were prompted to believe that our proceeding therein, was consistent with truth.[1]

In this manner Elias Hicks recorded in his Journal the culmination of his courting of Jemima Seaman. Elias, like most men, was reticent about affairs of the heart. No letters from the first period of their acquaintance have survived, but it is easy to see that if such were written they were feelingly expressed. "I feel my mind drawn at this time to salute thee," Elias wrote to Jemima after their marriage, "in that near and sympathetic affection and precious unity, that binds [us] together in that unutterable love, that neither time nor distance can wear out or erase. And my desires are . . . that so we may be as Epistles Written in Each others hearts." [2] In the same year, Elias told his love in words which must have been precious to her: "In the Sweet Influences of that Love that neither Distance, Nor Death, Can obliterate or Erase, do I salute thee with Endeared Embraces and fervent are the Desires and Prayer of my Spirit to the God and Father of all our Tender Mercies for [thy] Preservation . . . and that while I am absent . . . you may be the Immediate object of his Merciful and Paternal Regard.[3] But the written word could never completely convey his affection. "Oh my dear," he wrote, "my pen is not able, nor Language sufficient to Express the one half of the love wherewith my heart overflows towards thee at this time." [4] It is obvious that Elias' heart beat wildly when he received from Jemima Seaman "a mutual return of affection and good will." [5]

After he had acquired the carpenter's trade and had returned home, Elias found that the Hicks family had transferred from the fast diminishing Friends' group at Rockaway to the large and flourishing one at Westbury. Here in the Meeting already so necessary for his spiritual well-being, he first met Jemima Seaman of Jericho. Young people came together in a natural manner at Quaker affairs, much sociability was mixed with the gatherings for Worship and Business. Friends soon noted that Elias and Jemima attended Preparative, Monthly, and Quarterly Meetings whether held at Westbury, Cowneck, Bethpage, or Matinecock. The "divers opportunities" afforded by the nature of the Society proved sufficient for the two young Friends to "gain an intimate acquaintance" with one another.[6] Glances passed over the heads of elders, attention wandered from pious exhortations, hands touched in passing or while waiting upon the needs of guests following the meetings, and excuses were found to invite Elias to the Seaman homestead. All signs pointed to the fact that the young people were truly in love with each other, and that both families approved the attachment.

Jemima Seaman was the daughter of Jonathan and Elizabeth Willis Seaman. Her father was of the third generation following Captain John Seaman, one of the original settlers of Hempstead and a fellow magistrate with Elias' ancestor, John Hicks. Captain Seaman owned

a tract of twelve thousand acres of land on Long Island reaching
from "sea to sea." [7] He with his sons settled Jerusalem (Wantagh)
nine miles south of Jericho. The next generation moved to the north
shore near Oyster Bay, where there was a strong Quaker community.
The Seaman family were among the first Friends on Long Island,
securing membership before 1686.

On November 29, 1770, according to the time-stained pages of the
Westbury records, Elias Hicks and Jemima Seaman appeared in a
Business Meeting of Westbury Monthly Meeting and declared they
intended to take one another in marriage. This declaration was accompanied by written consent of both families. After a suitable time
for reflection, the assembled Friends appointed two of Elias' neighbors, John Mott and Micajah Mott, to "make inquiry into [his]
clearness in relation to marriage with other women, and to make
report at the next Monthly Meeting." In December, Elias and Jemima
repeated their intentions and asked for the consent of the Meeting.
John and Micajah Mott reported that Elias was "clear of marriage
engagements to other women." After due consideration the Monthly
Meeting gave its approval and appointed Robert Seaman, Jemima's
uncle, and John Mott to attend the marriage, see that all was done
in a proper manner, and report back.[8]

Jonathan Seaman's home at Jericho was large enough for the wedding as was the Widow Seaman's house in which Meetings for Worship were held, but for sentimental reasons the young couple wanted
to be married within the walls of the old building at Westbury.
Thus, according to the marriage certificate, "the Second day of the
first month in the Year of our Lord Christ one thousand seven hundred and seventy one," [9] Elias and Jemima sat in the Meeting for
Worship at Westbury which was to culminate in their marriage.
With Jemima on the women's side of the room was her mother,
two aunts, and a young cousin. On the men's side with Elias was
his father; two brothers, Stephen and Jacob; his cousin Benjamin;
John Hicks; Jemima's father; and two of Jemima's uncles. Future
neighbors of the young couple came from Jericho, as well as old

friends from Westbury, Hempstead, and Rockaway. After the gathering of thirty Friends had continued for a period in silence, Elias and Jemima came together to the front of the Meeting House, where, taking Jemima by the hand, Elias promised "with divine assistance" to be unto her a true and loving husband until death should separate them. Jemima made a similar promise after which both were seated facing the assembly where the marriage certificate was placed before them for their signatures. Words of commendation and advice were uttered as the worship continued, then the elders shook hands and friends and relatives came forward to felicitate the bride and groom. All present signed their names on the certificate.

Following the meeting, Jemima and Elias drove to her father's house in Jericho. Here Friends came again to greet the young couple and to admire Jemima's wedding dress, cut in the conservative fashion approved by Friends. The plain linen gown, probably spun and fashioned by Jemima herself, was softened by the fine lawn kerchief folded and pinned at each side of her waist. Her light-colored bonnet with soft crown and many pleats set off her happy face. Elias wore the shad-belly coat and collarless waistcoat of the day. His hand-knit stockings were tucked into high boots. The Meeting committee came also to the Seaman house to see that all was "consummated orderly," and one of them followed to Rockaway whither Elias took his bride. At the February Monthly Meeting the representatives reported that the marriage was accomplished in a manner agreeable to Friends. Elias and Jemima lived for only a few months at Rockaway, for in the spring they were invited by Jonathan and Elizabeth Seaman to live on the home place in Jericho. Here, through fifty-eight years of great joy—and some sorrow—Elias and Jemima dwelt.

The Jericho Turnpike runs from Brooklyn east to the furthermost point on Long Island, at Jericho it crosses the north-south road from Oyster Bay to Massapequa. In colonial times this road was a continuation of the Kings Highway which began at the ferry at the foot of Fulton Street in Brooklyn and ran through Kings County. In later days it was the road over which farmers hauled their produce from Queens County to the ferry for New York. Jericho was part of a large tract of land purchased from the Indians in 1648 by Robert Williams, an ancestor of Jemima Seaman. In early days it was called Lusum or the Farms. Friends were in the area by 1676, and when Elias and Jemima settled in Jericho it was a hamlet of less than a dozen houses scattered along the four roads. There may have been a tavern in the town, though it is recorded in later years that Elias Hicks kept open house for strangers so that liquor would not be publicly sold.

The farmhouses along the roads were covered from the ground to the ridgepole with cedar shingles bleached a soft grey by the winter storms, and shaded by locust and chestnut trees. Nearby were orchards made fruitful by scions taken from trees brought from Europe; beyond the orchards lay gentle rolling farm lands. Elias' neighbors were assisted by indentured servants or by Negro slaves brought to Long Island by the Quaker shipowners of Rhode Island. The Seaman house was large and commodious; John Comly, a Quaker minister of Byberry, Pennsylvania, on a visit to his friend, called it a mansion. The house was typical of those in the neighborhood, with two rooms facing the east and a long hall leading to the wing where the servants lived. A large kitchen with the necessary brick oven was at the rear. Four massive chimneys provided for the fireplaces which for many years heated the house. It was said that Elias Hicks loved to promenade up and down the long central hall, sometimes with his visitors, "and here with characteristic warmth of feeling he sped his parting guests, when the time of their departure came." [10]

The farmers lived well as recorded in the diary of Ann Warden, an English woman who visited in Jericho soon after Elias and Jemima were married. For breakfast "stores of butter, coffee, tea, and chocolate, with smoked beef, cheese and honey were served." At noon there was fish "in great perfection" and fresh asparagus; and the meats for the evening meal were followed by apple pie and custard.[11] The Jonathan Seaman farm contained approximately seventy-five

Whereas Elias Hicks Son of John Hicks of Rockway in the Township of Hempstead in Queens County on Nassau Island in the Province of New York. And Jemima Seaman Daughter of Jonathan Seaman of Jericho in the Township of Oyster bay in the County Island and Province aforesaid having Declared their Intentions of Marriage With each other Before Two several Monthly Meetings of the People Called Quakers at Westbury In the Bounds of Hempstead aforesaid According to the good Order Used and Amongst them Whose Proceeding therein After a Deliberate Consideration thereof And Having the Consent of Parents and Relations Concerned And Nothing Appearing to Obstruct Were Approved of by said Meeting

NOW These are to Certifie all Whome it May Concern that for the full Accomplishing their said Intention this Second day of the first Month In the Year of our Lord Christ One Thousand Seven Hundred Seventy one They the said Elias Hicks and Jemima Seaman Presented themselves in a Publick Meeting of the said People and Others at Westbury Aforesaid, And the said Elias Hicks taking the said Jemima Seaman by the hand did in a Solemn Manner Openly Declare that he Took her to be his Wife Promising to be unto her a True and Loving husband untill Death Seperate them And then and There in the said Assembly the said Jemima Seaman Did the likewise Declare that She Took the said Elias Hicks to be her Husband Promising to be unto him a True and Loving Wife untill death doth Seperate Them And Moreover the said Elias Hicks and Jemima Seaman She Assuming the Name of her husband As a further Confirmation thereof did then and There to these Presents Set their hands And We Whose Names Are hereunder Subscribed Being there Present at the Solemnization of the said Marriage and the Subscription In Manner as above said have also as Witness Set our hands to these Presents the Day and Year above Written

Elias Hicks
Jemima Hicks

This Certificate Recorded in Westbury monthly
Meeting Book in page 86 by
Samuel Willis Clerk

Philadelphia Seaman
Phebe Post
Henry Post
Elizabeth Willis
Phebe Willis
Martha Seaman
John Willis
John Post
Williams Seaman
Sarah Loines
Anne Willis
Phebe Willis
Keziah Willis
Mary Seaman

John Hicks
Jonathan Seaman
Elizabeth Seaman
Phebe Dodg
Mary Willis
Esther Seaman
Stephen Hicks
Robert Seaman
Silas Hicks
Rachel Hicks
Benjamin Hicks
Isaac Dodg
Henry Willis
William Willis
Jury Willis
Jacob Hicks

THE WEDDING CERTIFICATE OF JEMIMA SEAMAN AND ELIAS HICKS.
Jemima's signature on this certificate is one of the few known samples of her handwriting.

THE SEAMAN-HICKS HOME, AS IT IS TODAY. *Elias and Jemima lived here for all but a few months of their fifty-eight years of married life.*

THE HOME OF VALENTINE AND ABIGAIL HICKS. *Abigail, the fifth child of Elias and Jemima, married her second cousin and lived just across the road from her parents.*

acres of rolling land with some detached wood lots. In addition, Elias' father-in-law had the right to cut hay on the salt marshes ten miles south. Across the road from the nineteen-room farmhouse was the tanning establishment which Jonathan operated in addition to his farm. This included a bark mill, bark house, and shop; at the back of the lot was the spring and pond which supplied the water necessary in the treatment of hides.

Jericho, only twenty-five miles from Brooklyn, was isolated from the bustling life of the colonies.[12] A stagecoach traveling the length of the Island took three days to make the journey of one hundred and twenty miles. On roads leading away from the farm, Elias could drive for miles beneath overhanging boughs of chestnut, oak, and pine, through lanes bordered by thickets of alder and sumach. In the spring the landscape was a mass of white dogwood; in the fall it was bright with pepperidge and sassafras, and the yellow brilliance of smooth-shafted tulip trees.

Elias Hicks loved the land. He took satisfaction in looking after his stock and watching the round of seasons. He wrote in his *Journal* that life was only probationary, that he was a pilgrim with his gaze fastened on the glorious vistas of celestial abodes that lay ahead; still he delighted in the rolling hills, the streams and valleys, the sturdy trees and running brooks, and accepted them as gifts which the Divine Creator set before men to enjoy in the here-and-now. Elias enjoyed a hard day's work in the fields. He found an exhilaration in swinging his scythe through the stout marsh grass, or cradling the long stalks of wheat or rye. He exemplified the Quaker virtue of industry. He believed that man was accountable to God for the use of his time, and that an individual must administer to the best of his ability the responsibility that God laid upon his shoulders. The farmer at Jericho did not fail to have plenty of good fodder in his barns to feed his stock when winter was approaching "so as to render their lives comfortable as may be, whilst under [his] care." [13] Elias' barns were tight against the winds that howled in from the Atlantic. When about to leave home on a journey he spent many days making careful preparations so that he could leave in peace and quietness of mind. If he thought of matters relating to the farm while away from home he sent advice to Jemima concerning the fields to be plowed, manured, and planted; whether or not fence rails needed to be split and which fences needed repair; what animals to sell or butcher for family use. Elias believed that in spite of public service or unusual responsibility a man's first duty was to his family. "He who doth not take the necessary care for his own, and families' comfortable support," he wrote, "may be considered to have denied the faith, and in that respect is worse than an infidel." [14]

Elias Hicks abhorred idleness and thought that no portion of precious time should pass away unimproved. It irked him when his tenants took a day off to watch the horse races; he lamented the fact that few men seemed satisfied to give an honest measure of labor for their hire. It seemed to him that most men were more anxious to obtain the highest wage than to earn it justly. Often the oversight of the farm, a congenial task in itself, was made irksome and unpleasant for him by the lack of faithful workmen. "I am willing to do my part cheerfully and industriously," he recorded, "and then I can with more confidence, place my trust and dependence on a gracious and beneficent Providence, for a blessing on my labour; for if care and industry be wanting, there is nothing for him to bless." [15]

With a touch of scorn which the man who works with his hands from sun-up to sun-down has for the soft clasp of the clerk or city man, Elias believed that those who left Queens County for Brooklyn or New York City did so primarily to avoid honest toil. "I find it needful," he wrote one evening after he finished a hard day's work in the fields, "to do nothing to promote or encourage idleness, that bane of every Christian virtue; and especially at such a time as this, when most of our capable well-looking young men are running into cities and populous towns to engage in merchandise, or some other calling by which they may live by their wits, being unwilling to labour with their hands: although it is the most sure way marked out by divine wisdom for our truest comfort and peace here, and a right preparation for eternal joy hereafter." [16]

After his family increased in size, Elias had little time left "unimproved." The clothing of each member of the household was made from flax raised in his fields or from wool shorn from his sheep. Shoes were made from hides of his own cattle, and tanned in the Seaman tannery. Jemima braided and sewed the straw hats that were worn in summer, and the fur caps for winter wear were made from the squirrels which Elias shot. The pillow cases, sheets, and blankets, the quilts, towels, and tablecloths were all of homemade materials and manufacture. The winter ticks were stuffed with straw from the fields, the pillows filled with feathers plucked from geese that once waddled to the brook near the farmhouse. The leather for the horses' harnesses was tanned in the Seaman bark mill; handles of axe, hoe, fork, and flail were grown in the Seaman timber lot. It was fortunate that Elias and Jemima needed to purchase but few articles from the itinerant peddlers or from the Westbury store, for eggs sold at ten cents a dozen, butter at seventeen cents a pound, beef at five cents a pound, and cheese at eleven cents a pound. Potatoes brought twenty-five cents a bushel.[17] If a day was taken off for fishing, and the catch was larger than the family could use, the balance was sold at five cents a pound if shad, two cents if herring.

Help was as uncertain in the house as in the fields. Elias was sure that Jemima carried too heavy a physical burden, and now and again noted that he labored more in the harvest fields than was good for his bodily well-being. But the work was done, the barns filled, the family needs were met, and there was something left over to share with others. Elias had time to turn a hand to help a neighbor straitened in doing his husbandry; he gave of his surplus to those in need. When the Charity Society was formed in Jericho "to help among the blacks," his name headed the list of thirty contributors with a gift of ten pounds.[18] Elias refused to make money by speculation. In a year when most farms on Long Island had poor yield, his crop was

large. Buyers traveling over Queens County offered repeatedly to
purchase his surplus grain at steadily rising prices. Elias refused to
sell even at the unprecedented price of three dollars a bushel. Later,
when his neighbors, whose need was great, came to him for grain,
Elias sold for one dollar a bushel.[19]

As Elias went about his work, he noted with an observing eye
the wealth of spiritual illustrations in the world about him; to him
the spring time and harvest were marks of God's love and bounty to
men. He was thankful that God gave him the opportunity to con-
template His works in the beauties of the fields. Elias was accumulat-
ing a reservoir of ideas which in a later day made it possible for him
to answer the needs of those whom he addressed.

III

Settling in

at Jericho

ELIAS AND JEMIMA moved into the Seaman homestead in the spring of 1771. In addition to the young couple, the household consisted of the grandfather, John Willis; the grandmother, Abigail Willis; Jemima's father, Jonathan; and her mother, Elizabeth Willis Seaman.[1] There were busy days ahead for the young bride of twenty who was expected to assist with the care of the grandparents, help her mother, look after her husband, and share the multitudinous tasks of the Seaman home. Other responsibilities were added in the following October when Martha was born, first of the fourth generation to be under the Seaman roof, to be followed by David in February of 1773, and Elias Junior in 1774. Thus, within a span of four years, there were nine members of the family living in the Seaman homestead. Since Jonathan Seaman owned at least three slaves to help with the farm work and in the tanyard, it is probable that there was some Negro help with the housework.

Elias was satisfied that his move to Jericho was distinctly advantageous to him from a religious point of view. There were worthy

Friends in the neighborhood whose example developed in him a new seriousness of purpose; yet the farm work was so exacting that his spiritual progress was slow. Three years after his marriage when he was twenty-six, there was a profound change in Elias' outlook. He began to feel the "operative influence of divine grace" upon his mind; he realized that even though his youthful sins and vanities were laid aside, there remained much evil "which [was] not yet atoned for." Elias felt the judgment of God resting upon him. Like many a spiritual pilgrim before his day, he wrestled within his soul, frequently calling on "the Most High for pardon and redemption." He waited in watchfulness and deep humility, pleading that a way would open before him, hoping that he could experience reconciliation with God. At last "light broke forth out of obscurity and [his] darkness became as the noon-day." Much strengthened by "deep openings in the visions of light," Elias was conscious that his perplexities were resolved.[2]

The trials through which he passed in 1774 resulted in a rededication, on the part of the young Quaker, to the beliefs and practices of the Society of Friends. He was now willing to give more serious attention to those testimonies which separated them from their neighbors; he gave thought to major social concerns such as the holding of slaves, and the evils of warfare. Elias began "with weighty labour" to ponder, in the monthly business gatherings of the Friends at Westbury the advices and queries of the Book of Discipline, which were regularly used to remind Friends of the high level of Christian ethics to which they were committed. He accepted the current view of the Society that it was a spiritual remnant guarded from the intrusion of alien elements. "After a long Night of Apostacy, it hath pleased the Lord to call a people to freedom, and from under that darkness and Superstition that had overspread the Christian Churches."[3] Gradually, as he listened to the ancient phrases of the Discipline, Elias came to a deeper understanding of their meaning than many of his fellow members. Words came to him and he felt a concern to speak to some of the subjects engaging the Meeting's

attention. As he spoke, his understanding of the profound implications of the great truths pronounced by George Fox and those who
came after him was "much enlarged."

Friends were quick to avail themselves of the services of a young
person who showed a willingness to assist in the functioning of the
Meeting. The absence of any paid leadership in the Quaker group
made it necessary for Monthly Meetings to appoint standing committees such as Ministers and Overseers, as well as less important
committees for special tasks. In August, 1774, Elias received his first
committee assignment, a simple one and quite appropriate for a
young man in his fourth year of married life. He was appointed to
investigate the "clearness from others" of a young Friend, Obadiah
Wright, who desired to marry a member of Meeting, to move within
the limits of Flushing Monthly Meeting; consent of the living parents had already been obtained. Elias and Jemima drove over to the
John Wright farm on the Hempstead Plains where the parents were
consulted concerning wedding plans in order that they might take
care that no reproach arise, or occasion be given "by any intemperance, or immoderate feasting or drinking," and that all should be
conducted "with such modesty and sobriety as becomes a people fearing God." [4] Obadiah was reminded that marriage implies union, in
spiritual as well as in temporal concerns. At the next Monthly Meeting Elias reported that "no obstruction" stood in the way of Obadiah
Wright's proceeding with his marriage.

A few months later, Elias Hicks was appointed to a second committee, one which was to function for a number of months. It was
the custom among Friends, when their members moved to a new
community and grew strong enough in numbers to warrant the
building of a house of worship, to "open a subscription" in other
Monthly Meetings of the same Province and raise funds to pay for
the building. During the last quarter of the eighteenth century,
Quakers were steadily moving up the Hudson Valley and becoming
more thickly settled in Westchester and Dutchess Counties. Elias
Hicks was asked to assist in raising funds with which to help build

new Meeting Houses at Amawalk in Westchester County, and at
Nine Partners in Dutchess County. His committee work in this case
involved driving from farm to farm, discussing the subject with his
Quaker neighbors, or appealing to Friends as they talked together
on the Meeting House porch after the business sessions. Quakers in
the rural areas had little cash, and as Friends in Jericho were gathering in private homes for their First day morning worship, they did
not feel strongly about collecting funds for other parts of the Yearly
Meeting. Elias might have gone to some non-Friends for help but
this had been prohibited by the last session of the Yearly Meeting.
"Weighty Friends," thinking a resort to arms a possibility, did not
wish their fellow members to be under obligation to any who might
not be in sympathy, during such crucial days, with Quaker pacifism.
Elias' committee was able to report some immediate success in raising funds for Amawalk, but it was five years before the turn of events
and sufficient interest could be aroused to warrant the construction
of a large building at Nine Partners.

On a First day morning in 1775, Friends were gathered in the
house of the "two Widows Seaman" for their morning worship.[5]
Warm sun came through the windows and rested upon the motion-
less figures of men and women who had driven in from the neighborhood farms to gather in quiet waiting upon God. The women,
in their neat dresses, green or blue aprons,[6] shawls and black hoods,
sat on one side of the main living room; and the men in their high
boots, black coats, collarless waistcoats, and dark breeches, sat, with
their black beaver hats on their heads, on the opposite side of the
room. In the silence the hum of a fly against the window pane could
be heard, or the movement of a child's dress as she pressed closer
to her mother.

The men found it difficult to keep from reflecting upon the work
of the week just past or the tasks that awaited them, or from speculat-
ing on the spirit of unrest which had seized the neighborhood. The

minds of mothers were torn between inward examination, consideration of the many duties that fell to them in their busy colonial house-
holds, and keeping a watchful eye on little people who found it hard
to sit on wooden stools for two hours at a time. Yet all strove to
"center down," to take all thought away from "creaturely activity,"
and to seek to enter the holy of holies where they might worship
the Lord in spirit and in truth.

Unexpectedly, toward the conclusion of the meeting, Elias Hicks
stood up under the stress of great emotion, uttered a few words, then
took his seat. Elias had wrestled "under close exercise and deep
travail of spirit" for a long time before he rose to speak in his home
Meeting. He believed, as did all his Quaker neighbors, that God's
revelation to man was as fresh and direct in Queens County, Long
Island, in the year 1775, as it had been to Amos at Bethel in the days
of King Uzziah, or to Paul as he heard the call to come over to
Macedonia. False prophets might come who claimed that they had
the right to utter the words, "Thus saith the Lord," as did Hananiah
in Jeremiah's day, but there were ways by which the chaff could
be sifted from the wheat and the true message be known. Although
he had spoken on subjects in Monthly and Preparative Meetings for
some time, Elias shrank from the prospect of speaking in the Meeting for Worship lest he mistake his guidance. For some weeks he had
tried to keep his mind quiet and "resigned to the heavenly call," resolved that if the call came he would be prepared to do his duty.
Yet when he first recognized a "secret, though clear, intimation" to
utter a few words, he was afraid and kept silent. Refusing to yield
to the intimation, Elias felt strongly rebuked in his mind and under
"judgment"; but as he "humbled [himself] under the Lord's mighty
hand" he was assured that God would forgive him as he had forgiven
Jonah if now he would be ready when the time came and God should
"require such a service of [him]." [7]

No Friend gathered in the home of the two widows Seaman
changed his or her expression when Elias Hicks rose to speak, but

a thrill passed through the gathered group. This breaking of the
silence, an act weighted with great significance, might mark the birth
of a new prophet in Israel. Jemima felt waves of emotion sweep over
her, a combination of pride, uneasiness, and fear; and in the subsequent silence her mind teemed with questions. Would Elias lapse
into silence in the following Meetings for Worship, or had a gift
in the ministry been conferred upon her husband? If such a gift was
to be his, would he, like John Willis of Jericho, David Sands of
Cowneck, and William Valentine of Hempstead, leave his family
for weeks, months, and even years at a time to follow his call by
ministering to Friends in other Meetings? What of the children and
the farm should he go riding the frontiers? As these questions passed
through Jemima's mind, conjectural yet prophetic, the prospect was
not altogether pleasing. Yet Jemima knew that Elias would obey if
the call came, and go wherever he might be sent; and that her lot
would be to cooperate in whatever measures were necessary, even
to shouldering alone the domestic burdens. She was thankful that
the members of the older generations were still at home with her,
and she steeled herself to meet the future.

When Elias returned to the farm after the morning gathering,
he felt in his soul deep "joy and sweet consolation . . . as a reward
for this act of faithfulness." [8] He turned anew to the reading of the
Scriptures, knowing that a living prophet must measure his utter-
ances by the truths revealed in the Old and New Testaments, since
the truth of God was always the same. During the long winter evenings he saturated his thinking with the great themes of prophet
and apostle, and filled his mind with Biblical phrases and illustrations. But Elias was not satisfied with reading the Bible; he knew,
with other Friends, that it was possible to rediscover the most important religious truths independent of the written word. The Quakers held that there was a Divine Light within man, a "radiance from
the central Light of the spiritual universe, penetrating the deeps of
every soul, which if responded to, obeyed, and accepted as a guiding

star, would lead into all truth and into all kinds of truth." [9] Elias
plumbed the depths of the inner well of his spirit. He waited in
silence, endeavoring to hear and understand the voice of God speaking inwardly. He knew if he could make contact with the Divine
Illumination he would have a priceless gift of truth to share with
those about him. He realized that he must go down through the
maze of worldly impressions, habits, thoughts, and traditions, and
come to the innermost sanctuary of the soul where God freshly revealed Himself.

Elias was anxious that he should not mistake his guide. He heard
Friends speak of young men and women who did not "dwell in
the root," or "went beyond their call"; and of others who spoke so
inarticulately that their fellow worshipers could not comprehend their
meaning. Such speakers were not meant for the highly important
and dignified office of minister. Elias did not wish to speak too readily
nor mistake the sparks of his own kindling for divine impressions.
Thus in quietness and inward calm he waited to see what lay before
him, "resigned to the heavenly call, if it should be made clear . . .
to be [his] duty." [10]

In this period of spiritual apprenticeship, Elias experienced an
increase in divine knowledge. Meanwhile he threw himself with
even greater energy into the work of the Meeting. "I was also deeply
engaged," he wrote, "for the right administration of discipline and
order in the Church, and that all might be kept sweet and clean,
consistent with the nature and purity of the holy profession [the
Quakers] were making." [11] This was time-consuming work for a
young man with heavy family obligations, who was expected to help
the Seamans with the work of the farm and tannery. It meant attendance at First and Fourth day Meetings for Worship in Jericho,
Preparative and Monthly Meetings for Business at Westbury, and
the acceptance of an occasional appointment as a representative to
the Quarterly Meeting. As the Yearly Meeting, which lasted several
days, was held in nearby Flushing, his name soon began to appear

on the lists of representatives, and on committees appointed by that
body. The Friends were testing out the leadership possibilities of the
young farmer of Jericho.

Elias Hicks had evidently acquitted himself in his various appoint-
ments with wisdom, for he was soon named to a responsibility which
required tact, firmness, and good judgment. Friends in New York
Yearly Meeting had been troubled for some years over the holding
of slaves by their members. Quakers have been thought of as "vir-
tually the conscience of the eighteenth century and pioneers in almost
all humanitarian endeavors"; [12] but the practice of slave-holding had
become established among them before they realized the iniquity
of the institution. Quaker landowners, as all colonial proprietors,
needed far more help than was available to cultivate their large tracts
of land; Quaker craftsmen could not find enough white apprentices
to assist them in their shops; Quaker shipowners found the importation of slaves to be a lucrative business; and Quaker families, like the
Hickses and Seamans, welcomed the Negroes as domestic help. Because the need was so great and because of an increasing number of
slaves coming into the Atlantic seaports, "it required more virtue
than even the Quakers were yet prepared to exert, in order to defend
them from the contagion of this evil." [13]

In 1776 Elias Hicks was appointed by the Monthly Meeting on a
committee to visit Friends who held Negroes as slaves. This was not
an easy task, as Friends held various opinions concerning the methods by which the evil practice might be overcome. Following the
impassioned pleas of John Woolman in his visit to Long Island
when Elias Hicks was a boy, New York Friends proceeded cau-
tiously to "discourage . . . the further purchase of Negroes." [14] They
did not wish to take more drastic action lest to move hastily might
"cause divisions, and introduce heart-burnings and strife amongst
[the members] which ought to be avoided, and charity exercised
and persuasive methods pursued, and that which makes for peace." [15]
The Yearly Meeting held at Flushing in 1773, which Elias probably

attended, directed that Friends should be disowned if they continued to "buy or sell Negroes or otherwise dispose of them so that after they come to the age of eighteen or twenty-one according to their sex, they or their Posterity are kept in bondage." [16] In 1775, the Yearly Meeting directed subordinate groups to appoint committees to visit "all who have slaves and inquire as to their education, and give counsel," as "all in profession with [Friends] who hold Negroes ought to restore them their natural rights to Liberty so soon as they arrive at a suitable age for freedom." [17] It was because of this minute that Elias accepted his first responsibility to combat slavery.

As the young Quaker and his fellow committee members drove from farm to farm in Queens County, they discovered that there were a good many Friends whose consciences were not yet enlightened. Men who owned slaves, and whose fathers had owned slaves before them, had remained silent when reform steps were proposed. To face these men on their own lands and ask them to free their slaves at great personal loss to themselves, and to go to the added expense of providing for the education of minors not yet able to fend for themselves, was no easy task. At the end of the first year, Elias' committee was forced to report to the Monthly Meeting that "there appeared a great unwillingness in most of them [the slave owners] to set their slaves free," although "the chief of [them] have done it under hand and seal." They added that a few had made an endeavor to provide education for Negro minors, and "some few are not yet disposed to take the advice of Friends." [18] The success of the committee was measured by the fact that papers of manumission were drawn up for eighty-five slaves owned by members of Westbury Monthly Meeting in 1776 and 1777. [19]

Elias probably influenced members of the family in their attitude toward their slaves. In his first year of visiting under the concern, his own father, John Hicks, reported to Westbury Monthly Meeting that he had freed his slave, Tom Leenor, with whom Elias had played as a boy; and that Charles and six other minors had received their manumission papers, to take effect when they arrived at the proper age. Elias' brother Samuel agreed to free his Negro man James, the action to take place in 1778 when he finished an apprenticeship to which he was bound. The Seamans also agreed to free the three slaves which they owned. Westbury Monthly Meeting was moving rapidly toward a reconciliation between the preaching of its ministers that God dwelt in all men and the conduct of its members.

As Elias visited the farms in his neighborhood on appointment by the Preparative and Monthly Meeting, he became more and more conscious of the rising tide of emotion which was engulfing the colonies. All Long Islanders, including the Quakers, seemed withdrawn from the earlier phases of the conflict between the mother country and her distant provinces. "The agitation excited by the Stamp Act, and the succeeding legislation which thrilled Massachusetts and stirred her to action, did not easily penetrate to the secluded farmsteads or the busy harbours of Nassau." [20] Elias never mentioned the Boston Tea Party or the Battle of Lexington.

The Quaker merchants of the port of New York maintained close connections with the wealthy merchants of London and Bristol. Attending the Yearly Meeting at Flushing, they warmly supported the pleas in the annual Epistles from London Yearly Meeting that Friends "be preserved out of all enmity, strife, and party; which arise not from the spirit of the prince of peace," and that they give thanks "for kings and for all that are in authority, that [the Quakers] may lead a quiet and peaceable life." [21] Friends were urged by many of their leaders to refrain from any connection with those groups in the Province who were forwarding protests of grievances to Parliament, and to avoid entanglement in the animosities of party conflict. All Friends, however, did not see eye to eye on the question of dealing with Great Britain, and families were divided. Elias' brothers, Samuel and Stephen, joined the gatherings of the Sons of Liberty, while the other three brothers attended the sessions of the Loyalists who planned means by which the Province might remain true to the crown. Years later, Elias wrote that he was left as an umpire or moderator between the family factions. In 1773, the Yearly Meeting at Flushing answered the Eighth Query, "We do not bear arms, or pay trophy money, nor are anyway concerned in Privateer, Letter of Marque, or in dealing in Prize Goods"; but found it necessary to add that "three or four in one Meeting are concerned in subscriptions towards the Militia." [22] Two years later some were unfaithful to the peace testimony and also were reported as serving in the militia.

In earlier days, Friends in the province of New York had been exempt from armed duty, except in case of invasion, but in 1773 the New York Committee of Safety, representing the Patriots, asked Friends to hand in a list of all male members between the ages of sixteen and sixty. After careful deliberation, the Meeting for Sufferings declined the request, not from "an obstinate disposition," but from "a truly conscientious scruple." [23] Because of the large number of Tory sympathizers, tension increased on Long Island during the spring of 1776. Both Hempstead and Oyster Bay town meetings refused to cooperate in the formation of a Provincial Congress, and Elias Hicks joined with the two hundred and five freeholders in Oyster Bay Township who voted against the forty-two attempting to organize a new government.[24] With most Friends he was against "looting and rebellion" and believed that the dispute could be adjusted through regularly constituted channels.[25]

As the probability of an attack by British naval forces upon the port of New York became real, the tempers of colonial leaders toward the men of Long Island became bitter. A proclamation was posted at Jericho denouncing a majority of the inhabitants of Queens County as "incapable of resolving to live and die freeman, and being more disposed to quit their liberties than part with the little proportion of their property that [was] necessary to defend them." The same proclamation indirectly struck at the Quakers for "remaining inactive spectators of the present conflict." [26] New Jersey troops under the command of the Continental Congress entered Queens County, homes were broken into, horses and cattle driven off, and one thousand muskets seized. About this time, Whitehead Hicks, Elias' second cousin, Tory mayor of New York City and Judge of the Supreme Court of the Province, was seized at his home at Bayside near Flushing and examined. He was paroled because he, as an officer of the crown, had repeatedly sworn to uphold the power of the king.

When contention came to a head and open warfare began, the Friends of Long Island were not molested by their neighbors, nor was overt pressure brought to bear upon them to enlist on either side. At Jericho the Friends sat amidst the rising storm and read in the London Epistle of the deep sympathy which English Friends had for the faithful "under their affliction" and those who "during a long enjoyment of ease and tranquility, in those once happy and flourishing countries . . . incautiously wandered till they [had] almost forgotten the true shepherd of the flock, Jesus Christ." [27]

The Provincial Congress, in organizing the State Militia, exempted from service certain categories of individuals, including Quakers; but when the British fleet anchored off the Narrows in mid-summer of 1776, some Friends and near-Friends enlisted on the Continental side. Elias' brothers, Samuel and Stephen, joined the men training at Cowneck, as did three other men by the name of Hicks. With them were men who answered to the names of Willis, Valentine, Hauxhurst, and Sands. When the Cowneck lists were drawn, however, those in charge made up a supplementary list of fourteen, labeled "Quakers," who did not serve. These included the names of Mott, Mitchell, Cornwell, Pearsall, Allen, Sands, Demott, and Kirk. When the Hempstead militia began to train in order to assist General Washington, it also included men with Quaker names, although it is possible they were not in membership at Westbury or other nearby Meetings. Among these were Birdsall, Seaman, Underhill, Jackson, Kirby, Wright, Cock, Titus, Townsend, Downing, Ketchum, and a half dozen others of the family of Hicks.[28] The rolls read like a list of Quarterly Meeting representatives.

Elias Hicks did not agree with his relatives and took the position long held by the Society at large. He believed that the "strength and preservation" of the membership "consisted in standing alone, and not [being] counted among the people or nations; who were setting up party, and partial interests." He was against war and bloodshed, which he considered actuated by the spirit of pride and wrath and not by that true Christian spirit which breathed peace and goodwill to men. No Quaker, it seemed to him, could "use any coercive force or compulsion by any means whatever; not being overcome with evil, but overcoming evil with good." [29]

IV

The Friends Face

the American Revolution

ELIAS HICKS was busy with his harvesting when General Howe landed 32,000 men on Long Island in August, 1776. The neighborhood was aroused. The Whigs hastened to support the troops of General Washington gathered around Brooklyn; several thousand Tories organized themselves into regiments to join the disciplined forces of His Majesty's Army. Most of the Quakers remained neutral, but some, who had gone so far as to side with the Patriots, left with the county militia. The Continental troops, driven from Long Island, withdrew from New York City, and for the remainder of the Revolutionary War the British occupied the Island.

Long Island, which was strongly Tory, experienced the tragedy of civil war. Before Howe landed, the Patriots raided the Tories, confiscated their properties, and imprisoned many individuals. Some Tories hid in the swamps. After British occupation, the Patriots were the sufferers. The British were not even careful of the property of those who professed loyalty to the king. Colonials from Connecticut and Rhode Island invaded the area in search of supplies and, led by former residents of Oyster Bay or Cowneck, slipped in and out with their fast boats keeping the inhabitants in a constant state of anxiety. As the people of Easthampton wrote to Governor Trumbull, they were "as a torch on fire at both ends." [1] The Friends shared in the anguish of the general population. Elias Hicks wrote of the period, "A war, with all its cruel and destructive effects, having raged for several years between the British Colonies in North America and the mother country, Friends, as well as others, were exposed to many severe trials and sufferings." [2]

The invading British forces took over public buildings and churches, including the Friends Meeting Houses. Troops occupied the Flushing Meeting House for seven years, placing prisoners of war under the rafters that once echoed the words of peace; later, the Meeting House became a hospital, then a storehouse. This necessitated holding the sessions of the Yearly Meeting at Westbury from 1778 to 1793. Here the grounds of the Quaker house of worship became a camping place for British troops, and Westbury the headquarters of Brigadier General de Lancey. The commander put a military guard about the Friends' building as a "protection," but, as this made the Quakers uneasy, the guard was taken away. From time to time officers and men attended the Meeting for Worship. British soldiers also occupied the Oyster Bay Meeting House; they broke up the benches, gallery, and paneling for firewood. The damage was so great the house became untenable; many Friends drove to Jericho to gather for worship with Quakers of that area.

Orders issued by the Patriots controlling Long Island, and by British officers in their turn, were not obeyed by conscientious Friends. In late spring of 1777, six Friends crossing from the Main to attend Yearly Meeting were incarcerated in one of the terrible prison ships of the British anchored off the Narrows. Offered freedom if they would take an Affirmation of Allegiance to the State, these Friends refused, "believing the taking of an Affirmation to either party while contending for the Authority of the Sword, would be inconsistent with the peaceable principles [Quakers] professed and endeavored to live in, and apprehending themselves Innocent they could not pay the Prison fees." [3]

Some weeks later, Justice Maloon and Sergeant Weeks rode to the Seaman farm and took from Elias Hicks, in lieu of a fine for his refusal to "go out at the time of the general alarm," "a pair of silver Buckles worth eighteen shillings, two pair of stockings worth eighteen shillings, and two handkerchiefs worth five shillings." Later in the same year, the justice returned with a warrant demanding Elias pay for work on military fortifications. On Elias' refusal, the justice took from him "a great coat worth one pound six shillings." [4] So much was taken from Friends by the military authorities that Westbury Meeting appointed a committee, on which Elias Hicks served, to collect a record of the "sufferings" of Friends due to distraint of goods. For several years such losses averaged £200 a year, and within the Yearly Meeting were as high, in a twelve month period, as £3,300. When Friends joined the armies, paid special levies as war taxes, used their wagons to haul military supplies, or otherwise took any part in the war efforts, the local Meetings took their cases under advisement. Unless suitable regret was expressed, the individuals concerned were disowned from membership. Elias Hicks served on several of the committees appointed to deal with such delinquents in Westbury Monthly Meeting. He agreed with the Book of Discipline; Friends should not "bear arms, or actively comply with any Military Service, or be concerned in Warlike Preparations either Ofensive or Defensive, by Sea or land, or deal in Prise Goods, directly or indirectly." [5]

In the spring of 1777 happiness came to the Seaman homestead through the birth of Elizabeth, the fourth child of Elias and Jemima Hicks. This joy was quickly turned to sorrow by the death of Jemima's grandmother on April 29, her father and mother on the 30th, and her grandfather a few weeks later. The Seaman property now passed to Elias Hicks. By this change he achieved an economic security and independence he had not previously known. He could give more time to the affairs of Friends; no doubt his standing in the Meeting was enhanced with his improved financial condition. Elias Hicks was never a wealthy man but always lived simply; from this time until late in life he was free from debt and not burdened with financial worries.

Included in the estate of the Seamans were three slaves whose manumission had been promised by their owners. Elias made affidavits for each one before the proper authorities. The first of these affidavits declared that he "Set free from bondage My Negro man named Ben Declaring him absolutely free for Ever without any Interruption from me or any person claiming him from or under me." [6] About the same time, Elias agreed to be guardian for the freedmen liberated by his father, to attend to their wants, to support them in their old age, and to draw his will in such a fashion that an amount would be left to sustain any who might need it.[7]

The availability of Elias Hicks for Meeting activities, and his growing stature in the community, singled him out as a coming leader among Friends. In his resistance to war hysteria, his refusal to share in military activity or to pay war levies, he demonstrated his adherence to the Friends' testimony for peace and good will; in his outspoken stand on slavery, he placed himself among the liberal element in the Society which recognized new social applications for ancient religious truths. His name appeared almost monthly in the records of Westbury Meeting as he reported for some committee or was appointed to a new duty. Elias spoke more frequently in Meetings for Worship, and his messages met with favor. In March, 1778, it was proposed that he be appointed to the Preparative Meeting of Ministers and Elders. The following month he received the accolade, without ritual or ceremony, which was to set him apart as a recorded minister and to lay upon him the chief task of his life.[8] Henceforth he would speak as the truth was revealed to him to ever widening gatherings in the order of true gospel ministry.

By setting Elias Hicks aside as a recorded minister, his neighbors in no way lessened his everyday responsibilities. A Quaker minister might be a tailor, like John Woolman, a sign painter, like Elias' cousin Edward Hicks, or a teacher, like his friend John Comly, but the gift of ministry carried with it little respect if it did not root in honest toil which provided the livelihood of the prophet. Friends thought that callings were bestowed by God, and all rightful callings were of equal dignity. Thus Elias was expected to continue his normal labors and to give such time in the ministry as the inward guide directed. As ministerial responsibilities grew, Elias Hicks continued to follow the plow, harvest the crops in his fields, tend his sheep and cattle. An added share of labor and responsibility came to rest on Jemima's capable shoulders.

During the months immediately following his recognition as a minister, Elias was active on committees of the Monthly Meeting which seemed to run the gamut of current Quaker interests. He reported on the clearness for marriage of several young couples, he visited Friends where there was cause for uneasiness because of violations of the Discipline, he helped to compile a list of sufferings, and drafted a fitting memorial for Jemima's uncle, William Seaman, a worthy elder. He collected funds for the building of a new Meeting House in New York City, renewed the deeds to certain pieces of property owned by Westbury Meeting, was named time and again as a representative to superior bodies. His usefulness extended beyond the circle of his own neighborhood. In May of 1778 his vocal contributions on the floor of the Yearly Meeting were so acceptable that he was appointed one of twenty-two members on a reorganized Meeting for Sufferings. This was the "weightiest" appointment he had yet received, for the Meeting for Sufferings, with a quorum of only ten, represented the Yearly Meeting when not in session, and discharged a number of stated duties. In war times it was directed "to extend advice and assistance to persons under sufferings . . . and to apply to the government, or persons in authority, on these and other occasions, as they may judge necessary." [9]

During the same Yearly Meeting, a problem arose which puzzled Friends and on which they could not find unity. When General

Howe captured New York City, British troops occupied part of the Pearl Street Meeting House for the storage of military goods. The Commissary paid to the Property Committee a small rental. When this transaction came to the attention of the Yearly Meeting, great uneasiness was expressed. Friends were not clear about keeping the money. No agreement was possible, and as information was received that Philadelphia Friends had faced similar problems during the occupation of the previous year, New York Quakers decided to send a delegation to Philadelphia seeking advice. Elias was named as a member of this important delegation.

On September 9, 1779, with his beloved friend John Willis, Elias Hicks left for Pennsylvania. As they planned to visit friendly groups on the way, each carried an appropriate minute of introduction, signed by the Clerk of Westbury Monthly Meeting. Elias' letter certified that he was a minister held in good esteem. "We took a solemn leave of our families," he wrote, "they feeling much anxiety at parting with us, on account of the dangers we were exposed to, having to pass not only the lines of the two armies, but the deserted and almost uninhabited country that lay between." Elias might proceed on his service his "mind . . . so settled and trust-fixed in the divine arm of power, that faith seemed to banish all fear, and cheerfulness and quiet resignation were . . . [his] constant companions during the journey." [10] Jemima, grieved by the loss of Elizabeth, the fourth child, who died of smallpox, and with care of the new born Phebe, began her schooling as the wife of an itinerant Quaker minister. With the multiple responsibilities of home, farm, and tannery on her shoulders Jemima had her dark moments of anxiety.

Friends were allowed to pass freely back and forth between the lines of the contending armies to attend Yearly Meetings and to make other visits, "a favour which the parties would not grant to their best friends, who were of a warlike disposition." [11] Thus Elias Hicks and John Willis did not anticipate any real difficulty as they approached the British army in possession of New York City, or the colonial forces holding Philadelphia. The first night the two Friends

stayed in a tavern by "Hellgate." The next day, they passed through
the outposts of the king's army at Kingsbridge and reached New
Rochelle. Elias wrote to Jemima immediately; the second night he
wrote again to assure her of his safety, and reported, "We are in
much the same state as when I wrote from hellgate, having nothing
to trust in for preservation. But the arm of Divine Providence Believing that his care is over all those that place their confidence in
him alone." "Beloved Wife," he added, "I feel much sympathy and
concern for thy preservation . . . and may the Lord our God watch
over us for good in this time of our outward Separation, and keep our
hearts pure unto him and one unto another." He concluded this
letter—the first to survive of many written away from home on the
work of the ministry—"My companion and Brother gives his love
please to Remember My love to all Inquiring Friends, and with dear
and tender affection I salute thee and our little ones with the kept
[*sic*] of our family." [12]

The two Quaker emissaries visited Meetings in Westchester, Purchase, Oblong, and Nine Partners, a good eighty miles north of New
York City. Then they turned west to the Hudson River, crossed
by ferry and followed the valley south to New Marlborough. Other
Friends on their way to Philadelphia joined them. As they traveled
in New Jersey, they went through towns in which grass grew in the
streets, and houses were desolate and empty. The party reached its
destination on Saturday, September 25, in time to attend the sessions
of Ministers and Elders in the Market Street Meeting House. Elias
Hicks and John Willis were warmly welcomed by Philadelphia
Friends and invited to share the hospitality of Henry Drinker and
his wife Elizabeth. These Friends lived on North Front Street below
Race, in a house which had a frontage of forty feet on the main street,
and a spacious garden in the rear. Henry Drinker was a member of
the shipping and importing firm of James and Drinker; his family had
already suffered because of the disturbance of the times. It was to this
firm that tea had been consigned at the time of the Boston Tea Party.
At Philadelphia the tea was not destroyed, but the company was forced

by public opinion to send it back to England, the firm loaning the captain enough money to see him home. Henry's father was one of seventeen Quakers taken into custody by the order of Congress for alleged Tory sympathy and exiled to Winchester, Virginia, where he remained for eight months. He was released and returned to Philadelphia the spring before Elias' visit to the Drinker home. Elias was strengthened in his own stand by his visit in this household.

During the Yearly Meeting, the Drinker home was filled with guests, as were most Quaker homes in Philadelphia. Elizabeth Drinker recorded in her Journal that she entertained James Mott of Long Island and three representatives from nearby Quarterly Meetings, while Elias Hicks and John Willis were in her home. On First day there were ten guests to dinner, on Second day thirty people enjoyed her liberal hospitality.[13]

A fever was prevalent in Philadelphia during this Yearly Meeting and John Willis was taken ill almost as soon as he arrived. Before the sessions concluded he was on his feet and presented the concern of New York Friends on the floor of the Yearly Meeting. Elias Hicks attended all the sessions the first four days, then in turn came down with the fever and was absent when the question of the rental money was raised. Elizabeth Drinker was kindness itself, staying with Elias through one entire day, summoning her physician, Dr. Cooper, to care for the invalid, and keeping away visitors who might tire the sick man. Meanwhile Philadelphia Friends discussed the problem faced by New York Yearly Meeting and recommended that the money received from the king's commissioner be returned.

After a few days' convalescence, Elias started back to Jericho. John Shoemaker, feeling uneasy about Elias' condition, took him to his house outside the city and insisted he remain through one cold rainy day. Though still weak, Elias attended a series of Quaker gatherings at Byberry, Middletown, Wright's Town, Plumstead and Buckingham. From Hardwick, he wrote back to Henry Drinker that he was in "a pretty good state of health," had just attended the funeral of a friend, and planned to visit some members of the nearby Meeting who were ill. He hoped that his recent host would not "pass through a more trying dispensation than hitherto he had experienced," sent his love to Dr. Cooper, and concluded, "My kind love to thee beloved friend, with thy kind wife and affectionate sister and your tender children." [14]

John Willis rejoined Elias at Middletown; the two friends crossed the "Drowned Lands," and attended a meeting there, but religious life seemed at a very low ebb. Again they went as far north as Nine Partners, before entering the territory between the two armies. As they approached the demarkation line they were stopped by a constable with a warrant for the apprehension of John Willis as a dangerous person. In the period that intervened before their examination, Elias visited the families of some distant relatives. When John Willis was arraigned for examination it turned out that his arrest had been instigated by two acquaintances, presumably Patriots, who had fled Long Island at the British occupation.[15] On their release, the two Friends continued southward through Peachpond, Amawalk, and Purchase, and reached Jericho after an absence of nine weeks, having covered in wartime, over rough colonial roads, 860 miles. They found all safe at home. Only one exciting event had occurred at the Seaman farm. Captain Daniel Young had taken from Jemima "two baggs with three bushel of wheat worth one pound ten shillings" [16] because she refused to pay a levy of three pounds to help build a fort at Brooklyn ferry.

Irritating problems continued to arise because of the war. The Yearly Meeting of 1780 accepted the advice of the Philadelphia Friends, but when Elias' committee endeavored to return the rental money to General Weir it was refused on the grounds that his receipts had already been forwarded to England.[17] Friends coming to Westbury for Yearly Meeting, traveling from the Main, had their conveyances taken from them by military authorities; Elias Hicks was named on a committee "to afford them assistance . . . with authority to call on the treasurer." [18] Friends to the north, in an area under the control of Congress, forwarded their quotas in Continental money. The Yearly Meeting, gathered in a town under British rule, refused to accept Continental currency and sent back word that the quotas must be paid "in the old money." [19] Large sums continued to be taken from members of the Society in lieu of war services, but after 1780 there was less distraint of goods, as the authorities passed legislation which allowed the Quakers to pay a sum of money for civilian construction in place of military service.[20]

Concerned for the condition of Friends in less populated areas, as well as on the frontier, Elias Hicks and William Valentine set out on a general visit on March 4, 1781. In the morning they worshiped with neighbors at Jericho, and in the afternoon rode their horses to Flushing. A sleigh, with hot soapstones in the bottom and a bearskin robe over the knees, would have been a pleasant vehicle in which to travel, but the two Quakers knew that many of the country roads in the back woods would be impassable with sleigh or wagon during the next few weeks. A part of the route followed Indian trails through the forest. On the 5th, they received from the commanding officer of the British troops their permits to proceed, and were ferried across the Sound to Frog's Neck. During the next sixteen days they visited among Friends in Westchester County, went briefly into Connecticut, and spent some time about Nine Partners in Dutchess County. Of these Meetings, Elias wrote in a notebook, "Although in many places meetings appeared in a low state, as to the life of religion, yet through divine favour, help was afforded, insomuch that I generally left them with the satisfactory evidence, that my way had been rightly directed among them." [21]

The 150-mile ride from Nine Partners north to Albany was a hard journey for the two Quaker emissaries. No longer did they meet many acquaintances known at Yearly Meeting. They crossed to the west side of the Hudson and rode through the ruins of Kingston, the first capital of the newly proclaimed Commonwealth, which had been sacked and burned by the British less than four years before. The roads were very bad. Sudden snow squalls and huge drifts frequently blocked the way. Now and again they passed militia men going to join General Washington, or men returning from the south who seemed to have had enough of fighting. When the travelers put up in Albany, they found that frontier town in great confusion. Early in the war the Indians, with their British allies, burned settlements in the Mohawk, Wyoming, and Cherry valleys; General Clinton retaliated by utterly destroying the main centers of the Iroquois civilization. In revenge the Indians were again on the warpath. They had already reached the Schoharie lands, were reported on the Mohawk River, endangering Schenectady. Families in Albany were packing their goods on flatboats and going down the Hudson. The fort to the north at Schuyler was abandoned as too difficult to defend.

These signs of war did not deter the two peace-loving Friends, who traveled to Danby, seventy-five miles east of Albany. In this newly cleared country, some of the houses were so hastily constructed that snow sifted on Elias' face while he slept in the loft of a pioneer's cabin.[22] Returning to Saratoga, Elias and William Valentine lodged in an inn managed by a family which had been driven out of Long Island. The innkeeper's wife was much surprised to learn that her guests had come from Jericho and proposed to return to the Island. She asked Elias how they dared to do this, and he replied that "as [they] took no part in the controversy, but were friends to . . . all mankind, and were principled against all wars and fighting, the contending powers had such confidence in [them] that they let [them] pass freely on religious accounts." [23]

Penetrating as far as the Vermont border, the two Quakers turned back from Hoosack and retraced their steps, visiting some Meetings missed on the way north, and revisiting friends made on the first part of their journey. Entering again the area that lay between the two contending forces they were stopped by army deserters who had just robbed and beaten one traveler. Elias, who was riding ahead, answered the robbers so mildly and pleasantly that their chief exclaimed, "Come, let us go, the Quakers go where they please." [24] William Valentine and Elias Hicks reached Jericho on May 15, after riding 850 miles, attending thirty-two Meetings for Worship and Business, and visiting ninety families.

A few months after the exertions of this journey, Elias came down with fever. His illness lasted so long and he was so exhausted, that many of his friends thought he would never recover. While in a state of great bodily weakness, Elias believed he was called to make a journey to a part of Long Island in which Friends were held in ill repute. He shrank from the projected task, but no turn for the better in his condition came until he yielded to the heavenly call. One night, during his convalescence, Elias had a vision. It seemed that he was performing the visit required. He came to a town in which he was not acquainted, yet one in which he must hold a religious gathering. As he cried aloud in his perplexity, a Negro answered his call and pointed out, in a distant part of the town, a place of meeting. The following year, when Elias was well enough to travel, his vision was realized. He found the town, recognized the direction in which the Negro had pointed, and, over the objections of his companions, rode to a certain house where a stranger welcomed the Quakers and offered them the use of a just-finished warehouse for a gathering place. As arrangements were being completed, a Negro entered. Hearing of the projected religious service, he leaped for joy, then hurried away to give notice of the plan. Elias disclosed to his companions the circumstances of his "vision." This "likewise had a very strengthening and incouraging effect on their minds." [25]

While visiting on the Island, Elias was increasingly conscious of the terrible suffering caused by the war. Frequent inroads were made on the inhabitants by the Patriots who crossed the Sound in their forty-foot whaleboats. These men attacked farmers reported to be in sympathy with the British, stole their goods and money, often torturing them in an effort to extract information concerning supposedly hidden treasures. Homes were burned and stock driven away. Escaped slaves hid in the swamps and likewise assaulted defenseless householders. In the latter part of 1782, after the birth of Abigail, their sixth child, Elias visited New York City and had an opportunity to see what the war had done to that port. He walked through the old Dutch quarter, where nearly a thousand houses had been burned when the American forces left the city. He noted that all schools were closed. He saw the results of inflation, with wheat at twenty-six shillings the bushel.

Friends were not molested by the authorities. General Pattison, the commandant of the city, ordered the enrollment of all male inhabitants between seventeen and sixty. "The firemen, and People commonly called Quakers, not being within the Description of Persons hereby required to take Arms, are nevertheless expected to exert themselves in any Cases of Emergency." [26] In 1782, the Friends were asked to take over the night patrol of New York. This they refused to do, not from a desire to escape a civic duty, but because they felt that their numbers—fifty-eight males—were not sufficient to patrol a city of 23,000. They also wrote the commandant that they could not "in conscience support or contribute directly or indirectly to the Practice or Business of War," and believed, "riotous and ill-dispos'd people would be under small Restraint from Persons who cannot submit even to Bodily Defense, and who wou'd therefore more likely meet with Injustice and abuse themselves than be able to control Boisterous and unruly men." [27]

During the summer most of the British troops were away from Long Island on active duty; in the winter they returned. Norwich was a general headquarters, but troops were quartered in many Quaker towns in Queens County. In Hempstead, then a village of a few houses and three taverns, the light-horse were stationed to gather forage for the army and be ready in case Brooklyn was attacked. The Hessian troops were more sociable than the English and often amused the children by making toys for them. At other times, they became boisterous, indulged in card and dice playing, used vile language, and made a nuisance of themselves. Tarleton's British Legion was stationed at Jericho and built a fort nearby called Fort Nonsense by the neighborhood. The Hessian Hanau Chasseurs came to the town in the winter of 1782–83. Some were quartered in the homes of Friends, others built huts made of boards pilfered from neighborhood barns.

Hens and geese belonging to Quaker farmers strangely disappeared, nicely split rail fences were used as firewood by the troops.

A page from the notebook of Quartermaster John Hausselt indicates the number of Friends' homes in which troops were billeted.[28] Elias, with four children in his family, and Jemima expecting her sixth child in the spring, were required to give up half a room to the judge advocate.

No.	Inhabitants' Names at Jericho	Offic[ers]	Troops Men	Rooms	£	Currency s	d
	Capt. de Walvenfeffs, Com'd [Commander]						
1.	Benjamin Townsend	1 Capt.	6	1½	1	7	9
2.	Richard Willits		12	1		18	6
3.	Jacob Willits		12	1		18	6
4.	Thom: Willits		12	1		18	6
5.	Gilbert Wright		12	1		18	6
6.	Zebulon Williams		18	1½	1	7	9
7.	Hiob Hago	1 Judge Adv.		½		9	3
	Lt. Colonels Compagnie						
1.	Frey Willits	1 Lieut.		½		9	3
2.	John Willits	1 Lieut.		½		9	3
3.	James Townsend	1 Lieut.		½		9	3
4.	William Johns		9	¾		13	10
5.	William Semans		18	1½	1	7	9
6.	Samuel Willits		12	1		18	6
7.	Simon Robins		9	¾		13	10½
8.	Jacob Robins		9	¾		13	10½
9.	Benjamin Robinson		9	¾		13	10½
10.	Elias Hicks	1 Judge Adv.		½		9	3
11.	George Weeks	1 Surg.		1		18	6
12.	Thom Place Paid for the last 6 weeks		6	½		9	3
	Capt. de Rodess Compagnie						
1.	Thom Jackson	1 Lieut.		½		9	3
2.	John Carpenter	1 Lieut.		½		9	3

	Inhabitants' Names	Troops			Currency		
No.	at Jericho	Offic[ers]	Men	Rooms	£	s	d
3.	Samuel Willits	1 Lieut.		½		9	3
4.	Willits Kerby		15	1¼	1	3	
5.	Jonathan Titus		12	1		18	6
6.	Jacob Vail		12	1		18	6
7.	Samuel Nicolas		9	¾		13	10½
8.	Isaac Titus		9	¾		13	10½
9.	1 Hospital Rich[ard] Willits			½		9	3
	1 Mean Gard. Jacob Carpenter			1		18	6
	1 Piquet F. Carp[enter] and Jackson			1		18	6
	Summa		202	25¼	25	9	3

Norwich the 26th March 1783   JOHN HAUSSELT, Qter. mastr.

Peace did not come officially until 1783, although there was no fighting on Long Island during 1781 and 1782. The whaleboat men gradually stopped their depredations. The young British Major André, who had stayed with the Quaker Townsends at Oyster Bay, was hanged for his part in the plot of Benedict Arnold. The Hessians in their bright blue uniforms, yellow waistcoats, and breeches with black gaiters, marched away to New York City for transportation. With them sailed 35,000 Loyalists bound for Canada and the West Indies. Among those who left New York were 1,004 Quakers who went to the Maritime Provinces in Canada.[29] At least six men by the name of Hicks were among the émigrés.[30] The Loyalists left their estates behind them, with most of their goods, to start life anew in a strange country. They learned through bitter experience the truth expressed in the London Epistle of 1779, "These sufferings have principally arisen from that confusion and distress which are inseparable from war, from the laws enacted for promoting military services, and from acts enforcing declarations of allegiance to those in power." [31]

V

Reform

and the Itinerant Minister

FRIENDS SUFFERED GREATLY during the Revolutionary War. The conflict disrupted the normal channels of intercourse between Meetings, the Society disowned members who aided the war effort, and Quaker Loyalists immigrated to Canada. Even before peace returned, members joined the host of Americans who poured out of the eastern settlements to take homesteads beyond the old frontiers. Under the impact of these changes, Quaker leaders recognized that renewed efforts must be made to keep Friends true to the principles proclaimed a century before. The Society proceeded at once to strengthen its organization. A Committee of the Yearly Meeting drafted a Book of Discipline replacing the Advices of London Yearly Meeting used until this time. The Ministers and Elders gathered a day before the business sessions of the annual meeting to consider deficiencies. Orders went to local Monthly Meetings to have papers of disownment read on First day mornings, in order that "in all cases of public scandal, endeavours be used to make the testification as public as the offence." [1] Elias Hicks served on committees directing these improvements. He enthusiastically undertook the task of strengthening the Society from within, making a more unified fellowship, and cultivating the hedge which separated Friends from non-Friends.[2] He spoke to the chief concerns of the Society at Jericho and Westbury, then in an ever widening circle.

One of these concerns was the revival of Quaker simplicity. In 1783, Westbury Monthly Meeting directed Elias "to labour with those whose love of Truth [was] not sufficient to keep them from the vain and reproachful superfluities so apparant." [3] He visited families whose houses were elaborately furnished, warned his fellow members to combat the spirit of ease and worldly mindedness, told the elders they must make clear that grasping after riches was an exceedingly hurtful tendency, and proclaimed to his neighbors that "plainness and simplicity were the true marks . . . of the Lord's people and children of every age." [4] On his visits to New York City, Elias perceived that a great change, which involved Friends, was taking place. Immigrants from all over the world crowded the port, expanding opportunities for trade. A Quaker, Robert Murray, head of the largest shipping firm in the country, rolled up to his office in a coach imported from England. Other Meeting members held partnerships in lines of packet ships, in commission business, and in merchandising. They belonged to the chamber of commerce and were officers of many civic organizations.[5] Elias was alarmed at the extensive commercial enterprises managed by these Friends. He frequently spoke in Meetings for Worship in the city concerning the danger of Friends becoming involved in debt, and of the scandal which could come to their families and to the Society as a whole if they were engaged "beyond their ability to manage." [6]

In their own home, Elias and Jemima were scrupulous about observing the testimony for plainness. Their furniture was simple, and their dress without ornament. When Jemima on one occasion indulged the older girls slightly by a change of fashion, Elias was troubled. Leaving on a journey, he wrote to her, "The manner of wearing their gown sleeves long and pined about the Rist wounded my mind . . . their dear Father prays that they may wisely consider the matter and if they can condescend to my desire whilst absent as to have these things removed it will be like Balsam to my Wounded Spirit." [7] Tradition states that Elias also objected to the women of his family cultivating flowers, but as time passed modified his views.[8]

Departures from Quaker simplicity, as well as corruption of other testimonies were due, Elias thought, to the ties that Friends made with nonmembers, especially in religious or civic activities. He urged that Friends keep separate from the world, "its spirit, manners, and maxims," [9] in order to avoid contention, envy, jealousy, and party animosities. Thus he cautioned Jemima, "I feel much sympathy and concern, for thy preservation, and that thou mayest avoid all un-necessary friendships and conversation with the World and Such of its inhabitants, that live in that Spirit, that Draws away the mind from the true watch that always ought to be kept up by us in this time of tryal." [10]

The newly revised Fourth Query asked if Friends were "careful to avoid the unnecessary use of Spiritous liquors, frequenting Tav-erns and places of Diversion." [11] On his journeys, Elias drew at-tention to the "hurtful and pernicious" practice of "dealing in ardent spirits, drinking strong drink, and handing it out . . . to workmen . . . by means of which many families [were] ruined." [12] Although he found it necessary to patronize taverns on occasions—and even held public meetings in them—Elias urged young people to avoid such gathering places. In a day when drinking of toasts was com-mon, he knew that the unwary might indulge to excess. On one occasion, he forcefully told members of the Society they ought not to sell a single bushel of grain to distillers.[13]

Quakers in New York pushed their efforts to free the slaves beyond the borders of their own Meetings. Elias Hicks, Silas Downing, James Mott, and Edmund Prior, acting for the Meeting for Suffer-ings, submitted a petition to the New York legislature urging that the importation of slaves into the state be prohibited. A bill which embodied the desire of the Quakers was passed in 1785.[14] Within two years, all members of New York Yearly Meeting granted manumission papers to their slaves. Elias visited Negroes set at liberty in Westbury Monthly Meeting. He found that some Friends had a "fair concern" for their former slaves, others took little interest in the welfare of these Negroes and made no effort to educate the children. Religious services for freed slaves were arranged for First day afternoons in several Meeting Houses.

The desire of Friends to maintain a hedge around their members, screening them from the corrupting influences of the world increased. Separate schools were established enabling the Society to uphold ideas which were at variance with those held by non-Friends. Schools came into existence, taught by Quakers, where curriculum and textbooks conformed to the desire for "a religiously guarded education." [15] The Yearly Meeting advised each local body of Friends to establish such a school. This was a lifelong concern of Elias Hicks. The Westbury committee, on which he served, conducted an investigation and reported to the Monthly Meeting, "Friends are sorrowfully affected at the schooling of their children, in being joined with those not Friends, and masters of not good example being employed, whereby our youth sustain great loss, in a religious sense." The Meeting built a schoolhouse, forty by twenty feet in size, "so near that master and children [might] attend meeting." [16] Tuition was six shillings per quarter. The committee requested assistance of English Quakers in securing a teacher for them who would be "a sober discreet Friend . . . properly instructed in useful learning . . . a young Man, unmarried . . . of an exemplary life and conversation; a very good writer, well vers'd in Arithmetic and with a competent knowledge of English grammar." [17] As an inducement for such a man to come to America, then at war with the mother country, the Friends offered to pay his passage, give him an annual salary of £200, and furnish him with a schoolhouse large enough for forty pupils. It is not known whether English Quakers secured such a paragon, but the school at Westbury kept. Elias sent his older children four miles to the school. It was necessary to suspend classes for two years due to the occupation of the building by British troops, but as soon as the soldiers withdrew the children returned.

Itinerant ministers bound the Society of Friends together, stimulated new life, and brought to nonmembers the Quaker interpretation of Christianity. Dependent on spiritual strength that came from an inward cleansing of self and a complete dedication to use by the Spirit, these ministers were a great power. The Quietist attitude was unsuited for great spiritual adventure or missionary conquest, yet the real strength of Quakerism in the eighteenth and early nineteenth centuries rested in the hands of these builders and preservers of the Society.

Week by week, month by month, dedicated men and women, recognized by their local Meetings as ministers, traveled the roads and trails from Georgia to Maine. To the neighboring island of Nantucket, between 1701 and 1780, came 576 public Friends, many of whom afterwards sailed on to Long Island. A stream of itinerant ministers from Great Britain added the weight of their messages, except during the actual war years. Many of these visitors remained for months, some for years. Nearly every Meeting had at least one recorded minister who visited beyond the local area. At New York Yearly Meeting, held at Westbury in 1781, certificates—indicating approval of local Monthly and Quarterly Meetings—were presented by six men and two women. Among these were George Churchman from Nottingham, Pennsylvania, who became a close friend and correspondent of Elias Hicks. In 1786, among the thousand attenders at Yearly Meeting were Nicholas Waln of Philadelphia, John Storer, and John Townsend of London. In the short period between 1782 and 1786, Westbury Monthly Meeting granted six certificates to approved ministers, including Elias Hicks, for service in the ministry through their own Yearly Meeting, Rhode Island Yearly Meeting, Philadelphia Yearly Meeting, and "the Southern governments."

The great work of the ministry required inward search in holy silence until the pure light and love of God arose within. With other

Friends, Elias believed that guidance sufficient for the needs of men came from the wellsprings of the Spirit, that power necessary to overcome sin and to secure eternal salvation was bestowed by the grace of God. Thus Elias could use none of the methods open to the clergy of other churches for the preparation of his sermons— concordance, dictionary, sermons of older divines, notebooks of illustrations, or sermon outlines. All these aids he considered "creaturely activity." He wrote, "It is a great thing when ministers keep in remembrance that necessary caution of the divine Master, not to premeditate what they shall say; but carefully to wait in the nothingness and emptiness of self, that what they speak may be only what the Holy Spirit speaketh to them; then will they not only speak the truth, but the truth [will be] accompanied with power." [18]

Periods of quiet meditation were a necessary preparation for the Quaker minister that he might be a ready vessel for the Spirit's use. In that section of his *Journal* dealing with the everyday routine of farm life, Elias wrote, "I occupied myself in my usual business, not feeling any particular religious draft; except the necessity of keeping up the daily watch, that no intruding thoughts lead into temptation, or prevent daily converse with the God of my salvation." [19] At times, in the stillness of his room, or in the powerful silence which sometimes came amidst the bowed worshipers, Elias entered into that deep mystical satisfaction which sensitive spiritual souls have experienced through the ages, and which to them has been the supreme gift of God. Thus he could write, "I had not sat long before a perfect, sweet calm ensued, wherein my whole man was swallowed up in divine seraphic enjoyment; so that not only my mind, but also my wearied body forgot all its toil; and my soul was so inflamed with gratitude, to the all-bountiful Author of all our rich mercies and blessings, that praises and thanksgiving ascended as incense from the altar of my heart." [20]

The inward joy of communion with God came not by a man's seeking, only through God's mercy. At times the sense of illumination was withdrawn, leaving the minister for periods "in poverty of spirit" or "great dryness." [21] Sometimes the blessed experience of intense communion with God carried over from one Meeting to another. Attending a First day morning gathering at Flushing, Elias felt, "the canopy of love . . . to spread sweetly and very comfortably over the assembly [and he] parted with them in the fresh feeling . . . of thankfulness. Nothing particular occurred in the course of the week; but the precious savour that was witnessed in the two forementioned opportunities, remained as a . . . cause of humble gratitude." [22]

From Elias Hicks's own words it is possible to see how he developed his ministry. On taking his seat in the gallery, he tried to silence the thoughts of everyday life and approach God. If he succeeded in turning aside the things of the flesh, and if the combustible matter which filled the soul burned away, a vacuum occurred, a new birth took place, and power came from on high. But when Elias could not order his thoughts he had a hard suffering meeting, struggling with unprofitable thoughts and the cares of the world. On such occasions he found no peace of mind but sat clothed in darkness so real that it could be felt. Such times of poverty of spirit he called "a deep baptism with the dead." [23] Usually, on attending a Meeting for Worship, Elias was able to "center down." A thought would come into his mind which seemed applicable to those around him, and as illustrations from the Scriptures or daily life came from his memory, he would arise and speak. "Although I had to sit . . . in the forepart of the meeting," he wrote, "in much weakness and depression, both of body and mind; yet as I abode in patience and resignation to my allotment . . . after a time . . . a small opening presented . . . and as my eye was kept steadily to it, I felt a necessity to stand up; and as I proceeded in guarded care, it opened a large field of doctrine . . . rejoicing the hearts of the faithful." [24] Often the minds of Elias' hearers "were humbled and contrited," sometimes those present "wept freely," or gave other evidence of being greatly stirred. Then the minister felt "it was a privilege to preach the gospel to the people in simplicity, plainness, and in the demonstration of the spirit"; these were "times of high favour," when God had "put a new song into his mouth." But the appreciative words did not turn the head of the Long Island minister. "Lay low, Oh my Soul!," he wrote in his Journal, "thou knowest that it is the Lord's power . . . that has raised thee from the dunghill where thou hadst plunged thyself by thy own follies . . . he who has plucked thy feet out of the mire . . . and set them on a rock." [25]

Why the call should come to visit one area and not another remained an unanswered question; but whether the call came to Elias to go North, South, East, or West, among Friends or strangers, he was convinced the ordering of his journey was in the hands of God. When an intimation pointed his mind toward a certain area, the impression would either die or return again and again with ever clearer insistence. Before he made a trip to New England, Elias had the desire to make such a visit impressed upon his mind for many months. Between journeys, he worked on the farm, feeling like "Mordecai when sitting at the king's gate," [26] waiting for service, yet without an open door. He was no doubt exhausted, drained dry by his constant speaking while on tour, and needed to fill the spiritual well before undertaking additional ministry. Prior to leaving home, Elias and Jemima would sit together for a period of silence until they were satisfied that the Lord would bless their separation. Elias must be sure that all was in readiness for his departure "that no occasion might be given . . . to reproach the truth, by any neglect or omission . . . and [in order] that all things might be left sweet and quiet at home, that so [he] might leave it with peace of mind, freed from every burden and care on that account; and be fully at liberty to devote [himself] wholly to the service . . . of his Master." [27]

The course of the journey was in the hands of God, as St. Paul found when he desired to pass into Bithynia and could not. Once, when Jemima was anxious to know when she might expect Elias home, he wrote that it was impossible for him to tell but he would press forward as the Lord permitted. Years later, hearing of illness among his relatives while he was on a trip through Pennsylvania, he sent word, "The news stirred near-feelings and sympathy with them, and would induce me to return home immediately if I were set at liberty from my religious obligations, but as that is not the case, I can only recommend them to the preserving care and compassionate regard of our Heavenly Father." [28] Under such a sense of divine call and direction, Elias Hicks, and all itinerant Quaker ministers, set forth, committed to "the perfecting of . . . persons who would be faithful to their inner Light, who would be sensitive to divine requirings of duty . . . and who would take up the cross . . . being *God's very own*." [29]

During the 1780s Elias Hicks traveled in the ministry mostly on Long Island. He went as far east as Montauk, where the Island juts out into the Atlantic Ocean. Here he held religious gatherings among the remnants of the ancient Indian tribes—the Massapequas, Shinnecock, and Montauks, and, by contrast, spoke at a worship service in the great Manor of St. George. He visited Shelter Island, so named because it had been a haven for persecuted Quakers in the early days. He spoke in the Dutch towns of New Utrecht and Flatlands, held Meetings at Rockaway and Hempstead where his father, John, was present. He preached at Matinecock Preparative Meeting of whose property he was a trustee.[30]

Immersed in spiritual exercises, Elias little realized the time-consuming responsibilities which filled Jemima's days. Their two sons, David and Elias Junior, were frail, requiring careful oversight. Thirteen-year-old Martha was a great help to her mother; Phebe played with Abigail, who was often underfoot. Elias wrote from New York, in June of 1784, urging Jemima to rest in quiet and patience while he was away. "Even though we cannot have the Enjoyment of an Outward Communion, yet as we are Concerned to keep in that in which the pure Unity Stands we shall oft feel each other as present in Spirit, and shall rejoice as we are made willing to Sacrifice for a Season that Sweet Communion that we Enjoy when in Each others company for his Sake and His Truth's." "I know," he added, "that in my Absence there is a Double care resting Upon thee, by which at times thou may Seem to be almost overwhelmed, but I beseech thee be careful of the better part, and if anything must suffer, let it be that which is temporal . . . that thou may grow in Grace and in the Saving knowledge of God our Savior." [31] The following September, Jonathan, their third son was born.

The malady which attacked the older boys was mysterious, and no medical care available could arrest the disease. Elias took his namesake to Saratoga Springs hoping the medicinal waters might help him, but, although the boy enjoyed the trip and was not overtired by the journey, he was confined to his bed soon after his return. In order to be of assistance about the house, Elias remained at home for the next three years. In February of 1787, John, their last son, was born, and in the same month David, the oldest, died.[32]

VI

A New Meeting
Hears Job Scott

A VAST SHIFT of inhabitants took place in the American Confederation of States, furthered by economic depression, the opening of new western lands, and population growth. As Friends moved into new areas, some of the older Meetings—such as Oyster Bay, Hempstead, and Rockaway—ceased to exist, but new centers of Quakerism developed. Jericho Friends petitioned Westbury Monthly Meeting for permission to establish a Preparative Meeting; the petition granted, the first business session gathered in the Widow Seaman's house May 17, 1787. The members immediately planned a new Meeting House, purchased land on which to build from Benjamin and William Wright, whose farm lay along the Oyster Bay road. Elias Hicks surveyed an acre and twenty rods which the new Preparative Meeting bought for £45. Tradition states that Elias also designed the building. It was similar to other Meeting Houses on Long Island, though quite different from the typical stone or brick buildings erected by the Quakers in Maryland and Pennsylvania.[1] The plain Meeting House, 36 feet by 33 feet, with "posts twenty feet high," [2] was a two-story, box-like structure with a high attic. Heavy hewn shingles, weathering to a beautiful silver grey, covered the outside of the building from ground to ridge pole. The windows on the north side were shuttered against the cold winds which swept down from the Sound as winter approached.

Elias and Jemima sat on different sides of the Meeting House. The division separating men and women was made by a partition; the upper section of this partition was lifted into the attic during Meetings for Worship and lowered when the men and women held their own business sessions. Posts supported the public gallery which projected about two-thirds of the distance over the room; and narrow stairways with solid sides, broken by platforms, led to the gallery. A single steep stair-ladder reached into the high attic where the hand-hewn rafters—bearing the marks of Elias' broad axe—supported the shingled roof. Three rows of seats, two upon a raised platform, composed the "facing benches," upon which the ministers and elders sat; plain wainscoting, half-window high, rose in back of them against undecorated walls. Above the facing benches was a narrow gallery, said to be used by appointed elders set aside to maintain good order among the young people who preferred to sit in the public gallery. Iron stoves fed by well-dried nutwood and supplemented by fireplaces built cater-cornered into two ends of the building, heated the structure. Wagon sheds, eighty feet in length and open to the south, stood by the road.[3]

The year after the Meeting House was constructed, Elias made a quick trip to Nine Partners and into Vermont. He went to investigate property that his father had already set aside for him. Some days after he left home, Elias wrote to Jemima, "send the deed which father had from Richard Willis for our Rite [sic] in Preston as it will be necessary for me to prove my Right, the Deed is among the papers in the trunk that Father kept writing in." He added, "It is a trial to turn my face again from thee and all my dear connections . . . bound up in a bundle of love with thee and the children."[4] A postscript followed in which he urged Jemima, as he had in two previous letters, to write to him. He even enclosed a sheet of paper as a gentle hint! While Elias was away his second son became progressively weaker and the boy was buried beside his brother in 1789. This was also the year in which John, father of Elias, died.

Jericho Preparative Meeting was soon advanced to the status of a Monthly Meeting, consisting of Jericho and Bethpage subordinate bodies.[5] The Meeting became the primary interest of the Hicks family. Elias served on four of the eleven committees which were immediately established to further the interests of the local organization. Jemima was appointed to the Ministers and Elders in 1793.[6] She frequently was a representative to the superior bodies and on several occasions, when Elias was out of the state on a mission, Jemima attended Yearly Meeting without him. New families joined Jericho Friends at almost every business session over a period of the next twenty years. When possible, Jemima accompanied Elias to extend the Meeting's welcome to these newcomers.

The year following his father's death, Elias made three trips under religious concern. He addressed a gathering of a thousand people in New York City, went as far north as Stafford, Vermont, where he found a congregation worshiping after the manner of Friends. As this group "appeared convinced of the principle of the inward light, as held by Friends," [7] he encouraged them to seek membership in the Society. Meanwhile the Hicks family had its first romance. Royal Aldrich, a young tanner from Uxbridge Meeting in Leicester, Massachusetts, settled in Jericho. Martha Hicks, now nineteen years old, soon found a new interest in life.

Elias labored on many disciplinary committees. Disownments at Jericho were very frequent, almost as frequent as applications for membership. Some members erred in paying the tax required by the Militia Law of 1786; young men and women fell in love with those who did not wear the Quaker garb and "married out"; on rare occasions a Friend gave way to passion and unbecoming language; now and then a member had to be dealt with for frequenting a tavern, attending a horse race, or visiting places of diversion. On occasion, the

Women's Meeting had a difficult case under care and requested help from the men. Elias was often appointed to render the desired assistance.

As was customary with recognized ministers, Elias did much family visiting, especially among the sick and aged. He noted on one occasion, "Most of this day occupied in a visit to a sick Friend, who appeared comforted therewith"; and a few days later, "I went to Setauket, about thirty miles distance, to visit a sick Friend, who had lately been received a member. We had a meeting with her and some of her neighbors, after which I returned home that evening." [8] During such opportunities he urged individuals to think about immortality, that they might "meet death with a peaceful and tranquil mind." [9] Friends were advised by the Discipline to make their wills while in good health in order to preserve family harmony. Elias had this concern on his mind and often drew up the necessary papers for his neighbors. He considered that the drawing of a suitable will required "sound judgment and discretion, therefore ought always to be done in time of health, with proper deliberation, and not in haste." [10] Another primary duty of ministers was assisting at Friends' funerals. Elias had a special gift for such occasions, and these services occupied much of his time. He normally attended one to two funerals a week when at Jericho, at least once he took part in three funerals on consecutive days.

After Jericho Monthly Meeting was established, and Elias Hicks became better known, his correspondence steadily increased. He exchanged letters with men whom he met on his religious journeys, and strangers wrote for his advice. A young man who was seriously ill urged Elias to call upon him, but Elias could only reply, "I am so circumstanced at present as not to see any reasonable way of paying Thee a visit . . . [so I] visit Thee with a few lines, having experienced in my Youth when about thy age, the Anxiety of a Sick Bed Repentance, then I was brought to see my great need of attending to the Operations of Divine Grace; that strove with me in my Early Days, Reproving me for my idle and vain conduct and for not living in the true fear of the Lord, and my cries in secret were to him for mercy, and I believe his ear was attentive to my Prayer." [11]

Although Jericho Friends had freed their slaves before the new Meeting was established, Elias continued his deep concern for the welfare of the Negroes of the neighborhood. He urged special religious gatherings for them in the new Meeting House. Such meetings were held at Westbury for a number of years, but, although the matter was brought up nine consecutive years in the Jericho business sessions, permission was not granted until a few Friends withdrew their objections. Westbury and Jericho were only four miles apart, but Quaker opinion on controversial social issues did not proceed at the same rate of speed everywhere. Meanwhile, Elias Hicks worked through the Charity Society, "for the relief of the Poor amongst the Black People; more especially for the education of their children." [12]

On a number of occasions, Elias interested himself in slaves owned by his non-Quaker neighbors. In 1790, he sent a letter to Joseph Lawrence urging that his slave Pompey be allowed to purchase his freedom for £50. Five years later another slave appealed to Elias for assistance, and knowing the owner had been a strong Patriot in the Revolutionary War, Elias wrote the man declaring that he "marveled" how one who once strongly proclaimed that "All men by Nature possessed Certain Unalienable Rights such as Life, Liberty etc.," [13] could now hold another individual in bondage. Such conduct, Elias added, tended to sap the foundations of the very government which the Patriot labored to establish.

When Jericho was set off as a Preparative Meeting, Friends agreed that the school funds—including half the value of the school building at Westbury—should be turned over to the new Meeting. The Preparative body named a committee consisting of Adonijah Underhill, Fry Willis, Elias Hicks, Jacob Willits, and Edmund Willis "to take care of the monies belonging to the school," and "to have the matter [of education] under care and proceed as way opens." [14] They used the money to erect a shingled school house on the Meeting's grounds. The Jericho portion also included sixteen spelling books, nine history books, nine copies of William Penn's *Advice to His Children,* and two copies of Barclay's *Catechism.* The first master taught "to the good satisfaction" of those in charge; Elias Hicks and Samuel Willis who served on the visiting committee thought that the school "was orderly conducted." It was agreed that the master's salary be raised from £11 to £13 per quarter, "if the number of pupils did not exceed twenty-six." [15] Elias Hicks was anxious that his own children have opportunity near at hand to secure an education qualifying them for the Quaker way of life.

In March of 1790, Job Scott, one of the most famous Quaker ministers of the century, visited Jericho, Westbury, and other Meetings on Long Island. He was born in Providence, Rhode Island, three years before Elias Hicks's birth on the Hempstead Plains. He became a schoolteacher, was recorded a minister four years before Elias Hicks was so designated, and was forty-two when he came to Jericho. Although Elias outlived Job Scott by thirty-seven years, and in that period occurred some fuller development of his ideas, his religious thinking was the same as Job Scott's. Job Scott was a true Quietist, often attending appointed Meetings for Worship in silence for fear that he would outrun his guide. He was uneasy about sermons preached in great warmth or animation, thinking that these were often given without gospel power. A few days before going to Jericho he wrote in his *Journal* a statement of Samuel Fothergill's,

The passionate preacher hath affected the passionate hearer: both have been in raptures, and neither of them edified. Mistake not the warmth of the passions, for the gospel authority. The first is like the rattling thunder, which frights, but never hurts; the last is like the lightening from the east, which illuminates, and, at times, breaks through all opposition, and melts every obstruction.[16]

On the other hand, when certain a given message was required of him, Job Scott, like other Quietist ministers, could deliver it with as much power and fervor as a Methodist exhorter. Three months before going to Jericho, Job Scott was at Sadsbury, Pennsylvania, and James Moore wrote of him in striking words:

Our Esteemed friend Jobe Scott from Rhode Island Government New-england Visited Sadsbury Who I think may be in a good Degree Accounted one of the Sons of thunder, for Before the Meeting was Scarcely Settled he arose on his feet pulled of his great Coat and hatt, and Began as truth opened the Way in avery Moving powerfull Manner in the Line of the Gospell, Saying be still for it is in Stillness and Silent of all flesh that god is to be Worshipp'd in Spirritt . . . Mentioning his own Expearience when god was pleasd first to visset him In his Yong Days by Drawing his mond Inward into an Awfull Silence . . . and so proceeded on for perhaps an hour. Except at times would Make a full stop to clear his passage for Delivery Wipe his face and get his Breath. And Being so powerfully Led . . . he had to stop pull of his other Coat and Neckcloath from about his neck Laid them Aside and Left only a small under Jacoat without Sleeves, unbutend that and so went on in Avery Moving and Encourageing menner. . . . I thought he seemed Like a Vessel Ready to Burst for Want of vent for a Sweat Ran of him Like Watter, and after a Short time he Rose Again and Went on . . . for perhaps three quarters or near an hour Longer.[17]

When Job Scott spoke, his purpose was to turn his hearers to the reality and wonder of the inward experience of God. Again and again he reiterated the message that salvation was "the birth, life and government of Christ in the soul." "The true doctrine has ever been," he said, "in all ages, Christ in man the hope of glory, a real union of the life of God in the life of man."[18] These words were central in the message of Elias Hicks.

To the two Quaker mystics, God was both transcendent and immanent, revealing Himself in the material world and to the soul of man. "My soul hath sometimes been enraptured," Job Scott declared, "while I have viewed and contemplated the operations of his hand in these things . . . the rocks and lofty mountains, the sturdy oaks and tall cedars; rivers, lakes and oceans . . . deserts and vast howling wilderness . . . the sun, moon, and stars in their courses. . . ."[19] The one long description of natural phenomena which Elias recorded

ended with the words, "The sensible traveler, look which way he
would, could scarcely help feeling his mind continually inflamed and
inspired with humble gratitude and reverent thankfulness to the great
and bountiful author of all these multiplied blessings." [20] To both
men, God was creator, sustainer, preserver; He was no absentee
deity, but active in His creation.[21] Both men abhorred Deism which
was to them a mighty gulf of darkness and unbelief. They could
not accept the thought of a remote, withdrawn divine power—a
mere First Cause. To the Quakers the Deist's universe was utterly
mechanical, not an organic whole pulsating with divine life.

When they came to describe God's self-revelation in man, Job
Scott and Elias Hicks broke into rhapsody. At this point they saw
the King of Kings reveal His infinite mercy and goodness to men.
"Religion," exclaimed Job Scott, "centers in the one word 'Emmanuel,' that is, God with man. And until something of this union
is livingly known, there is nothing known of true religion." [22] This
inward center of revelation, this Inner Light or inward law, was the
keynote of all Elias Hicks's sermons. He repeated the thought in a
hundred phrases, and emphasized it with simile and parable. He
turned to the Old Testament and found the concept in words of
Jeremiah concerning the law of God written in the hearts of men.
In the Gospels he discovered it in Luke's expression of the Kingdom
of God within the individual, and in the words of John concerning
the light that lighteth every man coming into the world. Elias found
the thought in the promise of Jesus that his followers should not
walk in darkness but would have the light of life. The words of
Paul seemed radiant to the Jericho minister with the certainty of the
union of the Spirit with man, the declaration that those who were
led by the Spirit of God should be called God's sons.

Many times Elias said, "Every one is enlightened by the same divine
light that Jesus was enlightened with; and we receive it from the
same source." [23] This light was a law, the "law of righteousness in
every soul . . . clear and perfect; so that every individual that at-
tends to this inward law, has the will of God manifested to him. For

no outward thing can manifest the will of God." [24] Therefore, to these Quaker Quietists, the immediate revelation of God was universal, given to all men and nations, whether they knew Christianity or not. "He has not left a rational creature, without a witness in his soul," explained Elias Hicks. "He does not send them away [to Scripture and priest] to find out what his will is: the knowledge, is within their own breasts . . . those who have never seen any written testimony of it; they have it as certainly as we have it." [25]

Since God was just, and His mercy universal, both Job Scott and Elias Hicks attacked the doctrines of predestination and election. Said Job Scott, "I am as sure there is no salvation out of Christ, as I am of anything in the world; I am also as sure that the common ideas of salvation are very greatly beside the true doctrine of salvation by Christ. . . . I am indisputably ascertained . . . that in all ages [salvation] has been a real birth of God in the soul, a substantial union of the human and divine nature." [26] And again, "We must, through the divine workings of God by his grace and spirit in us, work out our own salvation." [27] Said Elias, "God has [not] elected a certain portion to eternal life and a much greater class of his children to suffer eternal punishment." [28] "If we commit evil, we know that we love it more than we love our God. This is what makes us feel guilty. . . . It is our election, and by our election we must stand or fall; for none can be God's elect, but those who choose God for their portion." [29] The best that Elias could say of the traditional Protestant doctrines of election and reprobation was that they were strange, unsound, and dark beliefs.[30] These "doctrines," he said, "lead [men] to place too much trust and dependence on the external works of a *Saviour without them,* and an *imputative righteousness;* and not experiencing the *internal work of sanctification,* wrought by the spirit and power of a *Saviour within them;* which is a very dangerous error." [31]

Both Job Scott and his Jericho contemporary declared that the inward principle so wrought within men that it gave them the insight to distinguish between right and wrong, the evil and the good;

it gave each man "a perfect view of his state." [32] In a letter to a friend, Elias used the sentence, "Now God, or Christ (who are the one in a spiritual sense), is this light that continually condemns the transgressor." [33] The holy descending of the Spirit of God in the soul also gave power to follow the right. Job Scott and Elias Hicks both held the doctrine of perfectionism. Righteous living, even freedom from sin, was possible in the evil world around them because of the Light shining in their souls, pointing out the evil, guiding into the good, and giving strength to follow the better path. "The way of our return lies before us," said Elias, "through the grace of God . . . by which the internal sense of the soul is again arrested, and strict obedience to its dictates required; and if yielded to in uprightness and faithful submission, the external senses are thereby subjected and regulated, and every undue desire and passion subdued, and the creature returns a willing subject to the Creator, and primitive harmony is restored." [34] In a sermon he declared, "As long as we believe in the light, and continue to walk in the light, our intentions become settled and firm; that we will do nothing but that which is right." [35]

Walking in the light not only knit the individual to the Divine, but to all men. "In this light, this seed of God," said Elias, "there is unity . . . that love which he sheds abroad in our souls, to mollify our hearts . . . for in this it is we love all, and are ready to bless all, as He does." [36] In this sentence, Elias not only expressed the Quaker testimony against wars and revolutions, but also the Quaker belief in group mysticism. Catholics look to the teachings of the Church for their supreme guidance, Protestants to the Scriptures, the Quakers to the divine illumination of the brotherhood in a unity of love. The individual Friend might mistake his guidance, but in the corporate silence of the Meeting the will of God was known as well as it was possible for humans to apprehend it.

The thoughts of the two Quaker ministers upon the Inner Light was summed up by Elias, not long after Job Scott's visit to Jericho.

True Christianity . . . is nothing else than a real and complete mortification of our own wills . . . as [we] come to experience the self-denial, meekness, humility and gentleness of Christ, ruling and reigning in [us] . . . [we] become partakers of the divine nature, and know the *life of God* raised up in the immortal soul; which is the new birth, or *Christ formed in us,* and without which, as our Lord told Nicodemus, no man can see the kingdom of God.[37]

VII

Conflict

with the World's People

America was not a melting pot of religious beliefs in the colonial and post-colonial periods, for the religions did not mix. Each body of immigrants brought its national faith to the colonies, and in most places Anglicans, Catholics, and various Independent congregations lived side by side. Few, if any, of the separate denominational bodies were willing to admit that other communions possessed a valid approach to religious truth. The Great Awakening, with the resulting spread of revivalistic practices, created tensions and open conflict within older communions. In the bitterness which followed, men were not temperate in their language or their judgments. The Society of Friends shared the current religious animosities.

Quakerism was born in a period of persecution in Great Britain; there, during most of Hicks' lifetime, Friends were barred from public office, and from universities even longer. Each year New York Quakers were reminded by the London Epistle of Friends' financial losses due to their refusal to pay church tithes. Since early persecutions and current losses from tithing were attributable to the clergy, it is not surprising that the Quakers refused to consider ministers of the gospel as lambs of God. They called them hirelings and treated them with little understanding and less sympathy. Job Scott wrote, "I am sure they are ministers of antichrist. . . . The pains they take are for their own profit. They make a trade of preaching, they 'teach for hire, and divine for money,' false-prophet like. They crouch and truckle to the inclinations of their feeders." [1]

Friends came in conflict with the clergy at many points. As a consequence they forbade their members marrying communicants of other churches, disowned their associates if they were married by a clergyman, and testified against those who attended a church wedding. The Ninth Query condemned members for paying "Priest wages." [2] Clergymen, attending Elias Hicks's public meetings, were understandably shocked when he spoke of them as "merchants of Babylon, who [were] trafficking in the souls of the people . . . hirelings letting themselves out to the highest bidder." [3] Members of the Episcopal and Presbyterian churches were outraged when they heard their sacred ordinances called notions or mere opinions. Elias spoke of ecclesiastical rites as shadows of reality, the real substance being the inward regenerating power of the Holy Spirit. He attacked the institutions of higher learning which trained the clergy, as did all Quaker ministers of the time. "By merely turning to the light within us," he said, "we have a clearer evidence than all the books in the world can ever give us. For there is nothing but the spirit of God, that can teach us the things of God." At a later time he pushed the point so far as to say, "The light only can qualify a man to be a teacher. . . . It is no matter whether they can read or write in the least degree. The light in the soul can dictate more than all the books in the world; more than all that can be read or comprehended by the external senses." [4]

Speaking in Hempstead in 1784, Elias Hicks met a young Presbyterian minister named Thomas L. Moore. This young man attended one of Elias' public gatherings, strongly prepossessed in favor of the Society, although he thought the arguments which Elias used to support his position were laid upon very airy foundations. Elias spoke heatedly against the clergy. He declared that they had religious "merchandize to sell . . . that they were blind leaders, who, for a long time, by their carnal and lifeless teachings and doctrines, and many vain traditions, formed almost a total eclipse between God and [men's] souls." Thomas Moore wrote a protest to Elias suggesting that the Quaker's message had been illiberal, uncivil, and prejudiced. "However your desire . . . to take off the glosses with which Tradition has mingled religion," he set forth, "you might have been equally pointed, equally forcible, and yet perfectly civil." Thomas Moore could not understand the reason for Elias' attack. "Diverted of all prejudice against you, you saw me present at your Meeting and I can hardly suppose that even you can imagine a few railing invectives thrown out against a Society of which I account my privilege and glory to be a minister could answer any one good purpose." Mr. Moore admitted that human learning was not the only qualification for a gospel minister, but he declared that learning was an important qualification. "Learning," he wrote, "used for the glory of God . . . affords us the language in which to cloth our arguments and ideas. It teaches us the happy art of so censuring vice, as to render it despicable, and odious, of painting virtue and religion in its most beautiful colours. . . . A man can say a great many things without the assistance of this means but those who are present, will have great reason, to lament the want of it, and sincerely wish the preacher had been qualified with it." [5] Several letters passed back and forth between the two men, but neither could appreciate the views of the other. A dozen years later, Elias wrote, "It is a sentiment firmly established in my mind, both from historical facts and my own observation, that there is no one thing in the world that has done so much hurt to the children of men as that of an hireling ministry, therefore I consider it my duty . . . to expose it, and bear a full testimony against it, wherever opportunity presents, as the most baneful thing to the true interest of mankind." [6]

In 1791, Elias Hicks noticed over the door of a church in South

Hempstead words carved in stone, "The House of God." He considered it his duty to write to Andrew Onderdonk, a member of the church and a friend of Thomas L. Moore, objecting to the inscription. The title, "The House of God," he declared could be applied just as well to the stable where the beloved Christ Child was first swaddled, or to the mountain where he preached, or to the publican's house where he resorted, as to any house built in Andrew Onderdonk's day. All places were holy to the Quaker minister and all equally "The House of God." Andrew Onderdonk was a man of broad spirit. He answered Elias, "Why should Christians dispute because God, who sees not as man does, in His infinite mercy called one a Quaker, one a Presbyterian, one a Churchman. Let the spiritual Quaker permit the spiritual Churchman to worship their common master in the use of ordinances which he believes are the exact command of God. . . . I say let not the Quaker condemn these things in the Churchman who well knows that God is to be worshiped spiritually." [7] It was a long time before Elias could write, "All the professors of religion, the world over, if they would come to this . . . the light of truth in the heart . . . would all be Quakers. . . . Not that I would set the Quakers above others, but I consider the true Quaker, a child of God. Therefore, everyone under heaven, that does right, is a Quaker." [8]

In October of the same year, Elias Hicks, in company with Andrew Underhill, set out on a general visit within New York Yearly Meeting and surrounding parts. As soon as he had reached New York City, Elias wrote back to the older girls urging them to be obedient and respectful to their mother, and not to grieve her in anything. "Remember," he said, "your Creator who made you not to Spend your time in Play and Vanity but to be sober and to Live in His fear that He may Bless you. Be obedient to your Dear Mother, is my charge to you. . . . Love and obey your Tender Mother and Live in Love with one another and with your Little Brothers and Sisters. Let no Unsavory words be spoken among you but Live all in

Love together and then the God of your Father will Love and Bless you all." [9]

New York City had more than 30,000 inhabitants, and as Elias Hicks walked through the streets to the house of a friend, he saw many ships tied at the docks, ready to sail for distant ports, and great rafts of logs coming down the Hudson River. Stage coaches rattled by, headed for the Boston Post Road. He stepped carefully over the partially paved streets, while pigs and dogs hunted for scraps in the gutters. He regarded with displeasure the city gallows, stocks, and whipping post which stood between the almshouse and the debtors jail. The city public water pump was not far from the Meeting House on Pearl Street.[10]

Leaving the city and its vicinity, Elias and his companion went up the Hudson, then eastward into Connecticut and Massachusetts. They held religious gatherings in courthouses, in the homes of Friends, and in towns where no Quaker worship had ever been conducted. On one occasion, urged to prolong their stay and arrange additional gatherings, Elias expressed his satisfaction at the invitation but explained that he and his companion were not at their own disposal. In another public gathering, Elias saw "in an instantaneous and clear manner" that there was an individual in the throng who would never have "such an other opportunity." A young man present returned to his home, "his mind much affected with the declaration." He was taken ill and lived but a short time, "convinced that he was the person alluded to in the meeting." Thinking over the event, Elias wrote that his own "mind [was] established in the unerring faith of divine revelation, and that the Lord . . . still sees meet at times, to reveal His secrets, to His faithful devoted servants." Unbelief was so prevalent that it took great fortitude and strength of faith to make such a public declaration, yet he would have been under "condemnation" if he withheld the message given him. By his warning the young man was permitted to "use the few remaining moments allotted . . . him and thereby be prepared for his eternal state." [11]

At Hanover, New Hampshire, Elias had a very disagreeable session because some Dartmouth College students endeavored to break up his Meeting. Religious and moral life in American colleges was at the lowest ebb, with a spiritual deadness which evidenced itself in skepticism, ribaldry, and debauchery.[12] This was chiefly a reaction from the period of revivalism, as well as a backwash of attitudes created by the French Revolution. To Elias Hicks, "[It showed] the hurtful tendency of such places, some of them being mere seminaries of vice and licentiousness." [13] By December, Elias and Andrew Underhill had reached Danby, Vermont. Snow was two feet deep, forcing them to go at a footpace. They spent three days covering sixty-four miles. No mail having reached Elias from Jericho, he wrote urging Jemima to send him a line, suggesting letters be mailed to Troy so that he could pick them up on his return trip. He also hoped that Martha would find time to write him. To Martha, keeping company with Royal Aldrich, he sent a special word of caution that she "would keep in Humility and let the fear of the Lord dwell richly in [her] heart . . . that [she might] be Preserved Innocent and Chaste to the Lord." [14]

Elias could usually keep his mind centered on his call, but often on this trip he worried, not only about Jemima's health, but about conditions on the farm. Jemima had difficulty with the help, and Elias found it necessary to write her to discharge one of the hired men, not let him into the house again, and if trouble arose to notify the justice. On this mission, Elias saw a house on fire which reminded him of a fear he entertained "about a closet in the north side of the fire place." [15] He asked Jemima to inspect the closet and urged her to see that the chimneys were burned out on wet days.

The two Friends reached Lake Champlain and spent two weeks among Baptist congregations. Elias did not hesitate to argue against their doctrines of water baptism and personal election. Quoting St. Paul's first epistle to the Corinthians, the Quaker minister reminded the Baptists that the chief apostle to the Gentiles positively asserted that Christ sent him not to baptize. If so great a minister

had no commission or authority for such an ordinance, Elias declared
that such an act was not needful and could be no part of the task of
a gospel minister. He admitted that baptism was used by the Jewish
Christians but said this was merely condescending to the weak state
of their religion, just as Paul had for a time used circumcision. Christ
set men free from all signs and shadows—such as the ordinance of
baptism or the Lord's Supper—so that they could secure and enjoy
the true substance of religion which was Christ manifested in the
soul.[16] To meet the arguments of the Baptist lay preachers on absolute personal election, reprobation, and the impossibility of falling
from grace, Elias Hicks presented his interpretation of the problem
of evil.

"God's ordination, and God's creation, and God's will," said the
Friend from Jericho, "are always in perfect unison, and cannot be
diverse one from the other; and as all that he wills and creates
is immutably good, agreeably to his own declaration in the work of
creation; . . . whatever he ordains must likewise be immutably
good, therefore, if there is any such thing as sin and iniquity in the
world, then God has neither willed it, nor ordained it, as it is impossible for him to will contradictions." [17] Elias' interpretation of evil
rested on the dualistic Quaker concept of the nature of man, a com-
pound of body and spirit. Within the body, he declared to the Baptists, God places desires, propensities, and passions in order that man
may seek what he needs for the body. But the animal body, with its
propensities, is subordinate to the soul of man which is accountable
for the actions of the body. The soul is required to say to the body,
thus far thou shalt go and no farther. In their turn, the natural propensities within the body seek to gain ascendency over the soul. This
they will do unless the soul of man waits for the Spirit of God to
direct it, and so keeps the desires and passions of the body within
the bounds of reason and truth. Elias taught that man has perfect
liberty to choose good or evil, otherwise he would be a mere machine
and not a free spirit. The soul is on probation in order that it may
rise from a state of innocence to one of virtue and glory, worthy of

immortality. Those who elect of their own free will to turn from the spirit and law of God become like a corrupt tree, although the same justice, wisdom, mercy, and love are dispensed to them; by their evil choices, by following their fleshly inclinations, men bring forth evil fruit. But the human spirit that seeks to know and do the will of God is filled with divine light and love, and leads the individual from one degree of strength to another. Step by step, like climbing Jacob's ladder, the soul climbs from its probationary state on earth to heaven.[18]

Andrew Underhill and Elias Hicks left the Champlain area well satisfied. On the way home they crossed the Hudson River several times, once riding their horses over the ice. They were back on Long Island in the middle of February, after an absence of four months, during which they traveled 1,500 miles and shared in ninety-eight religious gatherings. Elias found no great change at home, ending his trip "with a mind full of peace and solid satisfaction."[19]

During the next few years, events moved along in their usual routine at Jericho. Elias smiled when he heard the familiar answer which was always given to the first Query, "Friends not quite clear of sleeping in Meeting." He knew from his own experience, that most Quakers had spent several hours doing the chores in the winter time before setting out on the drive through the crisp air to the Meeting House. He knew it was a severe test to sit in warm clothing, while waves of heat radiated from the corner fireplaces, without falling asleep. In the summer months Friends came to mid-week Meeting after working in the fields from sunup. Elias heartily concurred in the request of the Discipline that Friends should not chew tobacco or take snuff in the Meetings for Worship. He thought members should be disciplined if they made it a practice of "smoking Tobacco indecently, or too publicly, as in the streets, high Roads, or other places of Public or promiscuous Resort."[20]

Royal Aldrich and Martha Hicks were married in March of 1792, and moved into the house across the road a few hundred feet south of the Seaman homestead. Some months later, Elias met Royal's family and was especially pleased with Royal's mother whom he counted a sober, well-minded woman, worthy of high esteem. To Martha he wrote, "I have felt [thee], my dear Child, at times to be near to my life, and have had to believe that my Prayers for thy Preservation and Instruction in Divine Wisdom has been measurably answered, and tho thy care as to the outward is turned over to thy dear companion, yet my care for thy Immortal part is not one whit lessened." [21]

"Friends were clear of taking oaths, paying priests wages, bearing arms and other military services, lotteries and we don't know but clear of fraudulent and clandestine trade and of dealing in prize goods," wrote the Clerk of Jericho Preparative Meeting.[22] There was some uneasiness concerning the matter of taking oaths in spite of the fact that the state permitted Quakers to substitute an affirmation. Friends were cautioned to avoid holding up a hand when taking an affirmation or to use such a phrase as "so help me God." As Friends had taken no part in setting up the Confederation of American States so they took none in the establishment of the new Republic. They were forbidden "to accept posts of Profit or Honour in the government," and if guilty of violating this advice they were "not to be employed in offices of the church, or their collections received." [23] Occasionally it was reported that a member did take some minor office or accept some responsibility. Robert Nesbet of East Hoosuct [sic] wrote to Elias Hicks that it was difficult to keep Friends from "running to [the government] for help and assistance" when respected Friends of the first rank in his area served as justice of the peace.[24] It was hard to know where to draw a line. Elias himself served as one of a committee of six citizens of Oyster Bay to have charge of the marsh lands in 1797.[25]

The Long Island Quakers were much troubled by the movement of their members into other areas. When lands of the Loyalists were confiscated and put up for sale, the Yearly Meeting forbade its

members to buy. It held—as it did concerning lands of the Indians—
that the Commonwealth could not sell that for which it had not paid.
When lands were opened by the federal government west of the
Allegheny Mountains at a dollar an acre, Friends became uneasy.
Committees were appointed to labor with those who desired to
move, and if the change did not seem wise certificates of transfer
were refused. Elias Hicks agreed with other Jericho Quakers who
"were exercised under the consideration of the abundant moving of
friends from their habitations, and settling either in populous places
where many temptations present, or so far removed from being under the care of friends, whereby many . . . suffered almost irreparable loss in their spiritual condition and some in their outward
estates." [26] Elias tried to extend the hedge to include those who
removed. With other itinerant ministers he visited families on the
constantly moving frontier, held Meetings for Worship in log cabins, suggested the organization of Preparative Meetings, and endeavored to tie new groups into older Quarterly Meetings. He either
suggested, assisted, or was present at the formation of the new Quarterly Meetings of Nine Partners, Saratoga, Stanford, Ferrisburg,
Cornwall, and Scipio in New York state, and the Half Year Meeting
of Canada which was formed after Friends had crossed the St. Lawrence River and settled north of Lake Ontario. Elias realized that
the Monthly Meetings on the border of newly settled land had a
very difficult time and should receive every support the Yearly Meeting could give. Such Preparative Meetings were far apart; there
were many transfers of membership to examine, weddings to arrange and oversee in out-of-the-way places, and Quaker testimonies
and discipline to be maintained. Elias attended frontier Monthly
Meetings in which the business occupied from four to eight hours.

As Friends moved up the Hudson Valley and westward towards
the Great Lakes, Long Island no longer was a central place in which
to hold the annual sessions. As early as 1791, Elias Hicks was appointed on a committee to consider the removal of the Yearly Meet-

ing from Westbury to New York City.[27] In 1794 this change was brought about and the Yearly gatherings were held in the Pearl Street Meeting House. As New York Quakerism expanded, the influence of Elias Hicks and the demands upon his time for religious service increased.

VIII

"In Near

and Dear Sympathy"

JEMIMA HICKS experienced in 1793 many of the trials she anticipated twenty years earlier when her husband was called to the ministry. The April Monthly Meeting minuted a message to the Yearly Meeting at Newport, Rhode Island,

Our esteemed friend Elias Hicks, having in a solemn manner laid before us a concern that for some time hath impressed his mind to pay a religious visit in the love of the gospel to Friends in your parts . . . he being a Minister in unity with us and of an exemplary life and conversation we therefore recommend him to Divine protection and your Brotherly Care and sympathy.[1]

Elias urged Jemima not to endanger her health while he was away from home, even to let the business of the farm suffer if necessary, but with five children to oversee Jemima's hands were full. Phebe and Abigail were old enough to help her, but Jonathan, now in his ninth year, showed symptoms of the disease that had been fatal to his older brothers. John was six and Elizabeth, named after the child who died years before, was two. Jemima expected their tenth child in the autumn.

As soon as New York Yearly Meeting ended—the last held on Long Island—Elias crossed to the mainland. Here he met James Mott of Mamaroneck, member of a family devoted to him, and Hugh Judge of New Rochelle, from now on a constant correspondent. The three Friends reached Rhode Island in time for the Yearly Meeting at Newport. Elias was disappointed at the lack of spiritual life. This was due, he thought, to a few leaders dominating the conduct of the business and preventing the free circulation of concerns on the part of the less articulate. This was not the first occasion when he noted such a hurtful tendency among Friends.

The New York visitors were hospitably received as they made their way through Rhode Island, Massachusetts, New Hampshire, and Maine. At times the minister observed "the rawness of the young people," "the lukewarmness and indifference" of older members which came from a "want of dwelling in the root," an "absence of the perfect love which casts out fear," as well as the inroads made by "departure from true simplicity." But there were also "very comfortable, edifying seasons," when Elias was furnished with "ability to sound an alarm to the dead," "when the broken hearts were mended," and the "faithful labourers encouraged." There were even moments when God drew so close to the company of worshipers that "the glorious diadem of his holy presence" was felt, and "he was graciously pleased to distill heavenly dews for refreshing the weary travelers." [2]

In eastern Massachusetts, Elias came frequently in contact with the Universalists who were organizing as a separate denomination. He disagreed with their views on future judgment and immortality and clearly stated his own position. As a lad facing early temptations, Elias had thought if he yielded to sin and rebelled against the clear manifestation of God's will he would be forever cast out of the presence of his judge and his portion would be with the wicked.[3] In later years, he spoke of the awful approaching season when the pale-faced messenger would arraign the soul before the judgment seat of God. Here the soul would be required to give an account of the deeds done in the body, whether good or evil.[4] If men did not follow the light and elected darkness instead, at the day of reckoning the condition of the soul would be determined once and for all. Elias warned his hearers, especially those who were influenced by the teachings of the Universalists, to repent immediately and become subject to the Light, for continuity of life after death did not carry with it a continuation of opportunities for repentance and a fresh start. The time for decision was now.[5]

To Elias Hicks, hell was not a place, a gulf in some interior part of the globe, nor was heaven an area of certain limits in some distant and unknown region. He taught that the sinner carried his hell with him, the righteous already knew a heaven where God dwelt.[6] "Heaven," said Elias,

. . . is the place where the Lord God is pleased to commune with his creatures face to face, and no where else; it is everywhere God is. . . . The spirit must be separated from matter; when the body returns to the dust from whence it was taken; and while it sleeps in the bosom of the earth, the soul will be with God who gave it. . . . If we meditate in this inward divine law and obey its dictates, Heaven will be our portion, we shall live on angels bread. . . . It is his presence that makes Heaven; and when the soul is prepared to meet him there is life.[7]

The spirit within men is of the enduring substance of reality, Elias Hicks believed; he conceived of heaven not in terms of locality but of quality.

On this journey through New England, Elias and his companions visited such famous Quaker centers as New Bedford, home of the whaling ships; Sandwich and Scituate, among the oldest Friends' settlements in America; and Meetings on the island of Nantucket, whose members sent their ships off the coast of Brazil and into the Pacific after whale oil. They crossed the "great river Kennebeck" twice and reached Fairfield, Maine. Retracing their way, they attended Meetings in Massachusetts and Rhode Island. In late August, Elias wrote from Smithfield to Jemima, "Thou art an Everyday Partner of my mind, in near and dear sympathy." [8] Their separation

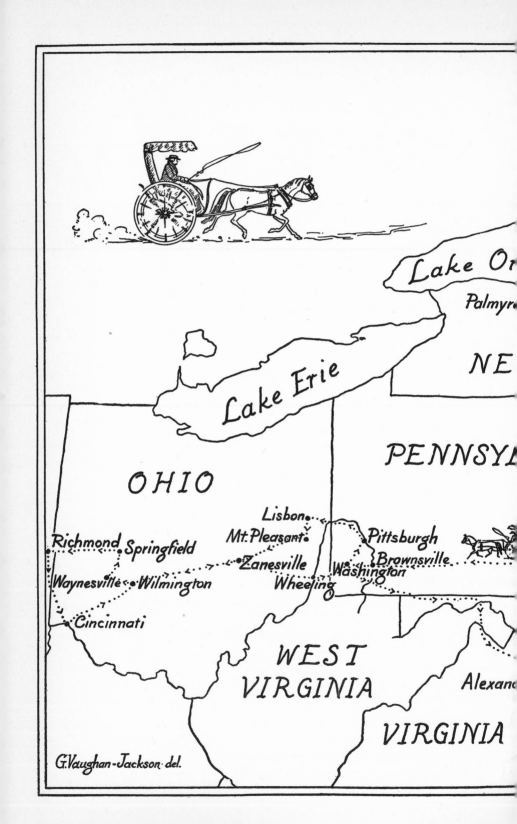

Lake Or[...]

Palmyr[...]

NE[...]

Lake Erie

PENNSY[...]

OHIO

Lisbon

Mt. Pleasant

Pittsburgh

Richmond Springfield

Zanesville Brownsville

Waynesville Wilmington

Washington

Wheeling

Cincinnati

WEST
VIRGINIA

Alexan[...]

VIRGINIA

G. Vaughan-Jackson del.

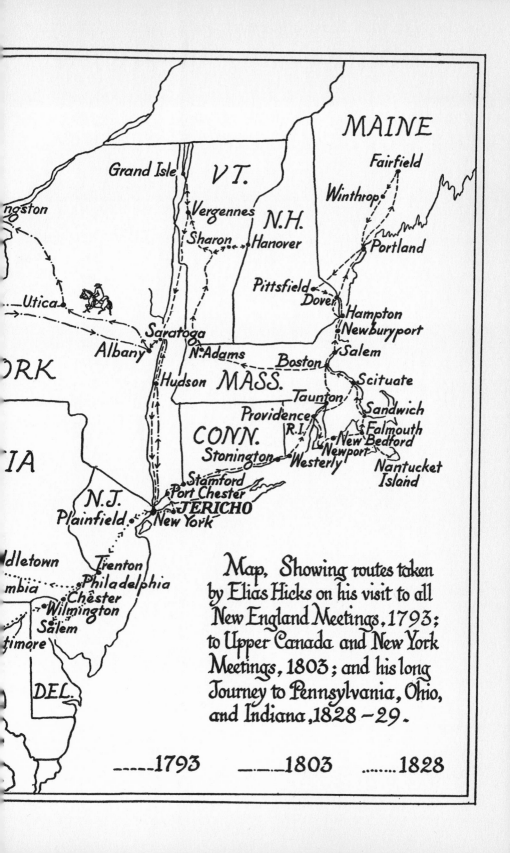

Map, Showing routes taken by Elias Hicks on his visit to all New England Meetings, 1793; to Upper Canada and New York Meetings, 1803; and his long Journey to Pennsylvania, Ohio, and Indiana, 1828–29.

----- 1793   ---- 1803   1828

seemed a heavy cross to bear, and the letters from home to Elias were few. He told Jemima, "My companion receives his packet of letters frequently, four, five, six at a time, which makes me feel as if I was forgotten by my friends, having received but two small letters since I left you four months before, and thou writes, my dear, as if paper was scarce *on very small pieces.*" [9]

In his letters to Jemima, Elias mentions some of the interesting members of New England Yearly Meeting with whom he stayed. There was Samuel Rodman of Nantucket, son-in-law of William Rotch, who had done so much to make the island the center of the whaling industry in America. William Rotch owned the *Bedford*, the first ship to fly the American flag in British waters. Outside of Providence, Elias stayed with Moses Brown on his estate of "Elm Grove." Brown was a man of strong character and interests. Before joining the Society of Friends he had built up a fortune through the slave trade, been a member of the State Legislature, and a Freemason. He became in time one of the most influential Quakers in New England, an ardent abolitionist, an advocate of broad educational opportunities, and a supporter of the new industrial development, which began in Rhode Island during his lifetime. Before Elias visited him he had assisted in founding the College of Rhode Island, also a school for Friends. The latter was short-lived, but Moses Brown contemplated a fresh beginning as soon as sufficient support could be secured. In Providence Elias hoped to visit with Job Scott, whom he admired and with whose religious thinking he had so much in common, but Job Scott had sailed for England a few months before on a journey from which he did not return.

The last Monthly Meeting attended in New England Yearly Meeting was at Richmond, New Hampshire; but instead of turning south, Elias and his companions went northward, crossing the Connecticut River near Hanover. In September, Elias wrote to Jemima:

. . . knowing that as the time draweth nigh, I would just Remind thee of ye little Company thou had at Little Elizabeth's birth, how Quiet and how Calm things were then conducted, that so the company thou

now calls in may be only such as thou hast cause to believe is living
in the Lord's fear. . . . I make no doubt that things will go well with
thee and the Prayer of my heart will be with thee, and I trust that he
that hath all strength and sufficiency will not leave thee in the hour of
Labour and Travail.[10]

On the day Sarah Hicks was born, her father was making his way on
horseback through the heavy forests which bordered the east side of
Lake Champlain toward Vergennes.

The next three weeks passed in a leisurely journey down the Hudson Valley, with excursions as far east as Troy. At Kingston, rebuilt
since Elias last saw it in ruins during the Revolutionary War, the
Quaker minister may have smiled to see a notice freshly posted on the
door of the old state senate building which read: "Ordred that for the
future no sleighs coming or going from Church on Sundays or other
days of Divine Service . . . shall go faster than on foot pace . . . and
no sleighs to ride through any of the streets during divine service." [11]
On November 11, following an absence of five months, Elias Hicks
reached Jericho to find Jemima, the baby, and the other members of
his family "in a pretty good state of health." This fourteenth journey in the ministry covered 2,200 miles by land and water, and enabled Elias to visit every Meeting of Friends in the New England
states, as well as some in the northern part of his own Yearly Meeting. It was the longest journey so far taken.

On his return to Jericho, Elias undertook the task of raising a
fund to assist Philadelphia Friends who were suffering from an epidemic of yellow fever. It proved to be the worst epidemic that had
swept any city along the coast. Each Quaker body in the New York
area sent money or supplies to the Meeting for Sufferings in Philadelphia for distribution among the afflicted.

Elias now revived interest in a concern which was once advocated
by John Woolman and Benjamin Lay but which had not caught fire
at the time. Elias declared that Friends should give up the use of rice,
sugar, and cotton because these commodities were the products of

men held in duress. He maintained that if families in the North
refrained from the use of these articles, the hold which slavery had
on the southern part of the United States would weaken. Jericho
Preparative Meeting endorsed his opinion with a minute which
read: "Tender scruples hath arisen in the minds of Friends with respect to the Traficing in or making the use of the produce of the
Labour of persons held in slavery from a feeling of commiseration
of their afflicted state." [12] Both the Monthly and the Quarterly Meeting approved the minute and, in 1794, the Yearly Meeting added its
endorsement. The Ninth Query was amended to include a section
which directed each Meeting to inquire whether or not its members
were implicated in slave holding by making use of the products of
slave labor.

A shadow fell over the home of Elias and Jemima in the spring
of 1794. The rolling chair long used by David and Elias Jr. was
brought out for Jonathan. John also showed signs of a like infirmity.
The boys' father remained close at home until December, 1797. Faced
with the problem of educating the younger children, Elias Hicks gave
an increasing amount of attention to the subject. He suggested that
parents should begin the training of their children as soon as they
"discovered propensities for improvement in the child." He thought
that six months was not too early since he was certain that a child
learned more in the first year of its life than in any other period. Many
times he repeated the sentence, "We must consider the education of
our children next to the salvation of our own souls; yea, equal to
it in all respects." [13] He helped to write the New York Discipline
which urged parents to be aware of the great and lasting importance
of a religious education, give liberally to establish schools, and make
provision for well qualified teachers able to instruct young people in
school learning and to excite in them a love of virtue by the example
of their own conduct.

Serving on the school committee at Jericho, Elias found it hard
to locate masters who were well qualified and willing to teach for
the annual salary of $250, even though a tenement in the village with

a garden could be had for $35 a year. No master stayed for long. Several times satisfactory school mistresses were secured and paid three-quarters of the amount given to their male competitors. There were usually about thirty-five pupils in the Jericho school, each paying twenty shillings per quarter for instruction in reading, spelling, writing, and arithmetic, with an extra charge for bookkeeping, accounting, surveying, or navigation. As cash was scarce, a daily rate of sixpence for schooling was established. Some income from bequests left to the Meeting was available to help pay the tuition of those who lacked the necessary funds. Elias Hicks taught the school on occasions between 1794 and 1798, filling in gaps between the departure of various masters. He was especially interested in teaching surveying, which he practiced widely in the neighborhood.[14] For instruction in advanced mathematics, Elias used his own copy of Nicolson's *The Navigators Assistant*. Before the children left the school for their homes, he enjoyed reading to them from his own books.[15]

After 1796, the masters of the Jericho school were guided by a series of regulations drawn up by a committee under the chairmanship of Elias Hicks.[16] As Quaker children walked down the country road they could see smoke rising from the chimney of the schoolhouse, knowing the master was ahead of them and had the building clean and warm. Their shouting and laughter was left behind as they prepared to take up their books and preserve a commendable decorum during school hours. They used the plain language, spoke to one another in a gentle, obliging manner, sought not to provoke their seat mates or complain about frivolous matters. When a slow pupil made a mistake they knew the master would frown if any bright pupil mocked or jeered when correction was necessary. As they went home for lunch, or left the building at the end of the day, the young people knew they must keep out of their neighbors' fields, resist the temptation to climb loaded fruit trees, and pass in an orderly and becoming manner on the highway. There was no painting or drawing in the little grey school, as Friends held art to be a mere copy of reality, and music was banished as a waste of time. No book of

plays or fiction found a place on the shelves of the schoolroom,
for those were thought by the Quakers to create a world of illusion
or contain licentious matter. Volumes in the Meeting House Library
were available for the use of the older boys and girls, who usually
attended school only in the winter term. These included the works
of George Fox, Robert Barclay, William Penn, John Woolman, William Law, and Benjamin Holme. Bibles from the press of Isaac Col-
lins, the Quaker printer of the first quarto edition in America, were
in use after 1791. The well-known textbooks of Lindley Murray, a
Friend in New York City, were acceptable to the school committee
as they were composed to animate piety and goodness and lacked
appeal for the corrupt mind.[17] While Elias' children were still attending the Jericho school the trustees asked the Meeting to exclude
children not members of Friends' families. The school was made
"select," and the corrupting influences of the world's people avoided.
Boys and girls who had one parent a member of the Society could
attend, however.[18]

The years from 1794 to 1798 passed smoothly in the little Long
Island village. "All Meetings for worship were held . . . though a
slackness appeared in some, especially in the middle of the week, and
not quite clear of sleeping." The Meeting at Half Hollow Hill was
continued on trial period after trial period. "Love and unity were
in a good degree maintained, but not so fully so with all as was
desired. . . . One instance of backbiting and spreading evil reports,
and some care taken." Richard Powell III was disowned because
he admitted "he knew money was laid on the horses before they
ran." There were "deficiencies in plainness." "The Scriptures were
frequently read in families." Micah Post went quite beyond the
example of Friends and was disowned for "giving way to corrupt
language, bearing arms, and marrying out." The Meeting for Sufferings in New York called attention to the great sickness and mortality
in that city, and a subscription was taken up. Sixteen pounds in money
was sent from Jericho to their distressed brothers, and twenty-five

wagon loads of wood. The Meeting, as usual, bought fifty copies of the annual London Epistles and distributed them among the members. "John Wright sent up to the Preparative Meeting a paper acknowledging he spake some hard and unbecoming Language in a Publick assembly to several persons. . . . His acknowledgement was acceptable." The children of the poor received attention. Edward Willis and Elias Hicks were asked to "assist the women in drawing a justification against Mary Ogden" who married out.[19]

During the years that Elias Hicks traveled through the Meetings of New York state he became increasingly aware of the educational needs of isolated families, of children who belonged to frontier Meetings or to Meetings so small that they could not afford to support good schools. He recalled the efforts of Moses Brown in Providence to establish the first boarding school for Friends' children in America. In spite of that temporary failure, Elias was convinced that a similar institution would succeed in New York if it had the backing and the authority of the Yearly Meeting. He introduced the subject on the floor of the Yearly Meeting in 1793, and the following year was named Clerk of a committee of fifty-six to proceed with the establishment of such a school. Elias knew the geography of the Yearly Meeting as well as any Friend, and worked with others to secure the purchase of sixty-six acres of ground next to the Nine Partners Meeting House at Millbrook, northeast of Poughkeepsie. Nearly £5,000 was spent on the school building, part of the money coming from English Friends. The boarding school was opened for boys and girls in December, 1796. Seventy boys between the ages of seven and fifteen, and thirty girls, seven to fourteen years of age, were in attendance. The rules of the school were much like those in force at Jericho. Elias' committee minuted the fact that "boys and girls would be boarded at a proper distance from one another, the school room of the boys to be a convenient distance from the girls to prevent improper familiarity; yet not so far separated but that an innocent and cheerful intercourse would be allowed and encouraged under suitable inspection at proper seasons."[20] The super-

intendent acted as the head of a family. No corporal punishment
was allowed, yet, in time—human nature being the same in Quaker
as non-Quaker boys—"some place of seclusion for refractory boys"
became necessary "where they could not have much light, but plenty
of air, and where they could be kept comfortably warm in pretty
cold weather." [21] Since pupils came from New York City and from
frontier towns, they appeared in a great assortment of costumes.
In the interest of the Quaker testimony on plainness, regulations
were soon sent home requesting that "an equality be preserved
amongst scholars . . . and that apparel consistent with simplicity be
used." [22] The matron was directed to remove unnecessary frills from
any garment that seemed overadorned, to advise parents to send
clothing that was plain, both as to color and make, and of a quality
strong rather than fine. Frequently, because of the difficulties of travel,
children remained at the school for two years without seeing anyone
from home.

Elias Hicks was a regular visitor to the school at Nine Partners.
Sometimes he helped the superintendent with his books or with
planning for the school farm. He visited classes. Lucretia Coffin Mott
later recalled being in a geography class when Elias came as a member of the visiting committee. The teacher asked one of the girls the
exact height of Chimborazo Mountain, and Elias rebuked her for
wasting the time of the girls. "Teach them something that will be
useful to them in after life," he said.[23] He often signed the report of
the committee, and appealed on the floor of the Yearly Meeting for
greater financial support. When at home, he liked to think of the
boarding school at twilight, when, according to the rules he helped
to lay down, the children were dismissed for rest and told to retire
to their bedchambers "in stillness; to avoid conversation, fold up
their cloths neatly and put them in their proper places and carefully
extinguish all the light except the hanging lamps; and were tenderly
and affectionately advised by their teachers to close the day with
remembering the gracious creator, that being the best preparation
for a quiet repose." [24]

IX

Light

Has Broken

On Monday, April 9, 1798, Elias Hicks sat in the home of a friend in Sadsbury, Pennsylvania, feeling lonely and depressed. An absence of nearly four months from his family, the effects of riding a thousand miles, and the knowledge that it would probably be another two months before he could return to the farm at Jericho caused his melancholy. He remembered a visit the previous week to one Friends' Meeting which was sunk so low in lethargy that nothing could ever restore it to life; in another, the spirit of worldliness so engulfed the members that religion was at the lowest ebb. He was exhausted from the labor of speaking once or twice each day, then riding ten to thirty miles to the next stopping place. Borne down by his fatigue and concern for the ministry, Elias took his quill in hand and wrote to his friend Gideon Seaman of Westbury, "I felt as though I were under the bottom of the Mountain, the Billows have gone over me." [1] Yet even as he wrote in the quiet of Second-day morning, Elias recalled the gathering at Richard Richardson's house, near the Potomac River, where his words had fallen on eager ears. Many of those present on that occasion would, he thought, be in their faith, "as a nail in a sure place." Elias remembered an assembly at Bush Creek in Maryland when others had eyes to see and hearts to understand. That too was "a solemn time, worthy of grateful remembrance." Thinking of these and similar Meetings, Elias added, "but the struggle has been continued, *light has broken.*" [2]

Elias Hicks was fifty years old, and twenty years a recorded minister. Many visits of a few weeks in length, and two longer journeys of four and five months on the road lay behind him. Now he was engaged in an extensive itinerary which took him through the most thickly settled Quaker areas. Leaving Jericho on December 12, 1797 in the company of an elder of the Meeting, Joseph Cooper, Elias Hicks rode to Brooklyn, crossed the horse ferry at the foot of Maiden Lane to New York City, and attended the Meeting for Sufferings. This was preliminary to the journey southward which took them, in gospel love, among Friends in Pennsylvania, New Jersey, Delaware, Maryland, and some parts of Virginia. It was a good time for a farmer to leave home; the crops were harvested and there was "good provinder" in the barn on the Seaman place. Jemima's responsibilities were many, but it was not likely that five of the children would again be down with measles as happened the previous spring. The land was at peace, and except for rapidly worsening relations with the Directory of the French Republic, international affairs were harmonious. The new government was well established, John Adams was President and Thomas Jefferson was Vice-President. The flag over the City Tavern, in which Elias sometimes held public meetings, had sixteen stars and sixteen stripes.

When he traveled by horse, Elias had a pair of saddlebags containing his clothing hung behind him, a silk oilcloth protected his hat, and an oilcloth cape covered his shoulders. When worn, this came low enough to shield him from rain and snow. Stout corduroy overalls protected his breeches and stockings. He wore a drab coat with a broad skirt reaching to the knees, and a black beaver hat with a broad brim. The coat had a low standing collar. His waistcoat was collarless, bound at the neck, reaching below his hips, with deep pockets and broad flaps. His breeches were open for a few inches below and above the knees, and closed with a row of buttons. His stockings were of black yarn, and his shoes were fastened with large silver buckles. In winter, Elias wore high boots, reaching the knees in front, and cut lower behind to make riding more comfortable.[3]

The sessions of the Meeting for Sufferings were filled with Quaker concerns. Some Friends of New York Yearly Meeting were taking greater interest in the Indians in the central part of the state. Contributions for the boarding school continued. The building of a large Meeting House, which might cost as much as £2,500, was under consideration for New York City. Friends expressed the desire that in the near future Elias Hicks would make a journey to isolated members in the frontier country, help establish new Preparative Meetings, and visit some of the Indian settlements. Elias was thankful when the sessions ended as he was eager to start the journey south which had occupied his mind for several years past. In hopes that Jemima would frequently send him news from home, he sent careful directions about letter writing, suggestive of the difficulties involved in the exchange of letters at the turn of the century. "May inform that as I desire to hear from you, as may be, now point out a Way for Conveyance of thy letters and therefore Propose thou Direct thy letters to the care of Samuel Fisher of Philadelphia, to be forwarded to John P. Ferris at Wilmington, and when sealed and thus directed Inclose them to the care of our Friend John Hadock of New York, who is willing to care of these and forward them . . . this being the present needful." [4] Several days later he added an interesting postscript on a letter to Jemima, "as thou writes but poorly, if thou should get Hallet or Royal to Write Superscriptions on thy letters it would make them more plain for conveyance." [5]

Taking in turn the Quaker Meetings as they came, the two friends from Long Island went down the Atlantic coast as far as Cape May, then turned inland, coming up the east coast of Delaware Bay. They visited the large groups at Mullica Hill, Woodbury, and Salem.

Elias spoke earnestly and forcefully of the danger involved in Friends becoming worldly and departing from true simplicity. He still believed the departure was due to Friends mixing in civil affairs, especially in holding public office. As a practical measure, he followed up a Meeting at Cape May by sending a letter to Jericho in which he told an Elder who had just been elected to public office that he should request to be released from the duties of eldership.[6]

At Haddonfield, the Long Island travelers stayed with Joshua Evans, a prominent minister of Philadelphia Yearly Meeting, who had visited Jericho twice within the previous ten years. Evans' attitude toward slavery was well known, as he had just completed a fourteen-months journey through the southern states. Elias Hicks asked many questions concerning the area into which he was going. In the home of his host, Elias noted that this Friend, who for forty years had preached against the evils of slavery, used no products made by slave labor. Before Elias left the home of Joshua Evans, the latter wrote in his journal, "We were visited by our beloved friend, Elias Hicks, of Long Island; his company and gospel labours at our meeting were very acceptable and edifying." [7]

Leaving Haddonfield, the two Quakers planned to go to Philadelphia, though for some reason Elias Hicks dreaded entering the heart of American Quakerism. This was his first visit in almost twenty years. As he had been ill during his previous visit, his knowledge of Philadelphia was scant. Perhaps he was overawed by the size of the metropolis, then the largest in America, by the stories he had heard of the wealth of its Quaker merchants, or by its intellectual reputation. Philadelphia at the time was second to London as the largest publishing center among English speaking people. To Hugh Judge, Elias wrote, "How I shall get along in this city seems yet much hid from me, though I feel fully resigned as to that, and witness at present a perfect calm and . . . quiet." [8] He could not dream of the uproar into which he would throw Philadelphia Quakers in later years, when Friends would be either ranged with him or against him. Elias and his companion rode their horses across the ice of the Delaware River and spent five days in Penn's city, much pleased to find an open door both in Meetings and among the families which they visited. The youth were very attentive to the visitors from New York; some seemed "under the forming hand, preparing for service," and others would no doubt "be as valiants . . . for the promotion of the cause of truth." [9]

While in the city, Elias stayed at the home of Samuel and Hannah Fisher. Hannah's parents, Thomas and Mary Rodman of Newport, Rhode Island, had entertained the Jericho minister on his visit to New England in 1793. Samuel was an active member of the shipping firm of Joshua Fisher and Sons which ran one of the largest and most successful lines of packet ships between Philadelphia and London. Like members of the Drinker family, with whom Elias stayed on his first visit to Philadelphia, Joshua Fisher and his three sons, Thomas, Samuel, and Miers, had been exiled to Virginia during the Revolutionary War. Samuel had been arrested for a second time on his return and confined for two additional years. While they were absent in Virginia, the family warehouses had been stripped of valuable goods by the Continental Army, for which the Quaker firm never received any compensation. Samuel and Hannah lived in a large mansion at 110 South Front Street, where they often entertained traveling ministers from America and Great Britain. They became fast friends of Elias Hicks'.

Elias was anxious to continue his journey to the south because he wanted to be back on Long Island in time for the spring Quarterly Meeting. He sensed that he was not really needed in Philadelphia since more experienced men were laboring in the city. He wrote Hugh Judge that Peter Yarnall, a well-known surgeon of Byberry, John Simpson of Bucks County, Richard Jordan, and Benjamin Beaver were all at work among Friends. John Wigham and Martha Routh of England were soon expected. He declared that Philadelphia Quakers had "been so continually visited that it looks as though there could be nothing left for [him] to do, for to preach any more to them seems as though it might be only a pouring water on a drowned mouse." He added, "perhaps I may have to *sit still* among them, if so I shall count it a favor." [10]

To Jemima, Elias wrote more intimately of impressions that troubled him greatly. The bustle of business was even greater in Philadelphia than New York, the streets—which were paved with brick and lighted at night—were filled with coaches, chariots, phaetons, light wagons, chairs, sulkies, landaus, and the stages leaving for North, South, and West. Ships crowded the docks along the Delaware, as much as one-fourth of all the exports from the country being loaded at these piers. The year's exports amounted to nearly twenty millions of dollars. Although the Quakers did not control as large a proportion of this trade as they had before the Revolution, much of it was still in their hands. Elias was exceedingly disturbed by all the abundance which he saw and by the oppressive toil after worldly goods.

The two Quakers left Philadelphia about the middle of January, held satisfactory gatherings in Chester and Wilmington, and proceeded down the Eastern Shore of Maryland. Again they were hospitably received. Methodists and Baptists opened their churches to them, though not all who wished to hear the visiting Quakers could be accommodated. The Friends were now in country which had long been under the warm Evangelical influence of Francis Asbury and Robert Strawbridge; thus their public gatherings were interrupted in a manner quite strange to the Quakers of the time— though one known to their ancestors a hundred years before. At St. Michael's Methodist Church when an aged ministering Friend was speaking, the local congregation kept up a loud groaning throughout the message. This so distressed Elias Hicks that when he rose to speak he addressed the group "concerning the necessity of inward and outward stillness as preparatory to the right performance of the great and solemn act of worship." He declared that those who broke into the message of the speaker with exclamations or other sounds were akin to the Pharisees. "Truth prevailed and silenced all noises." [11]

Near Third Haven, Elias Hicks and his companion came in contact with the Nicholites. These men and women, followers of one
Joseph Nichols of Kent County, Delaware, had developed a religious
body in Caroline County, Maryland, which paralleled the Quakers
at many points. Elias discovered that their religious services were
held in silent waiting for the Divine principle to strengthen and
direct their spirits. They held gatherings for discipline, but had no
hierarchy of Meetings. The Nicholites prohibited their members from
marrying those belonging to other religious bodies, from holding
slaves, and from engaging in any warlike activity. Their testimony
for plainness was so strict their members could not wear garments
which were striped, flowered, or colored. The women wore old-
fashioned bonnets of white cloth, straight and smooth on top. It
was not astonishing that they were called New Quakers. Much as
Elias approved of plainness, he felt the Nicholites, by insisting that
they could wear only white garments, made too great a matter of
dress. Shortly before he came to the Eastern Shore, four hundred
Nicholites asked to be taken into the Friends' Meetings. Others remained outside, fearing that in a larger sect their religious principles
would deteriorate. Elias could understand the hesitation of some,
and hoped that those who did join the Meetings would not "be hurt
by the great and prevailing deficiencies manifested" among the
Quakers whose Society they joined.[12]

Elias Hicks spoke at the old Third Haven Meeting House, associated with George Fox, William Penn, Wenlock Christison, William Edmundson and John Burnyeat, great Quaker leaders of the
seventeenth century. He was charmed with the old building, begun
in 1682, with its long slanting roof, shorter on one side than the
other. He noted with a carpenter's appreciation that the foundation beams were made from timbers two feet wide cut from the
virgin forest, and that the long horizontal clapboards had curving
irregular edges. The hand-made glass in the windows was bulging
and reflected several hues, while within all the benches, as well as
the wide floor boards, were put together with wooden pegs. The

members cherished a parcel of books which they had received from George Fox "as a token of his love." [13] Returning up the peninsula, Elias spoke in the courthouse at Chester, but found the audience very light, non-Friends whispering to one another during the silent waiting. A heavy-set woman sat passive as he began to speak, evidently hardened to his message, but gradually she softened and in the end bowed her head and wept so as to be heard through the room.

Elias was suffering from a cold and soreness in his lungs due to sleeping in strange beds, often between cold sheets in mid-winter. He was heartened while at Chester by the receipt of a package of letters, including two from John Hicks and one from his friend Hugh Judge. Hugh's letter had taken nearly six weeks to come from New York City, "but it served to quicken and brighten the chain of brotherly affection and friendship" [14] which bound the two men together.

Entering Baltimore Yearly Meeting for the first time, Elias came to the "Nottingham Lots," the area of Pennsylvania and Maryland long in dispute between William Penn and Lord Baltimore. Here Elias stayed with George Churchman at East Nottingham. He was the son of John Churchman, a famous itinerant Quaker minister whose travels had taken him at various times as far as Barbados, England, Ireland, and Holland. Elias was much interested in hearing George Churchman, with whom he had corresponded for several years, tell of the travels of his father, and of the work of his grandfather who helped establish the "Nottingham Lots." William Penn had located 18,000 acres of land between Chesapeake Bay and Delaware Bay which were divided into 500-acre plots. These were chosen by lot by those who settled the area. Penn sold the "lots" for eight pounds per hundred acres, or rented for two bushels of winter wheat paid annually at some navigable water or landing place on the Delaware. As most of the settlers were Friends, William Penn set aside one 500-acre lot as a commons, and within this acreage gave forty acres to the Quakers for the combined purpose of public worship, the right of burial and the privilege of education.[15] George's grandfather fortunately secured land just east of the Quaker plot. He helped to build the log Meeting House which served the Friends of Nottingham Monthly Meeting until the "Brick Meeting House" was constructed in 1724. George Churchman chuckled a bit in telling Elias about the long-standing dispute between the Penn and Baltimore families over the boundaries between the two proprietary colonies. The running of the Mason and Dixon line, when he was a boy, had placed the Meeting House plot and most of the Nottingham lots in Maryland and not in Pennsylvania!

Elias was surprised at the number of people who could be accommodated in the Brick Meeting House. A stone addition was added after a fire in 1748 which made the building one of the largest Quaker structures south of Philadelphia. A youth's gallery extended around three sides of the building, and Elias was pleased to see it filled. He gave "a rousing testimony [against] Friends . . . adopting the maxims and spirit of the world." He summed up this day's gospel in language that resembled George Fox's, "Truth reigned triumphantly in this meeting over all opposition and disorderly spirits." [16] Like Flushing Meeting on Long Island, East Nottingham had been occupied by one of the armies during the Revolutionary War. A hospital was set up here by General Smallwood of the American forces, a number of soldiers were buried in a corner of the Quaker cemetery. Because of his interest in education, Elias visited the Meeting school and asked many questions about the new boarding school which George Churchman and other Friends were attempting to establish nearby on the road to Chrome.[17]

After staying for five days at George Churchman's, the travelers continued on their way toward Baltimore. Just below the Brick Meeting House, they passed the Cross Keys Tavern. Here stagecoach passengers from Baltimore spent the night at the halfway point between that city and Philadelphia. Following the main road to the Susquehanna River the traffic was very heavy, as this was the chief route north and south.[18] Large covered wagons drawn by six horses

took up much of the road. The farms on each side of the way were
fertile, at that season of the year farmers were turning coopers and
making barrels out of oak and hickory timber with which the land
was covered. Elias noted the bark of the fine black oak and wished
he had it for use in his own tannery at Jericho. In his pocket, Elias
took from East Nottingham a minute of endorsement to read when
he returned to his home Meeting. "Our Friend Elias Hicks, of Long
Island," the minute read, "being now on a religious visit to Friends,
attending this meeting satisfactorily, produced a certificate from
their Monthly Meeting at Jericho date ye 6th of last month, expressing Friends unity with him as a minister. Also his companion, Joseph
Cooper, an elder, produced a minute from the same Meeting expressing the concurrence of his Friends in his present journey, these
were both read here to satisfaction." [19] Before crossing the Susquehanna, Elias attended a religious gathering at Little Britain where
he was "led into a large doctrinal communication, suited to the states
of many present." "The meeting was large and solid . . . edifying
and instructive," he wrote, "but too many, who have ears to hear, and
are led to acknowledge the truth of testimonies delivered, neglect
the practical part, which is the most essential . . . and are, therefore,
in a situation like those, who, seeing their natural faces in a glass,
turn away, and forget what manner of persons they are." [20]

Making his way to the several Friends' Meetings on both sides
of the great river, Elias Hicks met some "dark undisciplined spirits,"
who, though Quakers, had not attended Meetings for several years;
and non-Friends whom he felt were "loose careless minded people."
At Fawn he had a "profitable season," and at Bush Creek the "gospel
was preached in the demonstration of the spirit and with power . . .
and baptising influence." [21] At one of these Meetings, Friends were
still talking with amusement about the sermon of an "aged, worthy
woman," who, a short time before, declared, "concerning the tender
constitutions of young women . . . delicately brought up," so often
mentioned in contemporary literature, they would not have "weak
nerves, and be in need of medicine . . . if [they] would not sit up

unreasonably late at night, and would use [*sic*] themselves to rise
early in the morning,—make their own beds, and stir about in business."²²

In Baltimore, a city of 13,000, Elias and Joseph Cooper held religious services in the Eastern and Western Districts, among the
poor, at the almshouse, and several with the "black people." Again
Elias urged Friends to return to the ancient simplicity of the Society, which he insisted could only be secured by maintaining the
hedge which separated Friends from the world. He was disturbed
at the gay equipage of wealthy Friends, the elaborate furniture of
their houses—as it seemed to him—and evidences of the hurtful tend-
encies of pride. In Delaware and Maryland Elias Hicks saw Southern
slavery for the first time. The condition of the slaves in these states
was quite different from what he had witnessed as a boy on his
father's farm or had seen about Jericho. Elias was deeply moved
by the experience. At Sandy Spring and Indian Springs, west of
Baltimore, Elias in a plain and powerful manner pointed out the
sin involved in men holding their fellow creatures in bondage. He
declared both slave owners and their children would reap pernicious
fruit from the evil, fatal to their present and eternal well being. Those
engaged in the practice were unworthy of the respect of wise and
good men. At least one plantation owner was so struck by the address
given by Elias that the slaves on that plantation were set free.

Moving into Virginia, Elias Hicks was astonished at the numbers
who came to attend his appointed Meetings, especially those belonging to other religious sects. He soon learned, however, that some
came to see their neighbors and discuss business affairs rather than
seek religious improvement. The Friendly custom of talking to one's
neighbors after worship and business, was in these Meetings carried
to excess. Friends remained outside the buildings chatting to one another instead of joining in the business sessions. It irritated Elias to
have people so concerned with the advancement of their temporal
interests that they paid little heed to their spiritual condition. "O
that we, as a people," he wrote in Alexandria, "were more weaned

from the world and its fading enjoyments, and our affections placed on celestial treasures; then would the light of the Church break forth out of obscurity, and her darkness become as noonday; thousands would then be gathered from the highways and hedges." [23]

Elias set himself a severe pace, on occasions riding twenty miles between break of day and ten in the morning in order to be present for a Meeting. Sometimes his horse could not maintain the speed with which he covered the rough roads; then Elias left the horse behind and proceeded on a borrowed mare. He traveled so swiftly that little mail reached him from home, but he wrote constantly. To Jemima he expressed the hope that she would act discreetly with Phebe, now a young lady of nineteen, who was seeing a good deal of Joshua Willets of Islip, Long Island. "As thou knows my mind Respecting young peoples' keeping company," wrote Elias, "[do] not suffer our dear daughters keeping late hours, nor be in secret with Young Men in the dark." [24] He was happy to receive letters from Abigail, Elizabeth, and Martha. To Martha he sent word,

I discover thou art not very healthy, but remember for thy comfort and encouragement that it is through many tribulations the Righteous inherit the kingdom. And thy Dear Father knows the good of affliction for before I was afflicted I went astray. I have no doubt but Every Dispensation of Divine Providence is for our Good, as we submit to the turning of his Holy Hand upon us, I hope the days of affliction will be days of solid improvement. [25]

In a letter to Jonathan and John, Elias said "it [was] their Dear Father's greatest desire for them that they remember their Creator in the days of their youth." [26] Elias could not know the prophetic nature of the rest of this quotation, for in a few years the silver cord was loosed, the golden bowl broken, the pitcher broken at the fountain, and the wheel broken at the cistern.

While among the Meetings in northern Virginia, Elias was distressed by the free thinking, infidelity, and Deism, which was like "darkness spreading over the minds of many as a thick veil." He went to a small Meeting in the Blue Ridge Mountains called the Gap,

THE JERICHO MEETING
HOUSE, BUILT IN 1787
Tradition declares that
it was designed by
Elias Hicks, who was on
the building committee.

THE INTERIOR OF
THE JERICHO MEETING
HOUSE. *Marks of
Elias' ax can
still be seen on*

near Goose Creek, attended by many non-Friends, a "raw, insensible people, void of any right idea or knowledge of true religion." [27] Many who came to hear him had been influenced by Thomas Paine's *Age of Reason*. Even some Friends were captivated by the "dark insinuating address" of the Revolutionary War writer who had been raised in a Quaker home. These Friends had their faith shipwrecked. This occasion so oppressed Elias that in the night he had a remarkable vision. He beheld the earth shrouded in darkness. Then a bright rainbow spanned the heavens from northwest to southwest. Elias believed the rainbow was a sign that God was still with His people though evil surrounded them. God would not utterly destroy His children.[28] To Friends gathered in the Fairfax Meeting House, Elias Hicks pointed out the great advantage of living a life of righteousness, not founded on laws, maxims and precepts of men, but on the witness of the Son of God revealed to the heart and soul of men through the Holy Spirit.

Before leaving Virginia, Fairfax Quarterly Meeting took recognition of the work of "our Beloved friend Elias Hicks . . . his company and labours of love hath been truly to our satisfaction, as also hath been the company and solid deportment of Joseph Cooper, his companion." And the Women's Meeting added, "The said Elias Hicks had good service amongst us, Expressing many useful Hints for our own improvement in the best sense." [29] Leaving Hopewell and the other large Meetings in northern Virginia, towards the end of March the two men from Jericho turned northward. When they came to the Potomac River they found it in flood. The approaches to the main river were under water and it was necessary for the travelers to walk along the tops of the rail fences, leading their horses by the bridles. At one point, Elias' horse fell into a deep hole, "but soon arose, and swam ashore." A Friend who accompanied the two northerners in a one-horse carriage got across the plain "by the horse swimming it." Since the carriage was a heavy one, this was dangerous, "but as night was coming on we led the horse with the carriage into the creek, and after violent exercise, being at one time drawn under water by the weight of the carriage, he took it safe over." [30]

Returning by way of the Maryland Meetings, Elias clearly opened a true gospel worship in them. At Pipe Creek he wrestled with the lusts of the flesh and found evidence of many disorders and want of unity in the group. He spoke so plainly to Friends of what he sensed among them that his host declared that the reason no members of Meeting came to visit him after the gathering was because he had so aptly described their failings.[31] At "Menallon," he found a crumb of consolation in a few honest-hearted Friends, who kept the testimonies of the Society; and at Warrington he noted that religion seemed at a very low ebb by the prevailing of a worldly spirit. He urged Friends to remember the light, spirit, grace, and truth of the Lord Jesus Christ, their holy pattern. The beautiful stone Meeting House at Warrington was constructed some fifty years before, with sloping slate roof, wide eaves, and deeply recessed windows. Many of the benches were without backs, and the walls were wainscoted half way to the ceiling. Inside, black walnut posts supported the roof.

At "Yorktown, it was like a little feast after a time of Fasting," [32] for nine letters awaited him from Jericho. A letter of greeting from Hugh Judge told of writing "mostly in my shop by candle light." [33] George Churchman notified Elias that his horse, left at East Nottingham because of lameness, was now well mended. Elias replied that he had been "asked to go to Hagar Town but . . . [his] baptism was so great in passing friends meetings in that quarter that [he] had no strength nor confidence to look much without the pale of the Society." He added, "Unless your Yearly Meeting opens some way for the strengthening of some of those Meetings . . . I see little prospect, they will be desolate. Discipline is at such a low ebb. . . ." [34]

With news from home, Elias' mind began to turn more and more in that direction. To Jemima he explained, "should be glad the ground at the plains should be ready for planting, be manured as well as may be with the Dung that can be collected, and if necessary Isaac may be employed a little to help out with it, but wish to do without much hiring this summer. A Spot for Potatoes may be Reserved on the plains, but would not have any ground plowed at home, except the stalk ground for oats and flax; and as to Rails I don't desire any got. Except some few may be wanted to mend fences where Necessity requires." [35] Elias urged Jemima to leave the care of the farming to his brother Joseph, even if she had little confidence in his ability. He added, "I don't doubt but he will do pretty well." Jemima was having difficulty with Esech, who was helping her, and Elias suggested that she consult Martha and Royal concerning the best way to deal with him. "Endeavor to get him to work and keep him steadily at it," urged Elias, "as I know of nothing so likely to be Useful to him. . . . Be kind to Esech in any case, help by counsel as way opens, as he is living with us without parents . . . thus if anything happens we may be clear and not have to reflect on ourselves for not doing our duty." [36] Elias' absence on long trips had evidently cut into the family treasury, for he informed Jemima, "James Carhartt has a bond of sixty pounds against me of money that belongs to a Dutchman, should be glad if thou hast enough money by thee to pay the interest thereof, thou could call upon Royal or brother Joseph and get some, and pay it the first of 5th month." [37]

Looking ahead a few weeks, Elias asked Jemima to meet him at Yearly Meeting, if Royal and Martha could stay at home, since she had not gone the previous year. He suggested she bring some summer clothing for him, and reported that the clothing in which he left home in December was so heavy he found it necessary while in Virginia to buy a pair of thin breeches. The only news he had to pass on was that Samuel Fisher's wife "was put to bed with two fine boys," and that the horse he had left with George Churchman, "was perfectly recovered and in good heart." [38]

By the middle of April, Elias and Joseph reached Lancaster, the largest inland town on the continent. At London Grove, Elias uttered a plea that Friends pay more attention to the inward monitor and live in their families in true simplicity. At New Garden, Kennett, and "Hockesson," he found a small living remnant; at Chichester, "it was a time thankfully to be remembered"; at Goshen, he again warned Friends that "their strength and preservation consisted in standing alone, and not to be counted among the people or nations." [39] At Uwchlan he struck at those who put their trust in natural religion or mere morality, declaring that such belief was no more than a religion of Atheists and led to the danger of self-righteousness, pride, and self-will. On the way to Burlington, Elias was ill, troubled with "the Gravel or dropsy or a species of both complaints which gave great distress. . . . ," he even doubted at times if he should get through with his life.[40]

John Hunt, a minister of Chester Monthly Meeting, was much moved when Elias spoke in his Meeting against a worldly spirit and all warlike contention. He considered Elias a "lively and powerful" figure.[41] Large crowded meetings at Middletown and Providence delayed Elias, who was tired and eager to get home. At Newtown "truth rose in victory, softening many hearts, and comforting and strengthening the faithful." [42] Elias attended the four-day session of Philadelphia Quarterly Meeting, held a special gathering for the youth, and one for the "black people." The homeward-bound minister and elder passed into New Jersey where they again found many tender minds, also some business gatherings held in indifference and with lukewarmness. At Trenton, "strength was made manifest in the midst of weakness"; and at Rahway, Elias "was wholly silent" —a rare occasion. There were no Friends in Newark so the called meeting was small and those who attended it were in "a loose un-cultivated state of mind." [43] On May 25, the Friends reached New York City, in time for the opening session of the Ministers and Elders, to which Elias had been appointed as a representative. After the first sitting he rode home to see Jemima and the family, and to assist Jemima in getting out to the business sessions of the Yearly Meeting. "Our rejoicing was precious, and mutual," he wrote in his Journal, "in and under a sense of the Lord's mercy and goodness, for whose gracious preservation and help, in this arduous journey, my spirit was made to bow in humble adoration and praise." [44] On this first southern journey, Elias was absent from home five months and two weeks, rode 1,600 miles, and attended 143 religious gatherings.

X

Shadows

of Dissent

RELIGIOUS LIFE ran sluggish in American Christianity during the last few years of the eighteenth century. It was a time of half-belief or no belief. The Episcopal Church had not recovered from its connection with the Tory party; the Methodists were hurt by Wesley's withdrawal of his English ministers at the outset of the Revolution. The works of Voltaire, Rousseau, and other French liberals became well known in the new Republic due to the alliance with France. Influential figures such as Benjamin Franklin, Thomas Jefferson, and James Madison were not communicants. As the new century began, Christian Rationalism, Universalism, and Unitarianism became more sharply defined. The liberal movement of thought brought about a conservative reaction led by Francis Asbury and William McKendree in the Methodist Church, and James McGready in the Presbyterian Church. In 1801 a new outbreak of revivalism began in the Cumberland Valley and spread eastward. Often both liberal and conservative forces were present in the same church body, causing conflicts and schisms.

In the Society of Friends three trends developed. One, representing a continuity of Quietist views, showed an increased emphasis upon the sufficiency of the Inner Light. Spokesmen for this point of view were Job Scott—until his early death in 1793, Elias Hicks, Edward Hicks, and John Comly. The second trend, less clearly marked but obviously an outgrowth of the new liberalism in the air, was attended by a rationalistic interpretation of the Bible. Representatives of this new trend were the Irish Liberals, Hannah Barnard of Hudson, New York, and, somewhat later, the Quaker New Lights of New England. The third trend was parallel with the Evangelical awakening and recaptured something of the first period of Quaker Enthusiasm. Stephen Grellet and David Sands of New York, as well as the majority of the English ministers who visited the United States between 1795 and 1835, represented this point of view. The first two trends often combined, but Evangelicals opposed both. They insisted upon the primacy of orthodox theological doctrines, including the infallibility of Biblical revelation. It was nearly a quarter of a century before an open clash between these two irreconcilable positions took place within the Society of Friends in America.

David Sands, born in Cowneck, Long Island, "more than any other prominent Minister of the eighteenth century, cultivated in the minds of Friends both in England and America the evangelical temper and habit of orthodoxy." [1] He was raised in the Presbyterian Church, joined the Society, was recorded a minister three years before Elias Hicks, and traveled extensively in New York Yearly Meeting, and in Europe. Stephen Grellet, another of "the formative [Evangelical] leaders who gave expression to this tendency among Friends, and who pointed the line of march in this general direction," [2] was a French Catholic, educated in the College of the Oratorians in Lyons. He immigrated to America at the time of the French Revolution, joined Friends in 1796, and moved to New York City in 1799. The work of these powerful ministers, who visited many Meetings in New York state, was seconded by a number of visitors from Great

Britain with similar messages. Among these was Thomas Shillitoe, a former Anglican, who became a bitter enemy of Elias Hicks.

The theological climate within the Society changed with different speed in various Yearly Meetings. Job Scott, closely akin to Elias Hicks in his thinking, died in Ireland at the age of forty-two. He left a Journal and many other papers which were placed before New England Yearly Meeting for possible publication. This body had already issued two of his works, but before the *Journal* could be edited the thinking of the Yearly Meeting had so changed that it first hesitated and then refused to sanction the printing of the *Journal* of its most famous liberal. Meanwhile, the Meeting for Sufferings of New York Yearly Meeting, strongly influenced by Elias Hicks, secured a copy of Job Scott's manuscript and published it in 1797.

Because of the different points of view presented by various ministers, it was directed, in 1800, that a new statement be read each year in Preparative, Monthly, and Quarterly Meetings of New York. "That all contention and personal reflection be kept out of our Meetings, and that Friends be careful to keep out of heats and doubtful dispositions in the ordering and managing of the affairs of Truth, but that the same be conducted in the peaceable Spirit and wisdom of Jesus." [3]

Yellow fever broke out again in New York City in the summer of 1798; Hugh Judge wrote to his Jericho friend that the city was in a panic with sixty-three deaths in a single day, hundreds fleeing to the country. Three of Hugh's children were violently ill for ten days; the parents while nursing them hardly slept two hours in twenty-four. Most Meetings were reduced to two or three in attendance. Elias sent his sympathy, writing that this calamity came from the hand of God, though few would so recognize it but would ascribe it to natural conditions and thus lose an opportunity for learning. In the fall Hugh sent word that city Friends were returning to their homes, although rural Quakers would not venture into the city to sell their foodstuffs. Later he added, "I would stain a little more paper," and reported that Meetings still were poorly attended. Elias replied that Friends who had "forsaken their habitations need wisely consider what and where they fled too." [4]

Phebe Hicks, now twenty, married Joshua Willets of Islip on the south shore in the fall of 1799. Abigail, Elizabeth, Sarah, and the two invalid boys, Jonathan and John, were still at home. In August of the following year, Elias and Jemima welcomed with great pleasure their first grandchild, Elias P. Willets. Their happiness turned to grief two weeks later when Phebe died. The grandparents did what they could to comfort Joshua; Elias made it a point to stop frequently and see his son-in-law and grandson at Islip.

The following spring Elias Hicks and Edmund Willis were set at liberty to attend the sessions of Philadelphia Yearly Meeting and visit among Friends as the way opened. The trip to the Brooklyn ferry was made easier because of the new Jericho Turnpike just finished by a chartered company. On the way they passed wagon loads of Rockaway sand destined to be used on the floors of city homes. In New York the closely packed houses now extended as far as Union Square at Fourteenth Street.

While attending Philadelphia Yearly Meeting, Elias and Edmund again stayed with the Fishers. They too had suffered a severe loss in the death of their twin boys, but both families were consoled by "a firm belief that he does all things right." Elias was somewhat disappointed with the sessions of the Yearly Meeting, then the largest in America. He admitted that many weighty subjects were presented, but he thought that some Friends were too forward in speaking to the business while a lack of patience was exhibited by the leaders. Often agreements could not be reached and the business was postponed till the next year. A note in John Hunt's *Journal* indicates that the vocal communications of the Jericho minister were well received. "I got to the select Yearly Meeting at Philadelphia. Elias Hicks from New York Yearly Meeting was there, as a lighted candle, fitted, prepared, and qualified to search the camp; which he did (others assisting) in a manner and degree surpassing all I ever heard." [5]

The New York Friends remained in the vicinity of Philadelphia for several weeks. On a First day at Market Street, Elias spoke on the danger of strife and contention, setting forth the grounds of unbelief, and the medium through which Deism and infidelity entered and darkened the mind. During this period he was uneasy about his daughter Abigail although he had no reason to feel that anything was amiss. In answer to his letter of inquiry, word came that she had been desperately ill, but was improved.

Leaving the city, the minister and elder held large gatherings among non-Friends as they made their way towards the foothills of the Alleghenies. "The Lord is about to call in from the highways and hedges," Elias wrote to Martha Aldrich. "But," he added, "we must know of going deeper than tradition, as traditional religion is no real worth without we have added to it that of our own experience and judgment, and that is only found by living our daily experience in that injunction of our dear Lord." [6] The course of the Schuylkill River was followed through Reading and north over the Blue Ridge Mountains to the east branch of the Susquehanna River. Here they turned to the west branch of the same river by Muncy. Elias became very weary during the long rides through the mountains, but he was confident that many hearts were reached and much error corrected. Thinking of his experiences with the frontier people he realized that itinerant ministers should be cautious in judging the spiritual condition of isolated families in scattered settlements. He saw that it was necessary to temper "hot zeal and hard censure and reproof" in order not to wound his hearers and so miss the opportunity to do them good. "Being much worn with travel," the two men from Long Island rested at Williamsport. A "blessed gathering" was held in the court house which was too small to hold the crowd. "My mind was so swallowed up in this days exercise," Elias indicated, "that while on my feet, I was scarcely sensible whether I was in or out of the body, that when I sat down my strength was much exhausted, and I was in such a state of perspiration that I was thoroughly wet from head to foot." [7]

With much effort they passed over the Bald Eagle Mountain and down into the Half Moon Valley—the center of Pennsylvania—where Friends met for worship in a log Meeting House. It took still greater effort to cross the main range of the Allegheny Mountains and reach Sewickly, northwest of Pittsburgh. They were now in the midst of Redstone Quarter, belonging to Baltimore Yearly Meeting. These frontier Meetings stretched from both sides of the Monongahela River almost as far west as Ohio. Conditions were primitive and much weakness prevailed. Elias was disturbed at Friends who were superstitious, believing in spirits, hobgoblins, and witches. Some of the leading families declared that damage had been done to them by their neighbors who cast spells which brought about periodic fits. There were many tales related of a boy, the Redstone Seer, who pretended to tell secrets and see individuals in distant parts of the world. He claimed to be able to describe their manner of life and the details of their homes. He also declared he could tell conditions and dispositions of persons, noting whether they were witches or not. Elias spoke strongly against such superstitions but "reasoning seemed to have no weight with them." "God forbid," he wrote, "that any, professing the name of a Friend, should ever thus desert the God of his salvation . . . and be given over to strange delusions." [8]

From Redstone the journey eastward was through the mountains south of Connellstown, Maryland, and north through Gettysburg, York, and Lancaster. At York, there were letters for Elias and he felt "the love that accompanied the letter from Jemima was better than wine." To Jonathan and John, he wrote a tender epistle:

My mind is often led forth . . . on your behalf, and fervant have been my prayers, to your heavenly Father and mine, that he would be graciously near to you . . . and then although your bodies are weak yet your minds would be strong and hereby you could come to know your Creator, and this our Lord and Savior Jesus Christ tells us is life eternal . . . now it is the mind or soul that can only live and enjoy this eternal life, our poor bodies whether weak or strong must all perish and go to dust. So that it is not such a great matter whether our Bodies are weak or strong if we are careful to love the Lord and fear him and have him for our friend which he will be if we try to do good always.[9]

For his cousin Isaac Hicks, then in New York City, Elias described the great chain of seven mountains he had crossed.

Much of the way in this tour has been rugged, mountainous and rocky . . . but we passed pretty cheerfully on, viewing with an attentive eye the wonderful works of that boundless wisdom and power (by which the worlds are framed). . . . Here we beheld all nature with its varied and almost endless diversification. Tremendous precipices, rocks and mountains, creeks and rivers, intersecting each other, all clothed in their natural productions; the tall pines and sturdy oaks towering their exalted heads above the clouds, interspersed with beautiful lawns and glades; together with the almost innumerable vegetable inhabitants, all blooming forth the beauties of the spring; the fields arable, clothed in rich pastures of varied kinds, wafted over the highways their balmy sweets, and the fallow grounds overspread with rich grain, mostly in golden wheat, to a profusion beyond anything of the kind my eyes ever before beheld, insomuch that the sensible traveler, look which way he would, could scarcely help feeling his mind . . . inflamed . . . with reverent thankfulness.[10]

The eye of the practical farmer and carpenter noted in the Redstone country timber so large that one tree contained forty cords of wood; other trees were forty feet high and eight feet in diameter, with branches spreading twenty feet from the trunk.

On July 18, after a journey through New Jersey, Pennsylvania, Maryland, and Virginia, Elias and his companions were at Cornwall, New York, much worn down with fatigue. In this Meeting Elias "had not sat long before a perfect, sweet calm ensued, wherein [he] . . . was swallowed up in divine seraphic enjoyment; so that not only [his] mind, but also [his] wearied body forgot all its toil." They reached Jericho ten days later, after an absence of three months and eighteen days, "with peace of mind attendant on a faithful discharge of manifested duty." [11]

Jonathan, an invalid for eight years, continued to fail during his father's absence. He was cheerful through all his weakness and suffering, but died the following spring as the apple blossoms were scenting the air outside his window. The sadness and loneliness caused by the death of their third son led Elias to remain close to Jemima's side for more than a year.[12]

It was during these months that Elias Hicks heard the story of the clash in London between Hannah Barnard of Hudson, New York, and David Sands, formerly of Long Island, now of nearby Cornwall. The report gave him grave concern. At the Yearly Meeting following his first long southern trip, Elias Hicks had assisted in preparing a minute recommending Hannah Barnard "to perform a visit in gospel love to Friends in Great Britain and Ireland."[13] A woman of superior insight and power, speaking with much natural eloquence, she was a gifted minister held in high esteem among New York Friends. Hannah Barnard spent several months in Ireland, coming in contact with many Liberal Friends with whom she felt strong sympathy. Her own ideas were strengthened and perhaps advanced by these contacts. At the same time, David Sands of Cornwall Meeting in New York, with warm Evangelical passion, traveled over the same areas of Ireland. He was not well received in Ulster or Dublin, coming in sharp conflict with the Irish Liberals. Completing a visit in England, Hannah Barnard asked for the same endorsement on her certificate for travel on the continent as had been given by the National Elders of Ireland. David Sands led the opposition against such an endorsement, and London Yearly Meeting refused her request on the grounds that she differed in some points from the beliefs and doctrines of English Friends.

The chief accusation brought against Hannah Barnard was a charge that she promoted disbelief in some parts of the Old and New Testaments. The Hudson minister declared that armed conflict was morally evil and therefore God could not have commanded the Hebrew people to make wars on other people or to utterly destroy the inhabitants of Jericho. Neither was she willing to admit that the command given Abraham to offer up his son Isaac as a sacrifice was a commission from God. Under questioning, Hannah Barnard said that there were parts of the New Testament—such as the miraculous conception—the truth of which had not been revealed to her. She fully admitted the power of Providence to effect this or any other miracle, but did not consider agreement with ancient historical events to be necessary for salvation, nor a requirement for membership in the Society of Friends. The Evangelical party, which was in control of London Yearly Meeting, insisted upon belief in the plenary inspiration of the Bible. Joseph Gurney Bevan maintained that the denial of a statement made by Moses undermined Christianity itself, since Jesus evidently accepted the Mosaic authorship of the first five books of the Old Testament. Bevan expressed the opinion, with which the weight of the Yearly Meeting united, that an individual holding views similar to those of the American visitor ought not to travel as a minister. Hannah Barnard was asked to cease preaching and to return home to New York; this she did, refusing to accept the usual fund to cover her expenses.[14]

Late in 1801, Hannah Barnard reached America, and Hudson Monthly Meeting considered the minute forwarded with her from London. She was again requested to be silent as a minister. While she was taking an appeal to the Quarterly Meeting, her home Meeting instituted disownment proceedings against her on the grounds that "she called in question the authenticity of various parts of the Scriptures." Hudson Meeting declared, "in common with other professors of faith in Christ, we have always acknowledged the Scriptures to be of divine authority and most surely believed by us. . . . She does not unite with the Society in acknowledging the truth of that part which relates to the miraculous conception and miracles of Christ: that she hath not only imbibed these erroneous and dangerous sentiments, but is assiduous in disseminating them among others." [15] Hannah Barnard was too tired to make an appeal to the Yearly Meeting—where Elias Hicks could have come to her aid—and accepted her disownment. She eventually joined the Unitarian Church though she frequently attended Friends Meetings.

Elias Hicks was much troubled by these events. He had been a member of the committees which drafted the New York Disciplines of 1783 and 1800. In the former, the only reference to the Scriptures was in the Query, "Are Friends careful . . . in the practice of frequent reading of the holy Scriptures?" In the latter, Friends were advised to teach the youth a due regard and esteem for the Scriptures, and to frequently read and meditate therein so that they would secure a firm belief in the Christian religion, especially in regard "to the miraculous birth, holy life, blessed example, doctrine and precepts, of our Lord and Saviour Jesus Christ." [16] Hannah Barnard had not denied any of these theological teachings. Yet at her trial she had been asked whether she could "affirm belief in the coeval divinity of Christ," in the miracles of Moses, and in Jehovah's commanding Joshua to kill the inhabitants of Jericho. She was also asked if she accepted the translation of the whole of the Bible as accomplished by revelation, and if Jonah had been in the belly of the whale for three days. To Elias Hicks these were not items of belief required for membership in the Society of Friends. He held that Quakers might differ in their thinking upon many religious topics; the only point of agreement required of all was the acceptance of the operation of the spirit of Truth within the soul. He quoted George Fox, who said in 1652, "The Scriptures were given forth by the spirit of God and all people must first come to the spirit of God in themselves by which they may know God and Christ . . . and by the same spirit they might know the holy Scriptures and the spirit which was in them and that gave them forth . . . and without it they cannot know neither God, nor Christ, nor the Scriptures, nor have fellowship one with another." [17]

Hannah Barnard declared in London, "Nothing is revealed truth to me, as doctrine, until it is sealed as such in my mind, through the illumination of . . . the word of God, the divine light, and intelligence, to which the Scriptures . . . bear plentiful testimony." [18]

Elias agreed, *"Nothing but this light"* he wrote, "is sufficient to produce the knowledge, on which . . . belief is founded . . . by faithful attention to . . . *the light within,* we come to know and believe the certainty of those excellent scripture doctrines; of the coming, life, righteous works, sufferings, death, and resurrection of Jesus
Christ, our blessed pattern." [19] Later he added, "Search the Scriptures. . . . But you cannot know them, by reading them merely;
but as you are directed by the divine Spirit. Under the influence of
that Spirit, you may not only read and understand them, but you
will be confirmed thereby. This Spirit led the ancients, and it will
lead us." [20]

The case of the two New York ministers, fought out on the floor
of London Yearly Meeting, marked a watershed which led eventually to a division within the Society. David Sands declared that all
Friends ministers must proclaim certain Evangelical doctrines.[21] Not
claiming infallibility herself, Hannah Barnard was condemned because she could not grant infallibility to others. With her position,
Elias Hicks agreed.

Because, with the early Friends, he considered the Inner Light
the primary authority, and all external aids—even the Scriptures—
as secondary, Elias Hicks was more sympathetic with the Liberal
views of his day than with the Evangelical current that captured the
Society in England and was making great inroads in some American
Meetings. He wrote, "I have highly esteemed the Scriptures from
my youth up, have always given them the preference to any other
book, . . . and I would recommend all to a serious and diligent
perusal of them." [22] He was afraid, however, that the Evangelical
party would idolize the Bible, trusting to the letter and not the
Spirit.[23] He saw that a literal interpretation of the Bible led to a divided Christendom. He noted that ministers of denominations who
held this position used it to justify wars, doctrines such as predestination, and outworn ordinances. He realized from his own reading that the Bible contained many contradictions and inconsistencies,
and believed that it was written by fallible men who were liable to

make mistakes about historical facts as well as misinterpret revealed teachings. "They were poor weak men, like ourselves," he said, "who wrote from memory, and that was the reason there were so many contradictions." [24] Thus, wrote the Jericho minister, "all that . . . books can do, is to point us to this great principle, the [Inner Light] which is only to be known in our souls." [25]

XI

Days of

Work and Sorrow

IMMIGRATION TO THE WEST followed three main routes—through the mountains by the Cumberland Gap and into Kentucky, by way of Pittsburgh and down the Ohio River, and north through the Genesee Valley of New York. The northern route was the easiest to travel but the last to be opened due to the hostility of the Iroquois tribes. It was necessary for a Friend desiring to move westward to secure a certificate from his Monthly Meeting. This document indicated that his affairs were in good order, and served as an introduction to any Quakers that might be met along the way. Meetings were often unwilling for their members to separate themselves from established groups. As early as 1792 Friends had moved into the Genesee Tract without the consent of their Monthly Meeting of East Hoosac in Massachusetts. Sufficient Quakers were soon in the area west of Seneca Lake to form their own group for worship and business. Other members crossed the St. Lawrence River and settled on the north side of Lake Ontario. For this section of "Upper Canada" [1] Elias Hicks and Daniel Titus of Westbury set out in September, 1803.

The two Friends covered the 410 miles to Adolphustown in two weeks. To Elias, this trip was a veritable going into the wilderness. On the road west of Albany there was heavy traffic. Stage coaches, containing from nine to twelve passengers, rattled by on the well-beaten track. Covered wagons, drawn by four, seven, and as many as twelve horses, transported heavy loads to the frontier. Taverns were located about a mile apart, kept by respectable men who were leaders in the new communities. Private accommodations were scarce, and Elias often found himself in a room in which several huge double beds were set up, each expected to hold four guests, whether they were acquainted with one another or not. Near Herkimer the party found an especially attractive inn where steak, bread and butter, eggs, and cheese were served for twenty-five cents.[2]

Crossing the St. Lawrence River was an adventure as well as a formidable undertaking. Making their way over logs and mudholes, Elias and Daniel came to Cape Vincent where flat-bottomed boats were waiting to ferry them and their horses to Wolfe Island. When they reached the island, the path proved so little worn that the two men had to get off their horses and feel for tracks made by other horses. The night was pitch dark, and when the men became separated by more than five or six feet they could no longer see each other. On the north side of the island other flat-bottom boats were ready, though one was so small it would hold but a single horse. The second half of the crossing was much exposed to winds blowing down from Lake Ontario, and the swell washed into the boats, keeping all busy bailing them out. "But," wrote Elias, "my confidence was in Him, who hath the winds and waves at his command, and we got over about one o'clock in the morning."[3]

Adolphustown Quakers, starved for vocal ministry, held ten religious gatherings for the Long Island Friends, and the courthouse doors at Kingston were opened that all who desired to hear might be accommodated. It was evident to the visitors that members of the Society in Canada enjoyed the privilege of a free, living, gospel ministry, but that they had permitted the cumbering cares of the world to divert them from improving their gifts, and thus, in a religious sense, they could be compared to the idle drones who live on the labors of the industrious bees. The visitors left their fellow Quakers, some whom they found to be distant relatives or members of Long Island families, "in much brotherly affection . . . their cheeks bedewed with tears" [4] after the farewell address.

Returning by the same route to the St. Lawrence, the party was able to cross the north strait without difficulty, but the wind was so unfavorable it was necessary to take lodging in the one small house on the south side of the island for the night. "Accommodations were very poor," Elias noted, "having to lie on the floor, and on benches; but having the best of company, peace of mind, and a firm trust in the divine blessing, it kept us comfortable and pleasant." [5]

Journeying at the rate of about thirty-five miles a day, the Friends covered northwestern New York and the Finger Lake district. Returning to Troy, after an eight weeks' absence, Elias was disappointed at not receiving any letters from home. He wrote to Jemima that he was either forgotten by his friends and family or that they desired to keep news of some disaster away from him. "But however I may be forgotten by my friends at home," he added, "I am not forgotten by the best of friends—for the Lord has been near." [6]

At Troy, Elias wrote a long letter to Hugh Judge, who had recently passed through the same territory. Hugh Judge indicated what a traveler might expect on leaving the main western road. Near Unadilla, Hugh Judge stayed in a new settlement where people lived . . . "in huts generally covered with bark, with . . . few chimnies or much fire-place, except a black stone placed against the logs a little higher than the back stick, so that there was plenty of smoke in the room." "We lodged one night," he wrote, "at a friendly man's cabin of one small room, in which was a weaver's loom and four beds. In this place ten or twelve of us slept, and rested well. But when the mind is intent on the great object of fulfilling its duty, no bed is too hard, nor food too coarse; these things are considered as nothing, nor worth minding." Hugh Judge mentioned "hunting up some of the scattered sheep of the family; some of whom had lost every mark of the Friend." "We lodged," Hugh related, "at a Friend's house (if house it may be called) that had not a single pane of glass in it, and no way for light when the door was shut, but what came down the hole in the roof where the smoke went out. Yet the Friends were very kind, the woman having six children, one of which was an infant. I thought the hardships which women go through in this western world were little known or thought of by their sisters in New York." Elias found similar conditions, longed to bind the isolated families of Friends into the framework of the Society, and was distressed by the hardships to which new settlers —especially the women and children—were exposed.[7]

From Easton, Elias wrote home asking for information concerning John's helpless condition, but no mail reached him until he arrived at Nine Partners, almost three months from the time he left Jericho. A few days later, in a Meeting for Worship at Crum-elbow, he was "void of any spiritual food" for those assembled. His mind ran on one of the parables, and he hoped there might be "a lad present, who would have a few barley loaves and fishes." Shortly thereafter a young man arose and gave a pertinent communication. This opened the way to the Jericho minister who enlarged upon the ideas presented, "all did eat and were filled, and many fragments remained to be gathered up." [8]

Elias' horse was worn out by this time, and at Hudson he purchased a new one. Instead of pressing homeward, however, the two men made a detour to East Hoosac, in Massachusetts, in order to report on the welfare of relatives in Upper Canada. Only then did Elias Hicks and Daniel Titus feel at liberty to return to Long Island. They reached Jericho the day after Christmas, having covered 1,575 miles, and having shared in approximately seventy-five religious gatherings.

The Seaman home in Jericho was a quiet place by 1804, in contrast to the activity of the previous ten years, when the children made a bustle with their coming and going. That fall Abigail received a proposal of marriage from her second cousin, Valentine Hicks, a partner of Isaac Hicks in New York City. After their marriage, Elias and Jemima found their house a pleasant stopping place when attending Meetings in the city.

Elias stayed at home for two years as John, the youngest boy, grew steadily weaker through the ravages of the same disease which caused the death of his three older brothers. In 1805 John died. Of his feelings or those of Jemima, Elias makes no comment in his *Journal*, which is blank for a two-year period. Long after he wrote:

All of our sons . . . were of weak constitutions . . . and were not able to walk after the ninth or tenth year of their age. The two eldest died in the fifteenth year of their age, the third in his seventeenth year, and the youngest was nearly nineteen when he died. But, although thus helpless, the innocency of their lives, and the resigned cheerfulness of their dispositions to their allotments, made the labour and toil of taking care of them agreeable and pleasant.[9]

It was Elias' firm belief in God as perfect in infinite wisdom, mercy, and love [10] which gave him the fortitude through the years to face the slow torture of watching his sons grow weaker and weaker. He could write of the everlasting arms which upheld him, for he had experienced their sustaining power.

Not long after John's death, Elias sent word to his good friend George Churchman at Nottingham, "Our only surviving son . . . deceased last 4th day, my wife and I are now left with only four surviving children out of eleven, the two youngest are with us." [11] To which George Churchman sympathetically replied, "though distant from each other the bond of fellowship which was hitherto forknowned and witnessed when together remains unbroken. . . . I send sympathy . . . what can we do better than patiently submit to all that is permitted . . . my own son died last summer on the ocean in his packet from London." [12]

These years of sorrow developed in Elias the tenderness he exercised with those about him, which lent his address an unusual quality, and which gave him the right to speak to others of faith and trust.

Walt Whitman wrote of the "pleading, tender, nearly agonizing conviction" of Elias' speech.[13]

Elias' character was forged in the fires of self-giving service and personal trial. It was written of him, "No man perhaps was more highly esteemed in his own neighborhood than was Elias Hicks, by all descriptions of people both as a useful citizen, a kind neighbor and a humble Christian." [14] In his fifty-seventh year, Elias was:

> In person erect, of commanding stature, and possessed in a remarkable degree that intangible attribute which denominates 'presence.' In social life he was dignified but kind, a little reserved in manner and gave the impression of great intellectual force, combined with a stern devotion to the convictions of duty. Affable in bearing, and inheriting the courtly politeness of the old school gentlemen of the century, his society was much sought by intelligent people of all classes, who were attracted by his rare and varied gift as a conversationalist. His public addresses were not adorned with flowers of rhetoric, nor polished by scholastic learning, but were plain, logical discourses, delivered with a natural earnestness and eloquence which seemed to inspire his audience with a measure of his own strong faith.[15]

The Yearly Meeting of 1804 sent down its usual caution to subordinate Meetings concerning the things of the flesh, reminding Friends that they should not fall under the spell of the fascinating spirit of the World. In the same year, the Meeting for Sufferings reported that its sub-committee charged with the duty of watching the "movements of the general government" had reported that a new bill was likely to pass which might affect Friends. The bill in question required "a duty for the express purpose of war." Friends were urged to see that no one yielded to such a requisition, since this would "infringe the precious testimony, we as a people bear for the Prince of Peace." Local bodies were directed to set up committees to "give service and assistance as may appear needful." [16] Elias wrote to Hugh Judge giving the further information that the "duty extraordinary" which Congress was about to impose consisted of a 2½ percent levy on all merchandise imported into the country ". . . for the special purpose of erecting a fund, to be deemed the Mediterranean Fund for carrying on war against the Tripolotan powers in the Barbary Coast." [17]

An extended number of social concerns claimed the attention of the Yearly Meeting. The fund for the care of the poor now amounted to £1,250. Elias was asked to help with its distribution. The Woman's Aid Society was incorporated in New York City to afford relief to destitute non-Quaker widows with small children. They gave, as need required, flour, clothing, candles, soap, tea, coffee, wood, molasses, sugar, meat, butter, bread, wine, potatoes, and cash. The African Free School, with many Friends on its Board of Trustees had nearly two hundred pupils. The Indian Committee took over the work formerly done by Philadelphia Friends in parts of New York and New Jersey. Sessions of the Yearly Meeting were devoted to considering a campaign against the use of products of slave labor, but no active steps were taken. Education remained a concern of Friends on the elementary and secondary levels. In New York City, the Association for the Relief of the Sick Poor, under the leadership of John and Catherine Murray, turned the efforts of many Friends toward the schooling of indigent youth. Several hundred children were under their care. This work was paralleled by the Society for Establishing a Free School for the education of such poor children as did not belong to, or were not provided for by, any religious society. Again John Murray was one of the moving spirits of this new body; De Witt Clinton, mayor of New York, was a trustee. Out of this organization grew the public school system of New York City.[18] Valentine Hicks served on its enlarged board.

Elias Hicks was busy at Jericho with the affairs of the local school, attended by his daughters, Sarah and Elizabeth. He searched for good masters, but on occasion when the right man was available the school committee did not have sufficient funds to pay the required salary. Elias continued his interest in the boarding school at Nine Partners, visiting it each year, and signing the report for the Yearly Meeting. More than twenty of its graduates had become teachers. The school was in a prosperous state, spiritually if not financially. Frequently there was a deficit at the end of the year due to unpaid tuition and board bills. This was remedied by making each Monthly Meeting responsible for any default in payments by Friends' families.[19]

The year 1806 was a memorable one for Elias because his cousin, Isaac Hicks, returned to Westbury. Isaac had gone to Manhattan Island in 1796, and in a comparatively few years had become the largest shipowner in that city. His *Solon* was the first vessel to carry the newly adopted American flag into the Black Sea; his *Sally Hicks* was known for many years as "Queen of the Whaling Fleet."[20] Isaac's house in Westbury contained an excellent library which was at Elias' disposal. Isaac made at least four trips as a companion of the Jericho minister.

Samuel R. Fisher wrote urging Elias to attend Philadelphia Yearly Meeting and inviting him to remain in his home, "affording satisfaction to our minds, hoping it may prove a seasonable renewal of our acquaintance and partaking of that love which goes beyond the force and expression in words."[21] This was a longer journey than Elias was as yet ready to undertake, but he did make a few short visits in the neighborhood of New York City. At Richmond, the Episcopal minister was kind enough to announce that Elias would hold a religious gathering although "it was the day they called Good Friday."[22]

When 1807 opened, Elias Hicks was in the midst of another journey among the New York Meetings. He passed through the port which was a place "of great stir and commotion," speaking "comfort and encouragement to the honest-hearted and truly exercised," and "to the careless, the unguarded and refractory, caution and rebuke."[23] He spent several days with the Mott brothers about New Rochelle, and wrote back to Jemima that, "Part of the way was the roughest I ever rode in a sled . . . pretty much through the wood where we almost stove our sled to pieces, broke the roller out . . . and shattered it otherwise, but being a mechanick as Paul was formerly, though not a tent maker yet a sled maker, and being furnished with tools at the house of a kind friend . . . I mended it up as strong or stronger than it was before." [24] In spite of the difficulties of winter travel up the Hudson Valley, Elias experienced many "glorious meetings," in which he felt "richly repaid for all the toil" involved in the journey. At Nine Partners, however, he found many whom he considered "mere birthright members" who were "dead weights" in the Meeting, as well as some convinced Friends who "lost their first love" and became "stumbling blocks" to others.[25]

Writing of his experiences near Poughkeepsie, Elias Hicks gave a partial description of the core of his religious message:

[He] was led, in a clear manner, to show the ground from whence all darkness and unbelief proceeded; that it was from a want of due attention to, and right belief in, the *inward manifestation of divine light,* which reveals itself in the heart of man against sin and uncleanness; and at the same time shows what is right, and justifies for right doing. Therefore while men disregard this inward divine principle, of grace and truth, and do not believe in it, as *essential* and *sufficient* to *salvation;* they are in danger of becoming either Atheists, or Deists . . . [or] becoming so blinded as not to believe in . . . the very essential doctrine of perfection, as contained in the clear, rational, and positive injunction of our dear Lord: Be ye therefore perfect. . . . *It is by obedience to this inward light only,* that we are prepared for an admittance into the heavenly kingdom.[26]

Returning to Jericho, after an absence of two months, Elias settled down for the rest of the winter. He learned that his friend Hugh Judge had moved from Little Falls in Harford County to Baltimore and that he was "under a load of cares and anxieties." [27] His health was also affected and he was growing deaf. Elias sent word that he appreciated the tribulations and spiritual exercises through which Hugh was passing. Such experiences he did not consider new nor strange since he regarded the world as a furnace in which men were "placed for their refinement," and if they did not continue to add fuel to the flames, and kept themselves "covered with the proof coat," all combustible matter would be burned away and they would be fit vessels for the Master's use. Elias observed that he also was in poor health, "afflicted with pain and weakness in his back" to such an extent that he could "hardly get to meetings in a halting manner." [28]

The next month, however, he went to Yearly Meeting, accompanied by Jemima, who, for the first time, was a representative from the Quarterly Meeting to the Women's Yearly Meeting.

In the late summer the minutes of Jericho Preparative Meeting stated that, "Elias Hicks hath a prospect of placing his two daughters, Elizabeth and Sarah, at the boarding school at Nine Partners." This was later approved and "an essay" was directed to be forwarded to the superintendent of the school recording the fact that consent had been granted.[29] On October 31, Elias, Jemima, Elizabeth, who was sixteen, and Sarah, now fourteen, set out in a carriage for Millbrook. Stowed away in the back of the vehicle were all the clothing and other items the girls would need for a twelve-month period. They were excited as they drove to Brooklyn to take the ferry, and their excitement increased while they stayed with Valentine and Abigail in New York City. On Sunday the girls accompanied their father to the Pearl Street Meeting House in the morning and to the Liberty Street Meeting House in the afternoon. In both gatherings Elias was moved to speak. Coming home from the evening service their horses stumbled over the poorly paved streets and, as it seemed to the girls, weird shadows were cast at every corner by the smoky oil lamps. On Monday morning the family drove northward, passing through the city of 80,000, hearing the bellmen as they walked ahead of the garbage wagons, and the cry of the water tenders who were selling fresh water drawn from the reservoir on Chambers Street, constructed by Aaron Burr's Manhattan Company. The air was filled with woodsmoke coming from multitudinous fireplaces in which hickory and walnut logs were burning. Small Negro chimney sweeps passed them crying out, "Swipe ho!" Farmers turned sidewise as they went by so that they would not knock against the wooden yokes from which buckets of milk were suspended.

Leaving New York City, the Hickses leisurely drove through the villages of Manhattanville, Harlem, and Greenwich. They visited Friends along the route, and it was a full week before they reached Nine Partners. After seeing Elizabeth and Sarah established at the school, Jemima remained to assist the superintendent, while Elias departed with two local Quakers to visit Meetings in eastern Connecticut. In December, Elias and Jemima were united and started back for Long Island. Their departure had been too long delayed, for winter weather made their return difficult. At "Hurlgate" blocks of ice made it impossible for the ferry to leave the dock, forcing the travelers to remain in New York for two days before attempting the crossing to Brooklyn.

Elizabeth and Sarah remained at boarding school the full year. During this time their father stopped to see them at least twice. Late in the winter he came by in a sleigh bent on visiting twenty-seven Meetings in Dutchess and Putnam counties. In August he was again at the school, spending some time with the superintendent. He thought well of James Mott, a young teacher of nineteen who had just joined the staff, and was pleased that Elizabeth and Sarah had struck up a friendship with Lucretia Coffin of Nantucket.[30] At this time the institution received its first map—one of the United States, and a small class was formed to study French, some indication that members of the committee, including Elias Hicks, were searching for an extension of the somewhat meager plan of Quaker education.

The girls enjoyed the months spent at Nine Partners, the delightful walks among the rolling hills in back of the red brick Meeting House, their books, and their many new friends. The pleasure and enrichment which his daughters found at the school confirmed Elias' conviction that Friends should provide for their children a guarded education in schools of their own establishment. To his mind it was more essential that children of Friends "be brought up and educated in the fear of the Lord, and in his nurture and admonition, than that they should make great advancement in scholastic science, or obtain the riches and popularity of the world; all of which were of momentary duration . . . especially when compared with the blessings attendant on a truly moral and religious life, and walking in the fear of the Lord." [31]

XII

Liberal and Evangelical

Travel Together

STEPHEN GRELLET, French émigré,[1] now a member of New York Yearly Meeting, passed little time in that metropolis. He arrived from Philadelphia in 1799, but during the next eight years spent more than half his time beyond the borders of the Yearly Meeting. His background and message were so alien to many in the New York area that when he asked for a minute to Philadelphia in 1805 there was considerable hesitation before his request was granted. "It proved a trying time to poor Stephen," Elias wrote to Hugh Judge, "he has much to bear and much to suffer . . . but way I believe will be made for him."[2] Three years later, on returning from a European visit, both Stephen Grellet and Elias Hicks were appointed to visit in the Yearly Meeting.

Elias Hicks was now sixty years old. He had served on countless committees at every level from Preparative Meeting to Yearly Meeting; as an itinerant minister during a thirty-year period, he knew the thinking of the majority of the members and had their confidence. He had a commanding appearance, a strongly developed personality, great intellectual force, and spoke with such convincing eloquence and power that enthusiasts compared him to Daniel Webster.[3] Just before setting out on this new commission, Elias received a letter of encouragement from John Murray, Jr., well-known philanthropist, educator, and a recent Clerk of the Yearly Meeting, who commended him warmly:

The master has endowed thee with a strong mind, thou hast talents and qualifications for eminent Service in the Church, and among the people at large . . . and as thou art greatly devoted to promoting the Redeemer's kingdom here on earth, I correctly crave thy preservation and right direction in all thy religious movements . . . that thy labors of love and zeal for the cause of truth and righteousness may be effectual to the gathering of many and the scattering of *none*. I cannot close this communication without the renewed expression of the unfained love that I bear towards thee and the anxious solicitude I feel for thy preservation, support, and encouragement.[4]

The committee rode over the deeply gullied roads of the Peekskill Mountains. "To look before," Elias put down, "it seemed almost impossible to get along without upsetting. We were near four hours going ten miles, but through favour we got there safe. We did not put up at an Inn until eleven at night after getting through the mountains." [5] The group had not attended many Meetings for Worship before it became evident that the messages of Stephen Grellet and Elias Hicks were quite different in nature. Elias spoke the language of John Churchman, Job Scott, and Joshua Evans. His ministry was concerned primarily with the Divine Light, inwardly known, the necessity of submitting to its guidance, of seeing the sin which it revealed, and using the power which came through it to find unity with God and man. This manifestation of the Divine Light of God in the soul was the new birth, or Christ formed in man.[6]

Stephen Grellet used theological terms unfamiliar to New York Friends. He placed new emphasis upon ideas loosely held by Quakers in former times. "I unfolded this great Gospel treasure," wrote Stephen Grellet, "Salvation through faith in Christ Jesus the Lord;

what he had done for us, without us, through the blood of his cross, His meritorious death and most holy and acceptable offerings of Himself for our sins, whereby we are reconciled to God." [7] Those who compiled his writings said that Stephen Grellet included in his beliefs:

> The Divine inspiration and authority of the Holy Scriptures, and . . . all that is revealed therein concerning the unity of the Godhead—the Father, Son, and Holy Ghost—the utter depravity of human nature in consequence of the fall; the pre-existence and incarnation of the Son of God; the proper eternal Deity and the real manhood of the Lord Jesus Christ; the need and efficacy of his propitiatory sacrifice, as an atonement or expiation for the sins of mankind; his mediatorial intercession and reign.[8]

These were the main Evangelical doctrines of the nineteenth century.

By contrast, Elias Hicks uttered the chief tenets of Quaker Quietism, "The ministration of the *Son and sent of God,* even the *divine word,* that was in the beginning with God, and was God, is only sufficient to effect that great and blessed end; and that, not by anything which he has *spoken, commanded, or done without us,* but what he *speaks, commands,* and *does within us;* we yielding and submitting thereto by faithful obedience." [9] In his addresses there was nothing concerning a propitiatory sacrifice, expiation of sin, mediatorial intercession, forgiveness or reconciliation as used in a technical theological framework. Stephen Grellet talked primarily of an outward act, Elias Hicks of an inward transformation.

As the party went through the Yearly Meeting they found many deviations and departures from the ancient simplicity of "[their] worthy predecessors," and many testimonies weakly supported. To Elias Hicks, the heart of Friends seemed opened and many precious opportunities came for seasons of "powerful visitation." [10] To Stephen Grellet, however, the experience was a time of great trial. "I became introduced," he said, "into very deep and painful trial; for Elias Hicks, one of our Committee, frequently advanced sentiments repugnant to the Christian faith, tending to lessen the authority of the Holy Scriptures, to undervalue the sacred offices of our holy and blessed Redeemer . . . though his assertions were often so covered that few understood him fully." [11]

Stephen Grellet was hardly more than half the age of the Jericho minister, and had joined Friends but thirteen years before, yet he wrote that he, "frequently . . . and earnestly laboured with [Elias Hicks]." Stephen added that Elias "promised that he would be more guarded; but vain promises they were and several times I felt constrained publicly to disavow the unchristian doctrines that he advanced." [12] Perhaps Elias did not take Stephen's protests too seriously —it is always easier for Liberals to be tolerant than it is for Orthodox —certainly he held no ill will against Stephen. He wrote to Jemima that Stephen continued to travel with him and that Stephen sent her his love.

The committee made its way through the Yearly Meeting visiting all the larger bodies of Friends except those in western New York and Canada. Both ministers, with their different backgrounds and points of view, understood the purpose of their commission according to their own experience. For Stephen the chief task was, "that souls might be 'won to Christ,'" and Stephen was alert to "the least tendency to lead away from him, or to lessen in the views of others the . . . completeness of his Divine attributes." [13] Elias was anxious to "promote a reformation" in the Society. He found in all classes there were many departures from ancient simplicity and integrity, from truth and righteousness.[14]

After two months' absence without any word from home, Elias wrote to Jemima that he "was led to query is the beloved of my bosom forgotten me or become strange." [15] He was anxious to get home and pushed rapidly to end the journey. Sometimes the company rode far into the night, put up at indifferent inns, and started off again at break of day in order to reach their next destination. While away from Jericho, Elias made only one suggestion concerning affairs at home. He knew of a John Brown in New York City who owned a machine to card and spin fine wool, so he wrote Jemima that she might ask Valentine Hicks, when he was traveling to New York, to take their wool to John Brown and thus save herself much labor. The workshop was beginning to displace household industries on Long Island. Elias heard from Hugh Judge. His two daughters were with him, "one a talented teacher beyond many of her years," and the other married to "a stiddy [sic] salted Friend." Elias answered, "your dear children promise fair to give you much comfort now in your declining years." [16]

While on this journey, Elias entered into the fullness of his powers as a speaker. Again and again in his *Journal* he used the phrase, "the house was not sufficient to hold the people," [17] or "many, in most places, appeared convinced of the truth and propriety of our doctrines and principles," [18] as well as "it proved the largest meeting ever held in that place." [19] Sometimes he gave fuller details, "I found great openness generally among the people . . . and I was made glad in believing, that the Lord was graciously near, and accompanied the word preached, with his heart-tendering power, comforting and refreshing the broken hearted, receiving the spirit of the contrite ones, and stopping the mouths of gainsayers." [20] It is evident that Elias Hicks "was gifted to an unusual degree with the strange quality called 'leadership' with which God endowed so many men to carry on His work in the world." [21] One who knew the Jericho minister at this period of his life wrote, "We were also personally acquainted with him . . . he was calm, dignified, and self-possessed, correct even to rigidity, in his morals, simple and unostentatious, he was one of the purest specimens of the genuine Quaker that it has ever been our lot to know. Not free, by any means, from the superstitions and peculiarities of Friends, often severe upon the weaknesses and vices of society, he yet, from his unostentatious and simple demeanor, and active benevolence, commanded general respect." [22]

James Mott, Sr., of Mamaroneck, New York, a friendly and judicial critic of Elias Hicks, addressed him not many months before the journey of 1808, "I am satisfied that the master hath conferred on thee a precious gift in the ministry, and I have often sat with peculiar satisfaction in hearing thee exercise it." He cautioned, however,

"When thou came to touch on predestination, and some other erroneous doctrines, I thought a little zeal was suffered to take place, that
led into much censoriousness, and that expressed in harsh expressions,
not only against the doctrines, but those who had embraced them";
and continued, "I have often thought if ministers when treating on
doctrinal points, or our beliefs, were to hold up our principles fully and
clearly, and particularly our fundamental principle of the light within,
what it was, and how it operates, there would very seldom be occasions for declamation against other tenets, however opposite to our
own; nor never against those who have through education or some
other medium embraced them." [23] This helpful advice Elias did not
always follow.

Before the circuit ended, some of the company were exhausted by
hard travel and much speaking. The task ended, Elias observed, "I
may say with gratitude of heart, that the same divine power that
attended in the foregoing part of the visit, was again manifested for
our help, in going through, and finishing the service . . . to the solid
peace of my own mind." [24]

Stephen Grellet left on a second trip to Europe after extensive service among Friends in the south and on the frontier. Before leaving
he wrote,

I have been also introduced into many exercises on account of our
Society in these parts. There is a cloud impending over us; a spirit of
infidelity is insidiously spreading; therefore I have . . . earnestly laboured, both in our meetings for Ministers and Elders, and in other
meetings, and with my dear friends in private also, that . . . we may
avert the impending calamity, which at seasons appears to me to be
coming, like an overflowing scourge, over our Society.[25]

Stephen Grellet did not recognize that men like Elias Hicks were
standing by the teachings universally held throughout the Society of
Friends in the days of their youth. It was the new emphasis the Evangelicals placed on doctrines considered nonessential by Friends in
earlier years which was "the cloud impending" over the Society.

Steadily, as each year of the nineteenth century passed, signs of tension grew more pronounced. The Quakers had passed from the first joyous period of Enthusiasm into the isolation of Quietism by the simple process of cooling off. Then they planted a hedge to shut out the world's people. Occasional thunder on the Quaker horizon in the new century warned of heavier storms to come. For several generations Friends listened to sermons which emphasized the Inner Light, the necessity of following its guidance, and the importance of queries and testimonies; now the emphasis was shifting to theological doctrines which early Friends called "notions." The sermons of Stephen Grellet and other Evangelicals were reinforced by books written by British Quakers which contained the new theology. Henry Tuke of England wrote two works, *The Faith of the People Called Quakers in our Lord and Saviour Jesus Christ,* and *Principles of Religion, as Professed by the Society of Christians, usually called Quakers,* both of which leaned heavily towards an orthodox position. "The point of emphasis," Rufus M. Jones wrote of these books, "has entirely altered . . . and the whole perspective has changed from that of the seventeenth century . . . Tuke raises evangelical doctrines into unprecedented prominence." [26] John Bevans, Jr., of England, writing at the same time, the *Defence of the Christian Doctrines of the Society of Friends against the charge of Socinianism,* emphasized the depravity of man, the historical accuracy of every part of the Bible, the miraculous conception, the doctrine of the Trinity, and salvation through the vicarious sacrifice of a holy Redeemer. These books were widely circulated in America before Stephen Grellet left on his second European journey. Tuke's *Principles of Religion* became the "standard book for the use of New England Friends . . . though there was a large and influential group . . . in that Yearly Meeting heartily loyal to the position expounded by Job Scott." [27] The change which took place in London Yearly Meeting gradually permeated the rest of the Society, "Religious teaching based on the Inner Light in the souls of men, which a few years before would have passed as sound Quakerism and genuine Christianity, was now called in question, and tested in the light of the doctrine of the infallible authority of the Bible. The new spiritual life . . . had begun to clothe itself in new forms derived from the prevalent Evangelicalism of the day." [28]

Elias Hicks strongly objected to Henry Tuke's statement that the Holy Scriptures were "communicated" to men under divine influence and inspiration.[29] Elias was willing to grant that "all Scripture given by divine inspiration was profitable" and able to make men wise unto salvation; but he could not admit that all parts of the Bible were inspired. The Jericho minister did not wish to lessen belief in the Bible, the history or the mysteries recorded, but he did not believe that "the record preserved concerning Solomon's building a house for Pharaoh's daughter was given by divine inspiration, any more than the record of the expense and building of the new Meeting House in New York." [30] Nor did he think the passages concerning Solomon's wives and concubines, and the stories of the cruel wars of the wicked kings of Israel were inspired writings. Elias declared these records were on a par with the histories of the cruel wars of Rome and those of modern times. Henry Tuke's insistence that all portions of the Bible were given by revelation undermined the real value of the Scriptures, Elias thought, and did more damage than "all the wit, sophism, and infidelity of Thomas Paine." Tuke's position was not previously held by Quakers, and it "gave a general alarm to friends in this country, as a sentiment subversive to their faith." [31] Yet London Yearly Meeting sent Hannah Barnard home for holding views similar to Elias'.

Many interpretations of Christianity swept over New York and other Eastern states in addition to the shifting emphasis within the Society of Friends. The older Calvinism was vigorously defended by Presbyterians and some Congregationalists; Arminianism, with its liberal view of the Bible, was dominant in the Episcopal Church and rapidly spreading to other denominations; Rationalism and French romanticism, with their exalted view of human nature, were also influential; Universalists and Unitarians were teaching the Fatherhood of God and the Brotherhood of Man. All these ideas beat against the Quaker wall of isolation, which was giving way at several points.

In the past Long Island had been spared the results of earlier theological controversies. "In the years when Connecticut Valley was writhing under the fiery eloquence of Jonathan Edwards, and White-field preached on Boston Common to fifteen thousand weeping hearers . . . the once persecuted Friends, in their plain houses, quietly awaited the movement of the Spirit." [32] Unity among the Friends could not last. Thomas Willis of Jericho was one of the committee appointed in 1808 to visit within the Yearly Meeting, and was much influenced by Stephen Grellet. Gideon Seaman of West-bury, who was also a member of the 1808 committee, took the Evangel-ical position. With the death of Job Scott at an early age, the dis-ownment of the Irish liberals under strong pressure from London Yearly Meeting, and the silencing of Hannah Barnard, Elias Hicks was forced into the leadership of Quietists who clung to the im-portance of the Inner Light as central in religious experience. Under attack from the rising Evangelical wing of the Society, Elias was obliged to define his position on doctrines which to him were secondary. As a liberal interpretation of the Bible and of theological doctrine was more consonant with the central position he gave to the concept of the Inner Light, Elias Hicks gradually became the chief exponent of Liberal Quakerism.

The leaders of a Quakerism experiencing internal conflict traveled over the same territory, and the emotions and intellect of their hear-ers was pulled from one side to the other as Friends ministers, with equal sincerity, expressed their contradictory views. The language used to express these conflicting thoughts was so different that the listeners could tell as soon as certain keynote phrases or words were used what would follow. It was the Blood of the Lamb, or the Inward Manifestation of the Divine Light; the meritorious death that recon-ciled to God, or Christ in man the hope of glory.

XIII

The

Quaker Idealist

"The condescending goodness, of a gracious God," enabled Elias
Hicks to "surrender all up to his heavenly disposal, to be anything or
nothing," as the Jericho minister wrote in 1808, "and in every situation . . . to be therewith content." [1] It was a source of satisfaction
to Elias not to be called upon to make any extended journeys during
the next four years. He went instead to Islip and watched his grandson Elias Willets. He made a quick trip into Upper Canada and wrote
from Albany about the new fashion of calling supper "tea." Frequently Elias Hicks made short journeys lasting from two to four
weeks among Friends and non-Friends on Long Island.

As Elias was spending more time in Jericho, Jemima was freed
from the oversight of the farm. Two of the girls—now capable young
ladies—were at home, and there were servants to assist with the
work.[2] Jemima was able to spend some time with Abigail and Valentine in New York City, to be a representative to the Yearly Meeting
Ministry and Elders, and to attend the business sessions of the superior
Meeting. In mid-winter of 1809, while she was with her grandchil-

dren in New York City, Elias wrote that he "anticipated her return with pleasure, if her visit was out." He added:

nothing appears among us but harmony, and good humor, except last evening dear Elizabeth undertook to wind some silk, which got so tangled as to be an over match for her patience which led her to call on Sarah's assistance, but as the snarls in the silk did not readily yield to Sarah's skill, it drove Elizabeth . . . to scold at Sarah a little for relief; and although this is no great attainment that a family of three persons should live together eight days without scolding, yet it might be considered a rarity in some families, wherein seldom a day passes, without some.[3]

In the same letter, Elias spoke of the bad weather and suggested that Jemima cross by boat to Flushing and then take the stagecoach to Jericho.

Joseph Talbot requested Elias Hicks to urge that the Meeting for Sufferings take up a subscription to help Scipio Quakers build a new Meeting House. Their old accommodations were small and "smokey," new settlers were moving into the area and joining the Society, but the newcomers had no money to contribute towards a building project. William Poole of Brandywine requested that Elias make another trip south and bring Jemima with him. Elias wrote to his friend George Churchman, now in his eightieth year, "In younger life it has often been grateful and encouraging to my mind, to behold my ancient friend, clothed with greenness and pressing with fervour of mind toward the mark of our high and holy calling. . . . In thy declining state . . . God will continue to be with thee. . . ."[4]

At the Yearly Meeting in the spring of 1810, Elias saw one of his cherished ideas defeated. A new revision of the Discipline was approved, and in that part of the Query cautioning Friends against dealing in prize goods a change was made. The former Query was used as a means of making inquiry concerning the use of goods produced by slave labor, and of discouraging the practice. The new edition carried no reference to prize goods, as the majority of New York Friends considered it impossible to distinguish any longer be-

tween goods produced by slave or free labor. Returning to Jericho
after the action was taken, Elias wrote an essay which "condemned
slavery almost as vigorously as any which had ever come from a
Quaker pen." [5] The twenty-four-page pamphlet contained the results
of Elias' meditation on the subject of slavery over a period of many
years. Samuel Wood, a Quaker printer in New York City, published
the work under the title:

OBSERVATIONS

ON THE

SLAVERY OF THE AFRICANS

AND

THEIR DESCENDANTS

Recommended to the Serious Perusal, and
Impartial Consideration of the
Citizens of the United States
of America, and others concerned.

Below the name of the author appeared verses from the Bible:

Open thy mouth for the dumb in the cause of all such
as are appointed for destruction.
Open thy mouth, judge righteously, and plead the
cause of the poor and needy.

PROVERBS XXXI, 8, 9.

Elias Hicks opened his "Observations" with the statement that
slavery had been so long established that many well-minded individuals by force of custom and education considered the institution consistent with justice and social order. Though custom or institution were of long standing, Elias stated, that did not "alter the
nature of justice or equity, nor make wrong right, or right wrong,"
even though that custom "might be sanctioned by the laws of man." [6]
Because the citizens of the United States boasted that the enjoyment
of liberty was the most precious of all their many blessings, Elias
insisted they must consider impartially the whole foundation on
which African slavery was erected.

In the first place, the prophet of Jericho wrote, it was universally acknowledged that man was a moral agent and so accountable for his personal conduct; and further, that every man was a free agent and thus born free, no matter what the situation of his parents. Then Elias, in a series of nineteen Queries and Answers, set forth his arguments against slavery. He maintained that the people of Africa were as free in their relations with one another as the different countries of Europe until their lands were invaded by outsiders; they "possessed . . . the same inalienable rights of life, liberty, and the pursuit of happiness." It was by fraud, force and purchase that the Negroes were taken by the Europeans, and "every child of an African, born in America, or elsewhere, according to revelation and moral justice [was] born free, and therefore suffers . . . cruel fraud, and tyrannical cruelty . . . while under the galling yoke of slavery." [7] The claim of slave owners, he continued, that the Negro was "a different and inferior race of mankind" [8] was only a cloak to cover the plantation owners' unrighteous conduct. Moreover, the slave could not be a different species or an inferior race of mankind, as the Southerners declared, for nature had an immutable law that two animal species could not unite and produce offspring. The extreme heat and humidity of Africa gave the Negro his color and curly hair; the primitive customs of the land made them appear less civilized and inferior to the whites.

To own slaves, wrote Elias, was to possess prize goods, for the slaves were taken by violence, in a state of war, and contrary to their own wills. Elias Hicks went further by declaring that in his judgment the legislature of any state had a right to abolish slavery without compensation to those who owned the slaves. Plantation owners might consider a Negro "real property," but to the Quaker no man could hold as property a rational being, and to buy or sell such an individual was a heinous and unrighteous act in the sight of God. To buy a slave was to become accessory to human theft and subject to the death penalty prescribed by Mosaic Law. Holding a man by force in the abject state of slavery was little short of murder, and anyone who followed this corrupt custom should be obliged to

set his slaves free, forfeit the purchase money, and make full satisfaction to the person he injured. As a practical step Elias urged that
the United States and Great Britain cease trade with the West Indies.
This would lessen the price of commodities raised in those islands,
decrease the demand for additional slaves, and in due course end the
traffic. He maintained that such action would be more effective than
passing laws concerning slavery itself.[9]

Having laid before his readers the Queries with their appropriate
Answers, Elias Hicks emphasized his points with a sketch portray-
ing the horror of slavery. "Suppose," he wrote, "the way for obtaining slaves from Africa was entirely intercepted, and no other place
opened for obtaining any, except in the rivers Delaware and Hudson
. . . that the slave traders were continually infesting the shores of
those rivers; that they frequently kidnapped, and sometimes by force
carried off inhabitants to the West Indies, and sold them as slaves."
Then he pictured the traders moving inland, burning towns and
carrying away men, women, and children. "We now view them all
hand-cuffed, two and two together . . . sold to the slave merchants
. . . going on ship-board . . . crowded down between the ship's
decks, stowed close to each other, almost worn out by the hardships
they have already suffered, their tender arms galled with their irons,
and nowhere to lie down to rest their weary limbs but on the hard
deck of the ship; and so closely stowed as to be almost suffocated."
Continuing his harrowing story, Elias went on to portray the white
slaves, "driven like a herd of swine to market . . . exposed to public
sale, and without regard to sex or age, examined by those brutal men
who are to be their purchasers, as naked as they were born; and when
one is struck off to any bidder, a red hot iron is ready to brand the
poor victem . . . husband separated from a beloved wife, and a
wife from a beloved husband, who had been for many years the joy
of her life . . . torn asunder, like bone from bone . . . without the
small indulgence of . . . the possibility . . . of ever seeing each
other again." He finished his ghastly picture with an account of
children torn from their parents, driven by cruel drivers, struck till

the blood ran, working in the fields under the lash, some falling exhausted between the rows of cotton. This dark portrayal Elias concluded with the declaration:

Is it possible there should be . . . a man with a heart so hard as to assent to purchase, and make use of the fruit of the labour of his fellow citizens, his kindred and friends, produced in the horrid manner above stated, and taken from them by the unjust hand of cruelty and oppressive force? Would not every sympathetic heart, at the sight of a piece of sugar, or other produce . . . be filled with anguish. . . . Would he not consider the individual who would dare to be so hardy as to traffic in and use the produce of such labour . . . the open and avowed enemy of both God and man? [10]

Elias wrote the "Observations" nearly twenty years before William Lloyd Garrison began his campaign which opened the main abolition crusade. The seeds of the later movement were contained in this pamphlet. The Meeting for Sufferings approved the publication. In the Preface to the second edition Elias Hicks expressed belief that though a man convey his so-called right in a slave to another, the title to a slave was invalidated because such possession was a criminal offense in the sight of God.

Copies of the pamphlet were widely circulated and reached English Friends. Martha Routh wrote from Manchester that she found the writing, "very acceptable and instructive," and she was forwarding a copy to Thomas Clarkson, one of the leaders in the abolition movement in Great Britain.[11] Thomas Burling of New York, whose grandfather William was one of the first to plead with Friends to give up their slaves, wrote to Elias, "Thy pamphlet on the most effective way to put an end to the slavery of the poor Africans was put in my hands. . . . Thy arguments are irresistable and I believe has merited being the first in proposing a rational plan but I fear will be a work of time before its accomplishment." [12]

The movement against the use of slave products was given a new impetus by Elias Hicks' pamphlet and sermons, and many Friends joined in boycotting rice, cotton, and sugar. "Abstinence from the use of slave-labor goods became a favorite Quaker outlet for anti-slavery energy." [13] James Mott, grandfather of the husband of Lu-cretia Mott, limited his family to maple sugar, always wore linen cloth, and never allowed the use of rice in his household. After the publication of "Observations," Elias Hicks "stood out as a notable friend and benefactor of the colored race in a generally hostile world." [14]

There were some Friends, however, who did not agree with the Hicks position. The gentle John Comly saw no value in following his advice. Jonathan Evans, a powerful elder of Philadelphia, who at one time had abstained from the use of slave products, gave up the practice and bitterly resented Elias' advocacy of this type of reform movement.[15]

On a number of occasions, Elias Hicks graphically described his experiences among Southern plantation owners on the floor of the New York Yearly Meeting. Once he told of the threat made by a slave owner to shoot him, but when Elias called on the man the next day they had an amicable discussion and parted in a friendly man-ner. After New York's 25,000 slaves were freed, most Friends in the state were careful to carry on further concern for the Negroes within the framework of the state laws. Some shared in the work of the Underground Railroad, especially the Quakers in upstate New York near the Canadian border. Although a branch line went through Long Island, there is no record that Jericho Friends were active in this phase of the antislavery movement. Elias Hicks supported vari-ous plans for colonizing freed slaves. At first he looked upon Haiti, rather than Africa, as the logical home for ex-slaves; but he was forced to admit that the southern colonization societies which then existed would not be willing to support "a kingdom of blacks so near as San Domingo." [16] He realized that a colony close to the United States might tempt Southern slaves to escape from their masters. In a later essay he urged collection of funds to buy the freedom of slaves and "purchase a tract of land in the Southwestern interior or unim-proved parts of the United States" where the freed slaves could be instructed in a republican form of government, set up a state of their own, and finally be admitted into the Union. "Nothing short of so doing," he wrote, "would be just recompense for the wrongs we have done them." [17] His advocacy of the establishment of a separate State for Negroes suggests a philanthropic concern rather than a permanent solution of the race problem. Friends in general "wished no more than other whites of their day and generation to associate with different races on terms of social intimacy." [18]

Elias Hicks visited settlements of the Montauk and Shinnecock Indians on eastern Long Island and held meetings in their "wickwams." He served for a period on the Indian Committee of New York Yearly Meeting and was appointed to visit the Oneida, Onondaga, Stockbridge, and Brotherton tribes in various parts of the state. He accomplished his mission but left no record of his impressions. His interest in the red men never seemed as keen as his concern for "the blacks." New York Friends repeatedly took subscriptions in their local bodies to purchase seed, farm and household equipment for these tribes; financial aid also came from London Yearly Meeting. The "work of civilization" was always hampered by the twin evils of rum and inertia. John Dean, sent by the committee on which Elias served to act among the Brotherton Indians as teacher and farm agent, reported "in a distance of seven miles there were nine stills, consuming thirty thousand bushels of corn a year . . . a murderous work." [19] In Elias' letters appears a phrase frequently used in Indian treaties which the Jericho minister acquired from his contact with the Indians, "it served to quicken and brighten the chain of brotherly affection and friendship." [20]

On his trip to Upper Canada in 1810, Elias stopped as usual at Nine Partners boarding school. He found all in good order and was pleased to sign the report of the committee. Three years later he noted that the income of the school was $2,997 and the expenses $2,996. With this statement before it, the Yearly Meeting directed that tuitions be collected each quarter in advance. The day school at Jericho was in

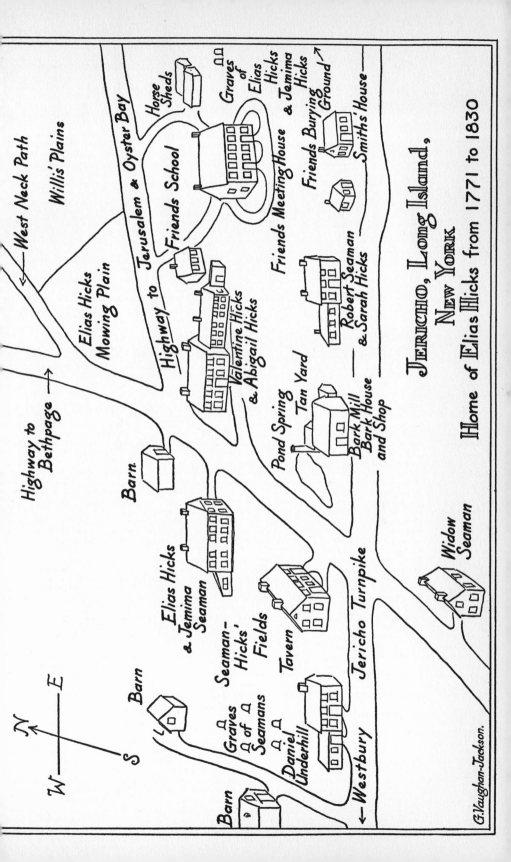

N
E
W
S

Highway to Bethpage →

West Neck Path

Willis' Plains

Elias Hicks Mowing Plain

Highway to Jerusalem & Oyster Bay

Horse Sheds

Graves of Elias Hicks & Jemima Hicks

Friends School

Friends Meeting House

Friends Burying Ground

Smiths' House

Robert Seaman & Sarah Hicks

Valentine Hicks & Abigail Hicks

Barn.

Pond Spring

Tan Yard

Bark Mill Bark House and Shop

Barn

Elias Hicks & Jemima Seaman

Seaman-Hicks' Fields

Graves of Seamans

Daniel Underhill

Tavern

Jericho Turnpike

Westbury →

Widow Seaman

Barn

G. Vaughan-Jackson.

JERICHO, Long Island, New York

Home of Elias Hicks from 1771 to 1830

better financial condition than the boarding school. It had a balance of $665.25 in 1811. The Yearly Meeting reminded Friends to consider all previous advices concerning the education of their children, especially regarding the employment of Quaker teachers so that the children of Friends would not "imbibe ideas and sentiments at variance with the nature of [the Quaker] profession . . . which being acquired in early life would be lasting." School committees were cautioned to give careful attention to the choice of books used, and wealthy members of Meeting were asked to "consider the claims which their brethren in religious profession possessing but little outward substance, have upon their Christian benevolence, that to those to whom a greater portion of wealth has been entrusted, may be found in the Spirit of Charity, good Stewards, ready to distribute, willing to communicate." [21]

Democracy in the Jericho Meeting continued to be real, every member rendering his due service. Elias Hicks, minister and carpenter, repaired the schoolhouse and sent in a bill for $1.12½ for work he did on the Meeting House. David Seaman, dignified Clerk of the Monthly Meeting, was requested to clean out the stables. Royal Aldrich purchased 160 feet of good nut wood for $8.97. Elias Hicks surveyed land needed to enlarge the cemetery. The Meeting warned its members against "the baneful effects resulting from the use of Distilled Spiritous Liquors," as well as the danger of "attending Places of Diversion such as Horse Raseing [sic]." An unexpected leniency appeared in the minutes now and then. When Fry Willis and Elias Hicks were sent to visit a young Friend who "had suffered his horse to run a race for a wager" they were told to deal with him with a "feeling of tenderness and sympathy." [22]

Twenty years before the anti-Masons formed a political party and nominated a presidential candidate, Elias Hicks spoke vigorously against all secret societies. In line with Friends' traditional opposition to oath taking, Elias insisted that it was not rational for a man to take an oath promising to keep the secrets of any organization. He argued further that God gave light to men in order that they might share it with their fellows, not put it under a bushel. If the Free-masons had enlightenment which was of value to society they should share it and "not cloister it up in secret." [23] In his sermons Elias usually added that lodges might easily become places where the membership spent their time in drinking and idle, even wicked, amusements. Other Friends denounced the "midnight orgies" of the Masons.[24]

In the decade which saw the rise of the Bible Societies, Boards of Home and Foreign Missions, the Friends maintained their aloof-ness. Elisha Tyson, the Baltimore philanthropist, declared that "princes, nobles and gentry" gave money to spread the gospel not because they believed in it, but because it was the "popular" thing to do.[25] John Hunt of Moorestown, New Jersey, said the very men who with great exertion and expense sent Bibles to the heathen in foreign lands did not understand the Scriptures themselves.[26] Elias Hicks' objections were more in accord with the wing of a Baptist denomination in the Midwest which maintained God did not need the help of human hands to bring His elect to repentance. Elias declared these new organizations were established "in the will and wisdom of men" and therefore would "fall to the ground." [27]

Attacks of the Friends on the clergy did not soften with the pass-ing years. Elias was as strenuously opposed to a hireling ministry in 1813 as he had been in 1784 when he argued with Thomas L. Moore of Hempstead. Writing to Samuel Cox of New Jersey, grandson of an old friend, he protested against the young man undertaking by "human science and creaturely requirements to prepare for the office of a minister of Christ." To Elias, such an idea was presump-tuous; he appealed to the young man to "study to be quiet, and mind his own particular business . . . in order to have real sanctification of heart." No one, Elias believed, could stay the hand of God from calling a man to the ministry, nor could a body of men by ordinances designate a servant of God. He pointed out to Samuel Cox that St. Paul, trained at the feet of Gamaliel, renounced his learning and de-pended wholly upon the immediate revelation of Jesus Christ. Paul did not go to Jerusalem to learn of the Apostles on receiving his call, but went into the desert of Arabia to be taught by the Spirit of God. "Seek the light of truth in thy own heart," Elias wrote his young friend, "keep to the light that convinced thee . . . avoid placing any dependence on man, or the works and wisdom of man, and fix thy whole reliance on God, and the operation of his light and spirit in thy own mind, as that is the only right source of spiritual strength and consolation to all who love him." [28]

Elias Hicks was opposed to the wave of camp meetings and other revivals which swept over parts of America during the first fifteen years of the nineteenth century. He wrote to Rufus Clark in New Haven, whose wife was a Methodist, that it was a great mistake to think "conversion from sin is effected by a sudden shock" to the mind. Such a belief, he held, led to spiritual pride and complacency. The one so converted was apt to think himself better than he really was, to show a fiery zeal which was temporary rather than lasting. True conversion and obedience to Christ, Elias held, came only through many deep baptisms of the Holy Spirit, sometimes over a period of years, preparing the soul for the kingdom of heaven.[29]

XIV

The Written

and Spoken Word

On "sixth day, 26th of 3d month, 1813," [1] Elias Hicks began to keep a home journal. Since the publication of George Fox's Journal, this form of writing had become second nature to Quaker ministers. The Journals were as distinct a type of literature as Yearly Meeting Epistles or Memorials to Deceased Friends. Elias' father owned several of the hundred Quaker Journals in circulation in 1764. In early manhood Elias purchased the first edition of John Woolman's *Journal*, the superlative American writing of this kind. These Journals, next to the Scriptures, were the most popular reading matter among members of the Society. Young Friends enjoyed the adventure tales of itinerant ministers, and absorbed the pattern of Quaker living from their reading. The Journals were a means of propagating the faith among non-Friends. "At every point of his unfolding Elias Hicks reveals the influence of Quaker Journals." [2]

Elias Hicks was not prepared to write a formal journal of his life in 1813, indeed he doubted the propriety of doing this at any time; [3] but he kept notebooks of his longer journeys which were put away in his cherry desk when he returned to the farm. In the travel diaries he described his experiences, his impressions of the various groups he met, and occasionally gives a summary of his sermons. In the early pages of the travel diaries he customarily noted the name of the family with whom he lodged and the distance traveled. The first page of a notebook reads as follows: [4]

> 2nd day night at William Shotwells Rahway
> 3rd day night at Sarah Shotwells, ditto
> 4th day night at Edward Vails Plainfield
> 5th day night at Henry Cliftons Kingswood
> 6th day night at Whatson Fells Solebury
> 7th day ditto at Moses Eastburns Buckingham
> 1st day [night] at Israel Lancasters ditto

Toward the end of the pages he began a column for distances:

Distance travelled	miles
From Jericho to New York	27
To Rahway	20
To Plainfield	9
To Kingwood [sic]	30
To Solebury Pen[nsylvania]	16
To Buckingham	4

Quaker ministers were cautious about speaking of expenses involved in their journeys so no one would construe their mission as a paid ministry. If financial means permitted, the minister paid his own expenses; if not, the home Meeting helped cover the cost. Twice Elias Hicks took at least one hundred dollars with which to begin a long journey. As demands on his services grew and long trips multiplied it was necessary to employ extra help on the farm. He hesitated to ask Jericho Monthly Meeting to cover his expenses, and thus sacrificed financially in order to give his services freely.[5]

It was Elias' custom to note his expenses along the way. These were typical: [6]

Ride to N.York Expenses on way [ferry?]	.54
From Rahway to Kingswood	.30

To Solebury Pennsylvania   27 d
To cost on way to Bedford   .31
I paid 90 cents for cloth for a jacket and
   75 cents for making it EH
Paid for shewing [sic] horses   40¢
   and in part pay for oats   25

Now and then he added special information in the midst of a list
of names or a column of figures:

To Myers's Inn
7th day [night] at Noah hanes's Wanes Ville here we continued
untill the following 7th day and lodged every night except one when
we lodged with our friend David Evans and the following 7th day
night we lodged at Samuel Stubbs at Elk [7]

Sometimes he jotted down on the margin of a page a message for
Friends on Long Island. "Job Carr and Wife Desire their love to
their friends." [8] Elias did not always keep a travel notebook, or remember to store them safely in the cherry desk. In the thirty-five
years which elapsed between the time he was recorded as a minister
and the day he began his home journal, he made at least twenty-one
visits of more than a month's duration. The cherry desk yielded
only fifteen notebooks; all he put down concerning a seven-hundred-
mile journey taken in 1807 was that he stayed with Abigail and
Valentine at the outset of his undertaking and was gone from home
for two months, attending "forty-five particular meetings, nine
monthly meetings, one quarterly meeting, and our meeting for sufferings twice." [9] The only comment he made concerning a thousand-
mile mission to Canada in 1810 was that the journey took place in the
summer. At a later date he condensed into a single paragraph his
attendance on both Philadelphia and Baltimore Yearly Meetings.
When Elias discovered that he had either not kept an account, or had
mislaid a record of several journeys taken between 1810 and 1813, he
proceeded to keep a detailed home journal.

A picturesque account of his life as a farmer and minister intro-
duces the home journal. He began with a plea that the affairs of the

world might not press so heavily upon him. "My worldly concerns engrossed much of my time to-day . . . how hard a master the world is; and from whose servitude I often feel strong desires to be fully redeemed; so that all my time may be more fully dedicated to the service of my heavenly master." [10] He could not escape the many tasks to be done. His much-worn carriage needed repairing, the garden required attention, and he wearied himself by building a stone fence. The Jericho minister abhorred idleness and sloth, wrote that he could never find an idle moment, and delighted in a reasonable portion of manual labor. However, at times he admitted "a less proportion . . . would suffice for him," since too great occupation with temporal affairs resulted "in poverty of spirit." [11] The home journal records that he stimulated his spiritual life, in spite of material demands on his time, by spending many evenings in Bible reading.

Now in his sixty-fifth year, and unaware of the exciting times that lay ahead, Elias began to muse on the swiftly passing days. He was troubled with rheumatism, probably brought on by the many long hours spent during all kinds of weather in the saddle. The farm work often was "attended with much care, and too much bodily labour for [his] time of life." [12] Yet he was proud that he could wield the scythe in the harvest fields nearly as well as in his youth.[13] Reflecting on the heavy schedule of Meetings he often set for himself, he recorded, "As old age and decline of life comes on, which is much hastened by our imprudence; accumulated diseases and a long record of increasing akes [sic], and pains rise up as so many witnesses against our past folly and indiscretion . . . as a just penalty of our former improper conduct." [14] In such a mood he wrote to his cousin, Edward Hicks, that he was trying to make a settlement with the world, and devote the little time left to him to the cultivation of the spirit; in the home journal he mentions that the "sands of life" might be running out for him, he hoped that he would remember to die and to enjoy a daily death to everything that would hinder him from walking in the path of duty. "Take care, oh my soul! and do not grow careless and forgetful when drawing near to the eve of life; lest the world and its cares get in and choke the bubblings of the celestial spring, through the abundant cumber that seems necessarily attendant on my present state in striving to help and comfort others." [15]

The home journal indicates how frequently Elias' farm work was interrupted, not only when he was called to take an extensive journey in the ministry, but by religious demands at home. In a two-week period Elias spent two First days at the Jericho Meeting, three days attending Quarterly Meeting at Flushing, and three days in assisting with funerals. This left six uninterrupted days for farm work. Of one funeral he wrote, "Attended the funeral of an acquaintance, a convinced person; it being his request on his death-bed." [16] One of the other two occasions of mourning Elias used as a vehicle for general advice rather than to give consolation to the bereaved. He warned Friends to abstain from following the customs and manners of others. "For in the awful day of final decision," he declared, "all our fig-leaf coverings will be torn off, and things will then appear as they really are; and we shall all stand in need of that substantial covering, represented by the coats of skins, which the Lord made for our first parents." [17]

Vividly as the home journal portrays the life of the Jericho minister, like all diaries of famous men and women much is omitted. Elias' eyes were so steadfastly fixed on his religious duties that all other activities were seen in relation to them. He never mentions the nursery of Friend Price at Flushing, which he frequently passed when the fruit blossoms were most beautiful. George Washington stopped years before to drink in their glory on a spring morning. Elias Hicks passed through Brooklyn more than a hundred times, and watched it grow from a town of 1,000 to a city of 15,000. He mentions a severe fire one First day morning when flighty non-Friends left the Meeting for Worship to watch the catastrophe, but although he stayed a number of times at the Traveller's Inn, he tells nothing about it. This inn was very popular with Quakers, and so large that the stables accommodated 150 horses at a time. Elias' letters to Jemima came regularly, but he thought it too commonplace to note that public postage was eight cents per single sheet for 40 miles, and twelve and one-half cents up to 150 miles. He was amused to learn on a trip to Kingston, New York, that sleighs could not travel faster than at a foot pace on the Sabbath morning; but he did not note in his journal that Friends of Philadelphia laid chains across the streets to prevent carriages driving by while Meetings for Worship were in progress.

During the first year, the home journal records a request laid before Jericho Monthly Meeting by Elias for a certificate of unity and concurrence to permit him to travel south. Five weeks passed before the local and Quarterly Meeting approval was secured, and before the Jericho minister could put his farm work in order so that he could leave with peace of mind. On the last mid-week Meeting Elias was able "to discharge another debt of love and care to [his] friends . . . and, through the prevalence of gospel love, it was made a tendering baptizing season . . . and they parted under a degree of the uniting influence of it." [18] Returning from this long southern mission, Elias fittingly closed 1813 with the words, "Another year is ended, Oh my soul, how hast thou improved it, and what progress hast thou made in thy heavenly journey?" [19]

By the time he was middle-aged, Elias Hicks was recognized as one of the two or three most effective Quaker ministers of the period. Immense audiences flocked to hear him, Quaker and non-Quaker. Those who knew him best wrote of Elias, "In declaring what he believed to be the counsel of God, he was bold and fearless, and his ministry, though unadorned with the embellishments of human learning, was clear and powerful. In argument he was strong and convincing, and his appeals to the experience and convictions of his hearers, were striking and appropriate." [20] A contemporary writer declared that the Jericho minister made a deep impression upon all who heard him; that he was "tall, his proportions muscular and athletic, his face of the Roman cast, intellectual and commanding, his voice deep, his gesture dignified and graceful. . . . [He] poured forth a strain of natural eloquence that is not often surpassed." [21]

Walt Whitman thought of Elias Hicks as that rare type of individual who occasionally appears among mankind stimulating the irrepressible aspirations of men as a little rill of fresh water from a perennial spring irrigates the soil. He wrote that Elias' nature was serious, reflective, deepened by spiritual intimations, and given a peculiar somber cast by the death of his four sons. He looked like a Hebrew prophet and had the spirit of one. The Camden poet, comparing his fellow Quaker to another eloquent minister of the day, said, "Elias was of tall and most shapely form, with black eyes that blazed at times like meteors . . . [he had an] inner, apparently inexhaustible fund of volcanic passion, [a] tenderness blended with a curious remorseless firmness as of some surgeon operating on a belov'd patient." [22] Others mentioned the prophet-like quality which Elias possessed. Hugh Judge spoke of his friend's abiding in the life and power of the eternal Word, of his filling many posts of honor with dignity, and of the affection that hundreds had for him. "His trumpet gave a clear and certain sound," Hugh asserted, "and all the living powers of my inmost soul [have] been bowed in adoration, worship, obedience and praise to that Power that raised him up, and committed unto him a dispensation of the gospel to preach." Yet in spite of the solemnity that gradually gathered about Elias as he passed middle age, Hugh could say of him, "He was pleasant and cheerful, but not light; solid and grave, but not gloomy." [23]

To those who listened to Elias Hicks, whether in a frontier cabin, a Maryland tobacco barn, a Pennsylvania courthouse, a district school, a wayside tavern, a Brooklyn hotel, or a shingled Long Island Meeting House, his words came with tremendous power. The governors of four states heard him speak, judges adjourned their courts that they and those in attendance might catch the message of the minister from Jericho, and twice the State House at Albany echoed his words. A stranger from England described Elias' speaking in appreciative words, "His appearance is simple, old fashioned and patriarchal, and he pours forth in his public discourses, in an astonishing and animated flow of plain, but powerful and penetrating language, a train of arguments that lightens, and sentiment that warms upon whatever it touches." [24] Elwood Walter, an intimate acquaintance, walked forty miles to hear him speak. Peter Cooper, New York philanthropist, declared that for his religious beliefs he was indebted to Elias Hicks as to only one other man. He admired the Quaker minister because "he was a pleader all his life for the rights of the underprivileged, he scorned outside authority and historical revelation, and placed salvation within the soul of man." [25] Elias' influence upon those whom he met was deep and formative; many were so impressed by his sincerity that they followed him implicitly in minor ways of living. On a visit to Samuel Fisher's home in Philadelphia, Elias casually mentioned that he was opposed to the use of gum-shoes, just introduced. For a generation the members of the Fisher family refrained from using rubbers.[26]

Throngs came to hear the Quaker preacher because he spoke with intense conviction. He knew deep openings in the light, he felt the life of God raised in his soul, he experienced the new birth, and he could say with the Founder of the Society, "This I knew experimentally." [27] Up and down the country, in good weather and bad, over newly laid turnpikes and through the roughest bypaths he traveled, repeating the message of God's nearness to men, His gift of the Light which revealed, guided, and gave power to strengthen men for their earthly pilgrimage and enable them to gain admittance to the heavenly kingdom. Such a faith was contagious; men and women were strengthened in their own certainties and their doubts dissolved; to many God never before seemed so real. Walt Whitman believed that there was an unnamed quality in back of Elias Hicks' preaching which emanated from his heart and reached the hearts of those in the audience, carried them with him, shook and aroused them. This sympathetic rapport rested on his powerful magnetic quality. His appeal was to the moral mysticism which is a part of human nature.[28]

Quaker ministers did not approve of the techniques of the revival meetings of their day, and rejected the emotionalism of Barton W. Stone and Thomas Campbell; but religious fervor was in the air and the more powerful Quaker ministers, like Job Scott and Elias Hicks, held their audiences spellbound. Walt Whitman described an occasion when Elias spoke before a fashionable audience in the handsome ballroom of the Morrison Hotel in Brooklyn. A large group had gathered—some out of curiosity—including many of the chief dignitaries of the city, wealthy merchants, judges, and officers of the armed forces. Richly dressed women were present, contrasting strangely with the small group of plainly dressed Friends sitting with Elias on an elevated platform. According to Whitman, after a stillness that was almost painful Elias arose and stood for a moment or two without uttering a word. He was "a tall, straight figure, neither stout nor very thin, dress'd in drab cloth, clean-shaved face, forehead of great expanse, and large and clear black eyes, long or middling-long white hair . . . still wearing the broad brim." Elias looked over the audience with his piercing eyes, then the words came from his mouth, "very emphatically and slowly pronounced, in a resonant, grave, melodious voice, 'What is the chief end of man? *I was told in my early youth,* it was to glorify God, and seek and enjoy him forever.' "[29] As Elias proceeded he spoke with increased fervor, finally he took his broad-brim hat from his head and almost dashed it down with violence on the seat behind him, and continued his discourse with uninterrupted earnestness.

Once in New York City Elias used a dramatic simile to gain the attention of his hearers. He remembered the manner in which men were called to order by the court crier, and arising he cried aloud three times, "O yes, O yes, O yes; silence all persons, under the pain and penalty of the displeasure of the court."[30] This unusual address caught everyone's attention. Then Elias explained that if a confused mass of people could quickly be brought to order in a court room, though they were present from different motives, how much more reasonable it was for men and women gathered together to worship the Judge of heaven and earth, to wait and worship in silence in order to hear the voice of the King of heaven.

Contemporaries wrote that Elias Hicks sometimes used a singsong voice heard at that period in Friends' Meetings, but after using this cadence for a moment or two he usually returned to his natural voice. This Quaker cadence was not dissimilar to the chant of a Greek Orthodox priest, or the rhythm of a revivalist warming to his subject. D. Elton Trueblood links this cadence to the prose poetry of Walt Whitman, and suggests the latter took his style from the preaching of the Quaker minister. "The oratory of Elias Hicks included passages which tended to fall into regular stress. The heavily accented periods were like the cadence of prose poetry which 'approximate, without quite reaching, metrical regularity.'" [31] As an illustration of the rhythm used by Hicks, Trueblood arranges a portion of a sermon the Quaker minister gave in prose-poetic form:

> And the law of God is written in every heart, and
>   it is there that he manifests himself:
> And in infinite love, according to our necessities,
>   states, and conditions.
> And as we are all various and different from one
>   another, more or less,
> So the law by the immediate operation of divine
>   grace in the soul,
> Is suited to every individual according to his
>   condition.[32]

When Elias spoke near Dover, Delaware, the rhythmic cadence was evident towards the close of another sermon:

> I want to increase this liberty among the people—
>   this liberty that God has given us,
>   and for which we are accountable to him.
> Having the privilege of learning and knowing,
>   if we do not act accordingly,

we shall be accountable;
for if God did not show his will clearly to us,
but left us to build on tradition
without clear evidence,
we could hardly be considered accountable creatures
in this state for the things that we do.
Here we should believe wrong things to be right.[33]

Elias Hicks used the peculiar Quaker phraseology which was an outgrowth of the isolation of Friends, their constant study of the Bible, and their emphasis on the writings of primitive Quakers. The meaning of words and phrases, puzzling to strangers, were well known to the Quaker listeners. When Elias was waiting in a religious gathering and no impulses stirred within his mind, it was as though the heavens seemed as brass and the earth as iron; or he felt himself to be in a state of weakness, he suffered with the seed in silence, or he sat in great poverty and want. If he centered down and after stripping himself of all secular thoughts, a religious theme came to his mind, then ability was received and utterance was given; or his mind was baptized into the states of those present, or a ray of light broke through. If he rose to speak, the testimony of truth went freely forth, or he was able to powerfully reach and tender the hearts. He divided the word suitably, or in a close line of searching the ability was afforded to clear himself among them. Then Elias might preach the gospel in clear demonstration of the spirit, he was drawn forth in a large doctrinal testimony, and in an open satisfactory time the rocks seemed to melt. After the Meeting concluded the Quaker minister had peace in his labors, truth reigned triumphant over all, he experienced a season of high favor, and it was all the Lord's doings. If he chanced to be among strangers who did not know the Quaker testimonies and did not warm to his message, he felt that the audience appeared insensible to the operations of truth; there was a spirit prevailing of darkness and ignorance, or his words did not seem to be in the life.

Many Quietist ministers formed the habit of circumlocution in relation to the words God and Christ. John Comly, the teacher of Byberry, used more than sixty such circumlocutions in his Journal, including such terms as: Divine Providence, Fountain of Good, Father of Mercies, Divine Architect, Heavenly Shepherd, Great Husbandman, and Supreme Legislator. Elias Hicks did not follow this practice to the same extent, but he spoke of Zion's King, Lord only Wise, Gracious Helper, King of Heaven, Divine Power, and blessed Author of every Mercy.

The hold which Elias Hicks exerted on his listeners, however, rested upon his natural eloquence, the freshness of his ideas, and his obvious sincerity. Many times he turned an expression which was picturesque and forceful. Sentences like these lingered with his hearers:

> To be a Christian is to be Christ-like.
> Religion and righteousness are the same thing.
> The world wars with the spirit.
> Little harlots call us away from God.
> When the mind becomes sensual, it is like the moon in eclipse.
> Heaven is everywhere God is.
> The business of life is to turn inward.
> Our hearts are filled with many guests—many beloveds.
> You are never tempted by a devil without you, but by a devil within you.
> It is only a light from heaven that can show us the way to heaven.
> Beware the lo heres, and the lo theres.
> I never committed any sin but that I loved it better than my God.
> The candle could not be often put out, unless it was also often lighted, which shows the mercy of God.
> The true Quaker is a trembler before God.

Elias Hicks' sermons usually took about thirty-five to forty minutes to deliver.[34] Sometimes, however, he spoke well over an hour, and he mentions once speaking for two hours when the congregation "was quiet and still, and every countenance seemed expressive of the solemnity felt, which united us together and clothed us with a mantle of love." [35] As time passed many of Elias' sermons were taken down by shorthand, although never with his permission. Since the subject with which he began often grew into an "open field of doctrine," the ramifications of his sermons were many. Speaking at Byberry on one occasion his topic or text was "Let brotherly love continue." An analysis of this sermon shows divisions as follows:

1. Love is above price:
   We see it in family life
   Where each child is trained according to his ability
   The older serve as examples to the younger
   Love binds the entire family together.
2. How can love be secured?
   It cannot be bought
   It comes only through faithfulness to the father's directions
   God teaches his children directly, acting within the soul.
3. We have fallen away from pure love:
   Because our sins—our beloveds—keep God's love out of our hearts
   Sin has taken the place of God in our hearts
   We must turn to God to allow him to dispossess the sin in our hearts.
4. Man in his fallen state is full of sin:
   In the silence we can empty our hearts of sin and in the vacuum created love will come
   We can enjoy a new birth
   This new birth is the birth of Christ in the soul.
5. To the want of love in the heart is due all the persecutions of the ages.
6. Only the finger of God can write in our souls:
   No outward thing can manifest him.
7. There are two natures in man:
   The body and soul have different propensities
   Our duty is to subordinate the propensities of the body
   We are free agents and can do so
   The trees of the Garden of Eden are a parable of the differences within man's personality
   Our bodily propensities must be kept pruned
   By following the example of Jesus
   By doing God's will, not our own
   Thus the business of life is to turn inward
   If we live in the light we shall do right.
8. Around us is a great evil, the sin of slavery:

The land is guilty of oppression
To use the products of slave labor is to be as guilty as to own slaves
Slavery is a sin
The speaker will still love those who do not agree with him in this.
9. [An addition made after a few minutes of silence] There are no
   fallen angels, only fallen men and women:
   Thus we must continue the fight for righteousness
   Be encouraged to be faithful.[36]

William Penn wrote of George Fox, "Above all he excelled in prayer . . . it was a testimony that he knew and lived nearer to the Lord than other men." [37] None of Elias Hicks' prayers were taken down until the last few years of his life. These are short, simple, and marked by deep inner feeling. He followed a sermon at Darby, Pennsylvania, with this prayer:

Most gracious and ever blessed God! Be pleased, O Lord to receive the feeble acknowledgements of thy poor dependent servant, as a return of gratitude to thee for thy abundant mercy. . . . Enable us, merciful God, to surrender all our hearts to thee . . . and renew in us a concern to worship thee in spirit and in truth; that so . . . thy will and not ours may be done in all things. . . . Grant that our knowledge of thee may be increased through the light and grace dispensed; that so it may not be ineffectual, O Father, of leading us off from all our false dependencies and trust in any thing but thee; and grant that the glorious light of thy countenance and thy holy spirit be our leader; and that we may not dare to look away from it for any support, but that we may press unto it more and more—seeking more and more to be united with the full and powerful operations and abidings of thy grace. Enable us to bow before thee, and go on rightly in the great work that thou hast called us to do; and that all may tend to thy glory, and to the peace and consolation of our souls. Unite us together, O Father, as the heart of one man, that we may join in praise and acknowledgement of thy goodness, and give glory and honour to thy great and excellent name, who remainest to be God over all, blessed for ever and ever.[38]

Through the written and spoken word Elias Hicks wielded tremendous influence among Friends, and he stirred new religious desires among many non-Friends who heard him. A later admirer wrote, "He assaulted superstition and bigotry with great force and boldness, often arousing fear and prejudice. He sought the truth and only the truth and cared neither for the cost nor censure or applause. His only reward was the approval of his own conscience, the . . . Inner Light, was his only guide." [39] A non-Friend, who was his contemporary, summed up his ministry,

through a long, laborious, and active life, few men have borne a more conspicuous part, or wielded a more powerful and enduring influence among those who were accustomed to attend upon his public discourses. He was a person of rough exterior, but of vigorous intellect; and making no pretence to elegence of style, he reasoned with much force, and addressed himself to the every-day common-sense, rather than the imagination of his auditors. That he was no ordinary individual, must be accepted by all who are capable of appreciation the extent of his exertions.[40]

XV

"The Tumultuous State

of Public Affairs"

THE NOISY CAMPAIGN of the "War Hawks" called forth a plea for peace in the New York Epistle of 1812. This message urged that all discordant passions be overcome by divine love. Seeds of contention were to be eradicated and the peace testimony maintained as war was the scourge of mankind. During the ensuing years of conflict, Elias Hicks mentioned "the alarm of war heard in the land," and "the frequent reports of blood and slaughter." [1] He cautioned Friends to stay aloof from the carnage, declaring it was inhuman and irrational for men to "deliberately imbue their hands in each other's blood for this world's honours and profits; and dare at the same time to call themselves Christians, although so utterly estranged from the real Christian spirit and life." [2]

Elias sought redress for those Quakers suffering from a heavy tax placed upon them by the state legislature in lieu of personal military service. Though few Friends entered upon war service, there was great divergence in their attitude toward the state levy. Some members suffered distraint of goods three or four times the amount of the tax, while others "actively complied, and paid the tax, justified themselves in so doing, causing considerable altercation in the Meeting." [3] Elias maintained that citizens must support the laws of the community if they would be worthy of living in a free country, but he declared they should not follow civil policy when it interfered with conscience. "Without fear, favour, or affection," Friends should stand "against every encroachment of the secular power . . . lest they become accessaries in the war . . . and bear a part of the guilt of shedding the blood of their fellow creatures." [4]

Elias Hicks traveled approximately 2,200 miles during the three war years. In 1813, with Isaac Hicks of Westbury, he undertook a 1,500-mile mission as far south as Virginia. In New York City they found prices steeply inflated because of the conflict. Flour and bread were very dear, hams were selling from fifteen to eighteen pence, fresh beef at fourteen pence per pound, all of which was exceedingly hard on the poor. At Elizabethtown, New Jersey, the governor and his wife attended Elias' appointed gathering and "the power of God's divine love was felt to spread over the meeting as a precious canopy." [5] At Burlington, Elias declared "that as none had ever been perfect in [the gospel dispensation] but the man Jesus Christ, we had not a right, as his professed followers, to take the example of any but his own, for our real perfect rule of life." [6] Three thousand individuals crowded into the Mulberry Street Meeting House in Philadelphia when he preached on his favorite text, "Christ, the hope of glory and light of the world." [7]

Samuel Fisher's son Miers, who was a wealthy Philadelphia lawyer, wrote in his Journal at this time that Elias Hicks was considered the ablest preacher who had visited that area in many years. He thought Elias' discourse was regular, consistent, and coherent, delivered in a voice that filled the largest building. At first the conservative lawyer thought Hicks was a bit radical on the economic side "verging to that spirit of equality which destroyed the French national system . . . but as he went on, his meaning became more obvious, that he was describing what the world would have been but for the fall

of man and would be again if the gospel were generally obeyed." [8]
Miers Fisher rode with Elias and Isaac to one of their appointed Meetings and dryly noted that "Elias was not remarkable for reserve in conversation upon common topics." [9] They discussed the works of Swedenborg, and Miers discovered that Elias owned at least one volume of his writings. Fisher felt that Elias' preaching contained much of the style and matter of the Scandinavian theologian.

Elias Hicks carried through a strenuous schedule while in Philadelphia. He held eleven religious gatherings in eight days, sometimes spoke for two hours at a time, and finished speaking wet from head to foot with perspiration. Heart-searching opportunities awaited the Long Island Friends among the Nottingham Quakers; a "concerned remnant" was discovered in Baltimore; but in Washington and Alexandria, "the people appeared very destitute of real religious engagements, their minds being so swollowed up in their political controversies, and other worldly concerns, that there seemed to be very little room in their thoughts for anything else." [10]

Elias was easy in mind about Jemima while on this journey. Valentine and Abigail had moved into a spacious house across the road from the Seaman homestead the previous year. To his son-in-law Elias sent many requests for chores to be done about the farm. From Baltimore, Elias wrote Jemima of a severe trial which came to Hugh Judge and his wife. Their daughter Rachel, who was a very promising teacher and minister, moved to Alexandria and there was "drawn off, and inticed to marry out of the Society with a rigid Methodist." From George Town he added that the roads were very indifferent, among the worst he knew outside of western Pennsylvania. "I told my companion," he said, "that if they mended their spiritual highways as they did their temporal ones they made rough work of it indeed. . . ." [11]

After returning to Jericho, Elias received a letter from Samuel R. Fisher in which the Philadelphian spoke of the illumination in that city over an American victory, "while on our particular part all things remain quiet." He recalled that during the Revolutionary War the homes of Friends were stoned because they refused to join in civic celebrations marking the defeat of the British. Samuel trusted that a "return of public tranquility" was near.[12]

As many of the 1,400 merchant and fishing ships lost by the United States during the War of 1812 sailed from New York City; Elias, "with many other Friends," collected relief for the poor of the port who were in "a suffering state, for want of the necessities of life," due to "the present tumultuous state of public affairs." [13] His final comment on the war period showed breadth and growth in his own judgment. "We should no longer love as man loves in his fallen state, from a selfish motive," Elias declared, "but we should love as God loves, with a disinterested love, and then we should love, not our friends and neighbors only, but our greatest enemies also; and we should become qualified sincerely to pray to God for them. We should then be brought to discover, that all such among Christians as pray for the downfall or overcoming of their enemies by force of war, or by any other means than pure disinterested love, pray not in a Christian spirit, nor by the leading and influence of the spirit of God." [14]

Sarah, the youngest daughter of Elias and Jemima, married Robert Seaman, a Jericho kinsman, in November, 1814. Her father spoke at her wedding, and afterward noted in the home journal his satisfaction that "four daughters, out of five, [were] agreeably married, in the comely order of Friends: the other [Elizabeth] yet single, a tender precious young woman, observing with pious submission her parents' counsel." [15] Sarah and Robert established themselves in a house south of the Turnpike, leaving Elias, Jemima, and Elizabeth in the old Seaman home. But the parents had no opportunity to become lonesome. Across the road were Abigail and Valentine with their three daughters, at the crossroads were Martha and Royal Aldrich, and now another daughter was settled nearby. At Islip, not far distant, fourteen-year-old Elias lived with his father Joshua Willets; on a recent visit the boy's grandfather noted with anxiety that his namesake was very frail and seemed to be developing the disease which proved fatal to his four uncles.

There were many visitors to the Jericho Meeting. That spring a Friend from England gave "a long, tedious, and lifeless communication"; and another Evangelical followed soon afterward with an address attended by so much "creaturely warmth and animation, as to render it unacceptable." [16] To nearby Flushing came Elias' cousin, the painter from Newton, Pennsylvania, Edward Hicks; and to Jericho came John Comly of Byberry with whom Elias "felt near sympathy and unity." [17] Comly wrote of his visit to Jericho, "Called to see that dear and worthy friend, Elias Hicks, at his own house, where simplicity and neatness prevail. . . . Dear Elias . . . rode with us after meeting, and was as kind and tender as a father in experience, and his meek and upright deportment was that of a humble follower of Christ. Lodged at his hospitable mansion." [18] John Comly indicated that Elias had many religious opportunities on Long Island and that his sound, energetic discourses resulted in a great openness towards Friends.

In the spring of 1815, Elias felt a call to visit all the families belonging to New York Monthly Meeting. Accompanied by Samuel Parsons and other Friends from the city, Elias "sat" with 244 families. As was customary in such visitations, Elias spoke or prayed with members of the group after a period of silence. In many families he seemed to speak directly to the "state" or condition of some individual present who was deeply perplexed in mind, wavering between a right and wrong decision, or filled with religious doubts. "Often," Elias wrote, "I felt the renewed visitation of the heavenly Father's love, in which the visited and visiter were united in the bond of Christian fellowship; which tended to inspire with strength to persevere and trust in the Lord. . . ." He met with "a variety of states and conditions," occasionally worshiping with families where "things were much out of order, and darkness spread over us as a curtain," but he usually could find words that gave "improvement and help." [19] The itinerant minister became very sensitive to the needs of young and old; on occasions a psychic quality developed from his openness to spiritual impressions, and Elias gave direct spiritual counsel applicable to only one member in the family. Young people were stirred to dedicate their lives more fully to the testimonies of Friends or to the work of the ministry. His great influence upon these families is shown by subsequent events.

Freed from heavy household responsibilities, Jemima went with Elias on nearby trips, sometimes traveled on her own concerns. She rode to Quarterly and Yearly Meeting, to Islip to see their grandson, to Nine Partners with Elias and Elizabeth on a visit to the boarding school. They hurried back to Jericho in time for Jemima to be present for the birth of Sarah's first daughter, Phebe.

Elias Hicks enjoyed reading history. In addition to a number of Quaker Journals, he knew the chief historians of Quakerism, Joseph Besse, John Gough, and Thomas Clarkson. From Isaac Hicks' library he took Charles Rollins, *Ancient History,* George Smollett's *History of England,* David Hume's *History of England,* and Joseph Priestley's *History of the Corruption of Christianity.* That spring, feeling indisposed, Elias Hicks borrowed from his cousin *An Eccleciastical History, Ancient and Modern,* by John L. Mosheim, Chancellor of the University of Gottingen. Although Elias refers only to that section of the *History* dealing with the fifth century, he no doubt read all the story of Christianity from the first through the eighteenth century. Mosheim held a middle position between the German Pietists and German Rationalists; he was orthodox in doctrine but moderate in feeling. A learned man, he was the most popular preacher of his age, and succeeded in transferring some of his success as a preacher to his work as an historian.[20] In his *Ecclesiastical History* the chancellor outlined the many different interpretations of Christian thought and doctrine held through the centuries by church leaders. He stressed the persecutions conducted by orthodox Christian bodies and gave rationalistic explanations of the miracles. He pointed out in century after century the corruption, licentiousness, and greed of the clergy. In summary he wrote, "The professors of Christianity, and more especially the doctors and rulers of the church, have done unspeakable detriment to the cause of religion, by their ignorance and sloth, their luxury and ambition, their uncharitable zeal, animosities and contention." [21]

Reading Mosheim gave Elias Hicks a broader understanding of Christianity, and strengthened his resolve that members of the Society of Friends should be tolerant of divergent points of view. The German writer provided the Jericho minister with new perspective in contesting the forces of authoritarianism which came with the Evangelical movement. "English evangelicalism . . . bore from the start the aspect of a conservative reaction, endeavoring to overthrow rationalism, the typical modern movement of the day. . . . In the matter of religious truth and our apprehension of it, Wesley," according to Arthur C. McGiffert, "simply went back to the old position of the absolute authority of the Bible. Instead of leaving every Christian man to discover such truth as the Spirit might reveal to him personally he insisted that the authority of the Bible must be recognized and its teachings accepted without question." [22] This position was anathema to Elias Hicks. He taught that the Spirit would lead men into all truth, and that revelation was a continuous process. He stood against all external authorities which would curb new revelations of truth, whether in the form of creed, sacred Scripture, or hierarchy. He was a true liberal.

In January, 1815, Isaac Hicks again set out on a visit with his cousin Elias to New England. Travel was easier than twenty years earlier when Elias visited all the Meetings in this area. A steam ferry now crossed from Brooklyn to New York, and 1,500 miles of turnpike stretched through the state. On this journey, as in other years, the Jericho preacher answered the spiritual needs of his hearers. "Truth reigned" many times; gatherings closed with humble prayer and supplication. On one occasion "all were so swallowed up in a profound solemnity, that when the Meeting closed, it was sometime before any removed from their seats." [23]

On the way to Portland, Maine, Elias wrote Jemima, "It has not thawed any on the sun side of houses in a number of days, but we are so well clad we suffer but little." [24] Elias, who had visited so many inland spots in America and Canada, and Isaac, whose ships had gone as far as China and Russia, had much to talk about between religious gatherings. Elias, like John Comly, approved of Isaac's having retired from the cares of the commercial world and having settled at Westbury. Comly contrasted Isaac with wealthy Philadelphia Friends who after settling in country places made a show of grandeur in polished living.[25]

Elias wrote to Jemima of events along the way, of old friends visited. Their sled was twice buried in deep snows on the way to Boston, once breaking the "swiffle-tree." He confessed to leaving a letter Jemima meant him to mail lying on his desk. Sarah's baby had whooping cough when her grandfather left Jericho, and several times he sent back advice from aged Friends for Sarah's use, none of which proved of any avail. Elias asked Jemima to have one of the men put up a fence around the young pear and apple trees which he planted the previous spring, lest the sheep nibble the bark and kill them. His thoughts were probably upon those who might come after him, since, at sixty-eight, he could hardly expect in the normal course of events to enjoy the fruits of these trees himself. A new travel diary was added to others in the cherry desk. After some days' work spent on the farm the minister wrote, "Passed the present week mostly caring for my temporal concerns; yet not so much, I trust, from the love I have for the world or the things of it, but more especially from a sense of duty, that I may honestly provide for the outward welfare of myself and family, and have, through . . . frugal industry, a sufficiency when called from home . . . to keep the gospel free from charge, and that I abuse not my power in the gospel." [26]

A few days later he added, "As in my past winter journey, I witnessed summer and harvest, so now I may rest patiently in the divine promise, with the assurance, that as winter in due course has succeeded summer, so likewise summer by and by, in its turn, will succeed winter, and the time of the singing birds will come, and the drooping spirit will again rejoice in the Lord, and joy in the God of its salvation." [27]

XVI

Dissent

Moves Closer

TIME DEALT KINDLY with Elias Hicks. At sixty-nine an occasional spell of indisposition kept him from Meeting and made him think that his glass was almost run out, but he continued to pursue many interests. The Quarterly Meeting again appointed him to stimulate concern for the educational needs of Quaker youth. He worked with the Meeting for Sufferings preparing a memorial to the legislature concerning the state of Negroes. He advocated laws extending equality of citizenship to them, declaring, "they should have the full rights of civilized men. This is their just and righteous due, and these privileges, if duly and rightly administered to them, would bring them to be as good and useful citizens as those of any other nation." [1] He continued to have head-on collisions with clergymen over church ordinances and creeds, and denounced preaching for hire, hoping "to overthrow all their craft, by which they have their wealth." [2]

Elias was irked by the necessity of spending so much of his time working on the farm and overseeing his hired men. But he went into the fields at five o'clock in the morning; and "Peter Porcupine" wrote of Elias' ability to "cradle down four acres of rye in a day." [3] For many years Elias was a partner of Royal Aldrich in the tannery, but now he tried to lighten his responsibilities. He sent word to Royal to "draw in" respecting their mutual work "and not to purchase or lay in any more or greater stock of hides than would be suitable to his own occasion in carrying on the business in the future only by himself." "I am very anxious," continued the older man, "to bring my Temporal business to a close and be fully released from all worldly care." [4] Yet the Quaker minister found the days crowded. "So many and various are the avocations that almost continually engage my attention," he wrote to William Poole, "that I do not find time and opportunity to visit my friends . . . as often as I feel warm desires to do." [5]

Late in August, 1817, Elias Hicks began a new travel diary. Accompanied by his son-in-law, Valentine, Elias journeyed over well-known roads on a southern tour of duty. They attended the sessions of Baltimore Yearly Meeting; the Clerk endorsed Hicks' certificate with words of appreciation, and Elias noted in his diary that, "we parted from each other with thankful hearts." [6] To Jemima he sent word, "Yearly Meeting closed about an hour since. . . . [I] entreated . . . Friends for the removal of those many and great deviations that were apparent among them in the splendor of their houses, household furniture, their dress and adress, and manner of living." He added a postscript to his third namesake, the son of Abigail and Valentine, "tell little Elias that Grand Father wants to see him." [7]

On the return journey to Long Island, young people flocked to hear Elias. He was able to reach across the gap that separates youth and age, and touch the hearts of a new generation. "I felt a great power of love flow freely towards them, which caused my heart to rejoice, and I was made glad in believing it was the Lord's doing." [8] Elias' fame was so widespread that those in charge of an appointed gathering at Mulberry Street Meeting House in Philadelphia asked members not to take seats until non-Friends found places. A tremendous crowd collected, many standing in the yard outside the

Meeting House, others leaving because there was no room. When Elias reached the building he had a hard time forcing his way to the facing benches. The Meeting lasted for several hours and not even the rattling of fire engines and the accompanying cries interrupted its solemnity. Elias was deeply moved, his whole being "filled with a flow of heavenly love." At the close of the worship, he wrote, "All being eager to take me by the hand, as they could get near me, such a time I never witnessed before, for when I reached out my hand to them, I often had two of their hands in mine at once." [9]

Gatherings continued to be large as the two Friends made their way through the New Jersey centers of population. At Salem, the judge adjourned the local court and came with the lawyers and others in attendance to hear Elias Hicks. After an absence of four months, in which nearly one hundred religious services were held, the Long Island Friends were back in Jericho.

Sabbath observation was uppermost in Elias' mind at this time. He came to the conclusion that all "blue" laws were an unwarranted interference by the state in religious matters. To him the First day of the week was no holier than any other day. Though it was his custom to come in from the fields on both First and Fourth days, change his clothes, put on his gloves, and attend Meetings for worship, he was not averse to working on the farm before and after Meeting if the crops required attention. William Poole warned him that he was in advance of his time and his attitude would be misunderstood by many. On somewhat similar grounds, Elias objected to a Thanksgiving Proclamation issued by the governor. He declared this was simply playing into the hands of ecclesiastical powers, the clergy using the magistrates to enforce their superstitious customs, and placing upon the citizens the yoke of hierarchical domination. Elias said, "[The Governor] has by recommending a religious act united the civil and ecclesiastical authorities, and broken the line of partition between them, so wisely established by our enlightened

Constitution, which in the most positive terms forbids any alliance between church and state, and is the only barrier for the support of our liberty and independence. For if that is broken down all is lost and we become the vassals of priestcraft, and designing men, who are reaching after power by subtle contrivance to domineer over the consciences of their fellow citizens." [10] The Jericho Friend was as forthright as Roger Williams in his insistence that there be no encroachment by the State upon the field of religion.

Elias Hicks exchanged letters with Phebe Willis, an Evangelical elder of Jericho Meeting, who wrote out of concern over his use of the Bible. Counting on her friendship, Elias answered her questions hastily, without redrafting his letter, believing she would be able "to apprehend the main drift of [his] arguments, and be willing to put the best construction on such parts as [might] seem erroneous." [11] This letter, written on scraps of paper in time stolen from his many avocations, was to cause Elias much trouble. It was published without his consent, its meaning misconstrued and misinterpreted. The letter indicated, however, the extent to which rationalism had affected Hicks' point of view, and the gulf that existed between the Evangelical approach to the Bible and his own. By contrast, he stated, "There is scarcely anything so baneful to the present and future happiness and welfare of mankind, as a submission to tradition and popular opinion, I have therefore been led to see the necessity of investigating for myself all customs and doctrines . . . either verbally or historically communicated . . . and not to sit down satisfied with any thing but the plain, clear, demonstrative testimony of the spirit and word of life and light in my heart and conscience." [12] He recited the long chain of quarrels and divisions in Christianity which grew out of different interpretations of the Scriptures, the resulting heresies, persecutions, and bloodshed. "In this condition things continued," he believed, "until George Fox was raised up to bear testimany to the light and spirit of truth in the hearts and consciences of men and women, as the only sure rule of faith and practice." And though George Fox and his friends were considered heretics, "their doctrines were in nowise derogatory to those written by men who were inspired by the same spirit in former days."

Elias explained to the Jericho elder that God was a God of justice and love, unchangeable in nature. He therefore gave to every man by means of the Inner Light a complete and sufficient rule of faith and practice; otherwise He could be charged with partiality, since the greater part of mankind never had a knowledge of the Christian Scriptures. God gave men in different ages some outward manifestations of His will. To Abraham and his family, God gave a peculiar system of ritual and outward shadows to which He required obedience. To later men, He gave Jesus Christ and his apostles to turn them from outward darkness to inward light; and in many ages He raised up reformers to call men back to the true inward guide. "And where any people have depended upon what has been written in former generations, such make no advancement, but just sit down in the labours of their forefathers, and soon become dry and formal, and fall behind those they are copying after or propose to follow." [13]

Elias wrote further to Phebe Willis that there were some in the Society who would call members away from the inward guide to the letter. This could only result in dividing and scattering Friends. "For considerable disputes have already arisen concerning passages of the first importance." He added, "My views respecting the Scriptures are not altered, although thus abused by others, and . . . I shall . . . call upon them as evidence of the truth of inspiration; and to show that the upright and faithful in former ages, were led and instructed by the same spirit as those in the present day." [14]

Elias Hicks merely restated the message of George Fox, who said:

Now the Lord God hath opened to me by his invisible power how that every man was enlightened by the divine light of Christ. . . . This I saw in the pure openings of the Light without the help of any man, neither did I then know where to find it in Scriptures; though afterwards, searching the Scriptures, I found it. For I saw in that Light and Spirit which was before Scripture was given forth . . . that all must come to that Spirit, if they would know God, or Christ, or the Scripture aright, which they that gave them forth were led and taught by.[15]

Elias Hicks and George Fox were one in counting the inward revelations of God's spirit as the primary authority, and the Scriptures as secondary.

Touches of sadness, bits of humor, and interesting sidelights on passing events occupy Elias Hicks' home journal during the next two years. He took more time to visit John Hicks at Brookline, Samuel Hicks at Mamaroneck, and Stephen at Rockaway. Stephen, the youngest brother, died in 1817; Samuel, Elias' oldest brother, the following year. After Samuel's death, Elias wrote, "I am now the last and only survivor of six brethren, and am myself . . . nearly three score and ten; therefore cannot expect many more days, as I continually feel time making ravages . . . which, as a faithful herald, exclaims repeatedly to the inward ear, 'prepare to die.' " [16] The following year, Elias Willets, the oldest grandson, fell a victim at the age of nineteen to the disease that destroyed his uncles.

Jemima had been married for forty-seven years when her husband wrote from Moses Brown's home in Providence:

Inasmuch as I have often felt concerned when thus absent, least thou should worry thyself, with too much care and labor in regard to our temporal concerns, and have often desired thee to be careful in that respect, but mostly without effect, by reason that thou art choice of thy own free agency as to be afraid to take the advice of thy best friend, lest it might mar that great privilege; I therefore now propose to leave thee at full liberty to use it in thine own pleasure with the addition of this desire, that thou use it in that way as will produce to thee the most true comfort and joy, and then I trust I shall be comforted, my dear, in thy comfort, and joyful in thy joy.[17]

Concerning himself, Elias added, "I am getting along in a complaining way in the body, but strong in mind and as able to go forth in spiritual welfare as in the day I first passed over Jordan." [18] Now that he was over seventy, Elias was exhausted with meeting people.

Their very kindness and warm hospitality wore him out. "Almost as soon as we retire from meetings to friends houses, many friends gather to see us wanting to be informed about many things, insomuch that the intermediate time between meetings is almost as exercising to body and mind in many instances as is my arduous service in meetings, that I have no time to be idle. And even while I am writing these lines, pain and wearisomeness is my constant companion, having yesterday and this morning rode near forty miles and had an arduous days labour in meeting today." [19]

It was still necessary for the itinerant minister to struggle against the weather. On a trip to Islip the winds swept in from the Atlantic Ocean with such force that Elias' high-wheeled carriage was nearly blown over, and he was forced to cling to the windward side to keep it upright. In the winter of 1819, with Valentine as a companion, Elias visited in New York state. The two men stopped at the boarding school to visit two granddaughters, Phebe and Mary, children of Valentine. At Hudson, Hannah Barnard was much pleased with Elias' message. She reported that his doctrines were similar to those which caused London Yearly Meeting to send her home twenty years previously. Elias wrote Isaac Hicks that he hoped Hannah Barnard, who had since joined the Unitarian Church, might be restored to the Society. More than once Valentine and his father-in-law were snowed in. Near Easton, leaving the home of Samuel Cary, the two men set out for a called appointment at a village four miles distant. It snowed heavily and only a few individuals came to the building where the worship was held. By the time the service concluded the snow was so deep the speaker and his companion could not return to the Cary's. A hospitable frontiersman, with a large family already under his roof, opened his house to Elias, Valentine, and five other strangers—one a New York Senator. The next day, at a pace not exceeding a mile an hour, the Friends returned to the home of their host. A few days later the men from Long Island were twice tipped out of their conveyance into a mixture of ice, snow, and water. Valentine, who was on the bottom, found himself somewhat stiff and sore, but, as Elias wrote to Abigail, "he is cheerful . . . still fat and hearty." [20]

In January, 1819, six years after beginning the home journal, Elias Hicks discontinued that record. He had written a detailed account of his activities as a farmer and Quaker minister from his sixty-fifth through his seventieth year. On the final page he answered a question which Friends and non-Friends often asked him. What is required of a Christian? He answered, "I was led to open to Friends the three principal requisites to the being, and well-being, of a Christian. The first being a real belief in *God and Christ, as one undivided essence,* known and believed in, *inwardly* and *spiritually.*" The second, "A complete passive obedience and submission to the divine will and power inwardly and spiritually manifested; which when known, brings to the Christian state, through a crucifixion of the old man, with all his ungodly deeds." And the third requisite, "in order for the preservation and well-being of a Christian, it is necessary that they often meet and assemble together, for the promotion of love and good works, and as good stewards of the manifold grace of God . . . and no temporal concern of the greatest magnitude ought to be considered as a sufficient excuse for omitting this great and necessary duty." [21]

In the summer of 1819, Elias made his first trip to Ohio. He left with Willet Robbins, going west by way of the Delaware Water Gap, Reading, Bedford, and the Redstone country. Late in August the two eastern Friends reached Mount Pleasant, the center of the Yearly Meeting which had been set off from Baltimore seven years earlier for Friends in the state of Ohio, Indiana Territory, and the adjacent parts of Pennsylvania and Virginia. The Meeting House at Mount Pleasant was one of the largest Quaker structures in America, holding three thousand people. The wooden panels dividing the men from the women were so heavy that four men were required to turn the wooden axle which raised the partition into the attic. By good fortune the acoustics were excellent and a whisper from the front benches could be heard in the corners of the structure. Iron stoves, recently introduced, heated the building more adequately than the old time fireplaces.

Elias took a major part in the sessions of the Ministers and Elders, and the Business Meetings, which lasted eleven days. Samuel Bettle, clerk of Philadelphia Yearly Meeting, expressed great satisfaction in becoming better acquainted with the Jericho minister. He told a friend that "he never met a man in his life that he had a higher esteem for . . . than he had for Elias Hicks." [22] They lodged together and Samuel Bettle had full unity with Elias' testimony. Friends considered a revision of the Discipline and gave thought to dividing the Yearly Meeting. It was estimated that 20,000 Quakers now lived west of the Allegheny Mountains, and the Friends in eastern Indiana wanted to establish their own superior organization. Elisha Bates, a prominent local minister, was not in sympathy with much that Elias preached, including his appeal to abstain from the use of slave products.

At the close of the Yearly Meeting, Elias carried out an extensive visitation of Friends' groups up the Ohio River. Then leaving Midwest Quakers, Hicks and Robbins stopped at Pittsburgh for a Meeting in the spacious courthouse. Near Uniontown they crossed the National Road, the first to be constructed by the federal government. Passing into Virginia, Elias visited old acquaintances in Winchester, Hopewell, and Goose Creek, then went into Maryland by way of Frederick, reaching Baltimore in mid October. Of Frederick Town he wrote Jemima, "this is as dark a spot as I ever was in . . . my doctrine was suited to their states but set them together by their ears, and the controversy rose so high amongst them . . . that the party in favour of [my message] sent a person eight miles after [me], desiring us to return and have another opportunity with them, but we did not." [23]

In Baltimore, the Long Island visitors were entertained by Gerard P. Hopkins, a wealthy merchant, and Elias Hicks spent some time visiting heads of families. Baltimore Quakers were suffering from an internal quarrel over property, but Elias refused to be drawn into the matter. He wrote Valentine that Christianity did not stop at the point of mere justice, but in addition called for forgiveness, forbearance, and love. He added that he was forced to write in haste as there was "little time for writing by reason of the continual coming in of friends to see us, that when at our lodgings the room is mostly crowded." [24]

At Brandywine, Elias stayed with William Poole and then spent a week attending all the Meetings in Philadelphia. In these gatherings, Elias spoke with great force, energy, and freedom against the grave departures from the plainness and simplicity required by the Discipline, the evidences of superabundant wealth, and the luxury of some living in idleness. These he considered marks of declension from the teachings of John Woolman and Nicholas Waln. His remarks were distasteful to many Philadelphia Quakers who considered the Jericho farmer either old-fashioned or a bit radical. Elias also pressed his concern for the condition of the African race, urging Friends in his usual impressive manner to abstain from the use of slave products. All admitted that he gave a very "close testimony," some feeling that he was unnecessarily harsh in his attitude toward those who purchased cotton, sugar, and rice. A few conspicuous and influential members of the Society soon indicated their displeasure with his remarks.

The first occasion when public disapproval was expressed came at Pine Street Monthly Meeting. Here the Jericho minister declared that the leaders of Philadelphia Friends "were going round and round, like the children of Israel, not advancing forward." [25] He called upon the youth of the Society to break with the traditions of their fathers and push forward the work of reformation. After relieving his mind in the Men's Business Meeting, Elias asked for permission to address the Women's. Jonathan Evans, a prominent elder, opposed the request; but as the weight of the Meeting approved, Isaac Lloyd, an elder, was appointed to go with Elias to the Women's side of the building. As soon as they left, Jonathan Evans declared that the session had been a very painful one to him, and suggested adjournment "although the business of the meeting was not gone through with; neither was it late in the day, nor more than usual dinner time." [26] Several Friends indicated their disapproval of adjourning the business session while the visitor was attending the Women's section. It was felt that such conduct was "an unprecedented circumstance," "unusual," and might give offense. Jonathan Evans pressed his point, his two sons and some others agreed with him, and without unity the Meeting adjourned.

After a considerable time, Elias Hicks returned from addressing the women of Pine Street Meeting, and was much surprised to find that the men had gone. Isaac Lloyd was also hurt at the conduct of the Meeting. A few Friends remained behind to speak to Elias, but his only comment on picking up his greatcoat was, "It was kind of them to leave my coat behind when they went." [27] Later, at the home of Samuel R. Fisher, Elias asked if "this was the way they served strangers when they came to visit them?" [28] Jonathan Evans called upon Elias Hicks, protesting his inciting the youth to disregard the admonitions of the elders. When Elias replied it was the elders who first opposed the views of John Woolman on slavery, Jonathan Evans answered that "John Woolman bore his testimony in simplicity, but never called his friends thieves and murderers," as Elias designated those who used the products of slave labor. To this accusation, and a further one that he misquoted the Bible, Elias replied that he would make no answer until Jonathan Evans expressed regret for not showing proper respect with Elias' concern to attend the Women's Meeting. Jonathan Evans would make no acknowledgement, "not being sensible of any error," and the two men parted.[29] Elias had made a bitter, implacable, and powerful enemy.

Elias Hicks and Willet Robbins went on to complete their 1,200-mile journey from Jericho, but news of the occurrence at Pine Street spread rapidly. As stated in a later document, "Elias Hicks had been an approved minister of the Society for nearly fifty years. He had been, at different times, extensively engaged in religious service, within the compass of nearly all the Yearly Meetings on this Continent, and was esteemed by his brethren in all parts . . . as a sound faithful minister of the gospel. At the very time when this open mark of disrespect was manifested he was traveling with Certificates of the unity and concurrence of his Monthly and Quarterly Meetings." [30] It was evident that "This circumstance created a great excitement among Friends generally, who came to the knowledge of it, as it was considered . . . a mark of great disrespect and public hostility to that eminent and dignified minister of the Gospel . . . who . . . had been universally approved and admired, wherever he had travelled in this part of the country; as was fully evinced by the unusually large congregations that assembled at his meetings." [31] These were the first rumblings of the impending storm.

XVII

Christ in You,

the Hope of Glory

ELIAS' VEXATION over the adjournment of the Men's Meeting at Pine Street was removed by an encouraging letter from Samuel R. Fisher. The Philadelphia Quaker sent word, "I rest satisfied in all thy labours amongst us. . . . There is general satisfaction over thy last visit and it is spreading wider in this city." [1] Jericho Meeting also minuted the return of Elias' certificate with a warm endorsement from Ohio Yearly Meeting and from local groups of Friends along his route.

On Long Island some Friends wanted to send their children to the rapidly expanding district schools; others were willing to accept the bounty allowed for the support of local schools. Elias opposed both procedures, and sent his children to be taught at the Friends' School. From observation he concluded that many public school teachers had no religious principles, were unconcerned, and vulgar in their lives and conduct. All the learning and science the young people would acquire from them would not make up for the danger done "to their tender minds." [2] Elias considered the law requiring universal taxation for maintenance of public schools arbitrary and inconsistent with the liberty of conscience guaranteed by the Constitution. He thought it was the duty of every parent to bring up his child in the way he thought right, independent of control by any outside organization, so long as the children kept within the bounds of civil order. The minister declared that many took pride in their superior acquirements of worldly knowledge, "studying to be accounted learned in the sciences of this world," which he considered were "as trivial as the ribbons on the dear young women's head." [3]

Elias was continually disturbed by many Quakers who had a passion for gaining wealth. He observed this led not only to a worldly spirit, but to "grinding the faces of the poor." [4] On the other hand, Elias chided the poor for aping the rich, declaring that this resulted only in poverty, debt, and distress.[5]

Elias was saddened by the sudden death of Isaac, Isaac who, since his retirement to Westbury, had meant so much to Elias,[6] but he was happy to have a visit from another cousin, Edward Hicks, the painter of Newtown, Pennsylvania. He accompanied Edward for a week in neighborhood visiting, and considered his cousin's gift in the ministry "searching and lively." [7] The two men discussed the developing breach between the Evangelical Friends and those of the old school, as well as that between wealthy city Friends and those in the country. Later, Elias was pleased to learn that Edward was "alert and closely exercised in guarding the frontiers from [those] seeking to make an inroad on the borders of Zion." [8] Thinking in terms of Biblical allegories, Edward Hicks painted nearly one hundred canvasses of the Peaceable Kingdom, expressive of his hope that the religious conflict which was daily growing more bitter would terminate in an ideal condition.[9]

Elias told Edward of the bitter struggle he had in his own Meeting with Phebe and Thomas Willis who had charged him with unsoundness. The contest was carried to the local Committee of Ministers and Elders which appointed a judicious committee that tried to quiet the fears of Thomas Willis and his wife, and bring them into unity with the majority of the Meeting members, but without success.

Elias wrote William Poole that he was also under attack by non-Friends who protested because the Quakers did not join in the new interdenominational societies. The Long Island preacher sent a rather harsh message to Willet Hicks, who was traveling in the ministry throughout England. "We can easily account for all the mighty stir there is now in Christendom for to promote reformation by the Institution of Bible Societies, Missionary Societies, societies for the propagation of the Gospel in ferren [sic] parts, peace societies by which the hirelings draw or wrench by their pious frauds, every little pittance they possibly can. But knowing as the old proverb says that money makes the mare go they know full well without it they can do nothing." [10] Hicks was certain that association with other Christian bodies, even in good causes, would result in breaking down the containing hedge.

On his last visit to Wilmington, he had heard Benjamin Ferris talk about the changed attitude of English Friends. They now desired "to soften down, indeed to obliterate some of the distinctions which our predecessors had raised as a barrier between us. Our English ministers frequented meetings of clergymen and others, they were applauded for their zeal in the cause . . . they were tickled with the plaudits bestowed upon them." Ferris contrasted this attitude with the day when Friends attacked the "English Ecclesiastics" for exacting tithes, and keeping Friends out of the universities. From this new association, Ferris believed, came the insistence of Evangelical Friends upon preaching the doctrine of the Trinity and holding the Scriptures as the only medium of divine revelation. Elias and Benjamin Ferris agreed that these religious associations used ill-timed measures, in the hands of unqualified persons, to further their aims. For example, rather than send missionaries to India, which had been conquered by Great Britain at the cost of a million lives, the two Friends advocated returning civil and political rights to the Hindu. Elias linked opposition to Bible Societies with his concern for the American Negroes. Friends were asked to send copies of the

Scriptures to Asia, yet were threatened with fines and imprisonment
if they tried to teach the one and a half million southern slaves to
read the Old and New Testaments. As Ferris said, "Let us set the
candle in our own candlestick, before we attempt to enlighten
others." [11]

Stephen Grellet, returning to New York in 1821, began at once
to attack Elias Hicks. "I find the adversary has sown his seed of
enmity to Truth," he wrote, "and enmity to those that love the
Truth; that spirit has spread wide its roots. On sitting in meeting,
instead of rejoicing among friends, as I had hoped to do in former
years, I wept bitterly. Elias Hicks has led many to imbibe his anti-
Christian errors." [12] Later, he noted, "I found that the greatest part
of the members of our Society, and many of the Ministers and Elders,
are carried away by the principles which Elias Hicks has so assidu-
ously promulgated among them; he now speaks out boldly, disguis-
ing his sentiments no longer; he seeks to invalidate the Holy Scriptures, and set up man's reason as his only guide, openly denying the
Divinity of Christ." Stephen added, "I have had many opportunities
with him, in which I have most tenderly pleaded with him; but all
has been in vain. When I saw him last winter I found that there was
no more room to plead with him." Stephen Grellet considered it was
his duty, therefore, to preach with greater intensity, "the Lord Jesus
Christ as the only Saviour; to expose the awfulness of the sin of unbelief, and the fearful condition of those who [had] trodden under
foot the Son of God, and counted the blood of the covenant, wherewith we are sanctified, an unholy thing." [13] Elias Hicks and Stephen
Grellet did not speak the same language, nor could either understand the other's point of view.

If Elias Hicks had a favorite text it was either the twenty-seventh
verse of the first chapter of Colossians: "Christ in you, the hope of
glory"; or the ninth verse of the first chapter of John: "the true light
which lighteth every man, that cometh into the world." The early
Friends taught that Christianity was not a scheme of doctrines but

an inward experience which led to a way of life. They held the generally accepted theological beliefs of their day, yet, as Arthur J. Mekeel says, "It was not the doctrines themselves, but what they did with them, the place they gave them, that mainly distinguished Friends from other Christians." [14] On occasions the Society stated its collective beliefs, but it was always understood that assent to doctrines was not the test of being a Quaker.

The early Books of Discipline contained little theology, rather testimonies concerning Christian living. These testimonies were completed during the period of Quietism. The first theological expressions to find a place in the Disciplines came by way of advice to parents in the London Epistle of 1732. Friends were urged to teach their children to read the Scriptures, "which plainly set forth the miraculous conception, birth, holy life, wonderful works, blessed example, meritorious death and glorious resurrection, ascension, and mediation of our Lord and Saviour Jesus Christ." [15] This sentence was soon incorporated in the Philadelphia Discipline. It was not used in the New York Discipline until 1810, and then reduced to read, "the miraculous birth, holy life, blessed example, doctrine and precepts, of our Lord and Saviour Jesus Christ." [16] Baltimore, less influenced by London than other eastern Yearly Meetings, inserted instead a statement that youth should revere the doctrines and precepts contained in the Scriptures, "inducing them to believe, that the same experience of the work of sanctification, through the operation of the spirit of God . . . is to be witnessed by believers in all generations." [17] In 1806, Philadelphia and Baltimore, but not New York, wrote into their Disciplines the additional statement that any person who "[denied] the divinity of our Lord and Saviour Jesus Christ, the immediate revelation of the Holy Spirit, or the authenticity of the Scriptures" should be disowned.[18]

Evangelical Friends were unwilling to consider belief in the Indwelling Christ the primary requirement for membership in the Society. They insisted that the five main points in their interpretation of Christianity be accepted on faith. Yet the doctrine of the supreme authority of the Scriptures and the total depravity of human nature were radically opposed to the Foxian concept of the Inner Light; the deity of Christ and his death as a propitiatory sacrifice were concepts on which Friends had never reached full agreement. Hicks and the Evangelicals united only on the necessity of personal repentance, and even here their approach differed.

Although Elias Hicks laid great emphasis on the experience of the Indwelling Christ, he added a note not found among first-generation Quakers—the place of reason. He wrote that all matters of truth should be "first brought . . . to the test of the light in our own consciences"; second, judged by the test of "the reason of things"; third, checked by the test of "consistency with the precepts and example of our Lord Jesus Christ"; and fourth, "if relating to our duty to our fellow creatures," examined in the light of the golden rule.[19]

When speaking of Jesus, the Jericho minister used many traditional theological phrases. Jesus was Son of God, Prophet, Messiah, Mediator of the New Covenant, Saviour, Second Adam, Lord from Heaven, Head of the Church, Blessed Example, and King of Kings.[20] Elias declared that Jesus was "wholly swallowed up in the divinity of his heavenly Father,"[21] and that God and Christ were "one in a spiritual sense."[22]

The Jericho minister taught that Jesus had a twofold nature, human and divine. The human body was born of the Virgin Mary by God's creative power. "As in the beginning of Creation, he spake the word and it was done, so by his almighty power he spoke the word and by it created the seed of man in the fleshly womb of Mary."[23] Elias wrote to Thomas Willis that "Nothing appeared to mitigate against" a belief in the Miraculous Conception, although in the past history of Christianity, "many . . . believed otherwise, and these at times stood foremost in esteem." He pointed out that wars and bloody persecutions arose because men held or denied this article of faith. "I examined the accounts," Elias added, "and I was led to think there was considerable more Scripture evidence for Jesus being the son of Joseph than otherwise; although it has not yet changed my belief." This examination of the Biblical records, Elias thought, kept him from judging others who did not share his interpretations. He could "feel the same flow of love and unity with them, as though they were in the same belief." [24] Later, when directly charged with denying the miraculous conception, Elias vigorously affirmed his faith in the Biblical account. He always insisted, however, that this belief was unessential to salvation.

The Long Island minister taught that Jesus, having a human body, was subject to temptation as all men, yet lived a perfect life, free from sin, sealing his doctrines and testimonies by his death on the cross. Thus Jesus became the perfect example for all men.[25]

Theologically, Elias Hicks was an Adoptionist. He believed that Jesus, having fulfilled the Law of Israel, at his baptism received a still greater measure of the Divine Spirit, and was thus prepared for a more important mission. "The first birth was a created birth; the last was a birth of love, of union. . . . It was the holy descending of the life of God in the soul." [26] In reply to a question, Elias answered, "Jesus Christ, in his *outward manifestation,* was more blest, and abundantly more glorified, than any other man, and was above all, and therefore was the representative of God on earth, visible to the external senses, although the power by which he did his mighty works, was the invisible power of God, conferred upon him for that end, he being the instrument through whom God, by his power, wrought all those mighty works." [27]

Through the years Friends had omitted the term Trinity because it was not found in the Bible. Elias Hicks said that the doctrine of the Trinity, held by many, was in error. He could not accept the thought of three distinct persons in one God, nor that each of the three was wholly God. Neither could he apply the word personality to God, for he considered this implied locality and limitation of place. To him, God was one without divisibility or distinction of person. "Wherever the holy spirit of God is," he wrote, "there is God, and where God is, there is the Holy Spirit . . . for God is a spirit and nothing but Spirit." [28] Although Jesus was wholly swallowed up in the divinity of his Father, there was a difference to Hicks; the divinity of the Father was altogether underived, being self-existing, but the divinity of Jesus was derived from the Father. "In the moral relation to be a son of man, the son must be . . . in the same nature, spirit, and likeness of his father, so as to say, I and my father are one in all those respects." [29]

The eternal spirit within Jesus, according to Hicks, was that spirit described in John which illuminated every man. Jesus possessed a greater measure of the Divine Light, an unlimited measure, because he had a greater work to do; but the twofold nature of Jesus was different from man only in the quantity of the spirit possessed, not in quality or kind. "We have all a manifestation of the Spirit, sufficient for our own end. He had the fulness of it, as we have our several allotments." [30] And since God was just and good each individual had allotted to him a proportion of the spirit sufficient to his needs. It was in regard to the mission of Jesus that Elias Hicks differed most markedly from the Evangelicals.

On May 12, 1820, there appeared in the *Christian Repository,* a weekly Presbyterian journal published in Wilmington, Delaware, a letter over the signature "Paul" charging the Society of Friends "with holding doctrines and practices inimical to the principles of the Gospel, as contained in the Scriptures of the Old and New Testaments." This was answered the following week by "Amicus," and through February, 1823, the debate on Christian doctrines between "Paul" and "Amicus" continued. When the discussions were completed the papers were published in a book of more than five hundred pages. "Seldom have the productions of anonymous writers excited a more lively interest . . . especially among Presbyterians and Friends." [31] Rarely, if ever, had as extensive a discussion of theological questions been carried on by a Friend, though attacks upon the views of Friends were older than Roger Williams', *New England Firebrand Quenched,* and *George Fox Digged Out of his*

Burrowes. During the period of the *Repository* articles, William Poole of Brandywine wrote repeatedly to Elias Hicks, asking his opinions on theological matters. Elias answered in full and William Poole said he was sharing these letters with several other Friends.[32] As William Poole was the uncle of Benjamin Ferris (who was "Amicus") there is little doubt that the latter used many of Elias' ideas. In fact many of the phrases and sentences used in Elias' letters to William Poole reappear in the articles of "Amicus." Benjamin Ferris was also assisted by Evan Lewis and Dr. William Gibbons, both well known to the Long Island Quaker. William Poole sent copies of the *Christian Repository* to Elias Hicks as they were published and comments upon the articles passed back and forth between the two men.

The Presbyterian minister who wrote under the name of "Paul" pointed out that when the Quakers wrote of the character of God, the nature and offices of Christ, the work of the Spirit, the way of salvation, and "other grand essentials of Christianity, [they] hide in a cloud of mysticism." [33] He complained that a visitor to Quaker Meetings heard much on the need for plainness in speech and dress, the danger of attending other places of worship, and the evils of joining Missionary Societies; but he heard little of the infinite evil of sin, the need of a vicarious atonement, the total depravity of the heart, the Trinity, the Divinity of Christ, the resurrection, universal judgment and everlasting punishment. "Paul" further declared that the Friends, in not accepting the traditional theology of the Father and Son as separate persons in the Godhead, denied the atonement, since the man Jesus could not make infinite satisfaction to God for the transgressions of men.

"Amicus," like Elias Hicks, declared that Friends held "the doctrines of the New Testament" in regard to the person of Jesus; thus they did not use the word Trinity, the phrase "three distinct and separate persons in the Godhead," or speak of God as a plural being. To do so to "Amicus" was not Trinitarianism but Tritheism.[34]

To Orthodox Christians, whether Presbyterian or Evangelical

Quaker, the atonement was central; but to Elias Hicks and Benjamin Ferris the cornerstone was the Indwelling Christ. In this they went back to the position of George Fox. According to Rachel King, "There is no logical need for the incarnation and passion in Fox's central religious conception. When Fox talks about Christ dying for us and redeeming us, he is simply using inherited terminology without coordinating it with his other thought." [35] Thus Fox spoke of the cross as within. Hicks used the same simile when he said the selfish dispositions of men, their self-love, must be nailed to the cross. "What is the cross?" he asked. "Nothing but an inward law written on the table of each of our hearts; the law of the new dispensation." [36] Hicks went as far as to say that the death of Christ on the cross was not essential to salvation. God foresaw that evil men would crucify Jesus; thus, "it became expedient that Christ should suffer persecution and death to seal the truth of prophecy." [37] God, in His wisdom, might have provided another means than the crucifixion of Jesus to awaken the consciences of mankind. To Elias Hicks, the outward death of Jesus was but a figure of the inward redemption of the soul from sin by the spiritual blood of Christ which gave renewal of life.[38] He shocked the Evangelicals when he wrote, "I have never been able to see how the sacrifice of the outward Body of Christ would do more for me than to prove . . . we ought to sacrifice everything relating to the body even life itself." [39]

Elias Hicks rejected what he considered to be some of the grosser concepts concerning the vicarious atonement. He taught that sin originated in man's self-will, not in inherited evil. He said that Adam made satisfaction for his sin of disobedience by showing penitence, and God's clothing his nakedness with skins was a symbol of the nakedness of the soul reclothed with the Holy Spirit. Hicks did not accept the commonly held doctrine that righteousness was ever "imputed." He believed that a man could only be made righteous by his own consent and knowledge, not by an act in the historic past. He went so far as to say "the perfectly just, all-wise, and merciful Jehovah [could not perform] so cruel an act as that of slaying his innocent and righteous Son, to atone for the sins and iniquities of the ungodly. Surely, it is impossible, that any rational being that has any right sense of justice and mercy, would be willing to accept forgiveness of sins on such terms! Would he not rather go forward and offer himself wholly up to suffer all the penalties due to his crimes, rather than the innocent should suffer?"[40] Hicks refused to use the words "satisfaction" or "merit" because they did not appear in the Bible. To him, legal offerings and sacrifices were but shadows, the saving flesh and blood of Christ not being outward but inward. All God desired was complete repentance and surrender of the human will in obedience. Neither did Hicks use the phrase "blood of Jesus Christ" which received so much emphasis by the Evangelicals. The work of Jesus Christ was figurative. "The blood which cleanseth from all sin," he said, "was the life of the soul of Jesus."[41]

In his correspondence with William Poole, Hicks defined his thoughts concerning the mission of Jesus, and his thoughts, on the whole, appeared substantially in the letters of "Amicus." Elias explained that Jesus while on earth demonstrated by his miracles, outwardly wrought, a complete figure of the work of God on the believing soul. As Jesus raised the dead to life, so the Spirit of God, working on the spiritually dead, enabled the human soul to conquer all evil, be purified, and ascend into paradise. Thus all were made alive and born again of the incorruptible seed and word of God.[42]

At one point Elias Hicks placed an emphasis not duplicated by "Amicus." Hicks said that Jesus had a special mission to the Hebrew nation. He was their Messiah and Savior since in giving men the Sermon on the Mount, and by his death on the cross, he fulfilled all the Mosaic Law and put an end to it and to all the ordinances of Israel; replacing them by the inward law of the Spirit, foretold by Jeremiah. This was a definite historical work for his race, a culmination of all the work of the prophets. He came to the lost sheep of the house of Israel. In his outward manifestation he was "limited to Israel."[43]

Hicks summed up his thoughts concerning salvation in the pages of his *Journal:*

Salvation is obtained by all who desire it, when they yield to the Christ within the human heart, crucifying the sins of the flesh, and doing the will of God. In our coming into the obedience of Christ, we take upon us his divine nature . . . and this is Christ in us the hope of glory. . . . Therefore all the varied names given in scripture to this divine light and life, such as Emmanuel, Jesus, sent of God, great Prophet, Christ our Lord, Grace, Unction, Anointed, &. mean one and the same thing; and are nothing less nor more, than the spirit and power of God in the soul of man, as his Creator, Preserver, Condemner, Redeemer, Saviour, Sanctifier, and Justifier.[44]

When Stephen Grellet concluded in the winter of 1820 that "there was no more room to plead with [Elias Hicks]" an explosion was not far distant.

XVIII

Religious Freedom

at Stake

IN THE SPRING of 1822 the correspondence of Elias Hicks was heavy.
William Poole wrote asking about his health, and Elias replied that
the "tincture of bark," the "Elixir of Vitriol," and the "preparation
of Nation" which Dr. William Gibbons gave him when last in Wilmington were effectively meeting his needs.[1] Hugh Judge sent affectionate letters from Indiana where he was on a religious mission in
a newly settled country. He had news of Jonathan Evans' discour-
teous treatment of Elias at Pine Street Meeting and wrote to assure
his friend of his loyal support. A friend had sent word to Hugh
that when Hicks was last in Philadelphia he had never seen such
crowds gather to hear a minister.

Elias was especially interested to learn from his Midwest correspondent that William Forster, a minister from England, had brought
up in Ohio Yearly Meeting a proposal for a convention of all Friends'
Yearly Meetings. The suggestion was received with little favor, but
carried over for a year.[2] Elias Hicks knew that orthodoxy of any kind
required conformity, and realized the increasing Evangelical influ-

ence would result in attempts to secure conformity in religious beliefs. Because he considered religion a personal relationship with God
and not an opinion about God, Elias Hicks opposed every effort
towards uniformity of religious expression or the formulation of a
Quaker creed. As early as 1783 Rhode Island Yearly Meeting had
proposed to New York Yearly Meeting that one Discipline be considered for the entire continent. Elias was on the committee to discuss the matter and joined in the report that "the time had not fully
come" to comply with the request.[3] In 1805 an effort was made by
the Meeting for Sufferings of Philadelphia Yearly Meeting to secure
a uniform Discipline, but nothing was accomplished. Twelve years
later, Philadelphia sent a request to other Yearly Meetings for a
conference which might promote uniformity of faith and doctrine.
Several English Friends then in the country heartily endorsed the
plan, but Elias Hicks spoke vigorously against it in New York Yearly
Meeting and the request was refused. Elias opposed the same plan
at Baltimore Yearly Meeting on the grounds that it would establish "a creed which would make the Society in America approach
the position of the English Friends by definite doctrinal statements." [4]
It was the judgment of Baltimore Quakers that some advantages
would arise from such a conference, but as Baltimore did not wish
to invite delegates from London the subject was dropped for the
time being.[5]

Elias was much disturbed by a letter from his long-time friend,
Gideon Seaman of Westbury, who reproved Elias for preaching many
things that were better not said. Elias replied that he expressed himself on controversial subjects only when individuals pressed him for
an opinion or misconstrued what he preached. Gideon charged Elias
with making statements about the place of the Bible, and the reality of miracles which, Elias said, were "absolutely false." The Jericho
minister reminded Gideon that his faith rested on the Inner Light,
that interpretation of many passages of Scripture was a matter of
opinion, and that certain theological ideas, held by some individuals
to be of first importance, were not necessarily essential.[6]

Edward and Elias Hicks exchanged a number of letters. Elias reported that Valentine's barn was struck by lightning and, but for a heavy rain, Valentine's as well as his own house would have burned. Shortly Edward's home and workshop were destroyed by fire, "not a small loss" to the painter.[7] Edward sent word that the "winds of envy and rage" were blowing against him; Elias answered that the winds could not overcome the Newtown minister for they "blew through a goat's horn instead of a ram's horn." [8]

From Pleasant Valley William Dean dispatched a note thanking Elias for his messages, especially those against slavery and the use of slave products. "There has not been a day since when in thy company," he declared, "but what I have gathered additional strength." [9] That spring, while the Greeks were struggling for their freedom against the Turks, many Americans were sending funds to assist them. Elias wrote a four-page leaflet in which he stated that it was a remarkable fact that it was much easier to arouse the sympathy of individuals for sufferers far away than for those near at home. "Tens of thousands of human beings," he commented, "much more innocent than the Greeks . . . [are] suffering ten fold greater oppression . . . than would have been the case with the Greeks had they not taken up arms." [10] Real justice would be better served, he thought, if Americans provided liberty for those within their own shores.

Jacob Willetts asked Elias' help with the boarding school. The number of pupils was on the decline and there was a deficit. Some objected to the restrictions which made the school "select," but Willetts thought it proper to take only children of Friends' families, or children with one parent as members. He considered the greatest need was new blood on the committee, and hoped alumni would be included. Most of the present committee, he wrote Elias, were well advanced in age and had lost interest in the school. He urged Elias to take the matter up at the next Yearly Meeting, believing "there are those amongst the middle and younger class of Society who feel disposed to use the same exertions that thou, John Mott, and Ann

Willis and others did in 1807 for the continuance of the school." [11]

Mason Luke ("Parson") Weems requested Elias' assistance in distributing books which he had written on George Washington, Benjamin Franklin, Francis Marion, and William Penn. "Knowing that thou art a sincere Lover of Human Happiness," Weems wrote, "I feel confident to write thee." He then explained that he had written his biographies "to shew the youth of the land the Blessings resulting from imitating their examples . . . knowing that Drunkenness, Gambling, Duelling &c are the Rocks that wreck and ruin thousands." "The People of this my native land," he added, "are a People great, yea, extraordinarily favor'd by God and now furnished with a fair opportunity to display all the Virtues and felecities that Rational Beings are capable in a State of perfect self control uncrushed by the Kings and uncorrupted by Hireling Priests. But these privileges will never be profitable to their proper ends of making ourselves a Mighty People in Peace and Happiness . . . unless we fear God and walk in his statues." [12] He asked Elias for names of merchants to whom he could send his books on a fifteen percent discount with the right to return unsold copies.

There were a number of visitors at New York Yearly Meeting in May, among whom were George Withy of England; Edward Hicks, Richard Jordan, and Joseph Whitall of Philadelphia Yearly Meeting. Joseph Whitall was a strong Evangelical Friend and, according to Edward Hicks, "enrolled himself among the enemies of Elias Hicks and his friends." [13] It seemed to Edward Hicks that "there were too many Friends like recruiting officers, trying to enlist soldiers, to strengthen their respective armies." Edward considered his cousin "a greater preacher than the rest of us." [14] At the conclusion of the sessions, Elias wrote John Comly, "Thy . . . affectionate letter . . . and its contents was truly cordial to my mind, it tended, with divers others of the like kind, from a number of my endeared friends in different parts of the country, to excite humble and renewed gratitude . . . at a time when many are rising up, in an underhand way, to asperse, spread evil reports, belie and almost stone me." He reported that the Yearly Meeting was about the largest ever held, and the Evangelical visitors "were mostly sealed in silence . . . and as they were withheld from communicating much for our help, so we escaped interruption from much speaking." [15] Before returning to Philadelphia, Joseph Whitall had a talk with Elias Hicks and pointed out where they disagreed on religious doctrines. Elias was in "a tender frame of mind" and wept during the interview. Whitall also expressed his views on Hicks' preaching to Thomas Willis of Jericho, but laid no complaint before his Monthly Meeting.[16]

On returning home, Elias Hicks had a heart attack, which he counted as one of his "indispositions." He described the attack to William Poole, "Such was the severity of my pains, which came on by intervals of from three to five hours, and sometimes more . . . that it disqualified me for almost all kinds of action for several weeks: so that I could neither write nor talk without bringing on those severe spasms of pain, which ran through the upper part of my breast in a direction to each arm, and so down to my elbows; which at times was so excruciating, that I lack for words to give to another a full idea of it." [17] The attack did not cause Elias to give up his idea of going south. He wrote Samuel Titus in New Rochelle asking him to be his companion; Samuel answered that he was in full unity with his friend and would like to accompany him, but he was not well enough to go. He warned Elias that men would attack him and make accusations against him, if not to his face then in a way calculated to do him harm and lay waste his labors. Samuel said that he sensed such attacks at the Yearly Meeting just closed, but the attempts were "defeated by [Elias'] never failing weapons of love and forbearance." He added that many would be "narrowly watching" Elias because of his ideas concerning the Scriptures. Samuel Titus considered that many of the ideas of his friend were not clearly understood, and were consequently likely to be misconstrued. He advised the Long Island minister to keep to "plain simple practical doctrines; not entering into subjects of argumentation . . . speculative notions and opinions." [18] William Ridgeway, about the same time, told Elias that evil people were waiting for him to make a slip; they were circulating stories that he doubted the divinity of Christ, which, Elias answered, "was an old story, and as false as it was old." [19] Samuel R. Fisher sent a warm invitation urging his friend to be his guest, declaring that a new mission by Elias, at his advanced age, should be one of the most fruitful he ever enjoyed. The Philadelphia Quaker trusted that neither the strong current of applause that awaited Elias, nor the spreading spirit of opposition, would influence his coming.

George Withy, the English Friend who was at New York Yearly Meeting, went on to Philadelphia and reported the temper of that gathering as well as what he had observed in New England. His reports were certain to make the next southern visit of Elias Hicks to Philadelphia more difficult.

For several years there had been an intellectual ferment in eastern Massachusetts. In the Congregational Church this led to a division and the withdrawal of the Unitarians; in the Society of Friends there was a brief New Light outbreak. This was part of the general nineteenth-century movement toward liberalism, which took one form among the Irish Liberals, as evident in the preaching of Hannah Barnard, and another form in the message of Elias Hicks. All opposed, however, the Evangelical attitude toward the Bible, stressed the guidance of the individual through the Inner Light, and were against a rigid enforcement of Discipline by the elders. In the thriving centers of Lynn and New Bedford, Friends accumulated considerable wealth and came in contact with non-Quaker groups which held Liberal ideas. The first stirrings of the New Light Movement began as early as 1815, and by 1820 the movement was very noticeable. Elias Hicks had visited New England with Isaac Hicks in 1816 and some of his ideas may have influenced the movement, but no direct connection can be discovered.[20] Stephen Gould, a Quaker watchmaker of Newport, wrote to Thomas Thompson, a Quaker druggist in Liverpool, that there was a spirit of Ranterism abroad among New England Friends. Micah Ruggles, Mary Newhall, a Recorded Minister, and Lydia Dean, who was once Clerk of the Women's Yearly Meeting, differed from the body of Friends on points of doctrine and were calling the authority of the Discipline in question. Gould wrote that Mary Newhall "charged some of the first standing . . . with a dead formality"; and said, "that the people were 'priest ridden,' and the ministers were 'elder ridden.'" The New Lights claimed, according to Gould, that they desired the Discipline should be more spiritually administered. He added, "the spirit of opposition to the discipline, as well as some of the fundamental principles of Society, which seems to have risen up with us and in several Yearly Meetings, in ours is much kept down by the Spiritual weight of promptness to act. . . . The malady (if so it may be called), is very deleterious in its effects. . . . It is Deism at root, under the form of Godliness, which strikes at all Church order and good government."[21] Stephen Gould sent his English Friend word that George Withy's powerful preaching helped stay the disease; thirty-five Friends were disowned in Lynn and nearly as many in Salem.

George Withy and Stephen Gould missed the real significance of the New Light Movement. Mary Newhall in the course of her preaching declared, "The stream does not rise higher than the fountain."[22] This was a striking way of stating the old truth, given by Fox and Barclay, that the Inner Light and not the Bible is the final authority in religion. The Spirit of God guided the writers of the Scriptures in their day, but the same Spirit acts upon the human soul in succeeding generations. Stephen Gould and other Evangelical Friends had moved away from this position, and attributed an absolute authority to the Scriptures which reduced the Inner Light to a secondary position. Mary Newhall was preaching more the concept of progressive revelation than a revolutionary thought. "The Mosaic dispensation," she said, "in which the performance of certain rituals constituted the required religion" was superseded by "the more spiritual dispensation of our Saviour," and this in turn by the "yet more spiritual and inward dispensation of the present day." [23] "This," Frederick B. Tolles comments, "was the doctrine that the religion of any given period is accommodated to the capacities of its believers, and that there has been a gradual refinement, a progressive purification of religion, starting with the primitive tribal cult . . . developing into the more spiritual religion of Jesus, and finally, in modern times, assuming an even purer and more elevated form, divorced from all outward observances and creeds." [24]

Elias Hicks understood as clearly as Mary Newhall the concept of progressive revelation. He had written to Phebe Willis, "The Lord is graciously willing to reveal himself as fully to the children of men in this day as in any day of the world, without respect to persons, as each is attentive to his inward and spiritual manifestations." And had added, "How much more reasonable it is to suppose, that an inspired teacher in the present day, should be led to speak more truly and plainly to the states of the people, to whom he is led to communicate, than any doctrines that were delivered one thousand seven hundred years ago to a people very differently circumstanced to those in this day, I leave to every rational mind to judge." [25]

With David Seaman as a companion, Elias Hicks set out for the south in early October, traveling with a minute from his Monthly Meeting to attend Baltimore Yearly Meeting, and "if way opened," to visit Friends' families in the two northern Monthly Meetings in Philadelphia. William Poole's last letter spoke of agitating times concerning religious matters in that city, with a spirit of enmity abroad. He longed to see Elias again, "his father in relation to . . . truth," and trusted that he would be as firm as Paul in going up to Jerusalem.[26]

Before Elias left for the south, Philadelphia Meeting for Sufferings was in session. As it adjourned, Samuel Bettle, the Clerk of the Yearly Meeting, asked a portion of the membership to remain. When this group settled, Jonathan Evans arose and said, "It is understood that Elias Hicks is coming on here, on his way to Baltimore Yearly Meeting. Friends know that he preaches doctrines contrary to the doctrines of the Society, that he has given uneasiness to his friends at home, and they can't stop him; and unless we can stop him here, he must go on." [27] Jonathan Evans said that his information came from Joseph Whitall who four months previously had been in New York. Evans also charged Elias with distributing books containing unsound doctrines. Joseph Whitall added that Elias had the approval of his own Monthly, Quarterly, and two-thirds of the New York Yearly Meeting.[28] Some expressed surprise, and one individual declared he had often heard Elias Hicks in public and never perceived in his communications anything contrary to the well-known tenets of the Society. Jonathan Evans, Joseph Whitall, and Richard Jordan stated that there could be no doubt of Elias' unsoundness; Joseph Whitall mentioned his speaking to Elias after the sessions of New York Yearly Meeting, and said he was ready to testify to the charges. It was suggested that a committee of two wait on Elias Hicks when he reached the city. Some did not consider the group had authority to act, but their opinion was overruled. Elias and David Seaman spent three months in New Jersey, in Bucks, Montgomery, Delaware and Chester counties of Pennsylvania. At the first opportunity, the Friends appointed to visit Elias on behalf of the Elders performed their function and seemed satisfied with their interview.

The New York Quakers spent some time with Edward Hicks, William Jackson, Hugh Foulke, and Emmor Kimber. From Edward Hicks' house, Elias sent word to Jemima that gatherings were very large, many Friends following him from Meeting to Meeting, and house to house. He asked her to have David, his Negro helper, cut the corn and dig the potatoes, and then added,

Now, my dear, let me remind thee of thy increasing bodily infirmities, and the necessity it lays thee under to spare thyself of the burthen . . . of much bodily and mental labour and exercise . . . that it may be, my dear, our united care to endeavour that our last days may be our best days, that so we may witness a state and qualification to pass gently and quiet out of time, into the mansions of eternal blessedness, where all sighing and sorrow will be at an end.[29]

Leaving Philadelphia, Elias held many Meetings on the way south. At Nottingham he visited George Churchman, now frail in body. During Baltimore Yearly Meeting, he had several conversations with Philip E. Thomas, president of the Merchants Bank, who was much interested in the material development of the country, especially transportation improvements. Thomas feared that the Erie Canal being dug across New York state would take a great deal of trade away from Baltimore. Elias left the city with the endorsement of the Yearly Meeting "expressive of their unity and satisfaction with his labours of love amongst them." [30] On the return journey, the Long Island Friends, and Priscilla Hunt of Indiana, attended the session of Southern Quarter on the Eastern Shore of Maryland, now belonging to Philadelphia. Here the Jericho minister learned that a new combination was forming against him in the City of Brotherly Love. He went on to Green Street where, with the permission of the Monthly Meeting, he undertook a visitation of its 140 families. This task, with attendance at other city gatherings, occupied approximately a month. When he retired to his lodgings at night, following public gatherings, thirty, forty, and sometimes one hundred Friends of all ages came to engage him in conversation.

While Elias was visiting the membership of Green Street, a small committee of elders again approached him concerning the charges made by Joseph Whitall, and new accusations made by Ezra Comfort and Isaiah Bell, who had heard Elias preach at Southern Quarter. This committee represented a gathering of the male elders of the five city Meetings. Elias refused to appear before this body on the grounds that they had no jurisdiction over him. He sent word that the first charges made against him by Joseph Whitall covered statements given some months before in his own Yearly Meeting, where no exception was taken to what he said. He added that Joseph Whitall, if concerned, should have taken the matter up with Jericho

Monthly Meeting, since both Philadelphia and New York Disciplines required ministers who were charged with unsoundness to "be admonished in love and tenderness by the elders or overseers where they live." [31] As to the charges raised by Comfort and Bell, Elias said they were not valid; furthermore, the Discipline required that if a Friend did not agree with a speaker, he was to take the matter up "privately and orderly" with the minister before mentioning his concern to others; when this was not done the action came under the head of "talebearing and detraction," a disciplinary offense.

In undertaking family visits, Elias had deposited his certificate with Green Street Monthly Meeting. Some members of that Meeting considered it would be wise for Elias to meet the city elders in order to speak against the charges leveled at him. This they thought he could do without admitting the right of the elders to demand an interview. Elias agreed to an appointment with the elders and took with him John Comly, the Assistant Clerk of the Yearly Meeting, Robert and John Moore, John Hunt, and some other Friends who had been present at the Southern Quarter. The city elders, however, refused to talk with Elias unless they could have "a select private opportunity," even though many of the friends he brought with him were ministers and elders from country Meetings.[32]

At this time William L. Fisher told Elias:

I have not been ignorant that surmise and suspicion relative to thy religious opinions have been afloat and have gained full credence among many holding the foremost place in Society; and though I truly believe thou art not looking to men for confirmation and encouragement, yet it has appeared right that I should say I stand a living witness to many of those important truths thou has promulgated. It was only through thy means and instrument that the scales began to fall from my eyes and I was enabled to see Christianity in all its simplicity and beauty.[33]

He added that many could bear the same testimony and trusted that Elias would not be moved by the opposition against him.

Ten of the city elders now signed a letter, addressed to Elias, charging him with "holding and promulgating doctrines different

from, and repugnant to those held by the Society"; repeating some of
the views they believed he preached; declaring that they "could not
have religious unity with [his] conduct, nor with the doctrines . . .
which he was charged with promulgating." [34] Elias replied that he
was charged with unsoundness in an unfriendly manner, contrary to
Discipline, that the charges were not literally true, and that he held
himself amenable to his own Monthly and Yearly Meeting for his
conduct. At the same time, the elders received an epistle written by
three members of Southern Quarter, and signed by twenty-two
Friends present at the same session with Ezra Comfort and Isaiah
Bell, stating that the charges made by the latter against Elias Hicks
were "without substantial foundation." They believed that "the sentiments and doctrines held forth by . . . Elias Hicks were agreeable
to the opinions and doctrines held forth by George Fox, and our
worthy predecessors." [35] Nine elders replied with a second letter addressed to the Jericho minister declaring that their views were not
changed by the correspondence. They thought Elias should be willing to see them privately in order that any cause of uneasiness might
be investigated. They still considered he was disseminating principles different from those held by the Society, and that the matter was
of such "serious magnitude, so interesting to the peace, harmony, and
well being of the society, that . . . it ought to claim the weighty
attention of [his] Friends at home." [36] Elias was advised by members
of Southern Quarter to treat the second letter "with silence as any
remarks from [him] might serve as fresh kindling to blow up the
flame into a higher state of combustion." [37]

Elias Hicks finished his work at Green Street and returned to
Jericho, "with feelings of thanksgiving . . . and with the enjoyment
of that precious peace, which is experienced by those whose minds
are stayed on God." [38] The contest with the Philadelphia elders,
according to Rufus M. Jones, "was the watershed that shaped the
course of the coming movements. . . . Here was the place where
a loving spirit, tender appreciation and methods of reconciliation
would have worked wonders if only those Elders had known how to

employ such forces. . . . The inability to maintain 'unity,' which
meant to these Elders uniformity of doctrine, pushed them over into
opposition to the man whose immense vogue and influence disturbed them. . . . Most Friends were from now on loyal sympathizers of Hicks *or* supporters of the opposing Elders." [39]

Repercussions were immediate. Their home Meeting disowned
Comfort and Bell; the elder of Green Street who signed the Philadelphia letter lost his position.[40] William Poole wrote Benjamin
Ferris that he felt the elders would not retain the respect of the
membership of the Yearly Meeting at large unless they made an
open and candid confession of their error. Abraham Lower thought
the attacks upon Elias Hicks recoiled on the heads of those who made
them. The Philadelphia *Evening Post* carried a tribute to "the ministry and exalted character of our ancient friend Elias Hicks," and
the writer was satisfied that "the misrepresentations which were
made concerning him, and the treatment he received . . . savoured
strongly of persecution and . . . three fourths of the society of which
he is an ornament hold the same opinion." [41] James Mott, Jr., husband of Lucretia Mott, sent word to his father that the rumors concerning Hicks' unsoundness were "unjustifiable prejudice, founded
. . . upon little else than the vague report of some, and the envy of
others." "Of what consequence is it," James Mott added, "if he should
differ from some of us in minor points, mere matters of opinion, in
which he may be correct, and we incorrect; certainly not of sufficient
consequence to make it necessary to call him to account, especially
when he is travelling in discharge of his ministerial duty." Elias'
friend continued, "I consider this an attempt for stretch of power on
the part of our Elders, which I hope will never be countenanced in
our Society: if it should be, we would soon have articles of faith to
which our ministers must subscribe. This however I believe will never
be the case." [42] He continued, "I most sincerely desire . . . that the
uninterrupted harmony that has prevailed in our society in this city
may not be broken or impaired, which is much more to be feared
than any injurious effects from Elias' doctrines or opinions."

On the way home, Elias visited William Logan Fisher, spent a
week end with John Comly, and continued to Long Island in "a very
peaceful and humble state of mind." [43] In Jericho two streams of
thought fused in Elias' mind. As a minister, and a member of the
Meeting for Sufferings of New York Yearly Meeting for a generation, he knew that the Philadelphia elders were wrong. They had
not followed either of the two courses allowed by the Discipline and
Quaker custom. It was permissible for them to send a message to
Jericho Monthly Meeting asking for an examination of Elias' views.
While he was in Philadelphia they also could have asked the Preparative Meeting of Ministry and Elders of Green Street Monthly Meeting, where his certificate was deposited while making family visits,
to conduct an investigation. This had been done years before by
London Yearly Meeting in the case of Hannah Barnard. Hicks knew
that the Philadelphia elders realized both Jericho and Green Street
Meetings would uphold him. He saw as he had never seen before the
danger of a hierarchy taking possession of the Society of Friends,
as the priestly minority in other religious groups in the past dominated the Christian Church. He knew that latitude on points of
religious doctrine was allowed within the Society of old. The Evangelical position now demanded uniformity in religious belief. Religious
freedom was at stake. In the time yet remaining to him, Elias Hicks
determined to point out the danger facing his beloved Society.

XIX

The

Evangelical Invasion

WHEN ELIAS HICKS left Philadelphia, Jonathan Evans and his followers believed that the Jericho minister was promoting a spirit of libertinism. To them, Elias' exaltation of the Inward Light was but a pretext for lessening the authority of the Scriptures, his views concerning Jesus both inadequate and derogatory to Christ's exalted office. It was the duty, therefore, of those holding authority, to prevent the promulgation of such opinions. John Comly, Green Street Friends, and the large majority of country members of Philadelphia Yearly Meeting regarded Elias Hicks as the preserver of values inherent in Quietist Quakerism, the champion of reason and of religious freedom. There were many not in agreement with Elias' particular views who nevertheless defended him.

Samuel M. Janney of Baltimore Yearly Meeting, Liberal Quaker historian, wrote at the time, "The doctrines I then held were those called Orthodox, but I could not endure the spirit of bitterness and party zeal by which those doctrines were too often accomplished." [1] Edward Hicks said of his cousin:

I will not pretend to say that Elias Hicks was entirely clear of those extremes to which eminent men are liable, in the heat of controversy, and the tenacious defence of some favorite speculations. . . . Therefore, it is among the possible circumstances that dear Elias was led to an extreme in the Unitarian speculation, while opposing the Trinitarian, then increasing among Friends. . . . But I have no recollection of ever hearing him in public testimony . . . when his speculative views or manner of speaking, destroyed the savour of life that attended his ministry, or gave me any uneasiness.[2]

And he added, "We have a large and valuable body of Friends, that are neither Arians, Unitarians nor Trinitarians, but firm believers in the plain, emphatical testimonies of Holy Writ, that *Jesus Christ* was more than a man, and more than a prophet, and are willing to rest their eternal all upon this immutable foundation, with the primitive Saints and primitive Quakers." [3]

Elias was no sooner out of Philadelphia than the Meeting for Sufferings produced a document which threw that Yearly Meeting into turmoil. Many did not approve portions of the articles by "Amicus," just drawing to a close; although "Amicus" issued a statement disclaiming any authority for expressed opinions other than his own, this did not satisfy the Evangelicals. At a session of this meeting, held a few days after Elias Hicks left Philadelphia, a paper was produced entitled, *Extracts from the Writings of Primitive Friends concerning the Divinity of our Lord and Saviour Jesus Christ.* It was a clear expression of the Evangelical position, and was originally prepared with the expectation of publication in Wilmington with the papers of "Paul" and "Amicus." A Friend suggested that the Extracts be printed for general circulation. Abraham Lower, John Comly, and others objected to the publication on the grounds that the document was an effort "to palm off a creed on the society," that the pamphlet "would be used to abridge the right of private judgement," and "that something was about to be got up calculated to trammel our conscientious rights." [4] These Quakers held that if such a document were issued over the signature of the Clerk of the Meeting for Sufferings, it would have the appearance of a definite creed drawn up and ap-

SHADOW-PROFILE OF ELIAS HICKS. *Elias is wearing the shad-belly coat and collarless waistcoat of the day.*

THE FRIENDS SCHOOL AT
JERICHO, BUILT IN 1793
*Elias occasionally
taught here for a term
and served on the
school committee
for many years.*

proved by the chief committee of the Yearly Meeting. If adopted by
the Yearly Meeting the document would stand as an official declaration of faith. Although the objectors were overruled and 10,000 copies
of the Extracts printed, there was some uneasiness about broadcasting
them over the existing opposition. It was decided to wait until after
the coming Yearly Meeting.

At the next Yearly Meeting the minutes of the Meeting for Sufferings contained the full copy of the Extracts. Great excitement immediately developed, a stormy scene ensued, one "pretty substantial and
solid old Friend from the country . . . cried out, 'Who hath required
this at your hands?'" [5] "The followers of Elias Hicks raised a great
clamour. The cry of a *creed, popery, oppression* &c. resounded from
all sides; one declared that the document was opposed to Quakerism;
another, that it was contrary to reason, scripture, and revelation; another that it had its origin in darkness, and was calculated to produce
darkness." [6] After two turbulent sessions, a compromise was reached
by which the Yearly Meeting directed the publication be suspended,
declared the Extracts were not to be circulated, but rejected the
proposition to strike the material off the minutes of the Meeting for
Sufferings.

William Poole and Elias Hicks exchanged letters upon the so-
called creed. Elias looked upon the event as a real "tryal and test of
our principles," and declared, "had there not been light to put to
silence that Mass of incongruous matter brought forward by a formidable overbearing part of the meeting for Sufferings as a Creed,
or test of the faith of the members of our Society it would . . . have
convinced every sensible member . . . that the glory of the Divine
presence had entirely departed from us, or as much so, as from any
of the formal professors of Christianity." He thought that Friends
might as well "have gone back and submitted to the Episcopal or
Presbyterian Creed as to have adopted that brought forward at that
meeting." In their correspondence over the Extracts, Elias used a
phrase much quoted from then on, "We *cannot,* and therefore *are
not* bound to believe what we cannot comprehend." [7]

The effort to publish the Extracts pointed up the extent of the powers which resided in the Meeting for Sufferings, as well as the fact that in Philadelphia it was not a representative body. The city Meetings had an excessive number of members, originally appointed for reasons of convenience; when a division of opinion took place the country Friends found themselves poorly represented in this weighty body. Friends had never believed in majority rule, but it was equally objectionable for a minority to assume the right to govern. The mystical liberalism of Elias Hicks appealed to country Friends as approximating the seventeenth-century position of the Society; the Evangelical movement was accepted by a majority of city Friends. The efforts of the city Quakers to gain control of the committee of the Yearly Meeting thoroughly alarmed country Friends who were fearful lest action be taken forcing them to accept untenable views. The timing of the Extracts indicated to them that the city elders of Philadelphia planned to use the document against Elias Hicks when he again visited that area. If the Extracts were approved, the elders could easily silence him on the grounds that he was unsound in doctrines officially promulgated by the Yearly Meeting, as twenty-five years before London Yearly Meeting silenced Hannah Barnard.

From its beginning, the Society of Friends had been an unusually democratic organization. In the Preparative and Monthly business sessions each member had opportunity to express an opinion on whatever claimed the attention of the group. This was group mysticism, experienced when the worshipers gathered under the leadership of the Spirit. The individual might mistake his guidance, but there was less likelihood of the group misinterpreting the Spirit. For more than one hundred and fifty years this theory of final authority proved sufficient. A common code of moral conduct was evolved in the Business Meeting and far-reaching changes made from time to time, as in the case of the testimony against slavery. But the Quaker method of arriving at decisions proved inadequate to cope with changes taking place in theological thinking. This was due to the insistence of the Evangelicals in forcing their opinions upon those

who did not agree with them; and the fears of the Liberals who foresaw disownment at the hands of the Evangelicals.

According to Howard H. Brinton, "The conflict burst into flame
when the elders, going beyond their accustomed prerogative as
guardians of behavior, attempted to become guardians of the theological opinions of those who spoke in Meetings for worship.[8]

Those who feared the Society was losing its democratic spirit had
made many efforts to weaken the power of the elders and the Meeting for Sufferings. The Yearly Meeting was urged to allow individual ownership of the Discipline. Customarily only one copy of
this book of ethical directives was allowed in each Meeting. William
Poole made the suggestion that the term of elders be limited to three
years, and members of the Meeting for Sufferings be likewise rotated,
"breaking a chain of influence . . . injurious to the Society." [9] Edward Hicks asked his home Quarterly Meeting that "a strict and
serious inquiry into the standing of the Meeting for Sufferings" be
made by the Yearly Meeting "for there was reason to fear that it
was becoming a dangerous aristocracy." [10]

Tension and conflict were increased by English ministers traveling with minutes from London Yearly Meeting. A two-way traffic
was always maintained between the two countries and Elias Hicks
spoke appreciatively of the labors of Mary Ridgeway of Ireland,
Susanna Horn, Mary Nastel, Isaac Stephenson, and others. The English ministers were sincere Christians who came to North America
at considerable sacrifice, remaining from one to seven years, separated
from their immediate friends and families. Edward Grubb, English
historian, points out, however, that after 1810 all those that came
westward were strongly Evangelical, with a burning passion to press
home their point of view. They came with their minds made up. Welcomed among wealthy city Friends, they made little effort to meet
and hear those who held the Mystical Liberal position. They reflected the great change which took place among English Friends
in the first quarter of the nineteenth century. Fresh spiritual life

clothed itself in new forms; clothing which was more akin to that worn by Bunyan and Baxter than Fox and Penington. "Religious teaching based on the Inward Light in the souls of men, which a few years before would have passed as sound Quakerism and genuine Christianity, was now called in question, and tested in the light of the doctrine of the infallible authority of the Bible." [11] Elbert Russell adds that these Evangelical English Friends were vigorous, aggressive, critical, and intolerant of opposite views.[12] Their insistence upon Biblical authority clashed sharply with the New York Discipline which spoke of "the same blessed experience of the work of sanctification, through the operation of the Spirit of Truth being witnessed now, as in former ages, by all who attend to its manifestations"; [13] or the Philadelphia Discipline which, as late as 1808, declared the Inner Light, "was the only foundation of true religious and worship." [14]

William Forster spent eight years in America, returning to England in 1826. He met Elias Hicks on several occasions and was thoroughly opposed to his preaching. In an interview with Evan Thomas, an eminent and distinguished minister of Baltimore, Forster expressed his view concerning dangers in Elias' teachings. Evan Thomas replied that, "Elias Hicks did hold some peculiar views, which, perhaps, were not entertained by Friends generally," but "they were honest opinions . . . and there could be no doubt [they] were sincerely entertained by him." Forster pressed him further on Elias' unsoundness and Thomas continued, "I have not felt it to be my place to sit as a watchman in the gate, to recollect and record particular words falling from the lips of any Friend, either in public testimony or private conversation." Evan Thomas declared that he was more concerned as to the source from which the testimony came, and if it seemed to be accompanied with Divine influence and power. From his long acquaintance with the Jericho minister he esteemed him "to be a consistent, faithful testimony bearer," and although he might not be in complete agreement with Elias, held him in brotherly love and believed Elias was called to the ministry by the Head of the

Church. In disagreement, Forster denounced Elias' views as unsound and declared, *"A separation must and will take place* in the Society in America." [15] Perhaps this was the first prophecy from an important minister of such a possibility.

Anna Braithwaite came to North America three times between 1823 and 1828. She was a woman of commanding presence, with a rich cultural background, speaking several languages. In New England Yearly Meeting she was warmly received, and Stephen Gould wrote that she met with no opposition. He reported it was quite otherwise in New York and Philadelphia where "wholesome discipline" was disregarded, New Light elements left on committees, and the government almost in the hands of the loose and disorderly elements.[16] For some months Anna Braithwaite preached Evangelical doctrines in New York state without meeting objection. Resentment became evident at her pointed allusions to reputed sayings of Elias Hicks. Twice she dined at Hicks' home, discussing theology freely into the evening. After Anna Braithwaite sailed for England an account of her interviews with Elias was published—no doubt without her knowledge—and this began a long written controversy between the two, eventually involving other Friends. The correspondence, with a statement by Joseph Whitall and a letter to Dr. Nathan Shoemaker of Philadelphia, was issued under the title, *Letters & Observations Relating to the Controversy Respecting the Doctrines of Elias Hicks,* in 1824.

The interviews and correspondence illustrate how impossible it was for a Friend with the Evangelical and one with the Liberal point of view to understand one another, or to come to any common agreement. In discussing the Trinity and the use of the Scriptures, Elias Hicks spoke of "the propriety of bringing even Scripture truth to the test of the Spirit in our own hearts, and rejecting all such parts as we do not see to be consistent with the attributes of the Almighty," and of the "impossibility of believing what [he] could not comprehend." [17] Anna Braithwaite was shocked when Elias suggested that parts of the Bible were translated erroneously, that it was necessary to believe only a small portion of what was written in the Scriptures, and that men should consider the writings of Confucius and certain other philosophers as divinely inspired as the Bible. She declared Elias said that the fullness of the Godhead rested in man and "in every blade of grass." Elias ended this interview with an assertion that the Discipline should extend to matters of moral conduct but never to matters of faith.

Elias declared to the English visitor that he could not see how the cruel persecution and crucifixion of Jesus Christ could expiate his sins. It was the grace of God which gave power to live a sober, righteous, and godly life. Hicks told Anna Braithwaite, "So long as I feel that peace, there is nothing in the world that makes me afraid, as it respects my eternal condition. But if any of my friends have received any known benefit from any outward sacrifice I do not envy them their privilege." "But, surely," he added, "they would not be willing that I should acknowledge as a truth, that which *I have no kind of knowledge of*." [18]

It was Elias Hicks' opinion that Anna Braithwaite did more harm by breaking unity and love amongst Friends than she could ever overcome.[19] What a pity it was, he thought, that she would leave her affectionate husband and her young and tender offspring to risk her life, when she proved unacceptable to most American Quakers. On Anna Braithwaite's second visit she was arraigned by New York Monthly Meeting for branding Elias Hicks an infidel. She replied, "I never called him an infidel. My breeding, if nothing else, would have prevented my dishonoring the gray hairs of that dear old man, whom I love with unfeigned sincerity . . . there are some [of his] sentiments against which I have spoken, and which I have called the sentiments of unbelievers." [20] At Flushing and at Westbury, Friends objected to her certificate being minuted.

Elizabeth Robson was made of sterner stuff than Anna Braithwaite. She was in the United States between 1824 and 1829 and had many pitched battles with Elias Hicks, whom she called "that poor deluded old man." [21] In Sandy Spring, Maryland, Roger Brooke declared that Elizabeth Robson was sowing seeds of dissension and the Meeting refused permission for her to make family visits. New York followed the same procedure. She corresponded with many leaders while in America, and did not hesitate to write to Priscilla Hunt, "It appeared to me that thy present state is a dangerous one. . . . I believe there is not anything more injurious to the cause of religion than exercising the reasoning faculties in order to comprehend divine truths." [22] Elisha Bates sent Elizabeth Robson word from Mount Pleasant, Ohio, that a separation would probably take place sooner than expected, confirming his belief that "like amputation the operation may be painful but it is necessary for health and preservation of the body at large." [23]

Elias Hicks wrote to his friend in Brandywine of an unusual circumstance in New York Yearly Meeting when Elizabeth Robson, Anna Braithwaite, and Richard Jordan endeavored, after occupying much time in the ministry, to adjourn the session. Thomas Wetherald of Washington and Elias Hicks were both in the gallery, and those assembled desired to hear them, so when Richard Jordan and Elisha Bates shook hands as a sign that the Meeting for Worship was concluded "contrary to anything ever before witnessed . . . not a solitary individual, among the more than two thousand, was seen to move!" A few minutes later a second attempt was made, but with the same result. "A profound silence now pervaded the whole of this large assembly, and, in breathless expectation, every eye seemed riveted with intense interest on the galleries. The whole meeting, simultaneously breaking through the rules of the society, remained fixed and immovable, as if controlled by some invisible power." [24] Finally Thomas Wetherald rose to speak, followed by Elias Hicks. These two then shook hands, and the Meeting quietly dispersed.

Ann Jones of Stockport in England was even more outspoken than Anna Braithwaite or Elizabeth Robson. She publicly declared that Elias Hicks' teachings were *"diabolical* and *luciferian* and *damnable,"* and she thought him an *"openly avowed"* infidel.[25] At Darby, her words were so harsh that the elders of the Quarterly Meeting met and addressed a long letter to her in which they condemned her conduct, "as inconsistent with gospel order, unbecoming a minister of the gospel towards their fellow-labourers . . . and calculated to sow discord among brethren, and produce disorder in the church." [26] With the fierce fervor of a crusader, Ann Jones returned a week later and repeated much she had previously said. Edward Hicks must have had Anna Braithwaite, Elizabeth Robson, and Ann Jones in mind when he wrote of the "great importance of superior women always being right, for when they get wrong they are so difficult to manage." [27] Of the visitors in general he commented, "The English Friends spread themselves over the continent, and where ever they went they separated husbands and wives, parents and children, brothers and sisters, and the nearest and dearest of friends." [28]

Although Joseph John Gurney did not come to America during this period, his books—five of which were published before 1828—were widely circulated. Stephen Gould wrote to Thompson in Liverpool that Gurney's works were the best books that had yet been printed on the peculiarities of Friends, though some Friends felt there were places where "they might be bettered." Of Gurney's *Letter to a Friend on the Authority, Purpose and Effects of Christianity, especially on the Doctrine of Redemption* he said, "they are all good . . . points plainly stated in them with respect to the Scriptures and the coming of our . . . Saviour, which in some former Yearly Meetings would have not passed, now there is no objection. . . ." [29] Elias Hicks ranked Gurney with the Presbyterian and Episcopalian clergy. Thomas Shillitoe, another English Friend who was shortly to become Hicks' most powerful opponent, later said of Joseph John Gurney, "I declare the author is an Episcopalian, not a Quaker . . . no Quaker in principle. Episcopalian views were imbibed from his education, and still remain with him. . . . He has spread a linsey-woolsey garment over our members." [30]

To many Americans, Elias Hicks was the great commoner standing against the wealthy, cultured, and urbane foreigners. I. Stephenson wrote to a nephew of Elizabeth Robson, "The prejudice against

English Friends is very great. I think entirely proceeding from warm attachment to Elias Hicks." [31] John Bunting told William Poole that almost every Meeting opposed the conduct of the English Friends, feeling they "left the real principles of Early Friends and were approaching nearly to other Societies as regard faith and doctrine . . . even these ministers contend that the more sure word of Prophecy . . . is nothing but the Scriptures." [32]

One result of the feeling created against English Friends found expression in the treatment of the annual Epistle from London. Until 1823, these Epistles stressed the need for obedience to the Light of truth, manifested by obedience to the testimonies; in that year Orthodox statements began to appear. New York Yearly Meeting, which usually reprinted fifteen hundred copies of the London Epistle for circulation among its members, discontinued republishing the document. In 1825 the Epistle was not read in the Yearly Meeting.[33] Baltimore also discontinued reprinting the London Epistle but read it on the floor of the Meeting. When New England Meeting for Sufferings learned that New York was not distributing the Epistle, it directed the printing of an additional three thousand copies in pamphlet form to be sent into New York state! [34] With bitterness engendered by conflicting religious teachings, the Quakers were fast losing the right to call themselves "The Society of Friends."

XX

"Reason Is the Recipient

of Revelation"

ACCORDING TO ELIAS HICKS, the Society of Friends was in a mixed, unstable condition after 1823. "I fear a great portion of the ministry amongst us is doing more harm than good, and is leading back to the weak and beggarly elements to which some seem desirous to be again in bondage." [1] Elias told William Poole that he was "slandered, reviled, and defamed, by pulpit, press, and talk . . . [called] a deist, seducer, socinian, [and] unitarian." These charges rested on the fact that he "faithfully and honestly bore testimony against those false and unscriptural, though generally acknowledged and applauded doctrines, of one God subsisting in three distinct and separate persons; the impossibility of God's pardoning sinners without plenary satisfaction; and the justification of impure persons by an imputative righteousness, &c." [2] He declared it was a falsehood that he denied the divinity of Christ. "If Christ is the power and wisdom of God," he said in the same letter, "then certainly Christ the Saviour is God. . . . I assert the unity of God and Christ; although nominally distinguished, yet essentially the same Divine Light; and I have ever believed that the divinity of God and Christ are one—but I do not believe in two divinities." Elias noted that his friend seemed alarmed by the stir and dissension which was taking place in some parts of "the favoured, but at the same time lukewarm and lethargic Society." It was his opinion that the shakings through which the organization was going would reveal any unsoundness and open the way to honest seekers for truth.

Stephen Grellet, who now moved his residence from New York to Burlington, New Jersey, looked on conditions otherwise. "I left New York very mournfully," he noted, "deeply was my heart affected towards very many of our religious Society. I feel very tenderly for a little remnant left there who love the Truth." After a few months' residence in Burlington, he added, "I feel peaceful in having come here; but my sadness is not lessened; the little dark cloud, which years past, rested chiefly over a small spot in Jericho, on Long Island, is now like a thick darkness over the land." [3]

There were many strange and novel doctrines preached at New York Yearly Meeting of 1824, according to Elias' way of thinking. These included, "our victory over sin is not to be known on this side of the grave; that the humanity of Jesus Christ prays to his own divinity; that not to believe that the crucifixion . . . was a sufficient atonement for the sins of the whole world, unchristians us, and renders us criminal." [4] The sessions, on the whole, were harmonious, but there were increasing reports sent up from subordinate Meetings of public Friends finding opposition to their ministry. The Yearly Meeting sent down an Epistle calling attention to such marks of disunity:

The numerous and increasing instances, of the want of love and unity amongst us, has produced deep exercise and concern. As children of the same universal Parent, as professed followers of the same Blessed Lord, and Redeemer, powerful is the claim upon us to love each other; and how strongly it is enforced by the nature of our religious compact— a society called from the spirit of the world . . . how firm should be the band that connects us, in religious fellowship. "By this shall all men know ye are my disciples, if ye have love one to another." [5]

After Yearly Meeting, Elias, Jemima and their daughter Elizabeth visited Meetings in Stanford and Cornwall Quarters. Elias wrote back from Little Esopus to the three daughters in Jericho that they were having a pleasant journey, "not a tongue has risen against us and we have been received with tokens of joy." They were among rugged mountains and on stony highways. "Packed in the carriage," he said, "tossed from side to side as to make our flesh feel sore, we pass cheerfully on in calm acquiescence to those bodily afflictions. Your mother and sister make some pleasant remarks on our up and down tossed condition." [6]

Elias went on to visit Baltimore Friends in time for their Yearly Meeting, and considered he never attended a better one. On the return journey he stopped at Brandywine to console his friend William Poole on the death of his wife. In Philadelphia, Elias was taken severely ill and for a time there seemed but little prospect of his recovery. Jemima was sent for, and on this occasion made her only trip south of New York. When Elias was able to be about he spoke in a number of the city Meetings, and at those in the nearby counties. These sermons were taken down by a stenographer and later published by Marcus T. C. Gould without Elias' consent. They made a volume of some 320 pages, entitled *A Series of Extemporaneous Discourses*. In these twelve sermons, given when he was seventy-six, the Jericho minister fully set forth his views on both social and religious issues. He was still shaken by his illness, for he said at Abington, "It is likely this is the last time I shall see you here, or tread this floor, but my love for you is such, that I desire, after my decease you may remember these things, and realize them in your own experience." [7]

At Trenton the legislature was in session and so many desired to hear Hicks that the governor and legislature offered him the use of the State House. In New York City, Elias spoke feelingly of the mercy and grace of God who revealed Himself to every man, "I know that God is no respector of persons, from my own experience, or he would not have looked upon me a poor careless boy, ignorant of his true character, and wholly unworthy of his mercy." Elias spoke of the possibility of reading many books, studying science, and yet being ignorant of God. "It is God's revelation to the rational soul of man which gives true knowledge of his character, and the true faith which is exercised; it is a rational faith, for reason is the recipient of revelation. Deprive men of reason and there is nothing for revelation to act upon." "My religion," said Elias, "is from experience. . . . His voice spake to me in melting and powerful strains: Cease to do evil, and learn to do well. Leave off the vanities of the world, and set thy affections upon things unseen and eternal. . . . I was dead in trespasses and sins, and deaf to all the calls of mercy. But his grace quickened me, and unstopped my deaf ears, so that I heard the words of peace and pardon." [8]

Elias wrote Roger Brooke in Sandy Spring that after the gathering at Pine Street, when he moved along the gallery taking friends by the hand, "My old friend, and once united fellow labourer with me, Jonathan Evans, refused to give me his hand. . . . No other friends refused me their hand, except two in N.Y." [9] Elias was cited the month after he left Philadelphia in the Preparative Meeting of Ministers and Elders of Western District. No case was made out against the visitor; Friends were asked to dwell in patience, cherish moderation, and be charitable toward one another. An elder, on his own initiative, however, brought what he considered to be Hicks' unsoundness before Western Monthly Meeting. After a very heated discussion the Clerk refused to forward any minute to Jericho. During the session Israel Yarnall exclaimed, "If it be understood by the report,—if it set forth and declare, that Elias Hicks, the last time he was in this house, preached doctrines contrary to the Holy Scriptures, and contrary to our first and primitive Friends, being present at that time, I stand here as a witness that it is utterly false." [10] An unbecoming disorder prevailed and complaint was made against Yarnall who belonged to North Street Meeting. He was disowned by this Monthly Meeting but reinstated by the Quarterly Meeting.

It is a matter of regret that Marcus Gould did not take down the first sermon Elias Hicks gave in Philadelphia in 1824, when Jonathan Evans refused to shake his hand. As Elias spoke strongly in some of the other sermons against those who did not deny themselves the use of slave products, it may be that it was at this point Jonathan Evans took offense, as he had done in 1819. Thomas E. Drake says, "His evangelical opponents may possibly have confused Hicks' free-produce ideas with his theological views." [11] Hicks declared that the denial of liberty to the Negroes was worse than the denial of common education and all other good things of the earth, while "here we are glutting ourselves with the toils of their labour!" A bit later he said the use of slave products made a man a thief. "They who strengthen the hand of the oppressor, evidently manifest a hatred to the oppressed. . . . What is the difference whether I hold a slave, or purchase the produce of his labour from those who do?" And added, "I say there is a black cloud hanging over us, and I can see no advancement that we can make till this greatest of evils is removed." [12]

Elias Hicks took the same matter up at Newtown. "Men and women," he said, "have reasoned themselves into a belief . . . that they may hold a fellow creature in slavery, and still be right. . . . It never was right, and never will be right." At Middletown, Elias said the American people were taking liberty from the Negroes, a crime only short of murder. "We have been the means of [their] degradation; it results from our wickedness and oppression." [13] It was such remarks as these that Jonathan Evans did not consider temperate or in the manner of the gentle John Woolman. Elias Hicks believed it was time for sterner measures.

Free Labor Societies were established in Delaware and Pennsylvania, free product stores opened in Baltimore. Elias secured fifty-two subscribers on Long Island to Benjamin Lundy's *Genius of Universal Emancipation*.[14] Ezra Michener of London Grove, Pennsylvania, asked permission to reprint Elias' *Observations,* and Thomas Fisher ordered five hundred copies of an edition which Elias had reprinted himself. An organization of New York City Negroes, wishing to honor Hicks for his work against slavery, named their burial society, "The New York African Hicks Association." [15]

Many letters came to Elias Hicks from well-wishers, as well as those who questioned his views. Answering these became a burden to him. He sometimes apologized to old correspondents like William Poole for the delay in answering their letters, as such a pile of writing accumulated on his desk. Cornelius Blatchly asked what Elias thought of the Shakers, and Elias replied that they were on a bad foundation since a state of communal sharing would promote idleness. Nathan Shoemaker sent his appreciation to Elias, writing "Thou hast been instrumental in enlightening my mind and . . . opening in a degree of clearness some things that hitherto had been to me mysterious and irreconcilable with reason and the common principles of justice and mercy." [16] Friends sent Hicks copies of *The Berean, The Christian Inquirer,* and the *Advocate of Truth,* all publications of a liberal nature.

Elias Hicks was much distressed by two letters. One was from Moses Brown, in Providence, taking him to task for remarks that he had made in his public ministry, for his conflict with Anna Braithwaite, and his letter to Dr. Shoemaker. Elias replied in humility that he had expressed what was in his heart, and that he regretted nothing that he had written. "But I stand always open to conviction," he wrote, "and if any person, even a child, should convince me of any error it contains, I shall cheerfully yield it up, and acknowledge myself wiser than when I wrote it." He then gave an interesting exposition of his use of the Bible. He said it was no contradiction to hold at one time "that the Scriptures were the best book [in the world]," and at another time that they had done "more harm than good." This paradox was evident if his writings were carefully scanned. He believed the Scriptures did more harm than good to those who held the Bible as the only rule of faith and practice, as such a view led to a divided Christendom, wars, and persecutions. But if rightly used under Divine Guidance the Bible was a blessing. In answer to an accusation of Moses Brown's that Hicks was out of unity with Friends, Elias answered that year by year for forty years he had secured certificates to travel, always endorsed with the unity of his Monthly and Quarterly Meetings. "What should induce thee to mention a wish for my returning into the unity of my friends," Elias asked, "when I have not been out of it? unless it be in [the case of] some few individuals, who have been led away from the truth, and on their parts have broken the unity towards me, without any cause given by me." [17]

Elias Hicks was more disturbed by a letter from Hugh Judge, now settled in Ohio, in which Hugh repeated all the Evangelical charges made against his old friend. Elias patiently called Hugh's attention to the conflicting statements of the conception of Jesus found in Matthew, Luke, Mark, John, and Paul. He wrote that these did not affect his belief respecting the miraculous birth of Jesus, but he presumed, "Divine Wisdom permitted these different sentiments to prevent our laying too great stress on mere written testimonies or even on outward miracles for nothing but the Spirit of God can teach us the things of God." He considered this to be Barclay's position. Elias believed in miracles, he was certain God did intervene in human affairs, and that all the wonders of the old covenant were to point out to the people that there was a living and invisible God. Thus he ended, "Sooth thyself, my dear friend, and be quiet and trouble not thyself on my account. If thee could be one day with me it would ease thee from thy troubles." [18]

Edward Hicks came to New York Yearly Meeting in 1825. He now found it lucrative to paint carriages for his Long Island relatives, Willet and Samuel Hicks, and their friends. Before the sessions began, Elias joined his cousin and they spoke at gatherings in the city. Edward's sermons reflect a deepening feeling of impending calamity. "It is a dreadful crisis," he exclaimed, "the spiritual Jerusalem seems to be invested from every side. We seem to be giving way to the same spirit which the Jews possessed at the seige of Jerusalem. They contended with each other. They fell into divisions, and strifes, and factions, and it is computed that more were destroyed by their own hands than by the Roman army." And later, "I am fully persuaded that if there was less tattling and scribbling, and more praying, there would be happiness among us. The spirit of bitterness and malignity is like the whirlwind, that threatens to carry us away in the tempest." [19]

The Yearly Meeting had received a letter from the Meeting for Sufferings of London Yearly Meeting, which indicated clearly the extent to which that body had accepted the Evangelical position:

Believing in the Divine authority of the Holy Scriptures, they therefore accepted as true the doctrines therein recorded, and were contented to receive that which infinite Wisdom had communicated to the inspired Writers. They were firm believers in the Divinity of our blessed Saviour . . . the eternal word . . . which became flesh, and dwelt among men. Their [the early Friends] writings also bear testimony to their belief that the Son of God offered himself a sacrifice for the sins of mankind, that he is our Intercessor and Advocate with the Father; and that the salvation of the soul of man is obtained by this propitiatory offering, through obedience to the sanctifying power of the Spirit.[20]

To Elias Hicks, and those who agreed with his position, this exposition of the position of early Friends seemed to leave out all that was distinctive in their message.

At Westbury Quarterly Meeting following the Yearly Meeting, one of the English Friends, assisted by two New York Quakers, attacked Elias Hicks in the Ministry and Elders, no doubt quoting the letter received from London. "At the meeting his enemies appeared in battle array," Edward Hicks described the contest, "and as Elias never turned his back upon an enemy, something like a drawn battle was fought when, as it often happens, especially in religious contests, both sides claimed the victory." But Elias was much hurt by this encounter, "and as soon as he got in the carriage and the glasses were put up, he threw himself back and wept like a child . . . [but] on the next day in the general quarterly meeting he appeared strong in the Lord." [21]

Disturbed as he was by the attacks of the English Friends, Elias Hicks could still optimistically write to Roger Brooke in Sandy Spring that he felt nothing was wanting "to restore peace and harmony, but a strict adherence to our salutary discipline, which if rightly executed . . . no disorder can prevail . . . as it provides ample means for a settlement of all differences, and disorders that may occur." [22] He reminded his Maryland Friend that for more than forty years he had carried out the provisions of the Discipline and had never known it to fail. As examples, he cited the disturbances within the Society caused by the French and Indian Wars, and the struggle to clear the Society of slaves. Hicks did not realize that a new problem faced Friends which the Discipline could not adjudicate.

Contention was much greater in Philadelphia than in New York. John Comly was convinced that the Evangelical party planned to crush by disownment all those who did not agree with them, as the Irish Liberals and the New Lights of New England were silenced. He knew that an active New England leader suggested to a Philadelphia elder that fifteen or twenty of that city's Liberals be disowned in order to quiet the rest. Comly noticed that conscientious men and women who were moderates, solid influential Friends acting as heads of committees, were gradually being replaced by others who favored the Evangelical party. "A spirit of crimination and recrimination" grew, "meetings for discipline exhibited scenes of disorder and confusion. . . . Personal reflections and unbecoming asperities were cast on characters who once stood fair and impeccable," he wrote. "Many tender hearted Friends, disgusted, alarmed, and grieved, absented themselves from these scenes of confusion and strife. . . . The solemnity of silent adoration was disturbed by denunciations from the gallery against infidelity and other imagined absurdities. Doctrines . . . unheard in meetings of Friends, were reiterated and enforced with threatenings on those who dare to reject them." [23] Elias Hicks sent word to Roger Brooke that he heard resoundings of the strife of tongues. He was not moved by the new teachings, much of which could not be explained or made intelligible to the hearers, and which to him resembled old manna gathered from past days.[24]

Thomas Fisher sent word to Elias from Philadelphia that his father, Samuel, was very feeble, and hoped for a visit from his Long Island friend in the near future. He told of the powerful preaching of Thomas Wetherald of Washington who had visited in the Philadelphia area. This strong advocate of rational religion believed so deeply in progressive revelation, that he acknowledged his personal creed might change from day to day.[25] Desiring to visit the home where he was so hospitably received over the years, Elias Hicks and Jesse Merritt, with minutes of endorsement, set off for Southern and Concord Quarters of Philadelphia Yearly Meeting in the fall of 1826. At Chester, Elias told his hearers that the disciples of Jesus were taught to believe, "through a revelation in themselves that Jesus was the true Messiah."[26] He added, "I believe that should [Jesus] come now, he would stand as great a chance to be crucified as he did in that day; for his righteousness would so exceed ours, that we should be unwilling to conform to the cross."[27]

At a crowded gathering at Pine Street, Philadelphia, Elias spoke of the need for brotherly love. "For to be a Christian, we must not only be possessed of love, but it must be the ruling principle of all our actions." He pleaded for "a religion of experience—a religion of love, arising out of the life giving presence of the Heavenly Father." He then repeated some of his main tenets, the innocency of man at birth, man's ability to follow God's will, salvation through an operative faith, the divinity of Jesus Christ brought about through union with the spirit of God, his unique place as Savior of the Jewish people, the divine Light and Life given by God to all men.[28] When Elias sat down, Jonathan Evans rose and said, "I believe it right for me to say, that our Society believed in the atonement, mediation, and intercession of our Lord and Saviour Jesus Christ— that by him all things were created, in heaven and earth. . . . Great efforts are making, to make people believe that Jesus Christ was no more than a man, but we do not believe any such thing, nor can we receive any such doctrine, or anything which goes to inculcate such an idea." [29] Another elder, Isaac Lloyd, united with Jonathan Evans. Elias remarked, "I have spoken; and I leave it for the people to judge —I don't assume the judgement seat." Willet Hicks then asked for a time of quiet, urging remembrance of the testimony that "the Holy Ghost would be sent, and that it would lead and guide into all truth." [30]

That afternoon, at Twelfth Street Meeting, a very large body gathered and Elias spoke on "Vanity of Vanities." The experience of the author of Ecclesiastes Elias turned into an argument for following the true light, which was the rock or revelation of the spirit of God. Thomas Wistar, an elder of this Meeting, expressed disapprobation when Elias finished, and again Willet Hicks pleaded for guidance of the spirit which would lead into love of the brethren. Two days later at Key's Alley Meeting, the disorder was even greater. Two Friends contradicted Elias' teachings. Philadelphia Pemberton declared that "Jesus Christ died upon the cross . . . and ascended on high, and is seated at the right hand of the Majesty in heaven, there to make intercession for us. And it is only through him, that we have access to the Father . . . it is only and alone through him, that we can be saved; therefore, my dear friends, look well to your standing." Wishing to prevent confusion, Elias added, "God is a God of order—and it will do me great pleasure to see this meeting sit quiet till it closes. We have, and claim gospel privileges, and that every one may be persuaded in his own mind; and as we have gifts differing, so ought everyone to have an opportunity to speak, one by one, but not two at once, that all may be comforted . . . if you love me you will keep strict order; it will be a great comfort to my spirit." Othniel Alsop then spoke feelingly of Jesus Christ as the mediator, but in a few moments there were marks of disapproval and the last of what he said could not be heard. Elias Hicks again asked for, and secured, order. He added, "It was only the inspired spirit of God, that enabled the primitive disciples to know God; and without this inspiration no man ever did know God. We learn, likewise, that the name is the *power;* and this is not contained in the five letters that spell *Jesus*—no one of common sense will suppose this. But it was the power of his heavenly Father that was in him, when active on earth. He tells us, that it was his Father that enabled him to do miracles . . . 'for my Father is greater than I.' " [31]

While Elias Hicks was making his round of visits in the two Quarters, both Pine and Twelfth Street Monthly Meetings lodged complaints against him because of the doctrines he preached, and because of the disorder that accompanied some of the gatherings. After much discussion, a minute was endorsed which stated that "the doctrines and sentiments of Elias Hicks greatly tend to the subversion of sound religious principles, and of wholesome restraints of moral and domestic discipline." [32] Isaac W. Morris and Jasper Cope were directed to carry the minute to Jericho Monthly Meeting, setting out immediately. The two Friends reached the Jericho Business Meeting a little late, just in time to hear certificates of approbation read concerning the southern trip of Elias Hicks from Southern Quarterly Meeting and Darby Monthly Meeting, Green Street, Abington, and Byberry. Morris and Cope presented their documents to the Clerk, John Ketcham, who informed the Meeting briefly of the contents. A committee was appointed to consider the papers and the Meeting continued "in harmony and concord." In the course of the session, Elias asked for the unity of the Meeting in making family visits in Jericho and Westbury neighborhoods. The request met with cordial approval. At the close of the business, the Jericho minister urged the Philadelphia messengers to go home with him to dinner, but they "pleaded a pre-engagement to dine elsewhere." The next month the letters from Pine and Twelfth streets were read and "unitedly reprobated by the meeting, as comprehending little beside falsehood and calumny, and were judged to be unworthy of a place on the minutes, and were accordingly rejected and no further notice taken of them." [33] Under Quaker discipline, Philadelphia could take no further action against Elias Hicks.

After this encounter, Elias wrote to William Poole, "I am now about retiring to the king's gate . . . there to await fresh orders and whether it may be to retire from the field of labour and rest for a while, and put my house in order, and be prepared to go hence and be seen of men no more on this stage of action; or, whether I may be called to some small chores of farther labour in the vineyard of the heavenly husbandman, suited to my declining years, I know not, but cheerfully submit to His Heavenly disposal." [34]

XXI

Climax

of Dissent

SECTIONALISM and a new tide of democratic sentiment were strong in the United States in 1827, soon bringing Andrew Jackson to the Presidency. The Disciples were organizing as a denomination, the American Unitarian Association was in its second year. Some Methodists were becoming restive under the power wielded by the Bishops and considered establishing a Methodist Church without Bishops. The development of new denominations was not a mark of weakness in Christianity, but a sign that old forms could not contain all its vitality. Kenneth S. Latourette points out that "never in any one century had so many movements emerged from within Christianity as in the nineteenth century, and never before had the Christian movement exhibited so great an influence upon mankind." [1] The regrettable fact concerning the Separation which began among Philadelphia Quakers in the spring of 1827 was the manner of its accomplishment. Projected as a peaceful solution of incompatible ideas, the Separation was marked by bitterness and animosities.

The blame for the events which took place has been placed on the shoulders of many individuals and groups of Friends—Elias Hicks, the English Friends, the Philadelphia elders, John Comly, wealthy and aristocratic city Quakers, democratic farmers in country Meetings, antislavery agitators, the Evangelicals, and the Rationalists. The real heresy lay in the lack of love shown by some of the leaders and by many of the followers. Neither party to the conflict possessed historical insight, both claimed to represent primitive Quakerism. The Evangelicals insisted that certain truths were absolutes, the Liberals that new truths might be revealed.

Edward Hicks oversimplified the situation, yet spoke an important truth, when he said, "The Orthodox spirit has most improperly and unjustly dubbed as Hicksites the great body of Friends constituting the Yearly Meeting of Philadelphia, when neither Elias Hicks nor his doctrines had anything to do with our Quaker revolution in Pennsylvania, which originated in a contest between the republicanism of William Penn, planted in America and cherished by the free institutions of our country, and the aristocracy of London Yearly Meeting. If we must have a nick-name there would be much more propriety in calling us Comlyites." [2] It was John Comly, Assistant Clerk of Philadelphia Yearly Meeting, who precipitated the division of that Yearly Meeting.

Early in the year, Comly, much distressed by the spirit of contention existing within the City of Brotherly Love and spreading into outlying areas, mingled with Friends in the city Monthly Meetings to ascertain whether there remained any grounds for a reconciliation. In the Quarterly Meeting of Ministers and Elders he found a domineering spirit. Elsewhere he discovered an evident wish to blow the sharp breath of incrimination on the coals of strife. Everywhere he met with coldness and inhospitality. He expected the Orthodox, through their control of important committees, would disown all Liberals. The Byberry teacher sorrowfully concluded that the Society must divide, and conceived a plan by which something could be saved from the wreckage. He thought those who were tired of contention, who refused to be dominated by a minority, should peacefully separate themselves. [3]

Inspired prophets never hesitate to act on their insights without weighing the possible results. The inward voice brooked no compromise, the consequences must take care of themselves. Comly did not foresee that a quiet retreat meant dividing families and friends, engendering bitter lawsuits over property rights. Certain his plan was the correct one, John Comly—a beloved figure to many—traveled through the Monthly and Quarterly gatherings pleading for a temporary separation. In due season, when peace and harmony developed, Comly maintained that Friends would again worship together. He convinced William Poole of the wisdom of his solution, and the latter passed the suggestion on to Elias Hicks. Hicks wrote that in such a time of intemperance and intolerance no one could remain neutral, lest by his neutrality he assist those who were opposing the truth, but passed no judgment upon Comly's plan. Edward Hicks insisted that his cousin "never united with John Comly's excellent Christian plan of re-organizing the Yearly Meeting, through its constituent branches, nor came into it, till after it was effected." [4]

Those who saw the situation as did John Comly, believed that harmonious action within Philadelphia Yearly Meeting was impossible. At the instigation of three English Friends, the Meeting for Sufferings appointed a Select Committee for visiting all bodies of Ministers and Elders to inspect theological soundness. The Meeting for Sufferings refused to accept changes in its membership; Philadelphia Quarterly Meeting ruled that Eldership was a lifetime appointment. On Green Street Meeting objecting, Philadelphia Quarterly Meeting dissolved it.

The Clerk of the Yearly Meeting, Samuel Bettle, refused to give any consideration to opinions expressed if the speaker opposed the publication of the "Creed" in 1823.[5] Country Friends thought the only way to secure the control warranted by their numbers was the appointment of a new Clerk. They hoped to elevate the Assistant Clerk, John Comly; thus, in 1827, they appointed a larger number of representatives to the Yearly Meeting than usual. Again they were outmaneuvered. The time of the first session was consumed in debating without agreement the merits of John Comly and Samuel

Bettle. Had the representatives been allowed to present a compromise Clerk at a later session, the Separation might not have taken place.

At the next Business Meeting, John Comly proposed that the Yearly Meeting—since it was not in unity—adjourn without stating a time for reconvening. Samuel Bettle was unwilling to permit this action, so the friends of Comly began holding evening gatherings in the Green Street Meeting House, planning an orderly retreat. At the last session of the 1827 Yearly Meeting, it was suggested, and without general consent approved, that a Select Committee be appointed to visit each Meeting to test the soundness of the membership. As only Quakers agreeing with the views of Jonathan Evans, Joseph Whitall, and Samuel Bettle were named to this committee, the Comly party was convinced that "the Yearly Meeting was now usurped by orthodox power, and henceforth to be under their control and direction, as Philadelphia Quarter was." [6] Meetings were continued at Green Street, an address prepared and sent to all Philadelphia Friends declaring that a division existed because of incompatible views. The authors asserted, "Doctrines held by one part of the Society, and which we believe to be edifying and sound, are pronounced by the other part to be unsound and spurious. . . . Measures have been pursued which we deem oppressive." Therefore a quiet retreat from the scenes of confusion was in order. They taught no new Gospel, nor proclaimed any message not held by their forefathers. The often quoted phrase, "Christ within the hope of Glory," was used, with a new and much-to-be repeated phrase, "GOD ALONE IS THE SOVEREIGN LORD OF CONSCIENCE." The essay ended with a call for a gathering of representatives in June to consider holding a separate Yearly Meeting.[7]

Many painful scenes were also enacted in the New York Yearly Meeting of 1827, and a great want of unity and love manifest. Elias Hicks told Isaac T. Hopper that it was the most distressing session he had ever known. This he considered to be the fault of the Clerk, Samuel Parsons, and of five English Friends in attendance. Andrew

Cook sent word to Benjamin Ferris that a large majority opposed the views of the "imported Brethren" and that this number grew daily because of their violent proceedings. He also spoke of the action of the Clerk, "who always took on himself the responsibility of deciding on which side of the question the weighty part of the Society lay . . . considering the opinions of seven or eight persons who sit on high seats weighs more than one hundred persons sitting below." [8]

The English minister, Thomas Shillitoe, often called the Quaker Whitefield, was most outspoken. He became a thorn in the flesh to Elias Hicks during the next two years. Elbert Russell notes that Shillitoe was a convinced member who brought into the Society many of the Evangelical doctrines of the Church of England. Rufus M. Jones says Shillitoe accepted Quaker ways and customs, and was as sensitive to inward guidance as Job Scott or John Comly, but his mind-set was different, and his eager passionate love for saving souls and for rebuking unorthodox opinions had disastrous effects upon American Friends.[9] Thomas Shillitoe had traveled widely in Great Britain and on the Continent, and was seventy-two when he landed in New York in 1826. He considered it his duty to stimulate Friends to precipitous action, and at his first gathering in Hester Street made clear his opposition to Elias Hicks, stating "he did not come to America to help [Elias'] unchristian cause." [10] Shillitoe visited Samuel Parsons in Flushing, and Gideon Seaman and Thomas Willis in Westbury and Jericho. Elias Hicks was standing in his doorway when Shillitoe passed through Jericho and invited the English minister to be his guest, but Shillitoe declined. Elias invited him to call, and Elias' friends urged such a visit, but Shillitoe did not accept the invitation. After a searching testimony by the Englishman in Jericho Meeting, Elias added, "It was the prayer of my heart in sitting down in this meeting, that as we had a dear friend with us . . . we might be edified and instructed by his ministry. How fully has the prayer been answered, how clearly has he been led to set forth the efficacy and sufficiency of the Divine light, as ye have often heard it held up in this place; I appeal to this assembly if it is not the same doctrine, that ye have heard these many years past." [11] The two Quaker mystics saw eye-to-eye when speaking of the true inwardness of Quakerism, but they parted company on the new theologies.

Thomas Shillitoe admitted traveling through America under the watchword, "Go not from house to house." [12] He effectively cut himself off from all who did not share his views, and made it clear that he was opposed to the rationalism of Quaker Liberals. He visited extensively in New York Yearly Meeting and in Canada; he was back in New York City in time for the Yearly Meeting of 1827.

Although feelings rose high, there was not the disorder rampant in Philadelphia. Shillitoe mentioned the treatment of the English ministers. Many objected when Elizabeth Robson desired to speak in the Men's Meeting, and when Samuel Parsons minuted consent several hundred left the building during her discourse. A strong effort was made, pushed by the English visitors, to have a Select Committee visit Monthly and Quarterly Meetings concerning soundness of faith, but this was disapproved by the Liberals, who were in a large majority.

Elias Hicks wrote to Roger Brooke, "It was in general a boisterous time, but very few pleasant flowers or salutary dews were witnessed . . . black clouds [soon] darkened the horizon, and the wind [began] to blow, accompanied at times with pretty sharp flashes of lightning, and loud peals of thunder, which tended greatly to annoy us, and interrupt the Solemnity of the Meeting, insomuch that it was doubtful whether our coming together was for the better or for the worse; but I don't know that any lives were lost." [13] Elias added that Elizabeth Robson was making a tour of Long Island confining her visits chiefly to Presbyterians and Episcopalians who seemed to unite heartily with her views. Edward Stabler of Alexandria, also a visitor at the Yearly Meeting, wrote, after mature consideration of the conflict in the Society he "came to a clear and decided judgment, that the deep, spiritual, and practical views of Elias Hicks, so little understood and so greatly misrepresented, were in accurate accordance with the Christian religion." To his wife he sent word, "I am now writing at the house of the dear old patriarch, Elias Hicks. . . . It may be truly said, that our hearts fare sumptuously every day . . . after the most tumultuous and uncomfortable Yearly Meeting that I ever sat in. I never saw the equal of the endeavours made by some in that meeting, to sow discord and confusion: but they were ultimately defeated in their purpose." [14]

Stephen Gould, on the Orthodox side, wrote to his friend in Liverpool that in New York Yearly Meeting there were "scenes of confusion, ranterism or jacobinism, unparalleled." He reported that at times six or seven people were on their feet at once, individuals thumped on the floor to express their approbation of actions taken, and youths clapped their hands. He mentioned that Thomas and Anne Willis of Jericho could not attend the sessions as they were "under dealing" by Westbury Quarterly Meeting.[15]

The June Conference was held at Green Street Meeting, Philadelphia, and issued an epistle recounting the five years of discord, the public opposition to ministers traveling with minutes, unjust charges of preaching infidel doctrines, seizure of power by an officious minority, and threats to the preservation of religious liberties. The epistle summoned, in October, "A Yearly Meeting . . . upon the principles of the early professors of our name, and for the same purpose that brought them together in a religious capacity." [16] Elias' old friends William Gibbons and Benjamin Ferris signed as clerks.

Elias Hicks did not attend the October General Conference or General Yearly Meeting, but Valentine was present. Elias sent word to William Poole, "In regard to the movements of my friends in Philadelphia and adjacent parts, I feel nothing but peace and quietness when I look towards them, for, I trust, I feel them in that love that casts out fear, but I have not, as yet, found it my place actively to put a hand to it." [17] Subsequent events indicate that Elias was not in full accord with John Comly's plan, rather, he agreed with Evan Lewis who wrote to Benjamin Ferris:

There is one capital error which the Pennsylvania Friends committed which I very much regretted at the time and subsequent event have only confirmed the opinion I have had of its policy and this was *withdrawing* from the Orthodox. When the division took place, which was unavoidable I admit, it ought to have been done by the minority departing from the body. And, as far as I can see, it appears clearly to me that it only wanted union in purpose, and concert in action, to consummate this object. If the liberals had marched in solid column, and by direct strength and numbers affected a breach in the ranks of their opponents they would have been compelled to yield and would have left the field! In New York Yearly Meeting the proportion of the Orthodox is probably not much different than at Pennsylvania, but here when a division takes place which will not be long, the minority will leave the majority in possession of the field *and this is as it should be*. The separation as it has been in Pennsylvania has given a pretext to the other party which they ought never to have had, and which they have used much to your disadvantage in the Western Yearly Meetings.[18]

Elias could hardly believe that all the stir and confusion among Friends was the result of "a little difference of opinion on abstract subjects." These difficulties seemed more like a judgment of God upon the Quakers, sent because so many were "glutting themselves with the fruits of slave labor." "How can we ask or hope for better days," he exclaimed, "until the greatly oppressed is redressed and relieved from cruel bondage?" He added in a note to Emmor Kimber, some months after Yearly Meeting, "Friends in our Island, since our European Friends have left us, are generally preserved in harmony and concord. . . . It would be cause of thankfulness and gratitude . . . if they should not be permitted to come again amongst us until they ceased from sowing the seeds of discord and dissention." [19]

Valentine and Abigail brought back a full report concerning the October gathering of Liberal Friends. About 2,400 were in attendance, the women meeting in the Green Street building, and the men in a long shed, 100 by 45 feet, erected nearby. Plans were made for a Yearly Meeting in April, 1828, ten thousand copies of a general epistle ordered, and a more personal epistle written for Baltimore Yearly

Meeting, soon to be in session. Valentine told his Jericho Friends that the Orthodox party was rigorously disowning every Liberal. In some cases two or three families, gathered in a private home, disowned several hundred Friends who continued to assemble in the Meeting House. Southern Quarterly Meeting, with its subordinate Monthly Meetings, was laid down by a simple minute. Valentine felt no greater example of the animosities aroused could be cited than the case of the Western District Burial Ground. This property had been purchased in 1817 by the five city Monthly Meetings. Each appointed trustees to hold title, and committees for managing the grounds and making arrangements for interments. The Orthodox party, acting on the thesis that Green Street Meeting no longer existed, endeavored to exclude their members from the grounds. Scenes were enacted which were disgraceful to the name of Friend. Green Street members came with ladder and axe to climb the wall and break the locks which Orthodox Friends placed on the entrance gate. "Idle disposed persons came to watch." Green Street Friends then prepared to erect a new gate in the wall, and while in the midst of these operations one of the Orthodox committee approached and was told "in the perfect manner of Friends . . . thee had better go away; thee will get dust on thee." A warrant was issued against the Liberal Friends by the mayor on request of the Orthodox. When bail for future good conduct was refused, several Liberals spent three weeks in jail. At the trial the judge ruled "neither Shotwell nor his companion were guilty of any offence . . . they had entered the grounds upon a clear claim of right." [20]

Early in January, 1828, Elias suffered from a severe infection caused by the bite of a cat. He was unable for some weeks to do any manual work or keep up his correspondence. However, the pains of the body were but preparation for "the passage through the Valley of the Shadows of Death," also "made death to the body as a mere shadow indeed to the upright in heart." [21] Elias spent the time in reading. Copies of *The Friend,* newly published by the Orthodox party in Philadelphia, showed how deeply the Society was stirred by the recent Separation. *The Berean,* though not published by Quakers, and *The Friend or Advocate of Truth,* gave the liberal point of view of the day. In reading *The Friend* Elias Hicks was disturbed by the many articles attacking his emphasis upon the sufficiency of the Inner Light. He was certain that the Society was born in protest against stereotyped theological doctrines as much as in opposition to priests and external sacraments. A return to a religion of "notions" would abrogate the reformation attempted in the seventeenth century. Reading such articles, Elias Hicks determined that he had one further service to render the Society. After the 1828 New York Yearly Meeting, he hoped to lay his desire for a right interpretation of Quakerism before all whom he could reach. He presented this concern to Jericho Monthly Meeting, which recorded, "Our ancient and beloved friend Elias Hicks in a weighty manner opened to this meeting a prospect that has been for a considerable time impressive on his mind to make a visit in the love of the Gospel to friends and others in some parts of this, Philadelphia, Baltimore, Virginia, Ohio, and Indiana Yearly Meetings." [22] The concern was united with.

Meanwhile, several Pennsylvania Friends desired Elias to attend the Liberal Yearly Meeting set for April, 1828, and urged he promptly send word of his coming since his presence "would have a gathering and settling effect upon some who are wavering." [23] Before going, Elias wrote that there would be difficulties in reorganizing the new Yearly gathering. He recalled how his own family divided during the Revolutionary War, "three against two, and two against three," while he stood between as a moderator. Those who stood for the old government were fierce and determined to rule those they called rebels and infidels; they believed they were right and that the Lord was with them, though Elias told these brothers that "they were or might be mistaken." [24]

Elias Hicks went to the reorganized Yearly Meeting, where he found Willet Hicks, Hugh Judge, and Edward Stabler. Comly noted that 120 Friends attended the gathering of the Ministers and Elders; the men's business sessions were held in the Green Street Meeting

House, the women's in the new Cherry Street building. The Byberry teacher recorded, "Dear old Elias Hicks was there, and feelingly addressed the quiet, attentive assembly." In spite of rain and snow nearly 3,000 Quakers were present. "Many cementing seasons were vouchsafed . . . and the business was conducted and resulted in harmony and brotherly kindness." Comly expressed his feeling that the Separation was necessary by adding:

In the present momentous effort to regain that liberty of conscience which Truth gives, we may again be set free from the shackles with which we have been trammelled by a gradually ascending hierarchy . . . The true liberty of thought, of speech, and of the press, which is entirely distinct from *licentiousness,* may be again restored and enjoyed, to the advancement of the work of righteousness and of the real happiness of mankind . . . a way is opening, in which the various and precious gifts and operations of the Spirit may be more freely exercised.[25]

The Yearly Meeting decided not to deal with or to disown any Orthodox Friends, but to consider that membership in the Orthodox or Liberal Yearly Meeting was "an exercise of free agency." The Yearly Meeting extended an offer to divide Friends' property in proportion to the members in each Monthly Meeting.[26] An epistle stressing "the *one holy principle of Divine life and light in themselves"* in contradistinction to "the airy speculations of the professors of an outward religion" [27] was sent to London Yearly Meeting. The Epistle, however, never reached the floor of the English Meeting.[28]

To many who attended the parallel Yearly Meeting at Arch Street, attendance seemed nearly as large as usual. In both bodies there was harmony and peace in contrast to discord and confusion of the previous years. Orthodox Friends adopted the "Creed" rejected in 1823, and issued a *Declaration* charging Liberal Friends with being activated by principles of unbelief and insubordination, holding anti-Scriptural teachings, and openly denying the fundamental doctrines of the Christian religion. In the *Declaration,* Elias Hicks was held chiefly responsible for the views of the Liberal party; many pages were devoted to analyzing his messages. Although the words of the Jericho minister were often quoted out of context, the *Declaration* did clearly set forth the main differences between the two groups of Friends. Arch Street Quakers also contended that Elias Hicks, by attending the "General Association of the Separatists held . . . at Green Street . . . [established] beyond all doubt, his unity with them . . . and by placing a record on their minutes of his company, the Separatists, as a body, have formally identified themselves with him and his anti-christian doctrines, a declaration of which he openly made in very palpable terms, in one of their largest meetings on the preceding day." [29] Although Elias Hicks was not responsible for the division in Philadelphia, nor consulted about it, he was always associated with it. The Liberals were from then on generally called Hicksites.

XXII

Days of

Respite and Strife

THE SOCIETY OF FRIENDS was fast becoming a society of enemies. Although while at the Liberal Yearly Meeting in Philadelphia Elias Hicks did not go to Arch Street, Stephen Gould wrote his English friend, "It is hardly likely Elias Hicks would have been admitted to enter the premises even to attend a Public Meeting." [1] Lydia Mott of New York took a seat in the Orthodox Yearly Meeting but, because of her previous attendance at the Liberal sessions, was told to withdraw or be put out by force. Friends from Baltimore who were at Cherry Street eluded the vigilance of the guardians of the doors at Arch Street Meeting because they were not recognized. Other Friends, seen to climb the wall or go through the graveyard, were discovered and escorted into the street.

The Jericho minister returned to New York by steamboat with two concerns on his mind. One was to work on an extended Journal of his life and religious labors; the other to visit as many Friends in his own Yearly Meeting as possible before the annual sessions began. This would be the first stage in discharging the duties of the minute granted him in March.

Elias Hicks was under great pressure from his friends to write a formal Journal. William Poole first made the suggestion in 1823 during the controversy over the "Creed." He urged Elias to write a work similar to Job Scott's. At that time, Elias was not prepared to undertake such a work, although he was in the habit of keeping notes of his various journeys, and had some account of his life at Jericho. He seriously questioned the propriety of adding to the mass of historical material already in existence, thinking it might "tend to cloy and shut up the avenue of better instruction." He also questioned "whether what is revealed to one generation is as likely to be as profitable to a succeeding generation as to that, to which it was particularly directed." Hicks declared, "Every generation must have more light than the proceeding one, otherwise they must sit down at ease, in the labours and works of their predecessors." [2]

Emmor Kimber followed Poole's suggestion with a request that Elias put "his writings . . . in such order and be so arranged that a clear and decisive testimony may be left behind." He thought there were many thousands in Europe and America who had no clear idea of the doctrines Elias preached, who were "longing for something to satisfy their minds, remove shackles from their souls." He urged Elias to begin such a work at once.[3] Poole wrote giving new arguments for a Journal, to which his Jericho friend answered with a touch of humor, "The abuse of a blessing is no argument against its being dispensed, but it must be first proved that the thing dispensed is a blessing and was intended to be dispensed as such by the Great Dispenser of all real good." Elias was uneasy lest later ages would misconstrue his writings, that they would lead to contention and controversy. He concluded, "Could I pen down something that might be useful to the present and succeeding generations and then be obliterated it might not be amiss, but as I am looking forward with faith that greater and brighter things will be opened to succeeding generations than I and the people of this generation can bear, this makes me unwilling to leave anything of my experience, that might tend to hinder the reception of those new and advanced revelations." [4] He would not have his works used as the Orthodox were using the writings of primitive Friends, to silence new openings of truth.

But reasons for undertaking a major work increased. Poole asserted that Elias' letters were so instructive he was sharing them with members of his family and others. "I have been solicited many times to have them copied, but I have not known thy mind. I hope they might be made use of in a later year in a Journal of thy life." [5] Some of Elias' letters were printed—as was his correspondence with Thomas and Phebe Willis, and that with Anna Braithwaite—without his consent. Stenographers appeared unsolicited at Meetings for Worship and took down his sermons for publication. Benjamin Ferris, "Amicus" of old, and Evan Lewis of New York, wrote asking questions about his life, indicating they looked forward to writing biographical sketches about him. Elias Hicks might have written a Journal in any case, but it was probably the contest with the Philadelphia Elders and the disputes with the English Quakers that tipped the balance. He now desired to leave a record showing that he traveled for fifty years in the ministry, always with the unity of New York Friends, and that his emphasis on the Inner Light as the essence of Quaker preaching did not change from the days of his first sermon.

Elias was comparatively free from work on the farm in the winter time. He gave directions to "David the couloured man that has long lived with me" as to what was necessary to do, and within the house Ellenor, the mother of David, helped Jemima.[6] Elias took from his cherry desk some thirty travel diaries of his journeys in the gospel ministry and wished that he had written, or not lost, diaries of nearly as many additional missions.[7] He had before him the long home journal of the six years, 1813 to 1819. In his firm, clear handwriting, on foolscap folded 13 by 8 inches, he began, "Having experienced many mercies and preservations, both spiritual and temporal, in passing through this probationary state, I am induced to record some little account of them, under a sense of humble gratitude to my gracious and merciful Creator and Preserver." [8]

Elias wrote of his family, which received "honorable mention" in Samuel Bownas' Journal, of his parents who "sustained a good character among their friends," of his early life at Hempstead and Rockaway. He recalled the death of his mother when he had been a mere lad, his apprenticeship, and then the struggles within his soul against outward temptations, and "the merciful interposition of divine love." He had known times "of deep openings in the light," when he was instructed and comforted, and when a self-denying way opened to him. He wrote of his marriage with Jemima and "the clear consoling evidence of divine truth [which] remained as a seal upon our spirits, strengthening us mutually to bear, with becoming fortitude, the vicissitudes and trials which fell to our lot." His thoughts were sad, but his memories pleasant, as he recorded the story of his four sons and three daughters who did not survive. He remembered the "heavenly call" that came to him to speak in the Meeting at Jericho, of his hesitation, and of "the joy and sweet consolation that his soul experienced" when he yielded and became a messenger. He recalled the hours spent "for the right administration of discipline and order in the Church." [9] His first journey in the ministry came vividly to his mind.

The hours sped along as Elias put down his experiences in lonely frontier cabins, on long horseback rides through forests and over steep mountains, crossing great rivers and struggling against whirling snowstorms. He wove into his account the travel diaries from the cherry desk, and when none could be found remembered what he could, or condensed a labor of months into a paragraph. He recalled the hospitality enjoyed along the road, the friends he met. He was glad to discover that he had written something of the messages delivered from that first journey when preaching "the gospel of Christ, the work of regeneration and the new birth," [10] to his fuller expositions of the Inner Light and all its meanings. Elias filled over one hundred pages of foolscap before he reached the years covered by the home journal. It was a relief then to use this journal as it was written, placing between the pages—sandwich style—travel diaries of the

same period. By the time he covered the years through 1820, his manuscript was nearly four hundred pages long. Then he set it aside to
finish another time.

Elias spent as much time as possible before New York Yearly
Meeting visiting Friends along the Hudson. At Nine Partners, looking out over a meeting which he had addressed many times since 1781,
he summarized his primary message. He urged his listeners to bow
humbly before God, open their hearts to Him, and accept the regenerating power from on high. No guide book—not even the Bible—
was necessary to show them the way to Him, for the same Comforter
which visited Jesus and his disciples would visit them. He warned
his friends that the time was upon them when men would say: "I
am of Paul," "I am of Cephas," or "I am of Christ"; but they need
not be disturbed for in their own experience they would know who
He was. In a touching manner the patriarch ended his address, "It is
likely that I shall never see you again . . . but my friends, I would
not have you believe one word of what I say, unless by solid conviction." [11] Ann Jones interrupted the solemnity of the occasion by
saying, "We have heard considerably said, and we have heard, under a specious pretence of preaching the Gospel, the Saviour of the
world denied, who is God and Equal to God. And we have heard
the Scriptures had done more harm than good. We have also heard
the existence of a devil denied." [12] Elias merely observed that he was
well known in those parts and the people present could judge of
what he preached. He added that the Scriptures pointed to the Spirit,
which he believed was the doctrine of George Fox. This exchange
was typical of all other encounters between Elias Hicks and Ann
Jones.

As the Jericho minister looked forward to the Superior Meeting,
he felt in agreement with Samuel Titus who sent word to him that:

The state of things in our Religious Society are so wonderfully changed
and still changing from what they once were that I don't anticipate the
same satisfaction in the company of my friends who I love that I once

enjoyed. There was formerly a peculiarly pleasant sensation felt in the approach of our Superior Meeting, as well as a solacing recollection of them after they were past, which now seems almost if not altogether vanished away and gone . . . the same dividing and separating spirit has obtained an entrance among us that produced such sad effects in many places.[13]

Titus wrote his old friend that members at New Rochelle would welcome a visit from him, but he would find some deserters. Many more would rejoice in his visit, however, and Elias could be assured that "now in our advanced age I feel no diminution of love and esteem for thee."

Elias Hicks spoke in as many Quaker groups as time permitted, informing the membership of events taking place in Philadelphia, preparing them to prevent a like occurrence in their own Yearly Meeting. He was determined that if a division took place, Evan Lewis' prophecy should be fulfilled, the minority Orthodox party leaving the Liberals in control of the Yearly Meeting. Elias had learned during his last Pennsylvania trip that a peaceful separation, as proposed by John Comly, was impossible. On the other hand he was not willing for a third of the membership to remain in possession of the buildings in which the Yearly Meeting was held, thereby claiming to be the original body.

Stephen Gould wrote to Liverpool, just before New York Yearly Meeting began, that, "a most sorry time is anticipated at the approaching sessions . . . some of the leading Hixites have already avowed their intention to separate from the body if, as they term it, the present system of intolerance is persisted in . . . that is, I suppose, if they fail in displacing Samuel Parsons and Richard Mott as Clerks. . . . I look forward with hope and trembling fear . . . it will be at best an awful time." Gould evidently expected a repetition of the same action by Liberal Friends in New York as in Philadelphia. He added, "Elias Hicks and Willet have been travelling up north . . . stimulating their friends to appoint their own representatives . . . the bitterness and wrath that exists in the more northern

ELIAS HICKS, AN ENGRAVING BY SAMUEL MAVERICK FROM A PORTRAIT
BY HENRY INMAN. *Personal sorrows, a lifetime of rigorous living,
hard work, and heartfelt concern over the growing schism in the
Society of Friends are reflected in this study.*

ELIAS HICKS' CHERRY DESK. *Here Elias carried on his voluminous correspondence and wrote his Journal.*

Quarterly Meetings exceeds all belief." The country Friends grumbled about the manner in which the English ministers traveled, "contrasting the rich and costly packets" in which they came to America "at the expense of their friends" with the humble way in which John Woolman went to England in the steerage.[14] Some commented caustically on the coach and footman used by George and Ann Jones.

Earnest, conscientious, but determined Quakers set out for New York Yearly Meeting in May, many with heavy hearts. As Friends gathered it was evident that division already existed. In sessions of the Ministers and Elders on Seventh day the representatives were split into two factions, one desiring the reappointment of John Barrow, a friend of Elias Hicks, one desiring John Browne. As unity could not be secured, John Barrow minuted that fact, stating he would continue to serve only until the body was united, which he trusted would be at its next sitting. Some of the Orthodox representatives objected to the presence of Friends from the Liberal Yearly Meeting in Philadelphia, but the majority would not permit their exclusion.

On First day, Thomas Shillitoe attended worship at Hester Street in the morning, Elias Hicks at Rose Street. In the afternoon the two ministers exchanged places, throngs attending all gatherings. Monday morning the business session began with the usual Meeting for Worship. A much larger number of Quakers from other Yearly Meetings were present than usual. Among the ministers were Thomas Shillitoe, George and Ann Jones, and Elizabeth Robson from London; Stephen Gould and Thomas Howland from Rhode Island; Edward Stabler and Thomas Wetherald from Baltimore; David Osborne from Ohio. Visitors from Philadelphia included William F. Miller and James Foulke. Elias Hicks addressed the assembly "in a very solemn and impressive manner." He pleaded for patience, recommended a humble reliance upon God, and "pointed out in feeling and perspicuous language the nature and excellence of true religion, wholly dependent for its origin and progress on the revelation and power of His Spirit." [15] Thomas Shillitoe and George Jones added brief remarks, then Samuel Parsons, the Clerk, read the opening minute, followed by the list of representatives. Before he could proceed to reading the reports from Quarterly Meetings, which was the next order of business, Thomas Shillitoe arose and objected to the presence of Friends from Philadelphia who were known to have attended the separated Yearly Meeting in that city, and thus already disowned by Arch Street Friends. He declared it was his right to make this request since, having deposited his certificate from London, he was now as much a member of New York Yearly Meeting as any other Friend. Henry Hull and some others present supported Shillitoe's point of view; but Nicholas Brown of Canada West urged the Clerk to proceed with reading the reports "then the business would be regularly before the Meeting, and the Meeting *properly opened,* after which the subject that had been mentioned might claim its attention." [16]

At this point, Friends noted that Samuel Parsons, contrary to custom, had not brought the minute book of the Yearly Meeting, but was reading from a notebook. The lists of representatives were on scraps of paper. Nicholas Brown voiced his suspicions that the Clerk did not have the reports from the Quarterly Meetings. Friends argued back and forth until Elias Hicks observed that such discussion was beneath the dignity of the Meeting. He stated that "he did not believe there was an individual present that had not about as good a a right to a seat in that meeting as any of those who had objected." [17] Willet Hicks proposed that the reading of the reports be postponed until the various Yearly Meeting Epistles were read, when the session could decide whom it would receive and whom it would not. The Clerk refused, however, to proceed with any further business until Thomas Shillitoe's suggestion was acted upon, and the debate raged for two hours. Again the Jericho minister spoke. "We had heard," he said, "a great deal about seceders, separatists, and so forth, and the terms had been applied to Friends of what was called the new Yearly Meeting in Philadelphia. He was of an entirely different mind

—[the Orthodox] were the seceders who had separated themselves from the great body of the society." He attended with the consent of his Monthly Meeting the body gathering at Green Street and at Cherry Street and never attended a better Yearly Meeting. Indeed, he felt this body "the best and most effective . . . [and] *the cream of the society* in those parts." [18] To Hicks, the Liberal body was the legitimate Yearly Meeting for Friends in Pennsylvania, New Jersey, Delaware, and the Eastern Shore of Maryland.

Joseph Brown, an Evangelical minister, now proposed that Friends who objected to sitting with members of the Liberal Yearly Meeting of Philadelphia adjourn to the basement. Nicholas Brown declared that it was evident a minority of those present had planned a separation, that some of this group had met previously to arrange for steps to be taken, and that the Clerk sided with them and would not carry out the will of the greater number of Friends present. He objected to any adjournment and called upon the representatives present to nominate a Clerk who would carry out the sense of the Meeting as a whole rather than act for a party. Samuel Mott was named, but as he made his way towards the Clerk's desk, Samuel Parsons held up a paper which he proposed to read. Fearing that this was a minute for an adjournment, Friends protested. Samuel Parsons assured Elias Hicks that the minute was not for an adjournment, and Elias urged the members to let the Clerk read what he had at hand so that "the meeting would judge it." [19] As the Meeting was not convinced, an uproar ensued. There were "hisses, shouts, clapping of hands, stamping of feet, nay—among some of the young people—" according to an Orthodox observer, "curses and imprecations combined to raise so horrible a din" that the voice of Samuel Parsons was drowned completely.[20] After finishing the reading of the minute which he had written that morning in his lodgings—a minute for continuing the Yearly meeting in the basement of the Meeting House, not for adjourning it—Samuel Parsons left abruptly, leaving the notebook and lists of representatives on the table.

Samuel Mott was pulled forward by many hands "over the tops

of the benches and the heads of Friends." When he reached the gallery, Elias Hicks reached forth his hand also and helped Samuel Mott "clamber over the railing to the Clerk's desk." [21] In the meantime, approximately one-fourth of those present withdrew to the basement; finding the doors locked they crossed the street to Rutgers Medical College, which had been hired in case of such an emergency. Orthodox Friends anticipated that they would be unable to obtain possession of the Yearly Meeting as their brethren had done in Philadelphia. The larger Yearly Meeting, with sixty-three of the eighty-three representatives present, continued under the new Clerk, Stephen Underhill acting as his assistant. They were handicapped for lack of the original minute book, though copies of all reports from Quarterly Meetings, with few exceptions, were secured.

On the same day the Women's Business Meeting divided. Abigail E. Thurston, the Clerk, held Liberal Friends firmly together and the Orthodox party, again approximately one-fourth in numbers, withdrew to the African Methodist Church as prearranged. In this body the books and papers remained with the Liberals. Tears were shed as members of the Society, long friends to one another, left for the gatherings of their choice.

The business of both Yearly Meetings was continued in unity, various committees being reorganized to carry forward the concerns of Friends. Each body approved an Epistle. The Liberal body directed that its Epistle be sent to all the Yearly Meetings on the Continent, except Arch Street, and to London. The Epistle mentioned the excitement prevailing in the sessions, caused by the presence of Friends from other Yearly Meetings, which was taken "as a pretext for the separation of a number of our members from the body." The events of the division were related and Friends warned that they might experience difficulties in subordinate Meetings; but they were urged, "on all occasions" to be "actuated by a spirit of tenderness and love towards those who have gone from us." They were to keep from "accusations and denunciations, and to concede to others those inestimable privileges which" they claimed for themselves, "never encroaching upon the rights of others." [22] The minutes of the Yearly Meeting, when circulated, also contained the request that "Friends give no just cause of offence . . . either in word or deed . . . and in all cases where the rights of property are involved, it is advised that Friends carefully maintain our Christian character, in the strict observation of justice and equity." [23] The Orthodox Epistle spoke of the "prevalence of a spirit of unbelief in some of the fundamental doctrines of the Christian Religion" which "produced a spirit of insubordination" and "ensnared . . . under the pretence of greater spirituality and religious freedom." [24] This Epistle urged members not to be discouraged by the smallness of their numbers, but to encourage one another and give advice and counsel where needed.

In the last session of Ministers and Elders there was growing feeling against the English ministers, who were generally considered responsible for the Separation in New York. This found expression in an Epistle, which was approved by the Ministers and Elders and directed to be forwarded to the corresponding body in London. It read in part:

This Meeting has been brought under exercise and concern on account of the movement of our Friends from England now on a religious visit to this country and apprehending their services in the line of the Ministry ought to cease as it is evident we have not unity therewith believing their labors have had a tendency to produce discord in our society. . . . And it appears that labour has been frequently extended in the course of their visits to different parts of this Yearly Meeting, without producing the desired effect, a committee was therefore appointed to inform them thereof, and a personal interview has in some instances been refused, they are authorized to communicate the above minute in writing to our subordinate Meetings, also to the Morning Meeting of Ministers and Elders in London.[25]

A copy of this critical Epistle was delivered to Thomas Shillitoe, who denied that the Yearly Meeting, where shortly before he had deposited his certificate, had any authority over him.

The division among New York Quakers reversed the course taken in Philadelphia. In Philadelphia, the Liberals, though in the majority, were the Separatists. In Elias Hicks' Yearly Meeting, the Liberals, also in a large majority, remained in the Meeting House, continuing the Yearly Meeting begun in 1696. The Orthodox were the Separatists.

XXIII

A

Long Journey

Two WEEKS after the conclusion of New York Yearly Meeting, Elias Hicks climbed into his wagon, said goodby to Jemima, and started on the western journey with his good friend Jesse Merritt. In the oft-repaired vehicle was a goodly supply of summer and winter clothing for this longest trip. In Elias' pocket was $130.[1] The minister was eighty years of age but still vigorous. The editor of the *Advocate of Truth* informed its readers:

It will be gratifying to our Friends at a distance to know that this aged and beloved minister of the gospel, has obtained approbation of the Monthly and Quarterly Meeting to which he belongs, to pay a religious visit to the meetings of Friends within New York, Ohio, Indiana, part of Virginia, Baltimore, and Philadelphia Yearly Meetings. . . . The undertaking of such a journey, at the advanced period of life to which he has attained, expresses strongly the devotion of his mind to the blessed cause of truth and goodness. . . . Such greenness in old age . . . such dedication in the service of God, and of his fellow heirs of immortality, when bending beneath the weight of fourscore years . . . convey a lesson of deep instruction.[2]

In New Jersey and the environs of Philadelphia, throngs came to hear Elias Hicks. Comly wrote, "Large meetings gathered, though in the midst of haytime and harvest. It was very satisfactory to have his company . . . and no doubt much prejudice was removed from the minds of many . . . who flocked to hear him." [3] At Downingtown, however, mounting opposition forecast the stormiest trip in Hicks' experience. Hicksite Friends, locked out of the Meeting House, gathered under the shade of apple trees. Elias noted that the excitement caused by the Separation resulted in far larger meetings of both Friends and non-Friends. Many Quakers who were "wavering, [and] halting between two opinions," were now convinced and "cheerfully united with Friends." [4] "Indeed," he wrote, "We have found nothing in the least degree to discourage or impede our progress, unless it be an excess of kindness from our friends, who can hardly give us up to pass on, without favouring them with a visit in their own houses." [5]

Meanwhile Thomas Shillitoe was also driving towards Ohio Yearly Meeting. Knowing Hicks would take the same general route, the English minister made it a point to call on local clergy and give them copies of the Philadelphia *Declaration*. Where there were Quakers, he warned them against Elias' views, "that they might not be taken by surprise should a request be made by his party for the use of any meeting-houses in the name of Friends." [6] In western Pennsylvania the two opponents came face to face. At Westland, after Elias finished speaking, Thomas Shillitoe greatly disturbed the gathering by his pointed opposition. A little later he called Elias an imposter. This so upset many worshipers that they requested the Elders and Overseers to deal with Thomas Shillitoe. "Friends relieved their minds pretty fully" at Quarterly Meeting to no avail.[7] On several occasions, in business sessions, the English minister opposed the reading of Elias' certificate, and once declared he would rather not have his own certificate read if the certificate of the Jericho minister was to be minuted. Elias wrote to Valentine that "our old friend Thomas Shillitoe" (Thomas was seventy-four and Elias eighty) "warned people to flee from us with their lives." [8] As a result gatherings were held in barns, out-of-doors, once in a courthouse lit by candlelight, and again under a canopy made of long poles covered with branches. Attendance at times was over a thousand.

Each step of the journey westward brought greater opposition. The previous year, Anna Braithwaite and Elizabeth Robson had traveled this route preaching that the Hicksites were Deists, were possessed of an insidious spirit, and taught many "damnable heresies." [9] They made wide use of the 1827 Epistles of Indiana and of North Carolina Yearly Meetings which attacked Elias Hicks by name. Indiana Yearly Meeting of 1827 sent a special letter to the Ohio Meeting for Suffering warning "against imbibing the pernicious sentiments . . . at present afloat," found in the sermons of Hicks. When the Meeting for Sufferings concurred in the use of the Indiana Epistle, dissension began, followed by division on the local level. As Hicks proceeded he found Meeting Houses closed against him with guards at the doors "like soldiers in a time of war." [10] Disorderly scenes occurred. When the Hicksites were in a majority the Orthodox left the building. At New Garden, Ohio, Elias urged his fellow worshipers faithfully to support the testimonies "as the eyes of the people were upon Friends," watching their movements in their time of trial "when confusion and breaches of unity destroyed the bond of Christian fellowship." The present difficulty, he declared, was due to a few individuals "who had gained influence in society, letting in the spirit of jealousy," and who in turn "began to accuse some of their friends of promulgating unsound doctrines, without any just cause . . . Several Friends from England, . . . blew up the fire of discord, until they brought about a division." [11]

Mount Pleasant, the seat of Ohio Yearly Meetings, was reached on August 27. The *Advocate of Truth* noted Elias' coming with appropriate words, "Our venerable friend and minister, Elias Hicks, has again passed through these parts . . . he appears to be given up to spend and be spent in the service of his Divine Master, not dismayed or discouraged by the frowns, the censures, or persecutions of his opponents . . . furnishing renewed confirmation to many minds, that he still continues to be the sound, faithful Friend, and genuine Christian." The editor added that many sober, unprejudiced persons, observing the fortitude with which the veteran of the church met harsh treatment, came to listen, judged for themselves, and were convinced of Hicks' views. "It has rarely, if at all, happened in modern times," continued this Liberal sympathizer, "that any preacher of the Society of Friends, has been so fully known to the public, on account of the opportunities afforded by his extensive travels and the wide circulation of [his] printed sermons." [12]

This kindly opinion was not shared by many in Mount Pleasant. In the few days before Yearly Meeting began, Elias spoke in nearby Friends' Meetings. At once he came in conflict with Elisha Bates, the most powerful Orthodox minister in the area. Bates was the author of *The Doctrine of Friends,* considered by the Philadelphia *Friend* the clearest and ablest exposition of Orthodox doctrines written in America.[13] Both Elisha Bates and Anna Braithwaite openly attacked Elias Hicks, the former endeavoring to convince his hearers that the Jericho minister "was . . . an intruder." [14]

Letters from Long Island now reached Elias. He had chided Jemima earlier for not writing to him while on this journey, saying, "If I do not receive some direct account from home . . . I shall be ready to conclude that my friends have forgotten me or turned orthodox." He was able to send word that "divers friends, whose names I have forgotten, and some who have never seen thee, but love thee on my account, desired to be affectionately remembered to thee." [15] Elias was saddened by a letter from Gideon Seaman of Westbury, charging the majority group in New York Yearly Meeting, led by Hicks, as seceders. Gideon declared the minority were treated as children, indeed "considered as nothing." He protested against Elias' view that "the church hath no right to interfere with its members, or exercise any control over them, in matters of faith and doctrine, but that everyone hath a right and must be at liberty to publish his own sentiments." [16] Gideon spoke of an inclosed communication from

Jericho and Westbury Monthly Meeting which puzzled Elias, as he knew nothing of this Monthly Meeting.

While Elias and Jesse Merritt had been journeying to Mount Pleasant, dissension had been rife at home. One quarter of the two thousand members of New York Monthly Meeting had withdrawn to form an Orthodox Meeting.[17] In the five Hudson Valley Quarterly Meetings, one-third of the membership also withdrew. Only one Monthly Meeting, that of Marlborough, contained a majority of Orthodox and so held the Meeting House. In Jericho Monthly Meeting, 211 members sided with the famous Liberal, nine withdrew and three were neutral. These nine joined with thirty-nine members of the 341 belonging to Westbury Monthly Meeting to form a new Monthly Meeting with the combined name.

On September 9, a committee of six Orthodox Friends waited upon Elias Hicks to present the paper to which Gideon Seaman referred. It was a statement of the thirty-one adult members of the newly formed Westbury and Jericho Monthly Meeting declaring that Elias Hicks was not in unity, that he promoted the Separation and "laid the new Yearly Meeting under the necessity of retiring from these disorderly persons, and all others who united with them." [18] They ordered him to return home without delay. Elias Hicks informed the committee that he knew nothing of the body which framed the document and which had no authority over him whatsoever.

The same day the most turbulent Yearly Meeting ever held on the American continent began its first session. When Elias Hicks reached the Meeting House where Friends had warmly welcomed him in 1819, the guards denied him admission. With twelve members of the Select Meeting the Hicksites held a session under the trees, "as did George Fox." [19] The Liberals were also excluded from the Meeting for Sufferings.

As the time for holding Meeting on First day approached, Friends and visitors occupied every seat in the large building, many gathered outside the open windows and doors. Elias broke the silence with an earnest exposition of those matters which seemed most important.

Scarcely was Elias seated before Elisha Bates denounced the Liberal views just pronounced, concluding with the declaration that Hicks was an intruder since he had been "officially recalled." After a second lengthy attack by Anna Braithwaite, Elias rose to reply but was cut off by the two ministers shaking hands. Elisha Bates demanded "in a loud and authoritative manner" that the building be cleared. Some of the Orthodox remained, however, and ate their lunch in the high seats in order to save them for their associates attending the afternoon session. Elias Hicks went to Short Creek Meeting where a peaceful gathering was held, as none of the Orthodox leaders were present. Elisha Dawson and Amos Peaslee, two Eastern Friends, remained in the afternoon at Mount Pleasant and were ordered to cease speaking by Jonathan Taylor and Elisha Bates. While both Amos Peaslee and Elisha Bates were on their feet "voices in different parts of the house exclaimed, *"Elisha Bates sit down—sit down, Elisha Bates sit down."* [20] Amos Peaslee finished his remarks and was followed by Anna Braithwaite and Elisha Bates. After the worship concluded a number of Orthodox Friends slept in the building all night, guarding the doors.

Monday morning forty men watched the doors in an effort to exclude all Hicksites, but the press became so great that many Liberals entered. After a short silence, Jonathan Taylor, the Clerk of the previous year, opened the business of the Yearly Meeting and his right to preside was at once challenged. Hicksite Friends claimed he was disqualified because he had chosen sides before Yearly Meeting. They nominated as presiding officer David Hilles, Clerk of the undivided Redstone Quarter. David Hilles, whose name was approved by many, endeavored to come forward as Jonathan Taylor read the opening minute. The pressure was so great around the Clerk's table that it was splintered into pieces. At the same time "some person upstairs made a noise like cracking a board which alarmed the people a little. . . . Thom White (not a member), thinking it not quite enough sport, broke a small board across his knee." Someone on the floor of the building cried, "The galleries are coming down" and many Friends rushed out of the building, some through the doors and some out of the windows." [21] Many Hicksites remained for a short session and then adjourned until early the next morning.

Elias Hicks missed this violent session as he was tired and spent the morning writing letters. To Valentine he sent word, "The Orthodox of this yearly meeting are, if possible, tenfold more violent than in any other part of the Society. Gideon Seaman, and his associates in the little upstart Monthly Meeting of Westbury and Jericho have sent a very preemptory order for me to return immediately home, and not proceed any further on my religious visit, by which they trample the authority of our Quarterly Meeting . . . under foot." [22] Answering Gideon Seaman's letter, Elias Hicks lost his temper for one of the few times in his life. He was filled with hurt feelings and righteous indignation. He began, "My poor deluded friend. . . . My spirit mourns over thee with sorrow and regret, and also over those of my friends in Westbury and Jericho Monthly Meetings, who have associated together to oppose the truth; for certainly you must know from your long acquaintance with me, that the accusations which you have adopted . . . were founded altogether in falsehood." He continued, "You know the order of my family, and also have known my great labour and travail for fifty years, in word and doctrine, in meetings and families of Friends . . . for the promotion of right order and discipline in society; and for this cause only have I now, in old age, left wife and children, and my beloved friends, with every tender endearment, for the promotion of the cause of truth and righteousness . . . you . . . have turned away to fables and false reports." [23]

Although the Meeting House was posted the next day with notices warning the Hicksites not to attend, the Liberal group was in session before the Orthodox appeared on the grounds. Elisha Bates demanded possession of the building in the name of the representatives of Ohio Yearly Meeting. He was told that Yearly Meeting was in session, that he, and all other Friends, were welcome to enter and share in the business. The Orthodox party then adjourned to Short Creek, leaving the Hicksites in possession of the Mount Pleasant building until the Yearly Meeting was over. The Hicksites sent an offer to divide the properties of the various Meetings equitably on a basis of membership, but the Orthodox leaders countered by bringing a suit against the Liberals for trespassing. Writs were served on a dozen Ohio Hicksites and one Eastern visitor, Halliday Jackson. They were required to appear at Steubenville, twenty miles distant, where a number of Orthodox members, including Elisha Bates, Jonathan Taylor, Samuel Bettle, and Isaac Braithwaite of England were also present. The Liberals were charged with trespassing, disturbing a religious society, and gathering to commit a riot.[24]

Thursday was a day of public worship. The Hicksites with many non-Friends from the surrounding country met at Mount Pleasant; the Orthodox continued at Short Creek. Elias spoke for three-quarters of an hour, followed by Mary Lukens of Chester County, Pennsylvania, and Amos Peaslee. When the worship was concluded, Elias spoke again, explaining the attack made upon him by members of Westbury and Jericho Monthly Meeting. He also read an Epistle, received the night before, signed by twenty Quakers from his own Monthly Meeting. This letter protested "against the unrighteous act [of the few at Westbury and Jericho]"[25] and showed that both his own Monthly Meeting of Jericho and the Quarterly Meeting of Westbury were in unity with him. Among the signers were Robert Seaman, Samuel I. Underhill, Samuel and John Willis, John Plummer, John Ketchum, William and Isaac Willits, Richard Powell, and Thomas Hubbs.

The two Yearly Meetings continued to their conclusions, each sending out an Epistle giving its interpretation of events. No writ was served on Elias Hicks, although he wrote to Valentine, "I have been expecting for several days past to have a writ of trespass served against me by the sheriff, for going on their meeting-house grounds, by which I may be taken twenty miles or more to appear before the judge, as a number of Friends already have been, although my mind is quiet regarding the event." [26]

Yearly Meeting over, Elias Hicks and Jesse Merritt set out for Waynesville, in the western part of Ohio. They stopped at Flushing where Charles Osborne, an Orthodox Minister, endeavored to prevent Elias from speaking, first, by praying on his knees for an hour, and second, by asserting that Elias was not in unity with his Meeting. Elias produced his credentials, but the Orthodox left the building while these were being read. The two travelers reached Waynesville in time for the session of Ministers and Elders of the reorganized Yearly Meeting for "Indiana, Illinois and the western and middle parts of the State of Ohio." The previous year, when Indiana Yearly Meeting had met at Richmond, Indiana, an Orthodox statement had been accepted chiefly through the efforts of Elisha Bates, Anna Braithwaite, and Elizabeth Robson. This statement was rejected by Miami Quarterly Meeting, whose members called for the reorganization of the yearly gathering "on its ancient foundation and according to our present discipline." In September, six to seven hundred Quakers met at Waynesville representing several Quarterly Meetings; Elias wrote home that all was held in harmony and condescension. In the minutes mention was made of "our ancient and beloved friend, Elias Hicks," and of "our beloved friend, Jesse Merritt who acceptably attended." [27]

Although Thomas Shillitoe followed the same route as Elias and Jesse, he did not again face the Long Island minister. Learning that Hicks was at Waynesville, Shillitoe drove an additional eight miles to avoid another meeting. While Indiana Yearly Meeting, Orthodox, was in session at Richmond—attended, according to Shillitoe, by four thousand Friends—Elias Hicks held Meetings in a large barn on an adjoining lot. The two elderly ministers made their way Eastward by separate routes, Elias Hicks by way of Redstone Quarter, northern Virginia, Baltimore, and Philadelphia; Thomas Shillitoe by way of Kentucky, North Carolina, and then up the coast to New York. Elias recorded large Meetings, made up of every description of persons, high and low, rich and poor, Romanists, and Protestants of almost every denomination. Elias was now fortified by an additional letter from Westbury Quarterly Meeting which said:

This meeting, being informed that a communication has been circulated within the limits of Ohio and Indiana Yearly Meetings, purporting to be from "The Monthly Meeting of Westbury and Jericho," repeating certain charges, long since investigated and disproved, but evidently designed to impeach the religious character of Elias Hicks, an approved minister now with our certificate, on a gospel mission to those parts; after deliberation, it was thought right for this meeting to furnish Friends in that section of the country with a renewed testimonial of our esteem and love for this aged and faithful friend to the cause of truth.[28]

Letters from home brought news that John Comly and Hugh Judge were visiting in different parts of New York Yearly Meeting. Local separations continued to take place. Elias noted that both parties used much the same arguments to justify their actions. In Philadelphia and New York, the Hicksites stressed their large majorities; in Indiana, the Orthodox did the same. Both sides claimed they were returning to the principles of primitive Friends. The greater bitterness in Ohio Yearly Meeting was evidently due to the fact that in this area only were the two parties equally divided.[29]

When the Long Island Quakers reached the northern Virginia meetings in November, they learned that Baltimore Yearly Meeting had divided the previous month. The Separation was peacefully accomplished with so few leaving to form an Orthodox Yearly Meeting that William Proctor, an Evangelical, could write to England, "Baltimore is the only Yearly Meeting on this continent, who can be said as a body to have espoused the cause of the Separatists." [30] A separation might have been avoided had not George and Ann Jones objected to the reading of certificates of visiting Liberal ministers and Epistles from Liberal Yearly Meetings. They left the building with only two of the fifty-three representatives following them. The minutes of the Liberal Yearly Meeting contained an excellent refutation of the belief that all Yearly Meetings must take sides during the period of contention:

Believing, as we do, that each Yearly Meeting of the Society of Friends constitutes of itself a body possessing not less of right than, from necessity, all the powers of self-government, we neither claim the right to control the judgment, nor to animadvert upon the proceedings of others; nor can we, upon the same principles, recognise the right or the power, in them, to control, or prescribe rules for our conduct. This meeting has not considered itself called upon to advance any new principle of faith; nor in its communications with other Yearly Meetings, with which it corresponds, to explain, or expound those principles which have constituted the bond of union among its members, since the first establishment of the Society; under a belief that these principles are well known, not only to our members, but to the well informed portion of all Christian denominations.[31]

In the Maryland and Pennsylvania Meetings the houses were rarely large enough to hold all who wished to hear Elias. Jemima, mindful of her husband's needs, sent two thicker neckcloths and a tight-bodied winter coat with John Hicks, who now took the place of the devoted Jesse Merritt. In Wilmington, Hicks was grieved to find William Poole in very poor health. At Haddonfield, where both bodies of Friends occupied the same building, Elias found the high seats completely filled when he entered for an appointed gathering. He described what followed in his travel diary: "Knowing, according to the common usage and comly order of the Society it was my right and privilege to take the first seat, as I had full unity of the Monthly and Quarterly Meetings of which I was a member, and a minister, and more ancient than those who had taken the first seats, I very respectfully proposed to them to give me a seat next the Women as I was an old man and a stranger, but they refused the request but had not confidence to look me in the face." [32] As in past years, strangers were deeply moved by the Quaker's addresses, and Elias mentioned "some gay and fashionable females, as well as some of the men, who appeared bathed in tears at the close of these solemn meetings." [33]

Towards the end of the long journey, Elias, tired and sometimes indisposed, held a gathering on almost every day of the week. On January 20 he reached New York City, finding Jemima, Elizabeth and several other members of his family waiting to welcome him. Elias had traveled for seven months and ten days, covering a distance of 2,400 miles. "My spirit was deeply humbled under a thankful sense of the Lord's preserving power and adorable mercy," wrote Hicks, "in carrying me through and over all opposition, both within and without. He caused all to work together for good . . . and landed me safe in the bosom of my dear family and friends at home." [34]

The editor of the *Advocate of Truth,* delighted to hear that Elias Hicks was safely home after his arduous tour, and knowing of the opposition which he encountered during parts of the journey, drew a sharp contrast between those who sided with Elias and those who maligned him:

When we are introduced to a man whose years have numbered the larger part of a century, in the whole course of which his most embittered enemies have not been able to point out a solitary blemish; when we behold him in the practice of every virtue that can adorn humanity . . . destitute of pride and worldly ambition, toiling in old age, not for perishable gold, but for the improvement of his fellow creatures . . . leading a life of patriarchal simplicity. . . . Can we do other than tremble for human nature, when we distinguish such a person delineated as an angel of darkness . . . [with] malediction heaped upon him with unsparing cruelty. . . . [His tenets] . . . are in conformity with the faith, originally maintained by the society of Friends.[35]

XXIV

The Minister

Closes His Journal

IN SPITE OF the Separation, Jericho affairs continued as before—at least on the surface. The Clerk recorded, "Love and unity in a good degree maintained with the exception of a few who have separated from us." The Meeting House authorized for Jerusalem, seven miles south of Jericho, cost slightly under a thousand dollars; members constructed horse sheds at Jericho. A half acre was also added to the cemetery. The school was in a flourishing condition with a balance in hand of well over a thousand dollars. Discipline was strictly maintained. One member was under dealing for "the unnecessary use of spiritous liquors," and one for "vending" the same. A Friend gave way to profane language and a "wide departure from dress and address"; another joined a military company. Almost every month some young man or woman was disowned for "marrying out." The Meeting received instructions from the superior body to rotate appointment of elders; individuals could be reappointed. Disownment proceedings were not taken against individual Separatists, but their defection was recorded. In an effort to make an equitable distribution of property with the Orthodox, Jericho Monthly Meeting allotted $246.66 to the small body of Quakers.[1]

Early in the spring, Jemima developed pneumonia. Nine days later, in the house in which she was born, she "passed away like a lamb, as though entering a sweet sleep . . . [ending] fifty-eight years in one unbroken bond of endeared affection, which seemed if possible to increase with time to the last moment of her life." Elias continued in his *Journal,* "To myself, to whom she was a truly affectionate wife, and to our children, whom she endeavoured, by precept and example, to train in the paths of virtue, and to guard and keep them out of harm's way, her removal is a great and irreparable loss: . . . the loss and trial, as to all my external blessings, are the greatest I have ever met with, or ever expect to have to endure."[2] At Jemima's funeral, Elias spoke of "their united concern for the strict and guarded education of their children," of their mutual endeavors to preserve simplicity in the home, and to maintain "their Christian profession . . . that they might, through the mercy of God, and by faithfulness unto him, at the close of time, have a mansion in heaven, where," he said, "I have no doubt the spirit of my dear departed companion now rests."[3] Sadly, Elias took from his cherry desk the *Journal of George Fox,* and there below the records of the deaths of David, Elias Jr., baby Elizabeth, Phebe, Jonathan, John, and the unnamed little one, wrote, "Jemima Hicks, wife of Elias Hicks departed this life the 17th day of 3rd mo., 1829, about 15 minutes past 7 o'clock in the morning, aged 78 years, 5 months, and 26 days,—and left an excellent savour behind her affording much comfort to her bereaved husband, and children, for the loss of so great a blessing, both as a Wife and Mother in confidence their loss resulted in her eternal gain."[4]

Thomas Shillitoe came from the South in late April, and attended a Business Meeting of the Orthodox Friends gathered in the home of John Titus. He could not have been displeased to hear a testimony of disownment against the aged Liberal solemnly read and approved. Elias Hicks, the testimony declared, was "formerly well approved" in the Society, but "for want of abiding in a state of humble watchfulness . . . he [became] exalted in his mind, and giving way to a disposition of reasoning, has indulged in speculative opinions, asserting that we must always take things rationally; and that we are not bound to believe any thing we do not understand." The document further alleged that Hicks denied the existence of the devil, the fall of man, and many other truths of Scripture, including the Divinity of Jesus Christ, his propitiatory offering for the redemption of man, and his bodily resurrection. "At length he became the leader of a sect distinguished by his name, yet, unjustly assuming the character of Friends." [5] The only comment Elias Hicks ever made on the action of Westbury and Jericho Monthly Meeting was to state that this group had no jurisdiction over him, "For how can they disown those who never attended their meetings," he wrote a friend, "nor never had seen inside their new-built meeting houses? Would it not be as rational and consistent with right order for a Presbyterian or Methodist society to treat with and disown us for not attending their meetings, and not acknowledging their creed?" [6]

Edward Stabler, Edward Hicks, John Comly, and Elias Hicks attended New York Yearly Meeting at the usual time and place in 1829. At least 2,200 Friends were counted going out of the gate, upwards of a thousand were turned away.[7] John Comly noted that Elias, "still occupied a prominent station of usefulness in the meeting. His discernment and wisdom still shone with conspicuous brightness in the various deliberations . . . while his condescension to the views and judgment of others, marked his Christian tenderness and forbearance." [8] On Fourth day, Elias pleaded for obedience to the Inward Light, declaring that he knew from his own experience that God revealed His will to men. "He has from my childhood showed me the way faster than I was willing to walk in it." [9] The Epistle of the Yearly Meeting proclaimed the dependence of Friends "on the sure foundation, 'Christ in us the hope of Glory'; as an active principle in the soul of men, bringing into subjection every propensity, producing in the obedient, the fruits of the kingdom of

God." [10] Reports to the Yearly Meeting indicated that 14,768 Friends retained membership with the Liberals and 5,351 with the Orthodox, while 743 remained neutral.[11]

Elias found it more difficult than ever to keep abreast of his correspondence. To William Poole he wrote, "The long interruption of our mutual and friendly correspondence has not arisen on my part from any diminution of that sincere love and regard that has subsisted between us from the time of our first acquaintance, but from causes over which I had no control." [12] Shortly thereafter word came that William Poole was dead. Elias sadly wrote Benjamin Ferris, "a real chasm in [his] most interesting correspondence" now existed, since he had exchanged letters with William Poole more frequently than with any other individual.[13] The Jericho minister sent a heartening letter to Rachel S. Hicks, daughter of Gideon Seaman, who took the Hicksite side at Westbury rather than that chosen by her father. Elias was grateful that her reasoning was so clear, her mind so firmly established. He urged her to "go on and prosper, keeping in remembrance the caution of the blessed Jesus, that if any who make a profession of his name, love father or mother, wife or children . . . more than we love him we are not worthy of him." [14]

Thomas Hazard, Jr., notified Elias of the death of the pioneer Quaker Liberal, Hannah Barnard. A young man sent a letter asking Elias' advice about studying law. He prayed for the minister's good health, and for the "furtherance of the work thy God has graciously been pleased to make thee an organ—a mighty minister among men —leading the people out of night into the bright and eternal day." [15] But as most lawyers entered politics, and Elias still considered "it inconsistent for any member of our Society to take any part whatsoever in the governments and policies of this world, which are all supported and defended by the Sword," [16] he no doubt advised the young man to seek another calling.

In 1817 Hicks had opposed the construction of the Erie Canal, preached against it, and went so far as to say, "If the Lord had intended there should be internal waterways, he would have placed them there, and there would have been a river flowing through central New York." [17] He now heard that Friends in Baltimore were interested in connecting their city with Ohio by rail. Although English Quakers had taken a leading part in developing the Stockton and Darlington Railroad, and though Philip E. Thomas, Clerk of Baltimore Yearly Meeting (Hicksite), was the moving spirit in the new Maryland project, Elias was much disturbed. He wrote to Philip Thomas, the first president of the Baltimore and Ohio Railroad, that his calling as an Elder was of "a more noble and exalted nature than to enlist in such low and groveling concerns." [18] Elias was certain that preoccupation with roadbeds, bridges, tunnels, ties, and railroad carriages, would stifle religious life. Elias also wrote the parents of James P. Stabler in Sandy Spring, who was directing the building of the line from Baltimore to Frederick, "It afforded me very pleasing sensations to be informed of dear James' improvement in health, but it excited some different feeling when informed that he had taken the place of Assistant Superintendent of the railroad company, a business that I conceive that principally belongs to men of this world, but not to the children of light, whose kingdom is not of this world." [19]

Feeling that duties growing out of the certificate of Jericho Monthly and Westbury Quarterly Meetings were not yet fully discharged, Elias Hicks, with Cornwell Willis as a traveling companion, undertook a last visit through New York Yearly Meeting. According to the *Friend,* his associates said, "It is his intent to prove, as he goes along, that the orthodox misrepresented him; that he holds the fundamental doctrines of Christianity, and that he is a true Quaker." This the *Friend* was certain Hicks could not do.[20]

The Quakers rode up the Hudson Valley, crossing the river occasionally.[21] Elias regretted that the Nine Partners boarding school, for which he had worked so strenuously, was in the hands of the Orthodox, although the Meeting House and the farm remained with the Liberals. At Albany, the state house was opened for a large gathering of non-Friends who "behaved themselves very soberly, becoming the occasion." [22] In Troy the Episcopal Church was loaned to the Quaker minister, at Rensselaerville the Methodist Church, and at Verona the Baptist. By early September, they reached Cayuga Lake, then continued on as far as Rochester. On the way back, Elias' route traversed that of Stephen Grellet, who was making an intensive visitation through the state. Stephen noted, "I then crossed over to Long Island, where I had meetings with the small remnants of our Society. Very little companies are left in those parts, where lately there were many Friends. . . . The Separatists (Hicksite) have very generally taken possession of the meeting-houses. . . . The Lord has chastened this people very sore." [23] In the fall he added, The Meetings "were rendered very labourious and exercising from the circumstance that Elias Hicks was travelling in these parts. It frequently happened that I had meetings in places where he had been one or two days before. The people had been brought under great excitement by the anti-christian doctrines he had delivered." [24]

Meanwhile, Orthodox Friends, desiring a more detailed and authoritative statement of faith than any formulated by a single Yearly Meeting, held a convention of official representatives from eight Yearly Meetings, under the Chairmanship of Elisha Bates of Ohio, in Philadelphia. The thirty-six page statement issued, *The Testimony of the Society of Friends on the Continent of America,* "was the product and climax of the whole orthodox movement from its beginning in the later part of the 18th century." [25] The document expressed the adherence of the Orthodox Friends to the generally held Evangelical Protestant doctrines. Liberal Quakers thought it "an anomaly in their history, and strongly excited a suspicion, that those who adopted it are not Quakers of the old school." So reported the *Advocate of Truth,* and added, "It is well understood by all those who are conversant in the history of the Society that the early Friends bore a clear and decided testimony against all creeds, and confessions of faith, and systems of religion." [26]

Cornwell Willis and Elias Hicks circled Lake Champlain, then came down the Hudson Valley in a leisurely manner to New York City. Here Elias believed his "labour and exercise in the gospel, to Friends and others in the yearly meetings of Philadelphia, Baltimore, Ohio, Indiana, and New York" were concluded.[27] Elias felt easy in his mind about Friends. In those areas where he was best known his point of view was strongly held. In New York Yearly Meeting two-thirds of the membership agreed with him; in Philadelphia Yearly Meeting the proportion was approximately the same; in Baltimore four-fifths of the Friends had chosen the Liberal position. In Ohio Yearly Meeting, which Elias only visited twice, one half of the membership were Liberals. Hicks did not reach Indiana until the division was an accomplished fact, yet in this newest Yearly Meeting some fifteen hundred Friends felt he was upholding the ancient faith. Of the three remaining American Yearly Meetings, those of Virginia and North Carolina were small and beyond the limits of Hicks' journeys. In New England Yearly Meeting, Elias made three extensive visits, but no organized Liberal movement followed his pattern. Evidently the extinction of the New Light Movement a few years before the main Separation began drew off those who logically would have followed the Liberal prophet.[28]

Elias was relieved when the last of the seven Evangelical ministers, who had done so much to provoke the Separation during the previous decade, now returned to England. He realized they would give a biased report of events in America, but Liberal Friends had given up any hope of having their position placed before London Yearly Meeting in a favorable light. Only the letters of Samuel Parsons, or those of other Orthodox correspondents, were received by the Meeting for Sufferings in London.[29] Individual American Liberals tried to make their position clear by writing to personal friends in England. Benjamin Ferris wrote John Grace that English Quakers seemed afraid to hear the Liberal arguments, refusing to read publicly any document sent from North American Hicksites, but "condemned them unheard." He pointed out in Philadelphia Yearly Meeting alone eighteen thousand Friends were refused a hearing by English Quakers because of the testimony of their opponents. He added that Quakers in Great Britain and Ireland could not form an impartial judgment upon the divisions in America because of lack of complete information, since they listened only to those who took great pains to prejudice their minds "by statements wholly devoid of any foundation in Truth." [30] Individual correspondence was no more successful than official Epistles.

Crossing to Brooklyn in November, Elias Hicks spoke at a gathering attended by Walt Whitman. Of this occasion Whitman wrote, "Though the differences and disputes of the formal division of the Society of Friends were even then under way, he never alluded to them at all. . . . Elias Hicks' discourse . . . was one of his old never-remitted appeals to that moral mystical portion of human nature, *the inner light.*" [31]

Elias was soon safely home, after a fifteen hundred mile journey. He then returned the certificate granted for the long journey, "performed to the peace and satisfaction of his own mind"; endorsed by two Yearly, five Quarterly, and eight Monthly Meetings. [32]

Only a few weeks of life remained to the aged minister. He wrote a delightful letter to Elias Wilbur, a young Quaker in Saratoga, New York, giving "encouragement in the way of well doing and [the] path of true and real virtue." He added, "After we took leave of thy father's hospitable roof . . . though we then separated as to the body, yet in mind I often feel him as though present, with grateful sensations for his kindness in accompanying us in our journey from place to place, through rough and smooth, with such cheerfulness and good will as tended to smooth the way before us and made our journey more pleasant." [33] He answered an affectionate letter from Thomas Leggett, Jr., of New York, containing six queries. The answer to the six questions covered many of Elias' doctrinal views, and was reprinted in various forms. One edition was endorsed by eighteen of his friends of long acquaintance who declared these were the sentiments they understood Hicks always maintained. [34]

The Jericho minister gathered the last travel diaries and other papers to complete his formal *Journal*. Then "E.H. . . . closed his Journal, and signed his name." [35] On the last day of January, 1830, he spoke at the Rose Street Meeting House on the text, "There is a spirit in man and the inspiration of the Almighty giveth them understanding." He desired this divine principle might find a lodgement in the minds of his hearers, he believed those who possessed it would be happy, for they would know a love stronger than death, and a courage enabling them to speak the truth plainly and fearlessly. He closed with the words, "As these things have opened upon my mind, I have spoken them to you. I have had much to say, and have laboured extensively among my fellow creatures, with a view to incite them to attend to the will of God, as manifested in their own hearts. And this is all any instrument can do. . . . With sincere desires, that life, light, and immortality may be your portion, I bid you farewell." That afternoon at Hester Street he spoke for the last time in New York City, ending with the words, "My prayer is, may the Lord bless your endeavours; And in unbounded love, I bid you, my friends, young and old, an affectionate farewell." [36] Few eyes were dry when the venerable leader took his seat.

Elias rode to Islip to visit Joshua Willetts and while in the home of his son-in-law had a slight paralytic attack. Elizabeth, noting that her father did not use his right arm, could not refrain from tears, but Elias quietly remarked, "Weep not for me." [37] He insisted on proceeding to Bethpage the next day, since notice had previously been given of his coming.

On February 14, Elias wrote a long letter to his old friend Hugh Judge, ending with the message, "Be of good cheer, for no new thing has happened to us; for it has ever been the lot of the righteous to pass through many trials and tribulations, in their passage to that glorious, everlasting, peaceful, and happy abode, where all sorrow and signing come to an end . . . in the fulness of brotherly love to thee and thine, in which my family unite." [38] Finishing the letter, Elias rose from his seat, and, walking toward the fire, suffered a severe paralytic stroke. Then, according to Walt Whitman, "Being assisted to a chair near the fire, he manifested by signs, that the letter which he had just finish'd, and which had been dropp'd by the way, should be taken care of, and on its being brought to him, appear'd satisfied, and manifested a desire that all should sit down and be still, seemingly sensible that his labours were brought to a close, and only desirous of quietly waiting the final change . . . the prospect of death brought no terror to him." [39] During the next two weeks, Elizabeth cared for her father, aided by Martha, Abigail, and Sarah, while ten grandchildren hovered about the door ready to run errands. Elias gradually lost the power of speech, though when asked if his mind was entirely easy he articulated the words, "All's well." [40] Often in his closing days, "His countenance assumed all that dignity and sweetness, for which he was so remarkable when sitting in Meeting." [41]

In the midst of editions which carried the words of the famous debate in Congress on state and national rights, between Hayne and Webster, the New York *Evening Post* carried a notice of the death, on February 27, "in the eighty-second year, [of] Elias Hicks, an eminent minister in the Society of Friends." [42] At a Meeting for Worship, which filled to the doors the building Hicks had helped to construct, a number of his friends spoke feelingly of his life and work. Although the weather was bad, many stood outside unable to find seats within. Elias Hicks was buried beside other members of his family on March 3.[43]

There was a spontaneous outpouring of tributes in the diaries of Friends and in the public press on the decease of Elias Hicks. Edward Stabler wrote, "The beloved and excellent Elias Hicks passed from his habitation . . . to an eternal state of bliss. . . . His life has exhibited a lovely example of the blessed effects of obedience to pure principle. How wonderfully he has been preserved in meekness and gentleness, amid all the tempests which have assailed him." [44] Hugh Judge noted, "that great and good man . . . our elder brother E. H. is now no more in the society of men . . . his abode was in the life and power of the eternal Word . . . and it is in a measure of the same life, light and power in which he moved and acted . . . he has stood at the head in the great and good, and glorious cause. . . . He will live in the minds and affections of hundreds, to whom he has been a blessing in the hand of God." [45]

The editor of the *Advocate of Truth* published a long obituary, saying in part:

When a veteran in the cause of religion and virtue descends to the grave, one who has braved the tempests which beset him, and escaped the shoals, on which piety is too often wrecked, the heart of the spectator is moved with reverential awe. . . . He taught no gloomy, mysterious, and unintelligible doctrines, but strove to inculcate the mild and regenerating precepts of the gospel. His . . . religion . . . was a vital principle which came upon the heart with resistless energy. . . . He was regarded with deserved respect by the whole of the society, until within a few years since. In the division which ensued, he was selected as the object of malignant envy, and the destined victim of unmerited persecution . . . in the dispute which has been so long waged, slander has never dared to sully the fair reputation of Elias Hicks, Friends and enemies have united in pronouncing him a good man, notwithstanding their dissent from him in matters of speculation. . . . In his intercourse with the world, he was affable and courteous, without bigotry, or the spirit of intolerant zeal, recognizing in mankind, but one common family, the offspring of a gracious creator. His charity was not bounded by the narrow limits of sectarian prejudices, or the less dangerous influence of religious enthusiasm . . . his life had been spent in deeds of mercy and of faith.[46]

It was fitting that within a few days of his death a gathering was held by the African Benevolent Societies of New York, at which the spokesman remarked on the "indefatigable exertions in the abolition of slavery" of Elias Hicks. The speaker declared, "for purity of life, sincerity of profession, active exertion in the cause of human improvement, few men can bear comparison with this friend of humanity." He added, "Some of you have received deliverance from bondage through the instrumentality of the deceased, and consequently the name of Elias Hicks will be remembered with the most grateful recollections, and it will be perpetuated among you as the benefactor of the oppressed." After recounting the years of labor spent in behalf of the Negro, the speaker told a story of the last days of Elias. "In the affliction and anxiety which pervaded the family, when he was first attacked with the paralysis, a quilted *cotton* coverlet was inadvertently placed upon his bed. As the weather was severely cold, his children being anxious to make him comfortable, used their constant endeavours to keep this coverlet upon him. But they perceived by his actions . . . that this coverlet annoyed him, because with his hand, which was not paralyzed, he continually attempted to remove it . . . as something exceedingly offensive. It was at last suggested by a friend present, that the reason why he removed it, was on account of its being the product of slavery." When the cotton coverlet was taken away and a wool blanket substituted, Elias Hicks, feeling the wool with his fingers, nodded his pleasure.[47]

During the succeeding weeks several articles or reprints from other magazines appeared in the *Advocate of Truth*. The most natural memorial, however, was that from his neighbors. In March of 1830, the Clerk of Jericho Meeting recorded, "It being proposed whether there was not something due from us, to the memory of our late beloved friend Elias Hicks, deceased, by way of memorial, the subject claimed the solid attention . . ." of Friends; a committee was appointed which brought in an essay the following month beginning with the words, "The memory of the just is blessed." [48] This was read, signed on behalf of the Meeting by Willet Robbins and Abigail Hicks, Clerks, and forwarded to Westbury Quarterly, to go on to the coming Yearly Meeting. The opening paragraph of this memorial summarized the life and chief tenet in the teachings of Elias Hicks:

We believe the example exhibited in the life and religious exercise of this our beloved Friend, is eminently calculated to set forth the efficacy and sufficiency of that divine grace, which, when believed in and obeyed, bringeth salvation.[49]

Appendix I: Genealogy of the Hicks-Seaman Families

1. ROBERT HICKS, 1580–1647
To Plymouth, Mass., 1621
→

2. JOHN, 1607–1672
b. England. To Hempstead, L.I., 1640
→

3. THOMAS, 1640–?
1st Judge, Queens Co. High Sheriff. 4,000 acres Little Neck
(His great-great-grandson was Edward Hicks, the painter.)
→

4. JACOB, 1669–1755
Rockaway, L.I. Captain of the Militia. (Great-grandsons:
Isaac Hicks, merchant; and Valentine, m. Abigail Hicks, 1804.)
→

5. JOHN, 1711–1789
Rockaway, L.I. Joined Friends.
→

6. SAMUEL   JACOB   JOHN   ELIAS
                                    1748–1830

---

1. JOHN SEAMAN, 1603?–1694/95
To Mass., 1630. Patent Hempstead, 12,000 acres. Magistrate.
A Friend, 1686. Settled Jerusalem, L.I.
→

2. JONATHAN, 1647–?
Patent Hempstead
→

3. JOHN, ?–?
Oyster Bay
→

4. JONATHAN, 1716–1777
Jericho, L.I. m. Elizabeth Willis, 1719–1777
→

5. JEMIMA, 1750–1829
m. Elias Hicks 1771
→

Children of Elias and Jemima Hicks

MARTHA	DAVID	ELIAS	ELIZABETH	PHEBE	ABIGAIL	JONATHAN	JOHN	ELIZABETH	SARAH	INFANT
1771–1862	1773–1787	1774–1789	1777–1779	1779–1800	1782–1850	1784–1802	1787–1805	1791–1871	1793–1835	
m. Royal Aldrich, 1792				m. Joshua Willets, 1799 →	m. Valentine Hicks, 1804 →				m. Robert Seaman, 1814 →	

ELIAS	CAROLINE	MARY	PHEBE	ELIZABETH	ELIAS II
1800–1818	1808	d. 1826	?	1812	1815

PHEBE ?; HANNAH, 1817; WILLET, 1818; ELIZABETH, 1820; ELIAS, 1826; MARY, 1828; WILLET H., 1832

Appendix II: The Religious Missions of Elias Hicks

Year	Minute From	Time	Companion	Miles	Meetings Held	Areas Visited
1779	N.Y.Y.M. & Westbury	9 weeks	John Willis	860	21*	N.Y. & Pa.
1781	Westbury	10 weeks	William Valentine	860	33	N.Y.Y.M.
1782	Westbury	2 weeks*		50*	7*	Long Island
1782	N.Y.Y.M.	7 weeks	Committee	660	20*	N.Y.Y.M.
1783	Westbury	11 days		170	4*	N.Y.Y.M.
1784	Westbury	5 weeks*		100	24	Long Island
	Westbury (cont.)	4 weeks*		240*	23	Long Island
	Westbury (cont.)	2 weeks*		110*	8	Long Island
1785	Westbury				2*	N.Y.Y.M. & N.J.
1788	N.Y.Y.M.		Committee			N.Y.Y.M., schools
1790	Jericho		Fry Willis	150*	16*	N.Y.Y.M., new Meetings
	Jericho & N.Y.Y.M.	3 weeks 5 days	James Parsons	591	9	N.Y. & Vt.
	Jericho	2 weeks		115	15	Long Island
1791	N.Y.Y.M. & Jericho	4 months 3 days	Andrew Underhill	1,500	98	N.Y, NJ, Conn., Mass., N.H.
1792	N.Y.Y.M.	1 month	Committee			N.Y.Y.M., new Meetings
1793	Jericho	5 months	James Mott	2,283	123*	N.Y. and all Meetings Rhode Is. Y.M.
1795	N.Y.Y.M.	2 months	Committee	850*	18*	N.Y.Y.M.
1796	N.Y.Y.M.		Committee			N.Y.Y.M. Q. Meetings
1797	N.Y.Y.M.		Committee			N.Y.Y.M., Indians

*Numbers marked with an asterisk are approximate. Otherwise the figures are given by Elias Hicks in his diaries, *Journal*, or letters.

Year	Meeting	Duration	Minister / Companion	Miles	Meetings	Places Visited
1797	Jericho & Westbury Q.M.	5 months	Joseph Cooper	1,600	143	Pa., NJ., Del., Md., Va.
1798	Jericho	2 weeks				Westbury, families
1798	N.Y.Y.M.		Committee			Nine Partners Q.M.
1799	Jericho	6 weeks	Amos Whitson	460*	32	Conn.
1800	Jericho (cont.)		Amos Whitson			N.Y.Y.M.
1801	Jericho	27 days		190	35	Long Island
1801	Jericho	3 months	Edmund Willis	1,630	90*	N.J., Pa., Va., Md., Del., N.J.
	Jericho	18 days				
1803	Jericho	3 months	Daniel Titus	1,575	75*	Upper Canada
1806	Jericho	20 days		70	30	Long Island, Staten Island
1806	Jericho	2 months	Thomas Willis	700	57	N.Y.Y.M.
1807	Jericho & N.Y.Y.M.	2 months	Jemima Hicks	400*	16*	N.Y. & Conn.
1808	Jericho	5 weeks	Charles Willits	245*	27	Hudson Valley
1808	N.Y.Y.M.	10 weeks	Committee	1,000	76	N.Y.Y.M.
1808	N.Y.Y.M. (cont.)					N.Y.Y.M.
1809	Jericho					Hudson Valley
1809	Jericho					Jericho, families
1809	Jericho					Westbury, families
1810	N.Y.Y.M.					Upper Canada
1810	Jericho					N.Y.Y.M. Q. Meetings
1812	Jericho	4 weeks			28	Long Island
1813	Jericho				20	Long Island
1813	Jericho	4 weeks	Gideon Seaman	300	25	N.Y.Y.M.
1813	Jericho	3 months	Isaac Hicks	1,500*	110*	N.J., Pa., Md.
1815	Jericho	2 weeks			17	Long Island, families

Appendix II: Religious Missions (Continued)

Year	Minute from	Time	Companion	Miles	Meetings Held	Areas Visited
1815	Jericho					N.Y., families
1815	N.Y.Y.M.	4 weeks	Committee & Jemima Hicks	484	14	Nine Partners Q.M.
1816	Jericho	3 months	Isaac Hicks	1,000	64	Rhode Is. Y.M.
1817	Westbury Q.M.					Long Island, schools
1817	Jericho & Westbury Q.M.	4 months	Valentine Hicks	1,100	97	Pa., Baltimore Y.M.
1818	Jericho	49 days	Samuel Willis	450	49	N.Y.Y.M.
1819	Jericho (cont.)	14 weeks	Valentine Hicks	1,084	80	N.Y.Y.M.
1819	Jericho & Westbury Q.M.	3 months	Willet Robbins	1,200	87	N.Y., Pa., Ohio, Va, Md., N.J.
1819	Jericho	5 days	Jemima Hicks & Isaac Hicks	40*	6	Long Island
1820	Jericho (cont.)	13 days			15	Long Island
1820	N.Y.Y.M. & Jericho		Committee			Northern Q. Meetings
1822	Jericho		David Seaman			Pa., Baltimore, Y.M., N.J.
1823	Jericho		Samuel Willis			Hudson Valley
1824	Jericho		Jemima & Elizabeth Hicks			Hudson Valley
1824	Jericho					Baltimore Y.M.
1825	Jericho		Samuel Willis			Eastern Long Island
1825	N.Y.Y.M. & Jericho					Scipio Q.M.
1826	Jericho		Jesse Merritt			Southern & Concord Q.M., Pa.
1827	Jericho					Westbury, families
1828	Jericho & Westbury Q.M.	7 months 10 days	Jesse Merritt & John Hicks	2,400		Philadelphia, Baltimore, Va., Ohio, Ind. Y.M.
1829	Jericho & Westbury Q.M. (cont.)	5 months	Cornwell Willis			N.Y.Y.M.

Notes on Sources

MATERIAL for the study of Elias Hicks falls roughly into five categories.

1. There are excellent books, mentioned in the Notes, on colonial and post-colonial Long Island. The standard Quaker histories of this generation by William C. Braithwaite, Rufus M. Jones, Elbert Russell, Howard Brinton, Frederick B. Tolles, John Cox, Jr., Edward Grubb, Arthur J. Mekeel, Thomas Woody, and Thomas E. Drake, and those of an earlier generation by Henry W. Wilbur, Allen C. Thomas, Albert C. Applegarth, Samuel M. Janney, Frederick S. Turner, Samuel L. Fisher, Thomas H. Speakman, William Hodgson, and Thomas Clarkson deal with the period 1748 to 1830, or some special aspect of it.

2. The printed journals of Job Scott, John Comly, Hugh Judge, Edward Hicks, Edward Stabler, John Hunt, David Sands, Stephen Grellet, and Thomas Shillitoe contain many references to Elias Hicks or supply information for comparison.

3. Magazines printed by Liberals or Orthodox are of great value. The most important are *The Christian Inquirer* of New York; *The Friend or Advocate of Truth, The Quaker,* and *The Friend* of Philadelphia; and the *Christian Repository* and *The Berean* of Wilmington, Delaware.

4. Controversial leaflets, the reports of the trials in the Court of Chancery and the Court of Appeals in New Jersey and the Court of Common

Pleas of Steubenville, Ohio, and the depositions made before the Vice Chancellor of the First District in Chancery in New York City throw light on the conflict in the Society of Friends.

5. Voluminous and primary manuscript material is preserved. This is widely scattered. The minutes of Jericho Meeting and School Committee are in a safe in that Meeting, those of Westbury are under the care of that body. Marietta Hicks of Westbury has valuable material. The Lillian R. Newell Collection of letters to Elias Hicks is at Glen Head. Minutes of many Monthly Meetings of New York Yearly Meeting, and records of the Yearly Meeting, are in the Joint Record Room at Friends Seminary, New York City. Several hundred Hicks letters, the original Journal, and writings of many correspondents of Elias Hicks are in the Friends Historical Library of Swarthmore College. Here also are valuable manuscript accounts of the Separation. Records of the several Monthly and the Yearly Meeting are in the Baltimore Record Room at Stony Run Meeting. The Baltimore Collection—that of the author—comprises letters and articles by Elias Hicks, letters of Caroline Hicks, Edward Stabler, Benjamin Ferris, Aaron Leggett, John Ketchum, and other friends of the Long Island minister. Morgan State College, Baltimore, has a manuscript article on slavery by Hicks. In the Library of the Society of Friends, Friends House, London, are the minutes of Devonshire House Meeting, London and Middlesex Quarter, the Meeting for Sufferings and the Yearly Meeting, Casual Correspondence, Letters to and from Philadelphia, Pen Pictures of London Yearly Meeting; and letters of Stephen Gould, W. F. Robinson, Thomas Thompson, and Samuel Parsons; the diary of James Jenkens; diaries of Elizabeth Robson and other ministers visiting the United States 1820–30.

List of Abbreviations and

Short Titles

Baltimore Col.

Baltimore Collection. Manuscripts, letters, and photostats in the possession of the author, Friends School, Baltimore, Maryland.

B.Y.M.

Baltimore Yearly Meeting of the Religious Society of Friends. The manuscript books of the Yearly Meeting and its subordinate bodies are kept in the Record Room, Stony Run Meeting, Baltimore, Maryland.

Disc. N.Y.Y.M. 1810

Printed Book of Discipline of the Yearly Meeting of Friends, held in New York, for the State of New York, and parts adjacent, as Revised and Adopted, in the Sixth Month, 1810.

E.H.

Elias Hicks of Jericho, Long Island, New York.

F.H.L.

Friends Historical Library of Swarthmore College, Swarthmore, Pennsylvania. Here are nearly four hundred letters written by Elias Hicks, as well as his MS Journal.

J.H.

Jemima Seaman Hicks

J.E.H.

Journal of the Life and Religious Labours of Elias Hicks, written by himself (New York, 1832). The printed *Journal* incorporates the home Journal (1813–19) and many travel diaries.

London Epistles	*A Collection of the Epistles from the Yearly Meeting of Friends in London to the Quarterly and Monthly Meetings in Great Britain, Ireland and Elsewhere, from 1675 to 1805* . . . (Baltimore, 1806).
M.M.	Monthly Meeting of the Society of Friends. A Monthly Meeting consisted of several subordinate or Preparative Meetings.
MS Disc. N.Y.Y.M. 1783	MS Book of Discipline, From our Yearly Meeting held at Westbury, Long Island for New York and places adjacent: from the 24th of 5th Month, 1783 to the 31st of the same inclusive (Westbury Vault, Westbury, Long Island, New York).
MS J.E.H.	The manuscript Journal of Elias Hicks in Friends Historical Library of Swarthmore College, Swarthmore, Pennsylvania. It contains approximately one hundred pages not found in the printed *Journal*. Page numbering refers to the nearest parallel in the printed edition.
MS M.H.	Seven notebooks of material collected by Marietta Hicks, Westbury, Long Island, New York.
MS Min.	MS minutes of the Religious Society of Friends. Minutes were kept by the Preparative, Monthly, Quarterly, and Yearly Meetings.
Newell Col.	Newell Collection. A collection of nearly 300 letters written to Elias Hicks in the possession of Mrs. Le Roy Newell, Glen Head, Long Island, New York.
N.Y.Y.M.	New York Yearly Meeting of the Religious Society of Friends. The manuscript minutes of it and its various committees are found in the Record Room, Friends Seminary, New York City.
Prep. M.	Preparative Meeting of the Society of Friends. It is subordinate to a Monthly Meeting in which membership is registered.
Q.M.	Quarterly Meeting of the Society of Friends. It is composed of several Monthly Meetings whose representatives meet quarterly to transact business.
Y.M.	Yearly Meeting of the Religious Society of Friends. It is composed of several Quarterly Meetings whose representatives meet annually to transact business for a district extending over one or more states.

Notes

PREFACE

1. Rufus M. Jones, *The Later Periods of Quakerism* (2 vols., London, 1921), I, 489, 490.

2. Jones, *Later Periods*, I, 439.

3. D. Elton Trueblood, "A Century Passes," in *Friends Intelligencer*, 1 March 1930, pp. 165–66.

I: A QUAKER BOYHOOD

1. E.H. to William Poole, 12 Sept. 1823, MS Hicks Letters, Friends Historical Library, Swarthmore College, Swarthmore, Pa. Elias Hicks' date of birth is established as 19 March, 1748 (New Time) by a comment in the *Advocate of Truth*, I, 136. "E.H. we are informed, was just 80 years of age on the day on which he opened his prospect to his Monthly Meeting." Elias' request for a travel minute for the western journey was granted on 20 March, 1828. *The Christian Inquirer*, III, 406, carries the same information.

2. Deed of Jacob Hicks, *Hempstead Town Records* (Hempstead, Long Island, N.Y.) Vol. III, 3 April, 1735.

3. *J.E.H.*, p. 7.

4. E.H. to William Poole, 12 Sept. 1823, F.H.L.

5. To the Friends of the period "creaturely activities" suggested the luxuries and vanities not permitted in their simple way of life. "Speak to the condition" was a phrase frequently used to suggest inward spiritual agreement.

6. *J.E.H.,* p. 8.

7. MS J.E.H., p. 2.

8. Walt Whitman, *Complete Poetry and Prose* (2 vols., New York, 1948), II, 471.

9. Their son, Samuel Jr., became the first bishop of the Protestant Episcopal Church in America.

10. Henry Onderdonk, Jr., *The Annals of Hempstead: 1643 to 1832; Also the Rise and Growth of the Society of Friends on Long Island and in New York, 1657 to 1826* (Hempstead, 1878), p. 66. (Here after cited as *Annals of Hempstead.*)

11. *Records of North and South Hempstead,* III, 168. John Hicks' sheep were evidently marked by a narrow slit made in the left ear, and two holes the size of half pennies made in the right ear.

12. Elias Hicks, *A Series of Extemporaneous Discourses* (Philadelphia, 1825), p. 116.

13. MS J.E.H., p. 3.

14. New York *Gazette,* 4 June 1750.

15. *J.E.H.,* p. 8.

16. *J.E.H.,* p. 9.

17. *J.E.H.,* pp. 12, 13.

18. MS J.E.H., p. 5.

19. Hicks, *Extemporaneous Discourses,* pp. 18, 151.

20. Henry W. Wilbur, *Life and Labors of Elias Hicks* (Philadelphia, 1910), p. 12.

21. Wilbur, *Life and Labors,* pp. 12, 13.

22. A phrase used by George Fox and later Friends to suggest the universality of the Quaker message, as well as the Quaker belief in the divine element within man.

23. In this period membership in the Society of Friends was the right of children whose fathers were members, even though, as in the case of Elias Hicks, the mother was not a member. In a letter in F.H.L. dated 12 Sept, 1823, written to William Poole, Elias Hicks made the statement, "My father was considered a member among Friends at the time of my birth, which in that day gave me the privilege of taking a wife in the Order of Society, and that established my membership." There is no rec-

ord of Elias Hicks being admitted to membership by convincement or request of parents, so he must have taken advantage of the customary rule to claim membership at his marriage.

II: HAND IN HAND

1. MS J.E.H., pp. 13, 14.
2. E.H. to J.H., 17 Nov. 1791, F.H.L.
3. E.H. to J.H., 6 Nov. 1791, F.H.L.
4. E.H. to J.H., 22 Aug. 1788, F.H.L.
5. MS J.E.H., p. 13.
6. MS J.E.H., p. 13.
7. MS M.H.; Benjamin F. Thompson, *The History of Long Island* (2 vols., New York, 1843), II, 41, 42.
8. MS Min. Westbury M.M., Nov. 1770; Dec. 1770; Jan. 1771; (Westbury Vault, Westbury, Long Island, N.Y.).
9. From a photostat of the original.
10. Henry W. Wilbur, *Life and Labors of Elias Hicks* (Philadelphia, 1910), p. 67.
11. MS M.H., I.
12. Except for the paved road and traffic signal, Jericho had changed little until 1952. The Seaman-Hicks homestead still stands, though considerably remodeled. Across the road is the stately home occupied by Valentine Hicks who married his second cousin, Abigail, daughter of Elias Hicks. The fields which Elias tilled are now part of the Underhill property where the Clerk of Jericho Preparative Meeting was living at the time of Elias' death. Daniel Underhill, his direct descendant, was Clerk of Jericho Monthly Meeting, 1949–51. At the crossroads stands the house where Royal Aldrich and Martha Hicks, Elias' oldest daughter, once lived. The "Memorial Park" next door, dedicated to those from the town who gave their lives in two World Wars, covers part of the acreage where stood the Seaman tannery. South of the crossroads stands the Willets house, in which Elias and Jemima worshiped before the Jericho Meeting House was built; and on the west side of the road, Phebe U. Seaman, daughter of Robert Seaman (a great-grandson of the Robert Seaman who married Elias' youngest daughter), now lives. In 1952 the invasion of small houses began.
13. *J.E.H.*, p. 181.
14. *J.E.H.*, p. 197.
15. *J.E.H.*, pp. 189, 190.

16. *J.E.H.*, p. 276. Elias Hicks agreed with his contemporary Thomas Jefferson in holding in low esteem all city life. He felt that great cities were nurseries of vice, where men and women lived by their wits without giving to society a real return of value.

17. A story has been handed down concerning the tempo at which life moved onward at Jericho and Westbury in pre-Revolutionary days. In March a woman Friend asked to purchase needles in the store. Answered the proprietor, "I'm out of needles just now, but in the fall I shall go to town to buy some."

18. MS Min. of the Charity Society, 6 July 1794 (Jericho Safe, Jericho, Long Island, N.Y.).

19. Wilbur, *Life and Labors*, p. 14.

III: SETTLING IN AT JERICHO

1. Dates for births and deaths of the Seaman family can be found in Mary T. Seaman, *The Seaman Family in America* (New York, 1928); the Seaman and the Hicks family in the Records of Westbury Monthly Meeting; and in William Wade Hinshaw's *Encyclopedia of American Quaker Genealogy* (Ann Arbor, Michigan, 1940), III.

2. *J.E.H.*, p. 15.

3. MS Disc. N.Y.Y.M. 1783, p. 3.

4. MS Disc. N.Y.Y.M. 1783, p. 36.

5. Henry Onderdonk, Jr., *Annals of Hempstead* (Hempstead, 1878), p. 98.

6. According to Amelia Gummere, white aprons were not worn by Quaker women at this period. Amelia M. Gummere, *The Quaker, a Study in Costume* (Philadelphia, 1901), pp. 133–37.

7. *J.E.H.*, pp. 15, 16.

8. *J.E.H.*, p. 16.

9. Rufus M. Jones, *The Quakers in the American Colonies* (London, 1911), p. xvii.

10. *J.E.H.*, p. 15.

11. *J.E.H.*, p. 16.

12. Merle Curti, *The Growth of American Thought* (New York, 1943), p. 124.

13. Albert C. Applegarth, "Quakers in Pennsylvania," in *Johns Hopkins University Studies in Historical and Political Science*, Tenth Series, VIII–IX (Baltimore, 1892), p. 67.

14. MS Disc. N.Y.Y.M., 1783, p. 71.

15. MS Min. N.Y.Y.M., Book I, pp. 57–58.

16. MS Min. N.Y.Y.M., May 1773.

17. MS Min. N.Y.Y.M., May 1775.

18. MS Min. Westbury M.M., Book C, p. 172.

19. MS Records of Discharge of Negroes, Westbury M.M., 1776–91 (Westbury, Long Island, N.Y.).

20. Martha B. Flint, *Early Long Island: A Colonial Study* (New York, 1896), p. 333.

21. *London Epistles,* Epistles of 1771, p. 305. See also Epistles of 1772–83.

22. MS Min. N.Y.Y.M., May 1773.

23. John Cox, Jr., *Quakerism in the City of New York: 1657–1930* (New York, 1930), pp. 73, 75, 76.

24. Henry Onderdonk, Jr., *Documents and Letters Intended to Illustrate Revolutionary Incidents of Queens County* (New York, 1846), pp. 25, 26.

25. The Quaker testimony was not only against war but against revolution. Jones, *Quakers in American Colonies,* p. 562.

26. Onderdonk, *Documents and Letters,* pp. 43, 44.

27. *London Epistles,* 1776, p. 323.

28. Onderdonk, *Documents and Letters,* pp. 58–63, 78–80.

29. *J.E.H.,* p. 77.

IV: THE FRIENDS FACE THE AMERICAN REVOLUTION

1. Martha B. Flint, *Early Long Island: A Colonial Study* (New York, 1896), p. 339.

2. *J.E.H.,* p. 16.

3. *Journals of the Provincial Congress of New York* (Albany, 1842), I, 972, 19 June 1777; I, 1027, 5 Aug. 1777.

4. MS Min. Westbury M.M., 28 Aug. 1777.

5. MS Disc. N.Y.Y.M. 1783, p. 49.

6. The release of Ben Willis is recorded in the Oyster Bay Town Records of 1778, the other two in the records of 1794 and 1799. See *Oyster Bay Records, Queens Co., N.Y.,* Vol. VII, 1764–95 (New York, 1938), pp. 226, 227, 241.

7. MS Old Pen Article (Jericho Safe, Jericho, Long Island, N.Y.). Elias Hicks' will, Liber G of Wills of Real Estate, p. 13, Surrogate's Court, Queens Co., N.Y.

8. The minute reads: "At a Monthly Meeting held at Westbury ye

29th of Fourth month, 1778, William Seaman and William Valentine report that they have made inquiry concerning Elias Hicks, and find nothing to hinder his being recommended to the meeting of Ministers and Elders, whom this meeting recommends to that meeting as a minister, and directs the clerk to forward a copy of this minute to said meeting." MS Minutes Westbury Monthly Meeting, Long Island, N.Y.

9. *Disc. N.Y.Y.M., 1810*, p. 30.

10. *J.E.H.*, p. 18.

11. *J.E.H.*, p. 16.

12. E.H. to J.H., 11 Sept. 1779, F.H.L.

13. *Extracts from the Journal of Elizabeth Drinker: 1759–1807*, ed. Henry D. Biddle (New York, 1889), pp. 121–28.

14. E.H. to Henry Drinker, 5 Oct. 1779, 8 Oct. 1779, F.H.L.

15. From the MS Papers of Catherine Post Underhill. "To the Commissioners of Conspi [rac] y. [Poughkeepsie] Quaker Hill, 29 Oct. 1779. Gentlemen, I have strictly inquired into the Political character of Mr. Willis and am Satisfyed both from Persons from L.I. in his neighborhood and also from men of character here that he is a Person of Such Standing that no Danger Will arise for his being Permitted to Return to L.I. Therefore Desire having your approbation that he may have a Certificate to Pass our Guard. I am Gentleman your Humble Servant. Jonathan Tompkins."

16. MS Book of Sufferings of Westbury M.M., 3 Dec. 1777 (Westbury Vault, Westbury, Long Island, N.Y.).

17. English Friends were asked to investigate the matter and reported back that the receipt was among the papers in the war office. There is no record that English Friends made any arrangement by which the money could be returned to New York; but a minute of N.Y.Y.M. of 1784 reads: "after having in vain used their endeavours to obtain the Vouchers given for the money, they [London Y.M.] had paid it into the Exchequer."

18. MS Min. N.Y.Y.M., May 1781.

19. MS Min. N.Y.Y.M., May 1779.

20. The first constitution of New York, adopted in 1777, exempted from the state militia "all such inhabitants of this state (being of the people called Quakers) as, from scruples of conscience may be averse to the bearing of arms, be therefrom excused by the legislature and do pay the state such sums of money, in lieu of their personal service, as the same may, in the judgment of the legislature, be worth" (Article XL).

21. *J.E.H.*, p. 20.

22. *J.E.H.*, p. 21.

23. *J.E.H.*, p. 20. The William Heath Papers in Massachusetts Historical Society indicate that not all military authorities shared Elias' views. Four Friends, going to Oblong under religious concern, were arrested in November 1781 and word sent to General Heath, and on to Governor Clinton, that "the Quakers always express much inoffensiveness and they do not meddle with Politicks but I have known some of them to Collect very good Intelligence if they will do it on our side they will on the other. . . . They have it in their power to do us much mischief under the auspicious cloak of Religion." After an investigation, directions were given to "let such pass as produce recommendations. . . ." William Heath Papers, XXII, 1781, 55; also XXIII, 262.

24. *J.E.H.*, p. 22.

25. MS. J.E.H., p. 23.

26. *Royal Gazette,* 22 Jan. 1780.

27. John Cox, Jr., *Quakerism in the City of New York, 1657–1930,* (New York, 1930), pp. 79–81.

28. From a photostat from Jesse L. Merritt, Nassau County Historian.

29. MS Box 18, Report of the Committee on St. Johns Settlement, 17 Jan. 1788, Library of the Society of Friends, Friends House, London.

30. John and Charles went to Annapolis County, Oliver to Digby, Sylvester to Granville Township, Gilbert to New Brunswick, and Samuel to the Maritimes. Hicks family records indicate that John and Charles were descended from Elias Hicks' great-grandfather, Thomas. Letter from Dr. Franklyn H. Hicks, Halifax, N.S., Canada.

31. *London Epistles,* Epistle of 1779, pp. 330–32.

V: REFORM AND THE ITINERANT MINISTER

1. MS Min. N.Y.Y.M., May 1782.

2. The Book of Discipline of 1783 spoke of Friends being of one mind, walking by the same rule, and preserving unity as the bond of Christian fellowship, pp. 2, 4. Later Disciplines, such as that of 1810, put the Quaker point of view more concisely by stating that Friends were a gathered people, "distinguished by peculiar principles and testimonies . . ." were rules to serve, "as an exterior hedge of preservation against the temptations and dangers to which [they were] exposed." *Disc. N.Y.Y.M. 1810,* pp. 5, 6.

3. MS Min. W.M.M., Book C, p. 279.

4. *J.E.H.*, pp. 159, 162, 193.

5. John Cox, Jr., *Quakerism in the City of New York: 1657–1930* (New York, 1930), pp. 113–45. Robert Murray's brother John was president of the New York Chamber of Commerce from 1798–1806. Elias Hicks' grandson Elias, son of Valentine and Abigail Hicks, was to be president in 1853.

6. MS Disc. N.Y.Y.M. 1783, p. 85.

7. E.H. to J.H., 6 Jan. 1798, F.H.L.

8. MS Old Pen Article (Jericho Safe, Jericho, Long Island, N.Y.).

9. *J.E.H.*, pp. 66, 90, 101.

10. E.H. to J.H., 11 Sept. 1779.

11. MS N.Y.Y.M., 1783, p. 83.

12. *J.E.H.*, p. 101.

13. Elias Hicks, *A Series of Contemporary Discourses* (Philadelphia, 1825), p. 149. Cider was not considered "hard liquor." At the time of his death, Elias Hicks had "fifty bottles cyder." Photostat appraisal of his personal effects, 19 May, 1830, Baltimore Col.

14. Thomas E. Drake, *Quakers and Slavery in America* (New Haven, 1950), p. 98.

15. A phrase in use by Friends for many decades to express the essence of their educational ideal. Howard H. Brinton, *Quaker Education in Theory and Practice* (Pendle Hill, 1940), pp. 53–58, 96–108.

16. Henry Onderdonk, Jr., *Annals of Hempstead: 1643–1832* (Hempstead, 1878), p. 103; MS Min. Westbury M.M., Book C, pp. 270–306.

17. Cox, *Quakerism in New York*, pp. 164–65.

18. *J.E.H.*, p. 296.

19. *J.E.H.*, p. 232.

20. *J.E.H.*, p. 104.

21. *J.E.H.*, pp. 135, 137, 176, 179.

22. *J.E.H.*, p. 170.

23. *J.E.H.*, pp. 122, 136, 269, 288, 366.

24. *J.E.H.*, pp. 97, 98.

25. *J.E.H.*, pp. 118, 247, 255, 258, 397.

26. *J.E.H.*, pp. 195, 323, 369.

27. *J.E.H.*, p. 371.

28. E.H. to J.H., 7 Dec. 1828, F.H.L.

29. Rufus M. Jones, *The Later Periods of Quakerism* (2 vols., London, 1921), I, 101.

30. The Matinecock deed indicated that the land "now is and so from time to time and all time forever hereafter, shall remain and continue to them [the Quakers]."

31. E.H. to J.H., 20 June 1784.

32. Under a ruling made as early as 1761, all gravestones were removed in Friends' cemeteries, so no stones were placed over the boys' graves in the new burial plot at Jericho. Evidently Friends did not always obey the rule when they buried on their own property. When Jemima Hicks' parents died, they were buried some little distance back of the house, on land which now is a lane running to a pasture on the Underhill property. Daniel Underhill declared that he could remember as a boy seeing stones under the locust trees, on which were carved initials of the Seaman family. The last of these stones, one bearing the letters "J.S." for Jonathan Seaman, was knocked down by a hay wagon in Daniel Underhill's youth.

VI: A NEW MEETING HEARS JOB SCOTT

1. The building committee consisted of Adonijah Underhill, Elias Hicks, and others. Three hundred pounds were collected to cover the cost of ground and building. Trustees to hold the property were Stephen Mott, Gideon Seaman, Elias Hicks, and Edmund Willis. Jacob Willits was the Treasurer.

2. MS Min., Jericho Prep. M., 7 Dec. 1787. A porch to protect the two south doorways during inclement weather was added in 1818. MS Min., Jericho Prep. M., 14 May 1818.

3. The cost of the land and building came to over £450.

4. E.H. to J.H., 22 Aug. 1788; 1 Sept. 1788, F.H.L.

5. Friends had settled at Bethpage as early as 1688, and held weekly gatherings after 1732. A Meeting House was constructed in 1744, a schoolhouse in 1786. It was twelve miles southeast of Jericho.

6. MS Min., Jericho M.M., 16 May 1793.

7. *J.E.H.,* pp. 30, 31.

8. *J.E.H.,* p. 150.

9. *J.E.H.,* p. 167.

10. *J.E.H.,* p. 250.

11. E.H. to a Young Man in Great Weakness of Body, 10 Jan. 1791, F.H.L.

12. MS Min. The Charity Society (Jericho Safe, Jericho, Long Island, N.Y.). Elias Hicks contributed funds to the Charity Society for more than twenty years. Soon after it began, the Society received a gift of £150 to provide books for Negro children.

13. E.H. to Lewis Cornell, 6 Feb. 1795, F.H.L.

14. MS Min. Jericho Prep. M., 16 Aug. 1787.

15. MS Min. School Committee (Jericho Safe, Jericho, Long Island, N.Y.), 12 Nov. 1789; 18 March 1790; 13 May 1790.

16. Job Scott, *The Works of That Eminent Minister of the Gospel Job Scott* (2 vols., Philadelphia, 1831), I, 351.

17. Henry J. Cadbury, "Coatless Quietist," in *Now and Then, Friends Intelligencer,* 1 Oct. 1949, p. 550.

18. Scott, *Works,* I, 15–17; see also 119–21, 137, 138, 197, 243–45, 247–49, 301–303, 362, 363, 367, 475, 495.

19. Scott, *Works,* I, 49.

20. E.H. to Isaac Hicks, 4 July 1801, F.H.L.

21. *J.E.H.,* p. 29; see also pp. 32, 33, 38, 53, 93, 96, 126, 266, 321.

22. Scott, *Works,* I, 43.

23. Elias Hicks, *A Series of Extemporaneous Discourses* (Philadelphia, 1825), p. 10; see also pp. 67, 158, 160, 161, 204, 220.

24. Elias Hicks, *Extemporaneous Discourses,* p. 163.

25. Elias Hicks, *Extemporaneous Discourses,* pp. 4, 5, 8, 119.

26. Scott, *Works,* I, 475.

27. Scott, *Works,* I, 482.

28. Elias Hicks, *Extemporaneous Discourses,* p. 117.

29. Elias Hicks, *Extemporaneous Discourses,* pp., 35, 36.

30. Elias Hicks, *Extemporaneous Discourses,* p. 117. See also *Sermons Delivered by Elias Hicks and Edward Hicks* (New York, 1825), p. 16; and *J.E.H.,* pp. 36, 48, 50.

31. *J.E.H.,* p. 83.

32. Elias Hicks, *Extemporaneous Discourses,* pp. 2, 15, 186.

33. E.H. to a Friend, 14 March, 1808, F.H.L.

34. *J.E.H.,* p. 151.

35. Elias Hicks, *Extemporaneous Discourses,* p. 173.

36. Elias Hicks, *Extemporaneous Discourses,* pp. 73, 74.

37. *J.E.H.,* p. 103.

VII: CONFLICT WITH THE WORLD'S PEOPLE

1. Job Scott, *The Works of That Eminent Minister of the Gospel Job Scott* (2 vols., Philadelphia, 1831), I, 20, 21.

2. MS Disc. N.Y.Y.M., 1783, p. 84.

3. *J.E.H.,* pp. 84, 218, 221. Baptist ministers on the frontier during this period were unpaid. See also William W. Sweet, *The Story of Religion in America* (New York, 1930), p. 312.

4. Elias Hicks, *A Series of Extemporaneous Discourses* (Philadelphia, 1825), pp. 104, 290.

5. Thomas L. Moore to E.H., 29 Jan. 1785; E.H. to Thomas L. Moore, 4 Feb. 1787. In his correspondence Elias Hicks refers to an earlier letter he wrote on 20 Feb. 1785 which remained unanswered (F.H.L.).

6. E.H. to Unknown, 14 March 1808. See also E.H. to William B. Irish, 3 Sept. 1820, F.H.L.

7. Andrew Onderdonk to E.H., 12 April 1791, Newell Col.

8. Elias Hicks, *Extemporaneous Discourses*, p. 204.

9. E.H. to J.H., 6 Nov. 1791, postscript, F. H. L.

10. Edward C. Mack, *Peter Cooper: Citizen of New York* (New York, 1949), pp. 16–18.

11. MS J.E.H., p. 35.

12. Sweet, *Story of Religion*, pp. 323–24.

13. MS J.E.H., p. 35.

14. E.H. to J.H., 6 Nov. 1791, F.H.L.

15. E.H. to JH., 28 Oct. 1791, F.H.L.

16. *J.E.H.*, pp. 207, 216–17.

17. *J.E.H.*, p. 161.

18. *J.E.H.*, p. 36. See also Elias Hicks, *Extemporaneous Discourses*, pp. 10–15, 66–68, 116–19, 126–30, 165–70.

19. *J.E.H.*, p. 38.

20. MS Disc. N.Y.Y.M., 1783, pp. 11, 46.

21. E.H. to J.H., 28 Aug. 1792, postscript, F.H.L.

22. MS Min. Jericho Prep. M., 9 July 1795.

23. MS Min. Jericho Prep. M., 16 Aug. 1792; 11 April 1793.

24. Robert Nesbit to E.H., 14 May 1791, F.H.L.

25. *Oyster Bay Town Records, 1795–1878* (New York, 1940), III. In 1794, John Comly, leader of the liberal group in Philadelphia, "relinquished his right to vote"; *Journal of the Life and Religious Labours of John Comly* (Philadelphia, 1853), pp. 53–54.

26. MS Min. Jericho M.M., 10 May 1792.

27. Meetings for Worship were held on Manhattan Island previous to 1681. They were conducted in private homes until 1696, when the first Meeting House was built on Green Street (now Liberty Place). Additional ground was purchased and a larger Meeting House and a school were built adjoining, facing Crown Street (now Liberty Street), in 1748. Elias Hicks helped raise funds to build a new Meeting House, constructed in 1776, on the southeast side of Queen Street (now Pearl). This is usually spoken of in the histories as the Pearl Street Meeting House. See John Cox, Jr., *Quakerism in the City of New York: 1657–1930* (New York, 1930), pp. 28–34.

VIII: "IN NEAR AND DEAR SYMPATHY"

1. MS Min. Jericho M.M., 18 April 1793.

2. *J.E.H.*, pp. 39–50.

3. *J.E.H.*, p. 11.

4. *J.E.H.*, p. 307.

5. E.H. to E. Chichester, 17 Aug. 1805, F.H.L.

6. Henry W. Wilbur, *The Life and Labors of Elias Hicks* (Philadelphia, 1910), p. 111.

7. Elias Hicks, *A Series of Extemporaneous Discourses* (Philadelphia, 1825), pp. 113–14, 137–38, 140–41.

8. E.H. to J.H., 28 Aug. 1793, F.H.L.

9. E.H. to J.H., 24 Aug. 1793, F.H.L.

10. E.H. to J.H., 17 Sept. 1793, F.H.L.

11. Act of the Justices of Kingston, in the County of Ulster, N.Y. MS Copy in the Kingston Historical Museum, Kingston, N.Y.

12. MS Min. Jericho Prep. M., 17 Oct. 1793. MS Disc. N.Y.Y.M., 1783 as amended. Thomas E. Drake, *Quakers and Slavery in America* (New Haven, 1950), pp. 115–16.

13. Elias Hicks, *Extemporaneous Discourses,* pp. 87, 88.

14. Existing copies of surveys by Elias Hicks include those for the Jericho Meeting house grounds, a tract now included in today's Meadow Brook Park, the churchyard of the Episcopal Church of Oyster Bay in which Theodore Roosevelt is buried, and for many farms in the Jericho and Westbury area.

15. Part of Elias Hicks' library is in Friends Historical Library of Swarthmore College, a part is owned by Phebe U. Seaman, Jericho, Long Island. In the Historical Library are the third edition of George Fox's *Journal* containing the Hicks genealogy in Elias' handwriting, the Journal of John Woolman, works of Joseph Phipps, Emmanuel Swedenborg, and Hicks' *Sermons.* At Jericho are copies he used of the works of William Penn, Robert Barclay, John Gough, and Lindley Murray. Other books mentioned in his *Journal* and not found in either collection include the works of Mosheim, Clarkson, Priestley, and Thomas Wetherald. After 1806, Elias Hicks had free access to the splendid library of his cousin Isaac Hicks of Westbury which numbered several hundred volumes, including the current English historical and religious books.

16. With the exception of an occasional year or so, Elias Hicks served on the Jericho School Committee from its inception in 1787 to 1807,

when the first volume of the school committee minutes end. Book II is lost. Book III begins in 1823, when Elias was 73, and his name is not mentioned. Royal Aldrich and Valentine Hicks both served on the committee during the later period. Valentine Hicks taught the school for at least a term in 1826. MS Books Jericho School Committee (Jericho Safe, Jericho, Long Island, N.Y.).

17. MS Min. Jericho School Committee, 13 May 1802. John Cox, Jr., *Quakerism in the City of New York: 1657–1930* (New York, 1930), pp. 107, 169, 170.

18. MS Min. Jericho M.M., April 1796 to Nov. 1796.

19. MS Min. Jericho M.M., 4 April 1796 to Nov. 1796.

20. MS Min. Jericho M.M., 18 June 1795.

21. MS Copy, Conclusion of the Committee respecting particular duties of Superintendent and Teachers at Nine Partners boarding school. Baltimore Col.

22. MS Copy N.Y.Y.M. Extracts, Nine Partners School Committee, 1795–1805. MS Min. Jericho Prep. M., 9 Nov. 1800.

23. Anna D. Hallowell, *James and Lucretia Mott* (Boston, 1896), p. 17.

24. Extracts N.Y.Y.M. 1806–1840, Nine Partners boarding school, 1811.

IX: LIGHT HAS BROKEN

1. E.H. to Gideon Seaman, 9 April, 1798, F.H.L. *J.E.H.,* 57–81.

2. E.H. to Gideon Seaman, 9 April, 1798, F.H.L. *J.E.H.,* p. 72.

3. Amelia M. Gummere, *The Quaker: A Study in Costume* (Philadelphia, 1901), p. 41.

4. E.H. to J.H., 13 Dec. 1791, F.H.L.

5. E.H. to J.H., Dec. 1797. According to local tradition it was Jemima's poor writing which caused a descendent to destroy all her letters while keeping those written by Elias Hicks.

6. E.H. to a Friend, 29 Dec. 1797, F.H.L.

7. Joshua Evans, "Journal," *Friends' Miscellany,* No. 1, Vol. X (Philadelphia, 1837), p. 200.

8. E.H. to Hugh Judge, 15 Jan. 1798, F.H.L.

9. *J.E.H.,* p. 60.

10. E.H. to Hugh Judge, 15 Jan. 1798, F.H.L.

11. MS J.E.H., pp. 63, 64.

12. E.H. to J.H., 12 Feb. 1798, F.H.L.

13. *Historical Sketch of Third Haven Meeting House* (Easton, 1932), p. 14.

14. E.H. to Hugh Judge, 3 March 1798, F.H.L.

15. *Bi-Centennial of Brick Meeting House 1901* (Lancaster, 1902), p. 59.

16. *J.E.H.*, p. 65.

17. The boarding school at Chrome lasted only a few years; meanwhile George Churchman became one of the founders, in 1799, of Westtown, the Friends' boarding school south of Philadelphia.

18. This route is still U.S. No. 1.

19. MS Min. Nottingham M.M., 24 Feb. 1798, B.Y.M.

20. *J.E.H.*, p. 65.

21. *J.E.H.*, pp. 65, 66.

22. Joshua Evans, "Journal," *Friends' Miscellany*, p. 187.

23. *J.E.H.*, p. 68.

24. E.H. to J.H., 15 March 1798, F.H.L.

25. E.H. to Martha Aldrich, 9 March 1798, F.H.L.

26. E.H. to J.H., Jan. 1798, postcript, F.H.L.

27, *J.E.H.*, p. 70.

28. MS J.E.H., p. 70.

29. MS Min. Fairfax Q.M., 19 March 1798; MS Womens Meeting Fairfax Q.M., 18 March 1798, B.Y.M.

30. MS J.E.H., p. 71.

31. *J.E.H.*, p. 73. The Hoovers, ancestors of former President Hoover, were members of Pipe Creek Meeting about this time.

32. E.H. to George Churchman, 7 April, 1798, F.H.L.

33. Hugh Judge to E.H., 21 March 1798, Newell Col.

34. E.H. to George Churchman, 7 April 1798, F.H.L.

35. E.H. to J.H., 5 April 1798, F.H.L.

36. E.H. to J.H., 20 April 1798, F.H.L.; Esech was probably an apprentice.

37. E.H. to J.H., 3 April 1798, F.H.L.

38. E.H. to J.H., 26 April, 1798, F.H.L.

39. *J.E.H.*, pp. 74–78.

40. E.H. to J.H., 16 May 1798, F.H.L.

41. John Hunt, "Journal," *Friends' Miscellany*, No. 1, (Philadelphia, 1837), X, 277.

42. *J.E.H.*, p. 78.

43. *J.E.H.*, pp. 79, 80.

44. *J.E.H.*, p. 81.

X: SHADOWS OF DISSENT

1. Rufus M. Jones, *The Later Periods of Quakerism* (2 vols., London, 1921), I, 281–82.

2. Jones, *Later Periods,* I, 277.

3. MS Min. Jericho Prep. M., 11 Nov. 1800.

4. Hugh Judge to E.H., August, September, October, November, 1798, Newell Col. Hugh Judge, *Memoirs and Journal of Hugh Judge* (Byberry, 1841), pp. 243–45. E.H. to Hugh Judge, 30 September 1798, F.H.L.

5. John Hunt, "Journal," *Friends' Miscellany,* No. 1 (Philadelphia, 1837), X, 295.

6. E.H. to Martha Aldrich, 29 May 1801, F.H.L.

7. MS J.E.H., p. 98.

8. *J.E.H.,* pp. 99, 100.

9. E.H. to J.H., 4 July 1801; E.H. to Jonathan and John Hicks, 4 July 1801, F.H.L.

10. E.H. to Isaac Hicks, 4 July 1801; MS M.H.

11. *J.E.H.,* pp. 103–5. Criticism still lingers at Jericho because Elias Hicks went on so many long trips. Jemima, in 1801, probably hearing similar criticism, signed Elias' certificate to travel—an unusual thing for a wife to do. Abigail Hicks and Martha Aldrich also signed this certificate.

12. The latter half of 1801 and all of 1802 are blank in Elias Hicks' Journal. Only two letters of his are preserved from this period.

13. MS Min. N.Y.Y.M. Ministers and Elders, 26 May 1798.

14. The source material is to be found in the Library, Friends House, London. MSS Devonshire M.M., Vol. 13, 1796–1802; Vol. 14, 1802–10; London and Middlesex Quarter, 1798–1812; Pen Pictures of London Y.M., 1789–1808, 1808–33. The MS Journal of James Jenkins, 1761–1821 traces the various trials. It is also at Friends House.

In his Journal, James Jenkins wrote of Hannah Barnard's trial, "Here an autocracy of Elders ruled with an exclusive sway, and with tenacious hands held all power in its group . . . these feudal chiefs always expected and often obtained the obsequious obedience of these humbler breathren." He also pointed out that in Hannah Barnard's case the members of the Ministry and Elders "were accusers, Judges, and Re-Judges"; and that the bulk of the membership knew nothing of what went on in Committee sessions. "We poor *commoners,* had only noticed the unusual circumstances of the protracted, and frequent meetings . . . who did not separate this year at the usual time."

15. MS Devonshire M.M., Vol. 13. Samuel M. Janney, *History of the*

Religious Society of Friends: From its Rise to the Year 1828 (4 vols., Philadelphia, 1867), IV, 39.

16. MS Disc. N.Y.Y.M. 1783, p. 83; *Disc. N.Y.Y.M.* 1800, p. 95.

17. *The Journal of George Fox,* ed. John L. Nickalls (London, 1952), p. 136.

18. MS Journal James Jenkins, Library, Friends House, London.

19. *J.E.H.,* pp. 122, 123.

20. Elias Hicks, *A Series of Extemporaneous Discourses* (Philadelphia, 1825), p. 17.

21. *Journal of the Life and Gospel Labors of David Sands* (London, 1848), p. 242.

22. Elias Hicks, *Letters of Elias Hicks* (Philadelphia, 1861), p. 227.

23. Elias Hicks, *Extemporaneous Discourses,* p. 6.

24. Elias Hicks, *Letters,* pp. 227–28. Jeremiah J. Foster, *An Authentic Report of the Testimony in a Cause at Issue in the Court of Chancery of the State of New Jersey* (2 vols., Philadelphia, 1831), II, 417–21.

25. Elias Hicks, *Extemporaneous Discourses,* p. 5.

XI: DAYS OF WORK AND SORROW

1. A term used in the Quaker records of the period to refer to the area north of Lake Ontario and Lake Erie, in contrast to the older settled region of the Maritime Provinces.

2. Francis W. Halsey, *The Old New York Frontier, 1614–1800* (New York, 1901). Alice M. Earle, *Stage Coach and Tavern Days* (New York, 1900).

3. *J.E.H.,* pp. 106–9. E.H. to J.H., 16 Oct. 1803, F.H.L.

4. *J.E.H.,* p. 109.

5. *J.E.H.,* p. 110.

6. E.H. to J.H., 14 Nov. 1803, F.H.L.

7. Hugh Judge, *Memoirs and Journal of Hugh Judge* (Byberry, 1841), pp. 245–48.

8. *J.E.H.,* pp. 113, 114.

9. *J.E.H.,* p. 14.

10. *J.E.H.,* pp. 32, 38, 43, 118, 172.

11. E.H. to George Churchman, 19 Nov. 1805, F.H.L. The living children in 1805 were Martha H. Aldrich, Abigail H. Hicks, Elizabeth, and Sarah.

12. George Churchman to E.H., 24 Dec. 1805. His son John, who died at sea, was the author of *Magnetic Atlas,* a correspondent of George

Washington and Thomas Jefferson, the second American to be admitted to the Russian Academy of Science.

13. Walt Whitman, *Complete Poetry and Prose* (2 vols., New York, 1948), I, 479.

14. MS of John Jackson, Sketch of Life and Character of Elias Hicks, F.H.L.

15. *History of Queens County New York* (W. W. Munsell Co., 1882).

16. MS Min. N.Y.Y.M. Meeting for Sufferings, 27 April 1804.

17. E.H. to Hugh Judge, 27 April 1804, F.H.L.

18. John Cox, Jr., *Quakerism in the City of New York: 1657–1930* (New York, 1930), pp. 176–82.

19. E.H. to Job Chaloner, 15 Feb. 1805; E.H. to John Allen, Jr., 22 Sept. 1806, F.H.L.

20. MS M.H., VII.

21. Samuel R. Fisher to E.H., 3 April 1806, Newell Col.

22. E.H. to J.H., 8 April 1806, F.H.L.

23. *J.E.H.,* p. 116.

24. E.H. to J.H., 16 Jan. 1807, F.H.L.

25. *J.E.H.,* pp. 121, 122.

26. *J.E.H.,* pp. 122, 123.

27. Judge, *Memoirs and Journal,* p. 303.

28. E.H. to Hugh Judge, 30 May 1807, F.H.L.

29. MS Min. Jericho Prep. M., 8 Oct. 1807; 12 Nov. 1807.

30. *J.E.H.,* p. 126. Lucretia Coffin became an assistant teacher at Nine Partners in 1808, at the age of fifteen, with a salary of $100 a year and board. The next year she became a regular teacher, which entitled her younger sister to free tuition. In 1811 she married James Mott.

31. *J.E.H.,* p. 281.

XII: LIBERAL AND EVANGELICAL TRAVEL TOGETHER

1. Etienne de Grellet du Mabillier was born in 1773 in Limoges, France, of wealthy parents who were members of the nobility. He was educated under Catholic tutors and at the College of the Oratorians at Lyons. The Family estates were confiscated during the French Revolution, its members scattered, and Etienne and his brother came to America. Etienne became a Friend through the preaching of two itinerant English Quakers, warmly Evangelical in their point of view. He joined North Meeting, Philadelphia, in 1796, and was recorded a minister two years later. He moved to New York City in 1799.

2. E.H. to Hugh Judge, 3 Aug. 1805, F.H.L.

3. Edwin W. Weeks, "Elias Hicks and Hicksville," *Friends Intelligencer*, 3 April 1937, p. 230.

4. John Murray, Jr., to E.H., 3 Feb. 1808, Newell Col.

5. E.H. to J.H., 10 Aug. 1808, F.H.L.

6. *J.E.H.*, pp. 10, 11, 30, 50, 62, 91, 92, 103, 132, 149, 153, 198, 200, 378, 412, 432.

7. Stephen Grellet, *Memoirs of the Life and Gospel Labours of Stephen Grellet*, ed. Benjamin Seebohm (2 vols., London, 1860), I, 147.

8. Grellet, *Memoirs*, II, 203.

9. *J.E.H.*, 190.

10. *J.E.H.*, pp. 127, 128.

11. Grellet, *Memoirs*, I, 142.

12. Grellet, *Memoirs*, I, 142.

13. Grellet, *Memoirs*, I, 142.

14. *J.E.H.*, pp. 126–27.

15. E.H. to J.H., 17 Sept. 1808, F.H.L.

16. Hugh Judge to E.H., April 1807; E.H. to Hugh Judge, 28 May, 1808, F.H.L.

17. *J.E.H.*, p. 113.

18. *J.E.H.*, p. 115.

19. *J.E.H.*, p. 120.

20. *J.E.H.*, p. 129.

21. Weeks, "Elias Hicks and Hicksville," *Friends Intelligencer*, 3 April 1937, p. 230.

22. William Logan Fisher, *A Review of the Public Relations of the Society of Friends. . . .* (Philadelphia, 1852), pp. 109, 110.

23. Henry W. Wilbur, *The Life and Labors of Elias Hicks* (Philadelphia, 1910), p. 205. James Mott, Sr., to E.H. 5 Aug. 1805, F.H.L.

24. *J.E.H.*, p. 128.

25. Grellet, *Memoirs*, I, 168.

26. Rufus M. Jones, *The Later Periods of Quakerism* (2 vols., London, 1921), I, 285.

27. Jones, *Later Periods*, I, 312.

28. Edward Grubb, *Quaker Thought and History* (New York, 1925), p. 80.

29. Henry Tuke, *Principles of Religion, as professed by the Society of Christians, usually called Quakers* (London, 1805), pp. 12, 16, 26.

30. E.H. to Unknown, 8 Oct. 1810, F.H.L.

31. E.H. to Unknown, 8 Oct. 1810, F.H.L.

32. Martha B. Flint, *Early Long Island: A Colonial Study* (New York, 1896), pp. 335–36.

XIII: THE QUAKER IDEALIST

1. *J.E.H.*, p. 126.

2. *J.E.H.*, p. 178.

3. E.H. to J.H. 31 Dec. 1809, F.H.L.

4. Joseph Talbot to E.H., Nov. 1808, Newell Col.; William Poole to E.H., 18 Nov. 1810, Newell Col.; E.H. to George Churchman, 12 June 1810, F.H.L.

5. Thomas E. Drake, *Quakers and Slavery in America* (New Haven, 1950), p. 116.

6. Elias Hicks, *Observations on the Slavery of the Africans and Their Descendants* . . . (New York, 1811), p. 3.

7. Elias Hicks, *Observations*, pp. 4, 5.

8. Elias Hicks, *Observations*, p. 6.

9. Elias Hicks, *Observations*, pp. 7-9.

10. Elias Hicks, *Observations*, pp. 20–22.

11. Henry W. Wilbur, *The Life and Labors of Elias Hicks* (Philadelphia, 1910), p. 90.

12. Thomas Burling to E.H., 25 July 1811, Newell Col.

13. Drake, *Quakers and Slavery*, p. 118.

14. Drake, *Quakers and Slavery*, p. 120.

15. Drake, *Quakers and Slavery*, p. 117.

16. E.H., to William Poole, undated letter, F.H.L.

17. E.H. MS Fragment, Morgan State College Collection, Baltimore, Maryland.

18. Drake, *Quakers and Slavery*, pp. 120–21.

19. Letter from John Burlingham of Worcester, England, then in America, 1811, F.H.L.

20. Called to the author's attention by Frederick B. Tolles, Librarian, F.H.L.

21. MS Min. Jericho Prep. M., 10 Sept. 1812; 9 Sept. 1813.

22. MS Min. Jericho Prep. M., 1812–15.

23. E.H. to David R. F. Jones, 14 Jan. 1802, F.H.L. Wilbur, *Life and Labors*, p. 103. *J.E.H.*, p. 361.

24. Ezra Michener, *A Retrospect of Early Quakerism* (Philadelphia, 1860), p. 133.

25. [John S. Tyson] Life of Elisha Tyson, the Philanthropist (Baltimore, 1825), p. 6.

26. Journal of John Hunt, *Friends Miscellany,* No. 1 (Philadelphia, 1837), Vol. X, pp. 389–90.

27. *J.E.H.,* p. 412. Elias Hicks, *A Series of Extemporaneous Discourses* (Philadelphia, 1825), p. 291.

28. E.H. to Samuel Cox, 5 Dec. 1813, F.H.L.

29. E.H. to Rufus Clark, 17 March 1813, F.H.L.

XIV: THE WRITTEN AND SPOKEN WORD

1. *J.E.H.,* p. 132.

2. Rufus M. Jones, *The Later Periods of Quakerism* (2 vols. London, 1921), I, 440.

3. As late as 1823, Elias Hicks shows by his answer to a query from William Poole of Wilmington that he did not approve of writing a journal. Bliss Forbush, "The Newly Discovered Manuscript Journal of Elias Hicks," *The Bulletin of Friends Historical Association,* XXXIX (1950), 17.

4. From a Manuscript of Elias Hicks, photostat travel diary of 1828, F.H.L.

5. As he grew older, Elias Hicks sold the tan shop, later sold forty acres of ground to Valentine Hicks, and thirty-five to Samuel Sherman. He borrowed $1,500 from Valentine Hicks in 1819 and paid $75.00 annual interest upon the note for the next ten years. He borrowed $810 from Royal Aldrich in 1822, and paid $226.12 in interest during the next six years. There were also two small notes, amounting to $96.50 against Elias Hicks when he died.

6. Written on the last page of the 1828 travel diary, F.H.L.

7. MS travel diary 1828, F.H.L.

8. MS travel diary 1828, F.H.L.

9. *J.E.H.,* p. 123.

10. *J.E.H.,* p. 132.

11. *J.E.H.,* p. 133.

12. *J.E.H.,* p. 152.

13. *J.E.H.,* p. 185.

14. E.H. to Abigail Hicks, 6 February 1813, F.H.L.

15. *J.E.H.,* pp. 154, 187.

16. *J.E.H.,* p. 155.

17. *J.E.H.,* p. 157.

18. *J.E.H.*, p. 138.

19. *J.E.H.*, p. 163.

20. The Memorial of Jericho Monthly Meeting of Friends Concerning Our Ancient Friend Elias Hicks, 4th month, 15th, 1830, MS Min. Jericho M.M.

21. Samuel M. Janney, *History of the Religious Society of Friends* (4 vols., Philadelphia, 1867), IV, 110, 111, quoting from the *Christian Examiner and General Review.*

22. Walt Whitman, *Complete Poetry and Prose* (2 vols., New York, 1948), II, 400, 468–87.

23. Hugh Judge, *Memoirs and Journal of Hugh Judge* (Byberry, 1841), p. 357.

24. Emanuel Howitt, *Selections from Letters Written During a Tour Through the United States in the Summer and Autumn of 1820* (Nottingham, England, 1820), p. 9.

25. Edward C. Mack, *Peter Cooper, Citizen of New York* (New York, 1949), p. 134.

26. MS letter from S. Rowland Morgan, great-great-grandson of Samuel R. Fisher, 14 Jan. 1949, Baltimore Col.

27. *The Journal of George Fox,* ed. John L. Nickalls (Cambridge, 1952), p. 11.

28. Whitman, *Poetry and Prose,* II, 482.

29. Whitman, *Poetry and Prose,* II, 479.

30. *J.E.H.*, pp. 248–49.

31. D. Elton Trueblood, "The Career of Elias Hicks," *Byways in Quaker History,* ed. Howard H. Brinton (Pendle Hill, Wallingford, 1944), pp. 89–90.

32. D. Elton Trueblood, "The Career of Elias Hicks," p. 90.

33. *The Quaker, A Series of Sermons* (Philadelphia, 1828), IV, 113.

34. Henry W. Wilbur, *The Life and Labors of Elias Hicks* (Philadelphia, 1910) p. 65.

35. *J.E.H.*, p. 384.

36. Elias Hicks, *A Series of Extemporaneous Discourses* (Philadelphia, 1825), pp. 154–84.

37. *Journal of George Fox,* p. xliv.

38. *The Quaker, A Series of Sermons,* I, 21, 22.

39. Edwin W. Weeks, "Elias Hicks and Hicksville," *Friends Intelligencer,* 3 April 1937.

40. Benjamin F. Thompson, *History of Long Island* (2 vols., New York, 1839), I, 341.

XV: "THE TUMULTUOUS STATE OF PUBLIC AFFAIRS"

1. *J.E.H.*, pp. 137, 190.
2. *J.E.H.*, p. 190.
3. *J.E.H.*, pp. 223–24.
4. *J.E.H.*, pp. 168, 197.
5. *J.E.H.*, p. 139.
6. *J.E.H.*, p. 141.
7. *J.E.H.*, p. 144.
8. MS Diary of Miers Fisher, for 1813, F.H.L.
9. MS Fisher Diary, 1813, F.H.L.
10. E.H. to Samuel R. Fisher, 16 June 1813, Newell Col.
11. E.H. to J.H., 7 July, 1813; 12 July 1813, photostats in Baltimore Col.
12. Samuel R. Fisher to E.H., 21 Oct. 1813.
13. *J.E.H.*, p. 197.
14. *J.E.H.*, p. 226.
15. *J.E.H.*, pp. 194–95.
16. *J.E.H.*, p. 184.
17. *J.E.H.*, p. 228.
18. John Comly, *Journal of the Life and Religious Labours of John Comly*, (Byberry, 1853), pp. 153, 158, 159, 165.
19. *J.E.H.*, pp. 212–14.
20. Alfred E. Garvie, *The Christian Preacher* (New York, 1923), p. 198.
21. John L. Mosheim, *An Ecclesiastical History* . . . (Baltimore, 1832), p. 63, 115, 166, 184, 214, 230, 362, 368.
22. Arthur C. McGiffert, *The Rise of Modern Religious Ideas* (New York, 1929), pp. 106, 109.
23. *J.E.H.*, p. 255.
24. E.H. to J.H., 13 Jan. 1815, F.H.L.
25. Comly, *Life and Religious Labours*, pp. 163–64.
26. *J.E.H.*, p. 267.
27. *J.E.H.*, p. 270.

XVI: DISSENT MOVES CLOSER

1. *J.E.H.*, p. 340.
2. *J.E.H.*, p. 314.
3. Elizabeth Bower, *Biography of William Cobbett, The Jolly Farmer* (New York, 1930).

4. E.H. to Martha Aldrich, 30 Sept. 1817, F.H.L.

5. E.H. to William Poole, 5 Jan. 1817, F.H.L.

6. *J.E.H.*, pp. 315–16. Baltimore Q.M. endorsed the Hicks certificate with the words, "his company and Gospel labours amongst us have been truly acceptable and edifying." MS West River Q.M., 1710–1822. Book 41, p. 474, Baltimore Y.M. Record Room.

7. E.H. to J.H., 17 Oct. 1817.

8. *J.E.H.*, p. 318.

9. MS J.E.H., p. 319.

10. Henry W. Wilbur, *The Life and Labors of Elias Hicks* (Philadelphia, 1910), p. 103. Elias Hicks, *Letters of Elias Hicks* (Philadelphia, 1861), pp. 38, 39.

11. Elias Hicks, *Letters*, pp. 43–50.

12. Remembering his study of Christian history with its long story of persecutions, Elias Hicks declared, "from a comparative point of view, [the Scriptures] have been the cause of four-fold more harm than good"; Elias Hicks, *Letters*, p. 44. This is meant in the same manner as William Temple's remark," A strong case could be made for the contention that on the whole Religion, up to date, had done more harm than good." William Temple, *Nature, Man and God* (New York, 1949), p. 22.

13. Elias Hicks, *Letters*, p. 47.

14. Elias Hicks, *Letters*, pp. 48, 49.

15. *The Journal of George Fox*, ed. John L. Nickalls (Cambridge, 1952), p. 23.

16. *J.E.H.*, p. 326.

17. E.H. to J.H., 19 Nov. 1818, F.H.L.

18. E.H. to J.H., 19 Nov. 1818, F.H.L.

19. E.H. to J.H., 17 Feb. 1819, F.H.L.

20. E.H. to Abigail Hicks, 18 March 1819; E.H. to J.H., 17 March 1819, F.H.L.

21. *J.E.H.*, p. 355.

22. Jeremiah J. Foster, *An Authentic Report of the Testimony in a Cause at Issue in the Court of Chancery* . . . (2 vols. Philadelphia, 1831), II, 44.

23. E.H. to J.H., 17 Oct. 1819, F.H.L.

24. E.H. to Valentine Hicks, 28 Oct. 1819, F.H.L.

25. MS Historical Review of the Rise and Progress of the Separation of the Friends of Philadelphia Yearly Meeting up to the Year 1827. Prepared by a Committee of the Meeting for Sufferings. Approved 30 May, 1847, F.H.L. (Hereafter cited as MS Historical Review . . . to the Year

1827, F.H.L.) MS Account of a Meeting at Pine Street in 1819 by Jonathan Evans, F.H.L. Foster, *An Authentic Report,* II, 39, 40.

26. Foster, *An Authentic Report,* II, 39, 40.

27. Rufus M. Jones, *The Later Periods of Quakerism,* (2 vols., London, 1921), I, 461.

28. MS Historical Review . . . to the Year 1827, F.H.L.

29. MS Jonathan Evans. Foster, *An Authentic Report,* II, 40. Evans wrote in 1801 that while his wife was on a visit to Baltimore he "felt entirely released as regarding the disuse of the products of slaves." MS. J.E. Emmor Kimber in a letter to E.H. noted that Hicks' address "cut Jonathan Evans to the quick which he manifested by restlessness and great distortion of countenance." 25 Jan. 1829, Newell Col.

30. MS Historical Review . . . to the Year 1827, F.H.L.

31. Foster, *An Authentic Report,* II, 40.

XVII: CHRIST IN YOU, THE HOPE OF GLORY

1. Samuel R. Fisher to E.H., 17 Nov. 1819, Newell Col.

2. E.H. to S. V. Smith, 24 May 1820, F.H.L.

3. *Sermons Delivered by Elias Hicks and Edward Hicks in Friends' Meetings in New York* (New York, 1825), pp. 133–34.

4. *Sermons . . . by Elias and Edward Hicks,* p. 135.

5. *J.E.H.,* pp. 193, 233–34.

6. *J.E.H.,* pp. 386–88.

7. *J.E.H.,* p. 389.

8. E.H. to Edward Hicks, quoted by Edward Hicks in *Memoirs of the Life and Labors of Edward Hicks* (Philadelphia, 1851), pp. 89–91.

9. Alice Ford, *Edward Hicks: Painter of the Peaceable Kingdom* (Philadelphia, 1952), pp. 40–41.

10. E.H. to Willet Hicks, 25 April, 1821, F.H.L.

11. MS Ferris Collection, F.H.L. *Letters of Paul and Amicus, Originally Published in the Christian Repository* (Wilmington, 1823), pp. 20, 24–28, 34. Elias Hicks, *A Series of Extemporaneous Discourses* (Philadelphia, 1825), pp. 26–29.

12. Stephen Grellet, *Memoirs of the Life and Gospel Labours of Stephen Grellet,* ed. Benjamin Seebohm (2 vols., London, 1860), II, 141.

13. Grellet, *Memoirs,* II, 148.

14. Arthur J. Mekeel, *Quakerism and a Creed* (Philadelphia, 1936), p. 9.

15. *London Epistles*, pp. 159–60.

16. *Disc. N.Y.Y.M. 1810*, p. 95.

17. *Book of Discipline B.Y.M. 1806*, p. 102.

18. *Book of Discipline Phila. Y.M. 1806; Book of Discipline B.Y.M., 1806.*

19. *J.E.H.*, p. 158.

20. *J.E.H.*, pp. 144, 190, 194, 317, 341, 353. Henry W. Wilbur, *Life and Labors of Elias Hicks* (Philadelphia, 1910), p. 154.

21. Elias Hicks, *Letters of Elias Hicks* (Philadelphia, 1861), p. 203.

22. Wilbur, *Life and Labors*, p. 111.

23. Wilbur, *Life and Labors*, p. 114.

24. Elias Hicks, *Letters*, pp. 81, 179, 204, 226. Wilbur, *Life and Labors*, p. 194. Jeremiah J. Foster, *An Authentic Report of the Testimony in a Cause at Issue in the Court of Chancery* . . . (2 vols., Philadelphia, 1831), II, 421, 422. E.H. to Harvey Fink, 13 Dec. 1827, F.H.L.

25. *J.E.H.*, p. 141, Elias Hicks, *Letters*, p. 82. "Jesus being a real and true man, and placed in a state of probation as we are, having our real and true nature, as to his manhood, and tempted in all points as we are, yet by his faithfulness to his heavenly Father he overcame temptation and lived free from sin, and by the pouring forth of the divine Spirit upon him, and he uniting with it, he became a partaker of the divine nature, and was born of God, and was then the Son of God with power; as no created being can be, strictly speaking, a son of God, but by being born of the Spirit of God." Elias Hicks, *Letters*, p. 94. "The children of men wanted a perfect example . . . he came forth to show them they might attain this life by living according to the manifestation of God's will, subjecting themselves to his commands, depending upon his power, and in this way living a righteous life. It is by his blessed example that we must be judged, for he showed us the way of righteousness by his doctrine and testimony, and sealed it with his blood." *Sermons . . . by Elias and Edward Hicks*, p. 25.

26. Elias Hicks, *Extemporaneous Discourses*, pp. 69, 70.

27. Elias Hicks, *Letters*, p. 75.

28. Elias Hicks, *Letters*, pp. 55, 56.

29. Elias Hicks, *Letters*, p. 203.

30. Elias Hicks, *Extemporaneous Discourses*, p. 10. Elias Hicks, *Letters*, pp. 71–72.

31. MS Ferris Collection. *Paul and Amicus*, Introduction.

32. E.H. to William Poole, 7 Nov. 1820, 2 Aug. 1820, 9 Oct. 1821.

33. MS Ferris Collection. *Paul and Amicus,* p. 156.

34. MS Ferris Collection. *Paul and Amicus,* pp. 350–51. Elias Hicks, *Letters,* pp. 55, 57.

35. Rachel King, *George Fox and the Light Within* (Philadelphia, 1940), p. 161.

36. Elias Hicks, *Extemporaneous Discourses,* pp. 29, 219, 220, 255.

37. E.H. to William Poole, 7 Nov. 1820, F.H.L.

38. Quoted, Rufus M. Jones, *The Later Periods of Quakerism* (2 vols., London, 1921) I, 454. Elias Hicks, *Letters,* pp. 67, 166–71. *The Quaker, a Series of Sermons* (4 vols., Philadelphia, 1827), I, p. 41.

39. E.H. to William Poole, 7 Nov. 1820, F.H.L. Elias Hicks, *Letters,* pp. 52–54. In a letter to Phebe Willis, Elias Hicks wrote: "I believe that nothing ever did or ever will atone for spiritual corruption but the entire death of that from which the corruption originated which is the corrupt will. . . . This is the true atonement which the creature cannot effect for himself, only as he submits to the operation of the life and spirit of Christ, which will enable the willing and obedient to do it."

40. Wilbur, *Life and Labors,* p. 232. Elias Hicks, *Letters,* p. 128.

41. *The Quaker,* I, 41. *J.E.H.,* p. 198. E.H. to Dr. Shoemaker, 31 March, 1823, F.H.L.

42. *J.E.H.,* p. 198. *The Quaker,* I, 196. Elias Hicks, *Letters,* pp. 76–77.

43. Elias Hicks, *Extemporaneous Discourses,* pp. 249, 253–55, 305. *The Quaker,* I, 68. William Poole to E.H., 6 Jan. 1821, F.H.L.

44. *J.E.H.,* p. 330.

XVIII: RELIGIOUS FREEDOM AT STAKE

1. Dr. William Gibbons to E.H., undated letter, F.H.L.

2. E.H. to Edward Hicks, 9 April 1822. Edward Hicks compared the suggestion to the formation of early Church Councils and the decline of Christianity. Edward Hicks, *Memoirs of the Life and Religious Labors of Edward Hicks* (Philadelphia, 1851), pp. 96–99.

3. MS Min. N.Y.Y.M., 1783, 1784.

4. "Elias Hicks," *The Encyclopedia Britannica* (11th ed. New York, 1910), XIII, 448. Samuel M. Janney, *History of the Religious Society of Friends* (4 vols., Philadelphia, 1867), IV, 176.

5. Janney, *History of the Society of Friends,* IV, 176.

6. E.H. to Gideon Seaman, 5 March 1822, F.H.L.

7. E.H. to Edward Hicks, 9 April 1822; E.H. to William Poole, 7 July, 1821, F.H.L.

8. Alice Ford, *Edward Hicks: Painter of the Peaceable Kingdom* (Philadelphia, 1952), p. 40.

9. William Dean to E.H., 14 Jan. 1822, Newell Col.

10. MS Elias Hicks, Morgan State College Collection, Baltimore, Md. Hicks suggested that land be secured in the southwest, the freedom of slaves purchased, a Negro state created and admitted to the Union.

11. Jacob Willetts to E.H., 17 May 1822, Newell Col.

12. Mason L. Weems to E.H., 26 March 1822, Newell Col.

13. Edward Hicks, *Memoirs*, p. 103.

14. Edward Hicks, *Memoirs*, p. 95.

15. E.H. to John Comly, 31 May 1822, Barclay White Collection, F.H.L.

16. Jeremiah J. Foster, *An Authentic Report of the Testimony in a Cause at Issue in the Court of Chancery* . . . (2 vols., Philadelphia, 1831), I, 246.

17. E.H. to William Poole, 8 Aug. 1822, F.H.L.

18. Samuel Titus to E.H., 9 Sept. 1822, Newell Col.

19. William Ridgeway to E.H., 10 July 1822, F.H.L.

20. MS Frederick B. Tolles, New Lights in New England, F.H.L.

21. MS Letters, Stephen Gould to Thomas Thompson, 1820–35, Library, Friends House, London, 20 May 1822, 18 June 1822, 24 Feb. 1823, 19–20 June 1823, 19 June 1824.

22. MS Frederick B. Tolles, New Lights in New England, F.H.L.

23. MS Frederick B. Tolles, New Lights in New England, F.H.L.

24. MS Frederick B. Tolles, New Lights in New England, F.H.L.

25. Elias Hicks, *Letters of Elias Hicks* (Philadelphia, 1861), p. 49.

26. William Poole to E.H., undated letter, F.H.L.

27. Janney, *History of the Society of Friends,* IV, 214. Foster, *An Authentic Report,* I, 247, 256–57. Ferris MS, F.H.L.

28. Foster, *An Authentic Report,* I, 356.

29. E.H. to J.H., 1822, F.H.L.

30. MS Min. Jericho M.M., 20 Feb. 1823.

31. *Book of Discipline Phila. Y.M. 1806,* p. 64. *Disc. N.Y.Y.M. 1810,* p. 24.

32. Janney, *History of the Society of Friends,* IV, 217–22. Foster, *An Authentic Report,* I, 247–52. James Cockburn, *A Review of the General and Particular Causes of* . . . *Disorder and Division* . . . *in the Society of Friends,* (Philadelphia, 1829), pp. 62–67. MS Historical Review . . . to the Year 1827, F.H.L.

33. William L. Fisher to E.H., 6 Oct. 1822, Newell Col.

34. Janney, *History of the Society of Friends,* IV, 220–22. Henry W. Wilbur, *Life and Labors of Elias Hicks* (Philadelphia, 1910), pp. 129–32.

35. Janney, *History of the Society of Friends,* IV, 223–26.

36. James Cockburn, *A Review of General and Particular Causes which have Produced the late Disorders and Divisions in the Yearly Meeting Held in Philadelphia* (Philadelphia, 1829), pp. 76–79. Janney, *History of the Society of Friends,* IV, 226.

37. Robert Moore to E.H., 14 Feb. 1823, Newell Col.

38. *J.E.H.,* p. 394.

39. Rufus M. Jones, *The Later Periods of Quakerism* (2 vols., London, 1921), I, 462.

40. Abington Quarterly Meeting confirmed the disownment of Comfort and Bell, but the Yearly Meeting reinstated them. Philadelphia Quarterly Meeting reversed the judgment of Green Street Monthly and reinstated the elder.

41. Philadelphia *Evening Post,* 22 Feb. 1823.

42. Anna D. Hallowell, *James and Lucretia Mott* (Boston, 1896), pp. 79–81.

43. Abraham Lower to William Poole, 17 Feb. 1823, F.H.L.

XIX: THE EVANGELICAL INVASION

1. Samuel M. Janney, *Memoirs* (Philadelphia, 1881), p. 21.

2. Edward Hicks, *Memoirs of the Life and Labors of Edward Hicks* (Philadelphia, 1851), pp. 91–92.

3. Edward Hicks, *Memoirs,* p. 87.

4. William Poole to E.H., 25 Jan. 1823, 20 June 1823, Newell Col. Jeremiah J. Foster, *An Authentic Report of the Testimony in a Cause at Issue in the Court of Chancery* . . . (2 vols., Philadelphia, 1831), I, 368–69; II, 102, 103. *The Friend,* Vol. I (Philadelphia, 1827), pp. 237–39.

5. Foster, *An Authentic Report,* II, 102.

6. *The Friend,* I, 238. For the wording of the "Philadelphia Creed" see *A Controverted Document; Extracts from the Writings of Primitive Friends Concerning the Divinity* . . . *Jesus Christ* ed. William Bacon Evans, (Mt. Holly, 1946).

7. E.H. to William Poole, 23 May, 28 May, 1823; 26 March 1824, F.H.L.

8. Howard H. Brinton, *Friends for 300 Years* (New York, 1952), p. 188.

9. William Poole to E.H., 13 May 1822, Newell Col.

10. Edward Hicks, *Memoirs,* p. 100.

11. Edward Grubb, *Quaker Thought and History* (New York, 1925), p. 80. Edward Grubb, *The Evangelical Movement and its Impact on the Society of Friends,* Reprint, *Friends Quarterly Examiner,* January, 1924, pp. 22, 23.

12. Elbert Russell, *The History of Quakerism* (New York, 1942), p. 304.

13. *Disc. N.Y.Y.M. 1810,* p. 95.

14. *Book of Discipline, Phila. Y.M. 1806.*

15. Samuel M. Janney, *History of the Religious Society of Friends* (4 vols., Philadelphia, 1867), IV, 177-78.

16. MS Stephen Gould letters to Thomas Thompson, Library, Friends House, London, Folio 29-32, Letters 1823-26.

17. *Letters & Observations Relating to the Controversy Respecting the Doctrines of Elias Hicks,* 1824, pp. 6, 7. *An Examination of a Pamphlet, Entitled, The Misrepresentations of Anna Braithwaite, in Relation to the Doctrines Preached by Elias Hicks* (New York, n.d.), p. 23. Anna Braithwaite, *Memoirs of Anna Braithwaite* (London, 1905).

18. *Letters and Observations,* p. 18.

19. Elias Hicks, *Letters of Elias Hicks* (Philadelphia, 1861), pp. 159, 188, 195-96. E.H. to William Poole, 21 Jan. 1826, F.H.L.; E.H. to Roger Brooke, 6 Feb. 1826, Baltimore Col.; E.H. to William Poole, 27 Aug. 1824, F.H.L.

20. Boston *Pearl & Literary Gazette,* 18 July 1835, p. 367. In a letter to Roger Brooke, Elias Hicks said Anna Braithwaite "called me a deist, and an Infidel . . . there appeared a very general disunity among friends with her company and services." 6 Feb. 1826, Baltimore Col.

21. MS Elizabeth Robson, Library, Friends House, London, No. 70.

22. Elizabeth Robson to Priscilla Hunt, 22 Aug. 1825, Library, Friends House, London.

23. Elisha Bates to Elizabeth Robson, 6 April 1826, Library, Friends House, London.

24. Janney, *History of Friends,* IV, pp. 251-52. E.H. to William Poole, 1 June, 1826. F.H.L.

25. *The Christian Inquirer,* New Series III (New York, 1828), pp. 38, 39.

26. Janney, *History of Friends,* IV, 247-50.

27. Edward Hicks, *Memoirs,* p. 136.

28. Edward Hicks, *Memoirs,* p. 106.

29. MS Stephen Gould, 1824, 1825, Friends House, London.

30. Thomas Shillitoe, quoted by Samuel Janney, in *History of Friends,* IV, 188.

31. T. Stephenson to Thomas Robson, 8 Jan. 1825, Library, Friends House, London, Port. 38–66.

32. John Bunting to William Poole, 6 June 1825, F.H.L.

33. E.H. to William Poole, 25 May 1824; 1 June, 1825, F.H.L.

34. MS Stephen Gould, 1826, Library, Friends House, London.

XX: "REASON IS THE RECIPIENT OF REVELATION"

1. *J.E.H.,* pp. 394–95.

2. E.H. to William Poole, 8 April 1822, F.H.L.

3. Stephen Grellet, *Memoirs of the Life and Gospel Labours of Stephen Grellet* ed. Benjamin Seebohm (2 vols., London, 1860), II, 150.

4. E.H. to William Poole, 25 May 1824; E.H. to Isaac T. Hopper, 1 June 1824, F.H.L. Hicks wrote to J. Wilson Moore that contention arose because many Friends desired to return to an outward rule, an apostasy of the early church, E.H. to J. Wilson Moore, 26 March 1823; 22 June 1823.

5. MS Min. Jericho Prep. M., 14 Oct. 1824.

6. E.H. and J.H. to Martha, Abigail, and Sarah, 21 July 1824.

7. E.H., *A Series of Extemporary Discourses* (Philadelphia, 1825), p. 146.

8. *The Substance of Two Discourses, Delivered in New York, 17 Dec. 1824, By Elias Hicks, A Minister of the Society of Friends* (New York, 1825). These were the first sermons of Elias Hicks to appear in print.

9. E.H. to Roger Brooke, 9 Feb. 1825, Baltimore Col.

10. James Cockburn, *A Review of the General and Particular Causes which have Produced the late Disorders and Divisions in the Yearly Meeting Held in Philadelphia* (Philadelphia, 1829), pp. 93–98.

11. Thomas E. Drake, *Quakers and Slavery in America* (New Haven, 1950), p. 117.

12. Elias Hicks, *Extemporaneous Discourses,* pp. 60, 176–78.

13. Elias Hicks, *Extemporaneous Discourses,* pp. 209, 237–40.

14. E.H. to Valentine Hicks, 11 June, 1827, F.H.L.; Henry W. Wilbur, *The Life and Labors of Elias Hicks* (Philadelphia, 1910), p. 86.

15. Thomas Drake, *Quakers and Slavery,* p. 118.

16. Nathan Shoemaker to E.H., 7 April 1823, Newell Col.

17. E.H. to Moses Brown, 30 March 1825, F.H.L.

18. E.H. to Hugh Judge, 17 Feb. 1823; 4 April 1825; 26 April 1825, Newell Col.; 24 April 1825, F.H.L.; E.H. to William Underhill, 3 Dec. 1823, F.H.L.

19. *Sermons Delivered by Elias Hicks & Edward Hicks in Friends Meetings in New York* (New York, 1825), pp. 50–51.

20. MS Casual Correspondence, Meeting for Sufferings, London Yearly Meeting, 4 Feb. 1825. Case 33, Library, Friends House, London.

21. Edward Hicks, *Memoirs of the Life and Religious Labors of Edward Hicks* (Philadelphia, 1851), pp. 103, 104.

22. E.H. to Roger Brooke, 6 Feb. 1826, Baltimore Col.

23. John Comly, *Journal of the Life and Religious Labours of John Comly* (Philadelphia, 1853), pp. 304–5.

24. E.H. to Roger Brooke, 3 June 1826, Baltimore Col.

25. Thomas Fisher to E.H., 12 Feb. 1826; 29 Oct. 1826; 14 Oct. 1823.

26. *The Quaker, a Series of Sermons* (4 vols., Philadelphia, 1827), I, 32. Again Marcus Gould followed Elias Hicks and took down sufficient of his sermons to fill two volumes of a publication which he entitled *The Quaker*. One sermon came out each month, 2,000 subscribers were secured before the first issue. In all, when bound, four volumes were printed. The second and third volumes contained sermons of Jesse Kersey, John Comly, Edward Stabler, Edward Hicks, Thomas Wetherald, Townsend Hawkshurst, and Abraham Lower, all Liberals, as well as sermons of Elias Hicks.

27. *The Quaker*, I, 33.

28. *The Quaker*, I, 49–72.

29. *The Quaker*, I, 72.

30. *The Quaker*, I, 72, 73.

31. *The Quaker*, I, 81–104, 105–25. *The Christian Inquirer*, New Series, III (New York, 1828). An account is found in *The Christian Inquirer*. During this trip, Elias Hicks found it necessary to take his seat from time to time because of exhaustion, and then continue his address. At Wilmington, he spoke morning and afternoon for a total of two and a half hours.

32. Cockburn, *A Review of General and Particular Causes*, p. 100.

33. Elias Hicks, *Letters of Elias Hicks* (Philadelphia, 1861), p. 199. Samuel M. Janney, *History of the Religious Society of Friends* (4 vols., Philadelphia, 1867), IV, 246. Philadelphia Quarterly Meeting sent a similar complaint by a committee to Westbury Quarterly Meeting in

August, 1828. The letter was referred to a committee which reported later that it was not suitable to read. *The Friend*, I, 252–54.

34. E.H. to Samuel Comfort, 29 March, 1827, F.H.L.

XXI: CLIMAX OF DISSENT

1. Kenneth S. Latourette, *A History of the Expansion of Christianity* (New York, 1941), IV, p. 6.

2. Edward Hicks, *Memoirs of the Life and Labors of Edward Hicks* (Philadelphia, 1851), p. 252.

3. John Comly, *Journal of the Life and Religious Labours of John Comly* (Philadelphia, 1853), pp. 306–12. Comly wrote of those whom he felt were introducing difficulties into the Society as "the orthodox party . . . intended merely as a term of distinction, and not as granting any peculiar soundness of faith" p. 309. Those who agreed with Comly were called Comlyites, Hicksites, Liberals, Separates, or Tolerants.

4. Edward Hicks, *Memoirs*, p. 252. See also E.H. to William Poole, 10 Feb. 1827, F.H.L.

5. Jeremiah J. Foster, *An Authentic Report of the Testimony in a Cause at Issue in the Court of Chancery* . . . (2 vols., Philadelphia, 1831), I, 82. Country Friends believed Samuel Bettle had outwitted them when the "Creed" was under consideration by leaving it on the minutes where it achieved a semiofficial standing. Elbert Russell, *The History of Quakerism* (New York, 1942), p. 311.

6. Comly, *Journal*, p. 332; the Separation is described, pp. 305–55. See also: Samuel M. Janney, *History of the Religious Society of Friends* (4 vols., Philadelphia, 1867), IV, 252–69. Foster, *An Authentic Report*, I, 265–82, 287–315; II, 102–9, 332–44, 462–71. James Cockburn, *A Review of the General and Particular Causes which have Produced the late Disorders and Divisions in the Yearly Meeting Held in Philadelphia* (Philadelphia, 1829), 187–221. Elbert Russell, *History of Quakerism*, pp. 311, 314–15. Rufus M. Jones, *The Later Periods of Quakerism* (2 vols., London, 1921), I, 435–87. MSS Ferris, Foulke, Lippincott, F.H.L. MS Evans, Baltimore Col.

7. Jeremiah J. Foster, *An Authentic Report*, II, 453–54.

8. Andrew Cock to Benjamin Ferris, 27 June 1827, F.H.L.

9. Elbert Russell, "The Separation after a Century," reprinted from *Friends Intelligencer*, 1928, p. 41. Rufus Jones, *Later Periods*, I, 281; II, 873–74.

10. Thomas Shillitoe, *Journal of the Life, Labours and Travels of Thomas Shillitoe, The Friends Library*, III, 351.

11. Shillitoe, *Journal*, p. 353.

12. Shillitoe, *Journal*, p. 354.

13. E.H. to Roger Brooke, 26 June, 1827, Baltimore Col.

14. Edward Hicks, *Memoirs*, pp. 112-13.

15. MS. Stephen Gould, year 1827, Library, Friends House, London.

16. Foster, *An Authentic Report*, II, pp. 455-56.

17. E.H. to William Poole, 2 Aug. 1827, F.H.L. For use of term General Conference or General Yearly Meeting, James Cockburn, *A Review*, p. 206. Samuel Janney, *History of the Society of Friends*, IV, p. 274-75.

18. Evan Lewis to Benjamin Ferris, 18 Feb. 1828, F.H.L.

19. E.H. to Valentine Hicks and Abigail, 11 April 1827; E.H. to Emmor Kimber, 21 Dec. 1827, F.H.L.

20. James Cockburn, *A Review of General and Particular Causes*, pp. 225-37. Of the eleven Quarterly Meetings which formed Philadelphia Yearly Meeting, Philadelphia was the only one containing a larger number of Orthodox than Liberals, seven were strongly Liberal, and two were fairly evenly divided. Elbert Russell, in *History of Quakerism*, p. 322, indicates that two-thirds of the membership went with the Liberals; the Foster report gives 18,485 Liberals, 7,344 Orthodox, and 429 neutrals. In the official class, 389 Ministers and Elders remained with the Orthodox group, and 260 with the Liberals. There were only 10 of 52 members of the Meeting for Sufferings who were Liberals, which that party felt indicated a disadvantage unwarranted by their numbers. Among the representatives to the last united Yearly Meeting in 1827, 118 were from the Liberal group and 45 from the Orthodox.

When a case involving property finally reached the courts in New Jersey, it was won by the Orthodox, appealed, and won again by a split decision, 7-4, each party to pay its own costs. The decision in favor of the Orthodox party was not made on the basis of doctrine, but on the grounds that one section of the Society had actually separated itself. This was the traditional decision given in similar court trials involving other denominations in America. The courts held that the body which remained in the church building and continued to meet at the regular time was the original body. Samuel M. Janney, *History of the Society of Friends*, IV, 14, 334. *Report of the Trial of Friends in the City of Philadelphia, June, 1828 . . . or the case of Edmund Shotwell . . . and others* (Philadelphia, 1828).

21. E.H. to William Wharton, 12 October 1827, F.H.L.

22. MS Min. Jericho M.M., 20 March 1828; MS Min. Westbury Q.M., 24 April 1828. *J.E.H.*, p. 398.

23. Emmor Kimber to E.H., 25 Jan. 1828, Newell Col.

24. E.H. to William Poole, 31 March 1828.

25. Comly, *Journal*, pp. 357, 362.

26. Comly, *Journal*, p. 363. After the New Jersey property case was decided in favor of the Orthodox, the state legislature passed a law providing for a proportional distribution of Quaker property on the basis of membership in each Meeting.

27. Epistle to the Yearly Meeting of Friends held in London, from the Yearly Meeting of Friends held in Philadelphia, by adjournment . . . 1828; quoted in Comly, *Journal*, pp. 636–38.

28. On the advice of a committee to inspect the source of the Philadelphia Epistle, London Yearly Meeting decided, "[they] could not receive [it] . . . [they] could have no unity with persons possessing opinions contrary to the sound and established doctrines of our Society. . . . The Yearly Meeting could not recognize, or have any intercourse with, any associated body on the continent of America, who were not formed according to the long established practice of our Society and whose profession was not according to our Christian principles . . . [and they would] so notify several Yearly Meetings in America," MS London Y.M., Vol. 23, pp. 242–44, Library, Friends House, London; also Meeting for Sufferings, Vol. 43.

29. *A Declaration of the Yearly Meeting of Friends, held in Philadelphia, respecting the proceedings of those who have lately separated from the society; and also, shewing the contrast between their doctrines and those held by Friends* (Philadelphia, 1828), p. 17.

XXII: DAYS OF RESPITE AND STRIFE

1. Letters from William Proctor to his brother and sister, 1828, Box 51, Library, Friends House, London.

2. E.H. to William Poole, 12 Sept. 1823; 7 Dec. 1823, F.H.L.

3. Emmor Kimber to E.H., 10 Oct. 1826, Newell Col.

4. E.H., to William Poole, 7 Dec. 1823, F.H.L.

5. William Poole to E.H., 7 Dec. 1823, F.H.L.

6. MS Last Will and Testament of Elias Hicks, Deceased, Surrogate's Court, County of Queens, and State of New York. Elias left David the use of interest on £350 "for his comfortable support during his natural life . . . as needs may require . . . and his mother Ellenor . . . the whole sum above named both principal and interest."

7. Six of the travel diaries are in F.H.L. Details of nearly thirty jour-

neys given in the printed *Journal* are so complete it is impossible that Elias Hicks could have remembered them. Nearly two-thirds of the printed *Journal* is devoted to the home journal, 1813–19. The year 1821 is blank, the years 1820, 1823, 1824, 1825, 826, and 1827 are condensed into a few paragraphs. There is no account of the Separation in Philadelphia or New York. Details concerning the writing of Hicks' Journal, and its printing by Isaac T. Hopper, are found in Bliss Forbush, "The Newly Discovered Manuscript Journal of Elias Hicks," *The Bulletin of Friends Historical Association*, XXXIX, 1950, pp. 16–26.

8. J.E.H., p. 7.

9. *J.E.H.*, pp. 7–16.

10. *J.E.H.*, p. 21.

11. *Sermons by Elias Hicks, Ann Jones and Others . . . at the Quarterly Meeting of Nine Partners and Stanford . . . 1828* (Brooklyn, 1828), pp. 8, 13–21, 74.

12. *Sermons of Elias Hicks and Ann Jones 1828*, p. 20.

13. Samuel Titus to E.H., 21 March 1828, F.H.L.

14. MS Gould, year 1828, Library, Friends House, London.

15. *Advocate of Truth*, (Philadelphia, 1828), I, 186. *The Friend*, (Philadelphia, 1827), I, 263.

16. *Advocate of Truth*, I, 186. Henry W. Wilbur, *Life and Labors of Elias Hicks* (Philadelphia, 1910), pp. 183–84.

17. *Advocate of Truth*, I, 186. Samuel Janney, *History of the Religious Society of Friends* (4 vols., Philadelphia, 1867), IV, 290.

18. *Advocate of Truth*, I, 187.

19. *Advocate of Truth*, I, 187–88. In addition to the description of the New York Separation in the *Advocate of Truth*, accounts are found in *The Friend*, I, pp. 263–64, 290–92, 310–11; Janney, *History of the Society of Friends*, IV, 288–293; Jeremiah J. Foster, *An Authentic Report of the Testimony in a Cause at Issue in the Court of Chancery . . .* (2 vols., Philadelphia, 1831), I, 175–209; II, 261–282; MS Min. N.Y.Y.M. (both Liberal and Orthodox), 1828; MS J. Foulke, F.H.L.; *Decision of the Vice Chancellor on the Application of the Orthodox Party . . . 1835* (New York, 1838).

20. *The Friend*, I, 263.

21. *The Friend*, I, 263.

22. Epistle N.Y.Y.M., 1828. Foster, *An Authentic Report*, II, 459–60. London Meeting for Sufferings replied to the New York Epistles "the said Yearly Meeting recognizes no body of persons in the City or State

of New York, as in connection with it as a religious Community except that on behalf of which Samuel Parsons acted as Clerk." MS Meeting for Sufferings, Vol. 43, 5 June 1828, Friends House, London. May 5, 1830 London Yearly Meeting made the same statement, MS Min. London Y.M., Vol. 23.

23. *Advocate of Truth*, I, 191. MS Min. N.Y.Y.M., 1828.

24. Epistle N.Y.Y.M. (O), 1828. *The Friend*, I. 279.

25. MS N.Y.Y.M. Ministers and Elders, 24 May, 1828. Thomas Shillitoe, *Journal of the Life, Labours and Travels of Thomas Shillitoe, The Friends Library*, III, 440–42.

XXIII: A LONG JOURNEY

1. Photostat, MS diary Elias Hicks, 1828, p. 32. Baltimore Col.

2. *Advocate of Truth* (Philadelphia, 1828) I, 136.

3. John Comly, *Memoirs of the Life and Religious Labours of John Comly* (Philadelphia, 1853), p. 361.

4. *J.E.H.*, p. 402.

5. Henry W. Wilbur, *Life and Labors of Elias Hicks* (Philadelphia, 1910), p. 196.

6. Thomas Shillitoe, *Journal of the Life, Labors and Travels of Thomas Shillitoe, The Friends Library*, III, 447.

7. Shillitoe, *Journal*, p. 450. *J.E.H.*, p. 405.

8. E.H. to Valentine Hicks, 14 August, 1828, F.H.L.

9. *Advocate of Truth*, I, 91.

10. *J.E.H.*, p. 407.

11. *J.E.H.*, pp. 408, 409.

12. *Advocate of Truth*, I, 215–16.

13. *The Friend* (Philadelphia, 1827), I, 117.

14. MS J.E.H., p. 411.

15. Wilbur, *Life and Labors*, p. 196.

16. *The Friend*, II, 127.

17. *Decision of the Vice Chancellor on the Application of the Orthodox Party to Appoint a Receiver* . . . (New York, 1835). Printed by Isaac T. Hopper. In addition to the decision, this volume includes all the correspondence which passed between the committees of the two New York Monthly Meetings.

18. Letter from Westbury and Jericho Monthly Meetings, Aug. 25, 1828. *Advocate of Truth*, I, 264–65.

19. Shillitoe, *Journal*, p. 457.

20. *Advocate of Truth*, I, 252–53.

21. Copy of letter, Susan D. Pierce to Sidney Darlington, 17 Sept. 1828, Baltimore Col. Accounts of the Separation in Ohio Y.M. are found in the *Advocate of Truth; The Friend; J.E.H.;* Wilbur, *Life and Labors;* Shillitoe, *Journal; Report of the Trial of Friends at Steubenville, Ohio* (Philadelphia, 1829).

22. Wilbur, *Life and Labors*, p. 50.

23. E.H., to Gideon Seaman, 8 Sept. 1828, F.H.L. *Advocate of Truth*, I, 265–66.

24. David Hilles and Isaac James were found guilty of disturbing a religious gathering and fined five dollars each. Several Friends were found guilty of intent to riot, fined 6¼ cents each and sentenced to thirty minutes in jail. They appealed and the Supreme Court of Ohio reversed the decision. Samuel M. Janney, *History of the Religious Society of Friends* (4 vols., Philadelphia, 1867), IV, 303–5. *Report of the Trial . . . Steubenville*, p. 339. *Advocate of Truth*, I, 261; II, 166, 360.

25. *Advocate of Truth*, I, 262.

26. Wilbur, *Life and Labors*, p. 50.

27. Minutes of Indiana Y.M. *Advocate of Truth*, II, 21, 22, 370. *J.E.H.*, pp. 416–17.

28. MS Min. Westbury Q.M., 23 Oct. 1828.

29. The Orthodox point of view is found in *The Friend*, I, 318–19; the Liberal in *The Advocate of Truth*, I, 147.

30. MS Letters William Proctor, Box 51, Library, Friends House, London.

31. MS Min. B.Y.M., 1828, Baltimore Vault, Baltimore, Md. Reprinted, *Advocate of Truth*, II, 23, 24. In spite of these idealistic sentiments, London Yearly Meeting refused to correspond further with Baltimore Yearly Meeting. "This meeting concludes not to hold correspondence with that body now represented by Philip Evan Thomas as its clerk. This step is taken under a feeling of painful concern for those who have organized a body of Separatists . . ." Vol. 23, London Y.M., 1829, Friends House, London. Philip E. Thomas had been clerk for years; a few hundred Orthodox withdrew.

32. MS J.E.H., p. 424.

33. MS J.E.H., p. 418.

34. *J.E.H.*, p. 425.

35. *Advocate of Truth*, II, 2, 3.

XXIV: THE MINISTER CLOSES HIS JOURNAL

1. MS Min. Jericho Prep. M., Meeting 11 Jan. 1827, 10 July 1828, 2 July 1829, 14 Jan. 1830, 8 Oct. 1829. Jericho M.M. 25 May 1828, 19 Nov., 1829. The sheds, 80 by 20 feet, cost $188.20.

2. *J.E.H.,* pp. 425, 426. E.H. to William Poole, 19 May, 1829.

3. MS copy of article from a "Poughkeepsie News Paper," Baltimore Col. *J.E.H.,* p. 426. *Advocate of Truth* (Philadelphia, 1828), III, 174.

4. Elias Hicks' copy of George Fox's Journal, F.H.L.

5. *The Friend* (Philadelphia, 1827), II, 318-19.

6. Henry W. Wilbur, *Life and Labors of Elias Hicks* (Philadelphia, 1910), p. 192.

7. J. Foulke to G.H., 21 Aug. 1829. *Advocate of Truth,* II, 204.

8. John Comly, *Journal of the Life and Religious Labours of John Comly* (Philadelphia, 1853), p. 434.

9. *Advocate of Truth,* II, 301.

10. N.Y.Y.M. Epistle 1829. This is in pamphlet form; or if needed in more accessible form is found in *Advocate of Truth,* II, 204.

11. *Advocate of Truth,* II, 205.

12. E.H. to William Poole, 19 May 1829, F.H.L. Elias Hicks, *Letters of Elias Hicks* (Philadelphia, 1861), p. 219.

13. E.H. to Benjamin Ferris, 17 June 1829, F.H.L.

14. E.H. to Rachel Hicks, Jr., 27 Dec. 1828, F.H.L.

15. Samuel Evans to E.H., 20 Jan. 1830, Newell Col. Elias Hicks, *Letters,* pp. 237-38.

16. E.H. to William Wharton, Dec. 7, 1828, F.H.L.

17. *Journal of Friends Historical Society* (London, 1908), V, fn. 86.

18. Wilbur, *Life and Labors,* pp. 98, 99. By January, 1830, the Baltimore & Ohio was running horse-drawn carriages on its tracks as far as Carrollton Viaduct. That summer the *Tom Thumb* made experimental trips 12½ miles to Ellicott Mills. In June, 1831, the *York,* built by a Quaker, Phineas Davis, in the city of that name, became the first steam engine to be operated for public convenience in America. Edward Hungerford, *The Story of the Baltimore and Ohio Railroad, 1827-1927* (New York, 1928), pp. 1-110. In 1837, Valentine Hicks became president of the Long Island Railroad Company with terminus at Hicksville, near Jericho, named for the railroad's president.

19. Wilbur, *Life and Labors,* p. 99.

20. *The Friend,* II, 312.

21. No account of this journey appears in the MS Journal of Elias Hicks. *The Bulletin of Friends Historical Association,* Vol. 39, 16–26.

22. *J.E.H.,* p. 428. According to the series of leaflets published under *Decision of the Vice Chancellor on the Application of the Orthodox Party to Appoint a Receiver.* . . . at the time of the Separation, the School Committee in charge of the Nine Partners boarding school was constituted almost entirely of Liberal Friends. The Superintendent, however, was an Orthodox, whose term expired April 1, 1829. The Superintendent barred the windows and doors against the Committee and so took possession of the school.

23. Stephen Grellet, *Memoirs of the Life and Gospel Labours of Stephen Grellet,* ed. Benjamin Seebohm (2 vols., London, 1860), II, 216–17.

24. Grellet, *Memoirs,* II, 222.

25. Arthur J. Mekeel, *Quakerism and a Creed* (Philadelphia, 1936), pp. 62, 63. In 1832, Elisha Bates received a certificate to travel in London Yearly Meeting. The extreme literalism of his use of the Bible, as shown by his many writings, helped to bring about a reaction in England. George and Ann Jones, and Elizabeth Robson opposed him. The Ministers and Elders of London Yearly Meeting did not wish to receive his certificate, but they were overruled by the Yearly Meeting. Bates said that Elias Hicks and Primitive Friends both taught the supremacy of the Inner Light over the Scriptures and that both were wrong. *An Examination of Certain Proceedings of the Society of Friends, Called Quakers* (St. Clairsville, Ohio, 1837), p. 77. Carrying his concept of scriptural authority to a logical conclusion, Bates was baptized while in England. He was disowned by Ohio Yearly Meeting.

26. *Advocate of Truth,* III, 405.

27. *J.E.H.,* p. 437.

28. The exact figures for Hicksite and Orthodox Friends in 1830 are difficult to ascertain, chiefly because no record exists of the total membership in some Yearly Meetings. Elbert Russell states there were between 35,000 and 40,000 Hicksites in America, "by far the majority of the divided yearly meetings"; see Elbert Russell, *The History of Quakerism* (New York, 1942), p. 322. He indicates that when the numbers of the undivided Yearly Meetings are included on the Orthodox side—Virginia, North Carolina, and New England—the two bodies were about equal; but unless New England was much larger than is evident, the Hicksites still had a wide margin. Rufus M. Jones says, "It is obvious that the

'Hicksites' had a decided majority in the meetings that separated"; see Rufus M. Jones, *The Later Periods of Quakerism* (2 vols., London, 1921), I, 480. Both agree that if Friends in Great Britain, Ireland, and on the Continent were added to the totals, there were more Orthodox than Hicksite Quakers in the world.

29. Meeting for Sufferings, Vol. 43; Casual Correspondence, Case 33, London Y.M., Library, Friends House, London. *Advocate of Truth*, II, 360.

30. Benjamin Ferris to John Grace, 20 Dec. 1829, Library, Friends House, London.

31. Walt Whitman, *Complete Poetry and Prose* (2 vols., New York, 1948), II, 477, 478.

32. MS Min. Jericho M.M., 17 Dec. 1829.

33. E.H. to Elias Wilbur, 1 Jan. 1830, F.H.L.

34. Elias Hicks, *Letters*, pp. 226–230. *Advocate of Truth*, III, 22–24.

35. *J.E.H.*, p. 438. A sub-committee of the Meeting of Sufferings of New York Yearly Meeting arranged the various travel diaries and the home journal in order, giving "diligent attention to the original manuscript." About ten pages in every hundred were omitted, the spelling corrected, and chapter divisions created. The Meeting for Sufferings approved the publication of the *Journal* which was printed in New York City by Isaac T. Hopper in 1832. The book immediately went through five editions. Because of Elias Hicks' testimony against the use of the products of slave labor, the *Journal* was printed on linen paper, and copyrighted to prevent cheap editions appearing on cotton paper.

36. Elias Hicks, *Two Sermons and a Prayer, Delivered at Friends' Meeting Houses* (New York, 1831).

37. *Advocate of Truth*, III, 107.

38. E.H. to Hugh Judge, 11 Feb. 1830, F.H.L. *J.E.H.*, pp. 439–42.

39. Walt Whitman, *Poetry and Prose*, p. 483.

40. *Advocate of Truth*, III, 108.

41. *Advocate of Truth*, III, 80, 108.

42. New York *Evening Post*, 1 March 1830.

43. The grave was opened after the internment, without the consent of Elias Hicks' family, in order that a cast might be taken of his head. *Advocate of Truth*, III, 112. A silhouette of Hicks was made by Richard Field in 1829, a portrait painted by Harry Ketchum without Hicks' knowledge. From these materials Henry Inman drew the portrait appearing in some editions of the *Journal*, and William Ordway Partridge

created the bust of Elias Hicks now in Friends Historical Library of Swarthmore College. *Friends Intelligencer,* 22 July 1911; May 1937.

44. Edward Hicks, *Memoirs of the Life and Religious Labors of Edward Hicks* (Philadelphia, 1851), p. 237.

45. Hugh Judge, *Memoirs and Journal of Hugh Judge* (Byberry, 1841), pp. 356–58.

46. *Advocate of Truth,* III, 78–80.

47. *Advocate of Truth,* III, 172–74, 177–80.

48. *Advocate of Truth,* III, 181–84. *J.E.H.,* pp. 444–51.

49. *Advocate of Truth,* III, 181. *J.E.H.,* p. 444.

Index